SALOPIÆ COMITATUS;
summa cum fide, cura et dili-
gentia descriptionem hanc ti-
bi tabula refert. A. Dni. 1577.
FOR DIÆ PARS
WORCESTRIÆ PARS
ORIENS
SALOP HALES PARS
DRATON
NEWPORT
WELLYNTON
WENLOK
BRIDGENORTHE
LUDLOW
DEWDELEY
Tong cast
Browne clee hill
Stitterstones hill
Bringewood chase

AN ENGLISH RURAL COMMUNITY

Myddle under the Tudors and Stuarts

AN ENGLISH RURAL COMMUNITY

Myddle

under the Tudors and Stuarts

DAVID G. HEY M.A., Ph.D.

Lecturer in the
Department of Extramural Studies
University of Sheffield

Leicester University Press

1974

First published in 1974 by Leicester University Press
Distributed in North America by Humanities Press Inc., New York

Designed by Arthur Lockwood

Set in Monotype Bembo
Printed in Great Britain by Western Printing Services Ltd, Bristol
Bound by G. & J. Kitcat Ltd, London

ISBN 0 7185 1115 8

The publication of this book has been assisted by a grant from the Twenty-Seven Foundation

Preface

I am most grateful for the help I have received from Professor Alan Everitt, who supervised the original Ph.D. thesis out of which this book has grown, and from Professor W. G. Hoskins, who introduced me to the writings of Richard Gough and encouraged my study during its early stages; and to Dr Joan Thirsk for her valuable comments upon reading through the original thesis.

I have received great help from my former colleagues in the Department of English Local History at Leicester University. Michael Laithwaite surveyed two buildings and made many useful general comments on the surviving architecture, and Richard McKinley and Charles Phythian-Adams helped to clear up many other difficulties. Mrs Marsden of the Tan House and Mrs Latham of the Oaks were most obliging in allowing me inside their property; the former rector, Rev. A. J. Ayling, kindly allowed me to examine the parish records in the comfort of his own home; and the staffs of the Shropshire Record Office and the Lichfield Joint Record Office have been unfailingly helpful and courteous. I am also grateful to Mrs Irene Ashton for so capably typing the manuscript.

D.G.H.

For Pat

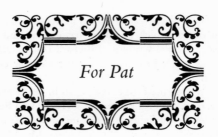

Contents

Illustrations

Tables

Maps

Plates

Acknowledgments

Plates 1–3 and 6–14: photographs by Geoffrey Drury; plate 4: Cambridge University Collection: copyright reserved; plate 5: Shropshire County Record Office. Saxton's map of Shropshire (1577) on the endpapers is reproduced by courtesy of the Trustees of the British Museum.

If any man shall blame mee for that I have declared the viciouse lives or actions of theire Ancestors, let him take care to avoid such evil courses, that hee leave not a blemish on his name when he is dead, and let him know that I have written nothing out of malice. I doubt not but some persons will thinke that many things that I have written are alltogether uselesse; but I doe believe that there is nothing herein mentioned which may not by chance att one time or other happen to bee needfull to some person or other; and, therefore I conclude with that of Rev. Mr Herbert –

> "A skillfull workeman hardly will refuse
> The smallest toole that hee may chance to use".

Richard Gough

Introduction

The community of Myddle would not have been singled out for special attention amongst local historians had it not been for a remarkable book, unique in our literature, that was written by one of its leading inhabitants at the beginning of the eighteenth century. In the year 1700, when he began his book, Richard Gough was a small freeholder living in the family's ancient tenement at Newton-on-the-Hill. He was by then a 66-year-old widower, living with his two youngest daughters, Joyce and Dorothy. He had had eight children in all, but two had died in infancy, two had died after their marriage, another son was a grocer in Shrewsbury, and the remaining daughter was married to a man in a neighbouring parish. He was a respected figure in the community, an intelligent and educated man who had served both his parish and his county in an official capacity, and who was interested in national events and issues as well as in all the human details of life in his own neighbourhood. He was a well-to-do yeoman, a staunch Anglican, and a supporter of the political settlements of 1660 and 1689. Though a judicious old man, he nevertheless spoke with the voice of the yeoman-freeholder, thus the insight that one gets into his local society is obtained from that particular point of view; one does not know the attitudes and thoughts of the labourers and poor husbandmen of his community.

Gough started by writing about the *Antiquityes and Memoyres of the Parish of Myddle*[1] in much the same vein as Camden (to whom he referred) and the other antiquarians of the sixteenth and seventeenth centuries. He describes the situation and bounds of the parish, the church at Myddle and the chapel at Hadnall, the patrons, the rectors, the clerks, and the fees and the dues. He then goes on to write about the lordship, the owners of the manor, the castle, park, and warren, the meres, commons and highways, and the manorial customs. He concludes with some remarks on the involvement of the parish in the Civil Wars.

All this is of some interest to the historian, but what follows made Gough's book one of the most valuable sources for the study of late-Stuart England that one could wish to find. In 1701, under the title of *Observations concerning the Seates in Myddle and the familyes to which they belong*, he wrote the individual histories "of all, or most part of the familyes in this side of the parish".[2] The major part of this work was completed within the year, but he continued to add bits until 1706. When he had finished, he had produced a book that is unsurpassed in describing the lives of the ordinary people of the late-seventeenth century – the complete range of a local community. So often, historians are only able to write about the great and the mighty, because the records of the humble and lowly are so scanty, but here, in Gough, is a vivid portrait of a community of men, women, and children that enables one to see what it was like for the ordinary villager to live in at least one part of England three hundred years ago.

Gough was writing from his own memories, recalling the numerous and varied incidents he had seen through what was then already a relatively long life. He also recounted some stories that had been passed on to him by his ancestors or had become part of the folk-lore of the community. Some of his stories are scandalous, some virtuous, but all of them are human and the sort of tales that bulk large in the reminiscences of people living in rural communities today. But what makes his work a great one, and what gives it cohesion, is his sense of history and his concentration upon the history of his community. His asides show that he consulted the various families whose pedigrees he was unsure of, he examined the parish registers, local deeds, and the manorial court rolls, he described changes in the local landscape, he puzzled over the meaning of place-names, but above all he was always conscious of both the contemporary and historical bonds of the community.

The only formal occasions when the whole of this community met together were when divine services were held in the parish church. Upon these occasions (as in other parish churches) an order of precedence in the seating arrangements was strictly observed. Shortly after the Reformation the gentry families began to install private pews in the nave, and they were followed by the farmers and craftsmen, and eventually by the labourers. The right to these seats descended with the possession of the particular farm or cottage to which they belonged, and in this way the social structure of the community was formalized. The gentry were seated in the most prominent places at the front, and the cottagers were crowded into the south-west corner. Such importance was attached to these matters that special parish meetings had to be called in cases of dispute or the erection of a new pew. These seating arrangements form the plan of Gough's book. He takes each pew in turn and writes about the individual histories of the families to which they belong. This is his central theme and the unifying factor in the life of the community. It is this, as much as anything else, that marks off Tudor and Stuart Myddle from modern society.

In this present work, Gough's writings have been supplemented from all the other sources that are available to the modern historian, and it is hoped that a great deal has been added to what Gough had to say. An attempt has been made to study in depth all the aspects of this rural community for a period of about six generations, between 1524 and 1701. Two theoretical objections may be raised. In the first place, it may be asked whether Myddle was in any real sense a community, or whether the unit of the parish was merely a legal framework with an artificial

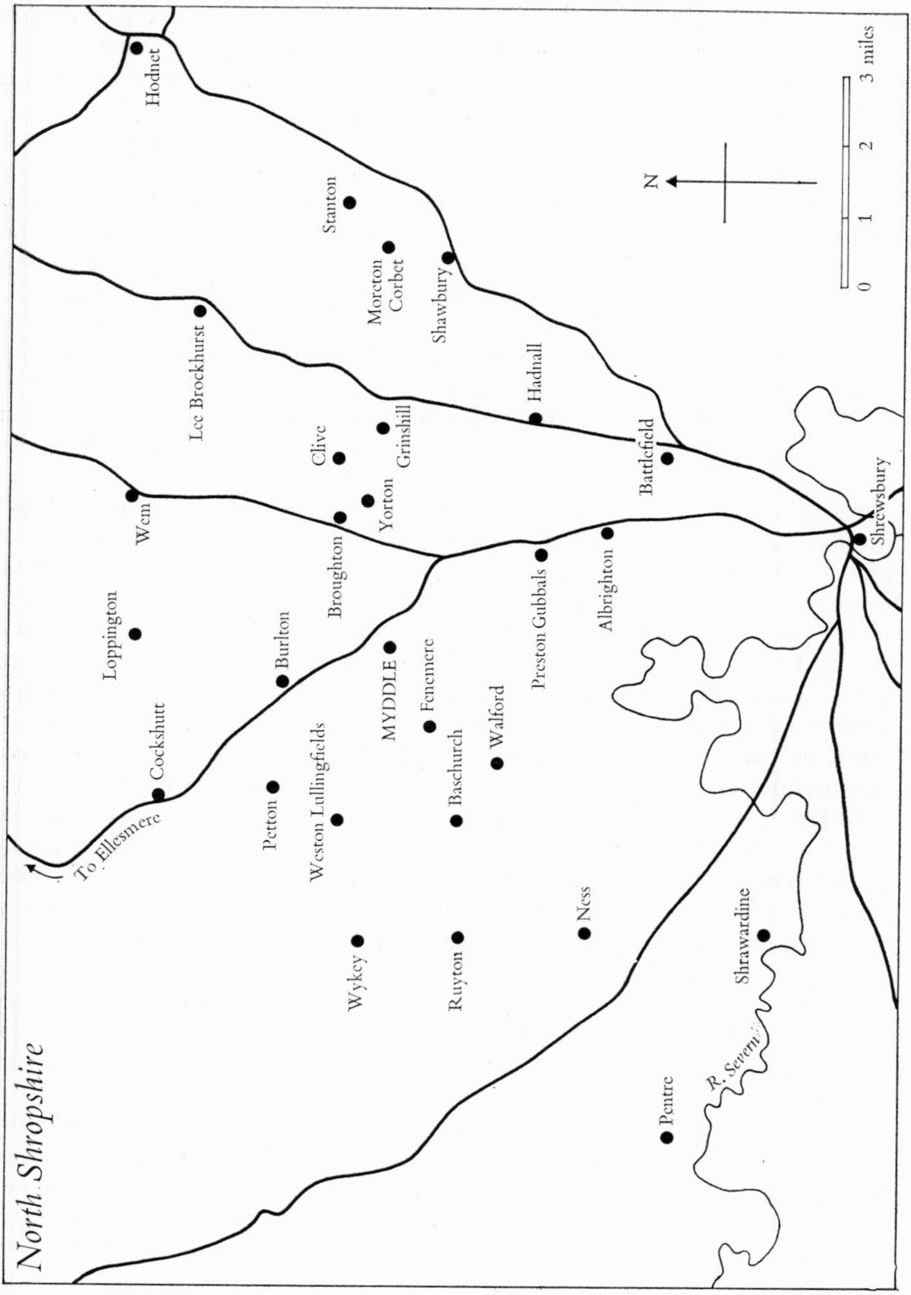
North Shropshire
Hodnet
Stanton
Moreton Corbet
Shawbury
Lee Brockhurst
Hadnall
Clive
Grinshill
Battlefield
Wem
Yorton
Broughton
Shrewsbury
Loppington
Burlton
MYDDLE
Fenemere
Preston Gubbals
Albrighton
Cockshutt
Weston Lullingfields
Baschurch
Walford
Petton
To Ellesmere
Wykey
Ruyton
Ness
Shrawardine
Pentre
R. Severn
N
0 1 2 3 miles

boundary. And, secondly, it may be questioned whether the period 1524–1701 has any validity as a unit of study, or whether this, too, is an arbitrary division that has been created solely by the chance survival of useful records. The first objection is more easily dealt with than the second.

Even when the chapelry of Hadnall is excluded, Myddle was a large parish of 4,691 acres, containing seven townships whose boundaries and organization were already anomalous by the sixteenth century. It was not an obvious geographical unit such as the single-township parishes of the arable east Midlands, where all the inhabitants were clustered together. There was also a great deal of contact and inter-marriage between people of neighbouring parishes. The people of Myddle had often lived in, worked in, or visited many of the surrounding villages and hamlets, and they were certainly conscious of belonging to a wider community than that of the parish. They also had some sense of county solidarity and spoke of it as their 'country'. Their friends and relations came from a fairly wide area in north Shropshire, and they were familiar with events and gossip from this wider district.

But only in their own parish did they know everyone. Gough was familiar with the detailed histories of families from all the seven townships, even though some of them lived two miles away. He himself lived in one of the small townships, a mile from the parish church, but he definitely thought in terms of the parish community. His whole book is based upon the assumption that he was writing about a group of people with a common history and common interests, and his own strong parochial attitude is revealed when he refuses to extend the benefits of his uncle's apprenticeship charity to the poor of Hadnall,[3] which was an independent chapelry bordering on his own township. The parish framework in Shropshire might have been in some respects an arbitrary one, but for many purposes it was the one that mattered. It was only in the parish church that large numbers of country folk met together. This gave them a sense of community and a consciousness that they belonged to a very local unit within the fairly wide district with which they were familiar. Anyone who has been brought up in a rural community will recognize this sense of belonging to a particular place within a wider neighbourhood. Professor W. M. Williams has described how in the present community of Gosforth (Cumberland), "The precise location of the parish boundary is very widely known and a very real difference is recognized between the people who live on either side of it, even where the actual distance is a matter of a few yards."[4]

This sense of community in Myddle must have been greatly strengthened by the long residence of several families, especially the yeomen and husbandmen of the leasehold tenements. Gough makes a division, according to size and value, between farms, tenements, and cottages. Some of the farms changed hands frequently and attracted outsiders, but most newcomers were from the wider area of north Shropshire, and a few gentry families were resident for several generations. The concept of the parish as the important local unit was given greater cohesion by the fact that these farms were usually held by minor gentry and substantial yeomen who rarely held land outside the parish. (The Atcherleys and the Downtons were the exceptions to the general rule.) Some of the cottagers were also resident in the parish for remarkably long periods, though, on the whole, this class tended to be the most mobile of all. But the backbone of the community was formed by the tenement-farmers, some of whose families lived in the parish throughout the 1524–1701 period, while others from this group inherited their holdings after marrying daughters of old families whose male line had come to an end. Gough's own family was established at Newton throughout the period, and he speaks respectfully of those whose names were even more ancient than his own in the local records. These families provided continuity and a sense of permanence for the community.

By the reign of Henry VIII the community was beginning to assume a special identity. Most of the names in the 1524 lay subsidy become familiar ones in later records, but the poll-tax returns of 1379 show that there had been no such continuity during the fifteenth century. It is the stability of a major group of families during the sixteenth and seventeenth centuries that is of significance during that period. Important changes in tenures during the sixteenth century helped to provide this stability by making the ordinary tenant secure in his possessions. This new security was accompanied by the clearing of immense stretches of woodland and the consequent abandoning of the open fields, which led to a pastoral form of economy. Men continued to get their livelihood in this way throughout the sixteenth and seventeenth centuries. There were, of course, other changes, especially when the population began to rise in the mid-seventeenth century, and the community was never a static one, but the period 1524–1701 can be seen as a whole, when the small tenement-farmer and the pastoral economy were the distinctive features.

This way of life continued for a while after Gough had written his book in 1701, but soon there were changes of a fundamental nature. By the time of the Tithe Award of 1838 there had been a large-scale conversion from pasture to arable farming, and a great deal of engrossing of the smaller tenements. The whole basis of the economy had been radically altered. The small tenement-farmer had largely disappeared and the community was sharply divided between a few rich farmers and the mass of the labourers. Most of the old names had vanished and the continuity had been broken. The Myddle of the nineteenth century was very different from the community of the sixteenth and seventeenth centuries.

It would have been an interesting task to discover exactly how this happened, but there are no records to enable one to date these changes precisely or to catalogue them in any detail. The parish registers cease to list occupations after 1660, the probate inventories peter out by the middle of the eighteenth century, Gough completed the bulk of his work in 1701, and, most important of all in this connection, there are no manorial surveys or rentals after 1656. One can only make general statements. This particular community cannot be examined in detail right to the end of its life, but it began to take a new form during the eighteenth century, and the dates 1524–1701 provide a framework during which a distinctive community was in existence.

It cannot be claimed that Myddle was *typical* of the rural communities of Tudor and Stuart England, for it is the *diversity* of such communities within the various agricultural regions that is interesting and important. But in one essential feature the parish of Myddle demonstrates a widespread phenomenon of those times, namely the continued importance of the small farmer. In the best corn-growing regions of the Midlands and East Anglia and in the vale lands that were newly enclosed for pasture, the small farmer was being driven out in the seventeenth century by low grain prices and the high cost of labour. But in the traditional pasture regions the yeomen and husbandmen were not only able to survive, but flourished during this period.[5] When A. H. Johnson discussed the disappearance of the small landowner throughout the country, he concluded that, despite the enclosing and engrossing of lands in the arable areas, the number of peasants in the country as a whole probably showed an overall increase during the Tudor and Stuart era.[6] The contrasting fortunes of arable and pastoral communities have been emphasized by local studies. At Sherington (Buckinghamshire) and Chippenham (Cambridgeshire) in the corn-growing area many smallholdings were engrossed in the seventeenth century,[7] but in the pastoral regions the continued vitality of the small farmer has been noted in a variety of local economies, such as in the Lincolnshire fens, the royal forests of Northamptonshire, or the Pennine districts of Lancashire and Yorkshire.[8]

The experience of the 'open' villages, where a strong freeholder class was able to resist enclosure, blurs this neat distinction between the arable and pastoral areas. Professor W. G. Hoskins has described the remarkable resilience of the peasants of Wigston Magna in the middle of the 'champion' or 'fielden' country in Leicestershire. While great changes transformed the economy and landscape of some of the neighbouring parishes, life in Wigston went on "with a monumental stability".[9] The lords of near-by Foston, Great Stretton, and Wistow destroyed the livelihood of their peasantry by enclosing the open arable fields and converting them to pasture, but the combined interest of the numerous small freeholders in Wigston prevented their lord from emulating his neighbours. Only in the 'closed' villages where the lord held a disproportionately large share of the land and where the peasants were few in number was the small farmer driven out; in the many 'open' villages where the property was divided into numerous small shares the yeomen and husbandmen managed to retain their way of life until well into the eighteenth century.

The "monumental stability" of life in Wigston was matched by the longevity of the peasant dynasties of Myddle. Both parishes contained "a solid core of middling-sized farmers",[10] and none of the 'peasant-gentry' families that rose from these ranks was ever rich and powerful enough to fulfil the role of squire. Neither was there much of a pauper problem until the pressure of immigration taxed local resources during the second half of the seventeenth century. Until then, both communities consisted largely of peasant farmers. But despite this important similarity, there were profound differences in the way of life of these peasant societies. Wigston lay at the very heart of the open-field system: it was a typical Midland nucleated village surrounded by its common arable lands, geared to the production of corn and to a mixed form of husbandry. It was always a large and populous village and by the end of the seventeenth century it was assuming an increasingly semi-industrial character. Myddle was very different. Its open fields were small and they were enclosed by agreement at an early date. The parish was relatively sparsely-populated, its settlements were widely scattered, and the farmers were chiefly occupied in raising beef and dairy cattle, with a few sheep and pigs, and the growing of crops for sustenance. The local crafts were never developed into an industry and the pauper problem in the late Stuart period was not as severe as in Wigston. The way of life of the arable farmer, cultivating his strips in a crowded, nucleated village, was alien to the Shropshire peasant who raised his animals in enclosed fields and upon the commons and who was more likely to live in a hamlet or an isolated farm than in the small village that lay at the centre of the parish.

Contemporary writers of the sixteenth and seventeenth centuries were aware of such differences, but as most of these chroniclers came from arable areas the woodlander has been persistently misrepresented as being both idle and lawless. Norden, for instance, wrote that "the people bred amongst woods are naturally more stubborn and uncivil than in the champion counties", and Aubrey thought of the woodlanders as "mean people [who] live lawless, [with] nobody to govern them, they care for nobody, having no dependence on anybody".[11] Whatever the truth of these harsh words when applied, for instance, to the remoter parts of the Kentish Weald, they were certainly an inaccurate description of the woodland communities of Shropshire. The characteristics that may be attributed to one woodland region need not necessarily have applied to all the others. Nevertheless, these regions had much in common and local historians are becoming increasingly aware of the value of studying communities as belonging to one or more definite types. The distinction between the 'open' and 'closed' nucleated arable villages has to be further refined so that rural settlements may alternatively be classified as, for example, industrial villages and hamlets, small market towns (whether flourishing or decayed), pastoral communities in the fens or in the Highland zone, and woodland parishes such as Myddle. These categories overlap, for few local societies conformed exactly to any one type, but it is more profitable for the historian to study Myddle in relation to other woodland communities throughout England than it is to compare such a parish with what are still commonly regarded as the 'classical English villages' of the Midlands.

Woodland communities originated either in former forest areas, like the forests of Arden, Dean, or Galtres, or they developed where there had never been a forest in the strict, legal sense of the word, but where large tracts of woodland remained uncleared until the sixteenth and seventeenth centuries. Myddle was a woodland community in the second, more general sense. These woodland parishes normally contained a parent village and several outlying townships that consisted of hamlets or a few scattered farms. The inhabitants generally held their land in severalty and by secure and, often, free tenures. Their security of possession and relative isolation from the centres of power made them more independent of secular and ecclesiastical control than was the case in the 'closed' villages of the 'champion' country. In the woodlands, the open-field system was abandoned early, and during the Tudor and Stuart period men earned their living there chiefly by rearing beef or milch cows, supplemented with subsistence farming and by-employments such as weaving or woodcrafts. In all these matters, Myddle may be described as a typical woodland community.

The physical environment of any sixteenth- or seventeenth-century society was of fundamental importance to its way of life, and the historian must start by studying the means by which people adapted themselves to it. But the patterns of regional culture are different from one woodland area to another, and every local community has its own individuality and does not altogether conform to the general type. Myddle and its neighbouring parishes did not have quite as many craftsmen as did some other woodland districts, nor was there much Nonconformity – at least, not before the nineteenth century. Woodland communities elsewhere differed in other ways; for instance, the royal forests of Northamptonshire contained a higher proportion of poor people than the surrounding arable villages,[12] whereas most woodland regions (including Shropshire) supported relatively few of the very poor, so that their labourers were less numerous and somewhat more prosperous than those of their rank in the 'champion' or 'fielden' zone.[13] The patterns of settlement, land-ownership and farming economy that were broadly similar in all the woodland areas did not invariably foster common characteristics in every aspect of life.

But though Myddle was different in some important respects from woodland communities in, say, Essex, Northamptonshire, or the Weald, it was broadly typical of its neighbouring parishes in the northern, lowland part of Shropshire, and it was comparable in many ways to the upland communities in the south of the county. The distinctive landscape not only of Shropshire but of the whole

Border region is one in which settlements are scattered and hamlets are more common than villages. The most obvious example of the normal pattern of several townships to one parish is provided by the name of Ruyton-XI-Towns, a parish a few miles to the west of Myddle, but Myddle parish, too, contained 11 townships before the chapelry of Hadnall was split from it. The experience of Myddle illustrates the usual manner in which the daughter townships of the Border region were colonized as farmsteads or hamlets by settlers who were offered generous terms to leave the parent villages to clear the surrounding woods. This piecemeal enclosure over the centuries, as woods were felled and swamps were drained, meant that the boundaries that were finally agreed upon made numerous twists and turns, and that the manorial structure was not always closely related to that of the parish. The resulting administrative anomalies that arose in Myddle were paralleled throughout Shropshire, and, indeed, throughout those other parts of England where the woods were cleared at a relatively late date.

In the parish of Myddle over a thousand new acres were brought into cultivation between the late fifteenth and the early seventeenth centuries. Similar contemporary schemes to fell the woods and drain the mosses and meres were put into operation in other parts of north Shropshire, especially on the Bridgewater estates in the lordships of Ellesmere and Whitchurch, and near by at Wem. These new lands were converted to pasture or meadow and the old open-field arable lands were abandoned to farming in severalty. Most of Shropshire's villages had once had an open-field system, and the evidence from Myddle parish suggests that the daughter townships also farmed a small area of open arable and meadow that was not fenced off into closes like the surrounding pastures. The enclosure of all these open fields occurred early and by agreement in Shropshire and there was no acute social distress such as that which accompanied so much conversion in the arable villages of the Midlands. Only seven parliamentary Acts were required to complete the process in the county in the late eighteenth century. The disappearance of the open fields was of little consequence when compared with the reclamation projects which provided the outstanding examples of improvement in the economy of the region during this period. The woodland clearances were used for grazing and the newly-drained mosses and meres were valuable for their peat and for their hay. Peat-cutting enterprises were associated with the drainage of Wem Moss (*c.* 1560) and of Brown Moss, near Whitchurch (by 1572), as well as of Harmer Moss in Myddle lordship, while the increased demands for winter feed that arose from the new emphasis on pasture farming made it profitable to drain meres for the purpose of growing hay. Both Harmer and a large pool of 200 acres near Wem were converted to meadow after they had been drained.[14]

From the sixteenth century onwards Shropshire's settlement patterns were made increasingly diverse not only as a consequence of this continuous process of clearing but as a result of the immigration of large numbers of squatters who began to erect cottages on the edges of the commons and unproductive land. Many of these cottages still survive (like the one in Myddlewood) in the form in which they were inhabited during the sixteenth and seventeenth centuries; others have been largely rebuilt, or encased in brick and stone. The pattern of immigration into Myddle broadly reflects the experience of the county as a whole, but the timing of this squatter movement varied from parish to parish. The first labourer's cottage to be erected in Myddlewood was built in 1581, but similar cottages were being erected in some other parts of the county a generation or so earlier. The first recorded example that has so far come to light was at Kenley, some ten miles south of Shrewsbury, in 1537. By the end of the century a dozen cottages had encroached upon Kenley common. On the Welsh border, to the west of Shrewsbury, squatters first appeared in the parish of Alberbury-with-Cardeston about the year 1540, and by 1584 they had enclosed a quarter of the central part of the heath. Other squatter settlements of the late sixteenth or early seventeenth centuries have been identified in Condover and Ford hundreds at Bayston Common, Exsfordsgreen, Lythwood, Pontesbury Hill and Preen Wood;[15] place-names that are indicative of the types of area into which the squatters were moving. Labourers were emigrating to woodland areas and setting up homes on the edges of the commons and uncultivated tracts of land in many parts of the country during the Tudor and Stuart period. A precise chronology of this movement has not yet been established, but the evidence from Shropshire suggests that this remote Border county was probably one of the last places to absorb these migrants. In the hundred of Pimhill (which included Myddle) the population rose by almost two-thirds between 1563 and 1672,[16] but most of this rise occurred after the first three decades of the seventeenth century. Some of the incoming labourers were housed in the existing villages and hamlets, but, more characteristically, new squatter communities, such as the colony that became established in Myddlewood, were formed on the edges of the heaths and commons.

But the central theme of the Tudor and Stuart period in Myddle must be stability rather than change. This stability only became apparent during the reign of Henry VIII. Shropshire appears to have been a comparatively poor county until that time, and Mr Trevor Rowley has recently pointed out how this is reflected in the large number of Norman churches that survive in the county, for few communities were ever wealthy enough to rebuild them in a Gothic style.[17] The stability of Myddle's farming families during the sixteenth century, in contrast to the previous hundred years, suggests an increase in prosperity that was no doubt associated with the new emphasis on pasture farming that led to the disappearance of the open fields and the cultivation of former wastes. It is not yet possible to say whether this stability of a central core of peasant families was widely paralleled in other Shropshire communities, but the signs are that Myddle was in no way exceptional, though the chronology would be different from place to place. Across the River

Severn at Ford, for instance, none of the fourteenth-century families still held land there in 1601, but during the seventeenth century there was a remarkable continuity in family ownership.[18]

This stability was enhanced by the soundness of the tenures during this period. Small freeholds were common in Shropshire and during the sixteenth century the copyhold tenement-farms began to be held on three-life leases. Some manors introduced this form of lease rather earlier than in the lordship of Myddle, and some retained the system until much later, but on the whole Myddle conformed to regional practice. In Bayston manor, for example, the three-life lease was normal from 1546 to the end of the seventeenth century, and the same system of tenure is well documented in Acton Burnell, Condover, and Kenley.[19] In each case, this method of holding land was terminated at various stages during the eighteenth century. As leases fell in, estate owners refused to renew them, for it was then more profitable to grow corn on larger farms. Some of the hedges were torn down, small farms were engrossed into larger ones, and the old pastures were ploughed up and converted to arable farming. The transformation of the agricultural system in the parish of Myddle not only exemplified the general trend throughout the county but reflected a national movement as a result of which the small landowner found it increasingly difficult to survive. In Shropshire, the three-life lease was rapidly replaced at Kenley after 1750 by tenancy-at-will; at Harley, holdings at will had become common by 1768, though it was not until the mid-nineteenth century that the process of creating a few large farms from the numerous small ones was completed; and though yearly tenancies were not introduced at Condover until 1799, they too soon became universal. Roughly the same story could be told at Acton Burnell, Bayston, Cressage, and Pitchford,[20] and the reports of the Board of Agriculture written at the close of the eighteenth century state that the size of farms had recently increased in all parts of the county, while the number of farms had diminished by about a third.[21]

As a result of the disappearance of so many farms many townships lost their status as administrative units as hamlets shrank and sometimes completely disappeared. In Myddle parish, most of the tenements that comprised Balderton township were engrossed into the hall estate by the middle of the eighteenth century, and Houlston was absorbed into Myddle township when its five tenements were amalgamated into a single farm. Daughter townships such as these were decaying all over the county. In Condover hundred, "Of the 61 hamlets which appear to have existed in the hundred at the time of Domesday Book, eight have since been deserted and 31 have shrunk to one or two farms apiece", while in Ford hundred, "Out of some 70 former hamlets nine have been deserted and 33 have shrunk to single farms".[22] Most of these decayed settlements shrank or disappeared as a result of the engrossing of the smaller farms during the eighteenth and early nineteenth centuries.

In this way the characteristic Tudor and Stuart farming economy of the Border region was destroyed. But before this happened Shropshire's woodland communities enjoyed two centuries of stability and mild prosperity. The following pages will describe the way of life of one of these communities, in so far as the available documents and visual evidence allow the tale to be told. Without Richard Gough's unique book, it would have been hard to breathe human life into the dry bones of this local society, but with the preservation of this rich and entertaining work the people of his parish have become the best documented of all the rural communities of Tudor and Stuart England.

CHAPTER ONE

Topography

1 · The site

The winding forest road that passes out of Shrewsbury in a north-westerly direction is an ancient route heading for Ellesmere. For five or six miles it twists towards the north until it passes the wooded slopes of Pim Hill (the meeting place of the hundred since the rearrangements of the twelfth century), and shortly afterwards it divides, the right fork following the eastern boundary of Myddle parish towards Wem, and the left one carrying on over Harmer Hill towards Ellesmere. This branch divides again after only a few hundred yards into a Higher Way along the ridge and a Lower Way that seeks shelter under the slopes, alongside what used to be a large lake (the Har-mere), until both ways join again on Myddle Hill and pass on out of the parish.

Another road, now much reduced in status, comes to join the Ellesmere road from the east, and after accompanying it for only a very short distance, drops down the hill to carry on west through Myddle village. This was once an important through road connecting the market town of Oswestry on the Welsh border with the new towns of Market Drayton and Newport that were sited right on the eastern borders of the county. Gough tells us that "it was usually the way of the Newport butchers to goe to Oswaldstree fayre, and there to buy fatt cattell, and to come the same day backe to Myddle and to ly att [the village] inne all night".[1] An estate map of 1650 confirms the route by naming it "Drayton Way".[2] But this road was much more ancient than the creation of these market towns, for its junction with the Ellesmere road has given Myddle its name. The Normans recorded it in Domesday Book as Mulleht, but the Saxon name was Mutla, and

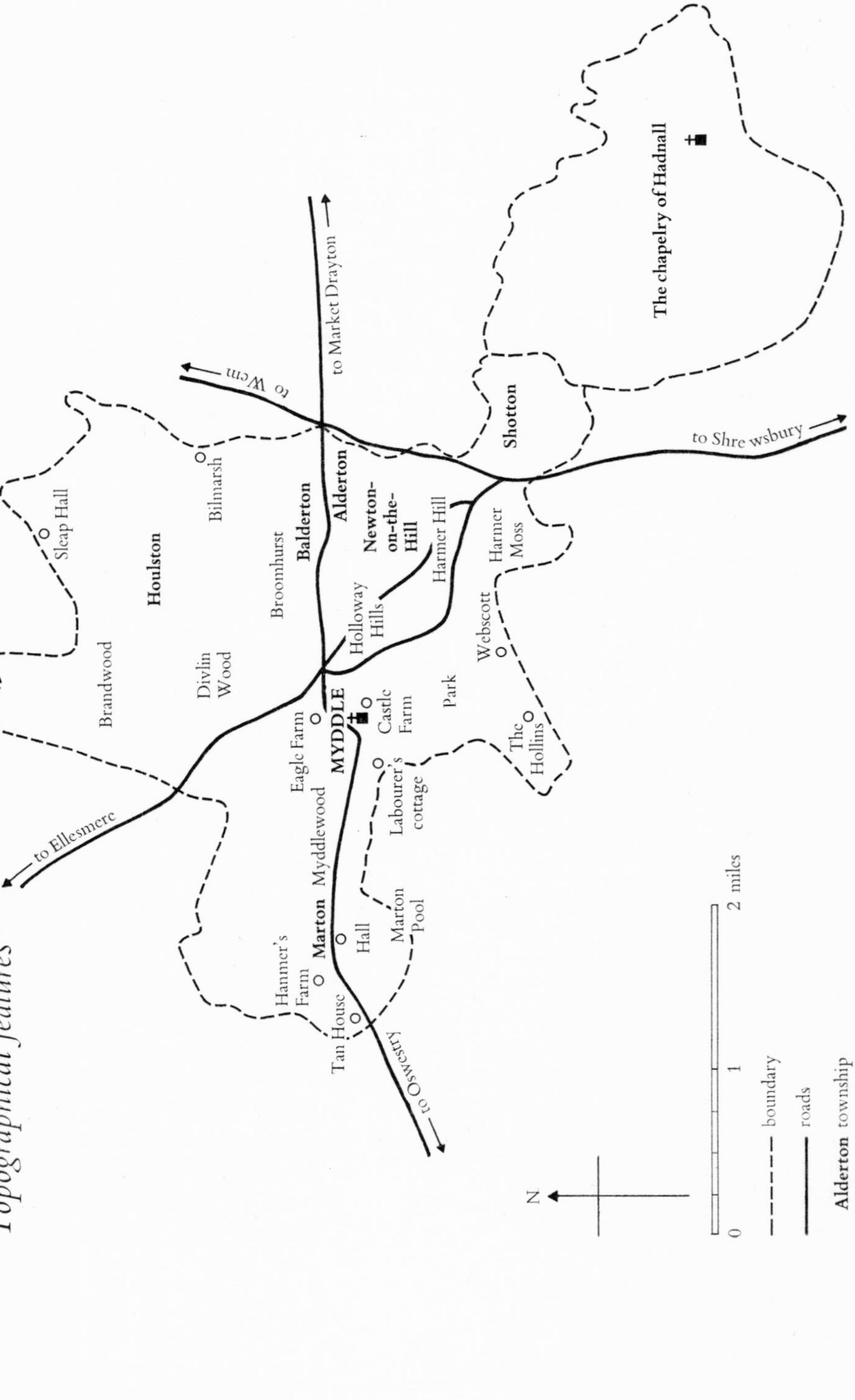

Topographical features

later, Muthla, before it became Muddle, and eventually Middle or Myddle. The name means 'a junction' where land was cleared and a settlement founded.[3]

From this parent settlement colonies were started in the surrounding countryside, so that by the time the parish boundaries were first marked out, no less than 6,903 acres came within its limits. Over 2,200 acres belonged to the chapelry of Hadnall, with which this history is not concerned. The rest was divided between the parent township of Myddle and the daughter townships of Marton, Newton, Houlston, Balderton, Alderton, and Shotton. The origin and development of these townships is dealt with in section 3 of this chapter.

The church and the castle are situated almost at the highest point of Myddle village, away from the junction and beyond the Pinchbrook stream, on a less exposed and more defensive site. The village straggles down from the church towards the stream, and in later times crept up the ridge on the other side. Throughout the parish the height of the land is generally about the 300′ contour mark, dipping slightly to the north-east. It rises to just over 400′ at Newton-on-the-Hill, but nowhere does it fall below the 270′ mark. North Shropshire has a gentle landscape, one that is still rural and peaceful for the traveller, with enough trees and variations of contour to please the eye, with the bold hill of the Wrekin rising dramatically to the south, and the misty slopes of the Welsh mountains framing the wide expanse to the west.

Myddle lies almost at the southern edge of the large lowland area of north Shropshire and Cheshire, far from the Pennines to the east, but not too far from the hills that bound it on the west, and within striking distance of the hills to the south of the county. It is an area that has been extensively glaciated. Two large ice-sheets met here on their way down from the Lake District and the Welsh mountains, with profound consequences for the landscape, and indeed for the whole farming economy. The glacial deposits have left a great variety of clays, sands, and gravels, varying considerably both in their composition and surface form. The modern soil-map is a jigsaw of patterns and colours that represent the complexities faced by the farmers of this parish. In practice that meant almost everyone. There is still no industry, and today many have to travel outside the parish to their jobs.

Almost all the north Shropshire villages were settled by the time of Domesday Book on or near the edge of the light brown-earths which occupied the gentlest slopes and were the easiest to cultivate. Thick woods were unlikely to thrive on these soils, which were more likely to produce an open canopy with a great deal of grass. Myddle was founded upon such a site and there were already eight hides of land cleared in the manor by the time of the Norman Conquest. In between the villages were expanses of heavy, ill-drained land, supporting only thick woods, glacial pools, and swamps. The distances between the villages varied according to the extent of this uninviting territory, while the narrow roads that joined one settlement to another twisted and turned round physical objects that were easier to circumvent than remove. The one-inch Ordnance Survey map reveals even on a casual survey the landscape and settlement patterns of a former woodland area. Myddle was never in a forest in the legal sense of the word[4] (though Hadnall formed part of the Wrekin forest until 1300), but north Shropshire has all the characteristics that one generally associates with a forest zone. There are numerous small villages and hamlets, woods and winding lanes, pools and drainage ditches, and frequent late place-names ending in '–green' and '–cote' (or '–cott'), with 'woodhouses', 'Hayes', 'Newtons', '–woods', and 'Leasows' (a west Midlands name for a woodland pasture), intermixed with the heaths and the mosses. The clearing of these woods and the drainage of these marshes and meres was pursued in fits and starts throughout Anglo-Saxon and medieval times, and in a more organized way during the fifteenth, sixteenth, and seventeenth centuries. In Myddle it occupied a good deal of time and energy during all these periods.

The brown-earths of Myddle parish are mainly those of the Clive Series, though some of the Hodnet Series can be found around Newton, and those of the Newport Series at Marton.[5] The Clive Series are "distinguished by the warm brown coloured surface passing to a grey or yellowish-grey weathering sandstone at no great depth". They are well-drained soils and most suitable for arable cultivation. The site of Myddle village was well chosen; it remained the largest settlement in the parish, and Marton and Newton, the two other places in Myddle parish that are on the brown-earths, were the largest of the secondary settlements that were colonized from the parent village.

The other main series of soils is the gley-soils, consisting of clay and loam, which are found in flat areas where natural drainage is unsatisfactory or almost non-existent. North Shropshire lies in the rain-shadow of the Welsh mountains and is amongst the drier parts of Britain, but the results of glaciation meant that the area had a great amount of stagnant water. Arable crops do not take kindly to these gley-soils, and even where they have now been artificially drained they are only used today as permanent pasture, except for occasional light patches that are suitable for growing corn. The Salop Series of gley-soils is found in Myddle parish on the low-lying lands to the south, around Webscott and the Hollins, with the Crewe Series stretching from Myddlewood over almost the whole of the northern part of the parish. This latter area was the last to be cleared and drained, and the place-names of the isolated farms – Brandwood, Bilmarsh, Broomhurst, and Sleap (a "miry place") – tell their own tale. Some of this land remained tenanted from the lord, but much was let out to freeholders (from at least the twelfth century) and eventually grouped into small townships.

In the very lowest areas, around Marton Pool and Harmer Moss, the soil is a peaty loam. Harmer was drained during the seventeenth century and converted into meadow and pasture land and a turbary, but Marton Pool was left for fishing and fowling, and today adds a touch of natural beauty to the rural scene. The parish boundary goes through the middle of it, and this joint ownership (the free-holders of Marton also had fishing rights) may have prevented any attempts to drain it.

Finally, in this short survey of soil conditions, mention must be made of the outcrop of sandstone which runs alongside Harmer Moss and breaks out again on Myddle Hill. This band of rock never carried enough soil to support a crop, but it has provided an excellent building stone for several centuries, and when all the other land was used up, nineteenth-century squatters found nooks and crannies in which to erect their cottages; a process that is now being repeated with modern bungalows.

These, then, are the basic soil types, but in a glaciated area such as this there are bound to be numerous variations upon these basic themes. The modern six-inch Ordnance Survey map marks several features that worked to the advantage of the farmer. Clay pits are marked in the brown-earth zones north-east of Newton and south-west of the church. There are two gravel pits south of Bilmarsh and another one in Myddle just north of the house by the higher well. And there are two sand pits south of the castle, another one in the south-west corner of the park, and a fourth at Marton. The Soil Survey also remarks[6] that alternating bands of marl and thin sandstone known as skerries are very well exposed in Bilmarsh Lane. There are fields called Marl Fields in this area, and in other places within the parish. There was much that was to the farmer's advantage once his land had been drained. It is a prosperous farming region today.

Gough also tells us that, "This place has the benefitt of good water for Marton, beside the large Meare that is neare it, has severall springs and pumps in the towne, and a cleare brooke in winter time running along part of the street. Myddle has two faire wells in the common street beside pumps and draw-wells, and a brooke running over crosse the street at the lower end of the Towne".[7] The smaller settlements on the gley-soils and at Newton were less fortunate, for they "have only pitt water" and a common well between Newton, Balderton, and Alderton. All this helps to explain why Myddle was chosen as the original settlement. It was a defensive site just off two main roads, with natural clearings and the best soils, and with a plentiful supply of water. It also shared with the rest of the area "great plenty of freestone" and abundant wood for building purposes.

2 · *The church and the parish*

The church of St Peter in Myddle was a Saxon foundation. Its dedication and the large size of its original parish (nearly 7,000 acres) compared with its neighbours would have made one suspect that this was so even though there is no architectural evidence to prove it. The documentary references, however, are quite clear. A priest is recorded in Domesday Book, and sometime before the Norman Conquest the church had been granted by Warin the Bald to the monks of Shrewsbury Abbey. The monks never appropriated the church, but presented rectors until the Dissolution, when the advowson passed to the Chambres of Petton and Balderton Hall, who in turn sold it to the Egertons shortly after their purchase of the manor in about 1600. From that time it continued in the hands of the lord.

Nothing of the ancient fabric survives. The original tower was a stone one as high as the wall-plate of the nave, with a wooden steeple on top. But this collapsed in 1634, and the present stone tower was erected.[8] The rest of the building was completely reconstructed in 1744 and extensively restored in Victorian times. So now, the only connecting link with the Saxon and medieval church is the use of the same commanding site by the present building, close to the castle at the top of the village.

The seating plans drawn up by Gough[9] suggest that the original church had no aisles, for his north aisle leads straight into the centre of the chancel. Then as the population increased and more space was needed, three arches were knocked out of the southern wall and a new structure equal in size to the old was added, with a great window adorning its eastern end. The present church follows the same plan. A further increase of population in Myddlewood in the late sixteenth and the seventeenth centuries led to more pews being installed, until there were 47 in all. The church was now taking as many seats as it could hold, the south door was permanently closed, and the font was moved just inside the north door. And as with any other church, the gentry occupied the front pews, the yeomen and husbandmen sat behind them, and the cottagers sat in the far corner at the back.

The Parsonage House stood on the opposite side of the street, next to Dodd's tenement. The manorial surveyor of 1563 claimed that it was concealed property of the lord's but was unsure how it had become so. "The parson of Myddle witholdeth my lord of a house and gardine in Myddle towne. Dod's and that weare all one thinge and Dod's is my lord's. The parson hath bin a good whyle in possession. It was granted to a clerk of that church (how I ken not) and so hath continued longe, but some say it was in consideration of a marriage". The lord took no steps to enforce his claims, and the house and garden continued as a freehold without even a chief rent. In the 1640s, Thomas Moore, the absentee rector, "regarded not the repaire of the parsonage-house and buildings, one large barn whereof went to ruine in his time", but his successor, Joshua Richardson, "built that part of the parsonage-house which is the kitchen and the rooms below it, in which hee made use of so much of the timber as was left of the barne that fell downe in Mr More's time".[10] The 1699 terrier[11] described it as: "The parsonage house, containeing four bayes; the back house or kilne, one bay; the barn, five bayes; the stable and beast house, two bayes . . . the garden containeing about the eighth part of an acre; the fowl yard containeing [the same]; the yard containeing about a quarter of an acre; [and] the fold yard containeing about a sixteenth part of an acre . . .". Nothing

The parish and townships

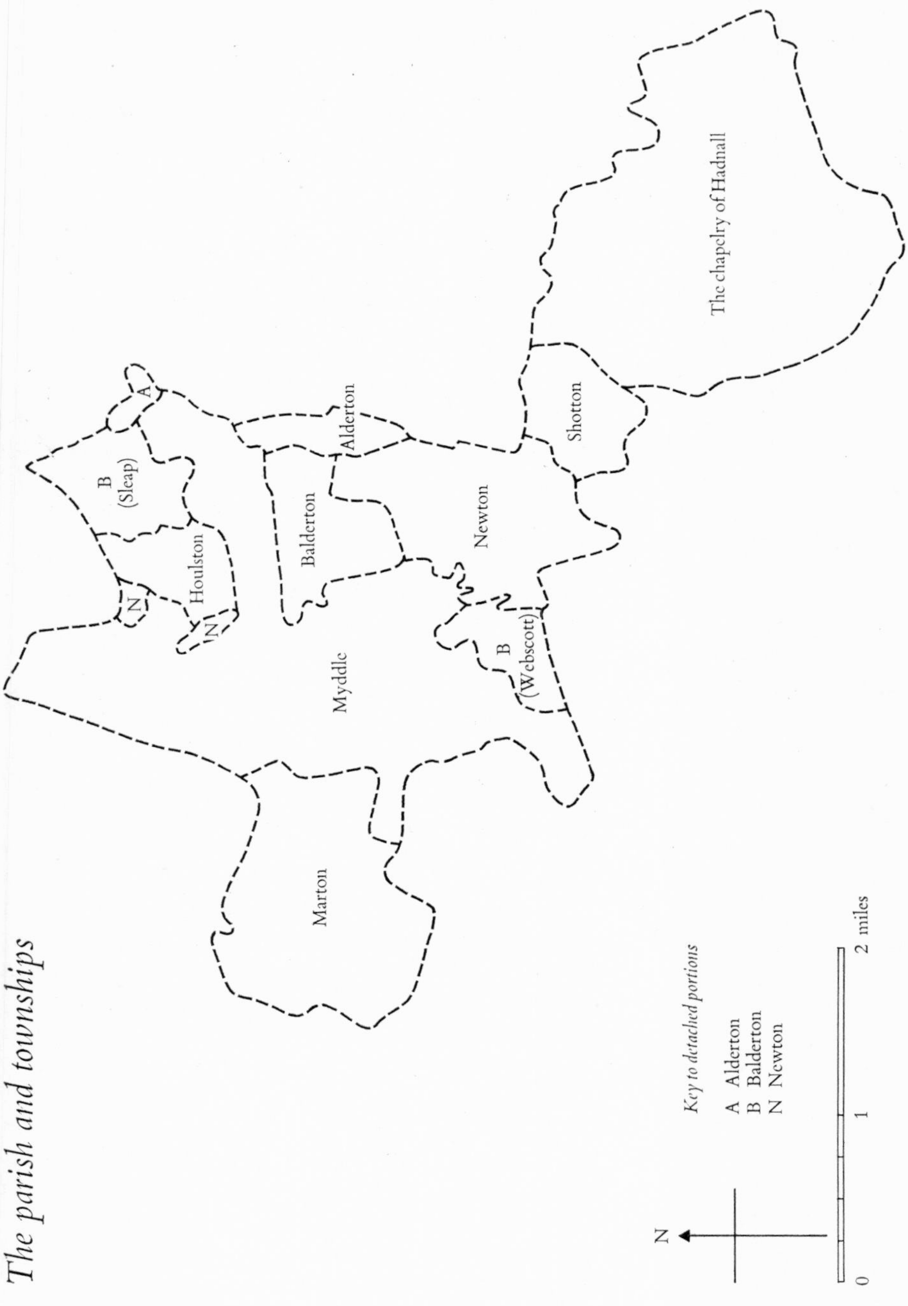

remains of this old building; the old and the new rectories stand there in its place.

The parson had no land of his own apart from this, but his parish covered 6,903 acres and the tithes made it a goodly living. Like most woodland parishes, Myddle was much larger than those in the arable east Midlands, but it was also one of the largest in north Shropshire. The area served by Myddle church was reduced by almost one-third when the inhabitants of Hadnall's Ease built a chapel of their own[12] to save themselves their "three long miles" weekly trek. But there was never any endowment to this chapel, and the mother church jealously guarded its parochial rights of baptism, marriage, and burial until the early years of the eighteenth century. The inhabitants of Hadnall maintained the chapel and a minister by their gifts, but they were still compelled to pay their tithes to the rector and to pay rates for the repair of Myddle church, even though they had no seats there. They naturally felt aggrieved over this and in 1693 petitioned the Bishop of Lichfield to order the rector to provide for "a competent curate to read divine service, and administer the holy sacrament". The bishop reluctantly replied that he had no legal power to do this and that they would have to be content with the £5 a year that they got from the rector as "of free gift".[13] The "thirty families" of Hadnall's Ease continued their separate existence and form no part of this history.

The exclusion of the townships of the chapelry – Hadnall, Haston, Smethcot, and Hardwick – leaves 4,691 acres. The parish boundaries reflect the pattern of the original clearings of the woods. Some farms like the Hollins, or Brandwood, or Sleap Hall, are obviously late appendages to the original nucleus. A modern planner would put them each in a different unit from that of Myddle, but when they were first cleared they were still cut off by woods and pools from those other settlements which look so much nearer to them today. Gough devotes a lengthy section to the brooks that acted as parish bounds; some of these were large enough to be obvious natural frontiers, like the Old Mill Brook at Marton, or Sleap Brook, but most of them were tiny and sluggish, little more than drainage ditches, and serving as bounds only in the absence of more obvious features. The boundary in the east was different in that for about a mile it followed the line of an ancient saltway heading towards Shrewsbury from the Cheshire salt-mines. But in the far north-eastern corner beyond Bilmarsh the parish boundary was pushed back a considerable way beyond the track to another stream. Gough was at great pains to be exact about the boundaries, and in 1626 Ralph Kinaston, the rector, was presented by his churchwardens at the bishop's visitation for not going on the perambulation.[14] This annual walk around the parish was essential in maintaining its integrity in the days before there were any detailed maps, especially in a woodland area like north Shropshire where there was a lot of late settlement and there were few natural boundaries.

3 · *The manor and the townships*

The lordship of Myddle did not cover the whole of the parish, even when one excludes the chapelry of Hadnall. The townships of Myddle, Marton, Newton, and Houlston all lay within the manor, but Alderton, Balderton, and Shotton were either separate in origin or cut off at some remote and early date. To Gough and his contemporaries the combined unit of Balderton and the lordship of Myddle was known as "this side of the parish", whereas Alderton and Shotton, together with the townships of Hadnall's Ease (Hadnall, Haston, Smethcot, and Hardwick) lay within the Liberty of Shrewsbury and formed "the far side of the parish". Despite this terminology, the inhabitants of Alderton and Shotton worshipped at the mother church and not at the chapel-of-ease. Geographically, the divisions do not make complete sense, for Alderton was physically united with the other townships of "this side" and was completely cut off from the rest of "the far side". An obvious demarcation line would have been along the narrow strip of the Newton–Shotton boundary which is in fact the only link between the two major parts of the parish, but Shotton continued to be attached to the parish church even though it lay on "the far side". These puzzles need an historical rather than a geographical explanation.

At the time of the Domesday survey Shotton was probably joined to all the townships of the chapelry in the separate manor of Hadnall. The name was recorded as Hadehelle, that is Headda's nook or corner, from an Old English personal name.[15] The Saxon owner, Godwin, had been dispossessed and the manor granted to Osmund under Rainald the Sheriff, who was the lord of 11 manors within the Domesday hundred of Baschurch. During the course of the next 150 years, large parcels from within the manor were granted to Haughmond Abbey. Gilbert, the Lord of Hadnall, gave the whole of Hardwick and a half of Hadnall township to the abbey in the 1150s, and his son-in-law, Nigel Banaster, made further grants.[16] Some of the smaller freeholders also followed their lord's example. The Banasters were to become leading landowners in Myddle as well, and it was probably they who were instrumental in building the chapel-of-ease at Hadnall.

The township of Shotton somehow became split off from the parent manor, but remained attached to Myddle church. This event probably took place before the chapel was built. By the sixteenth century the township consisted of just one farm. But to add to the confusion Gough writes: "It is thought that Smethcott did formerly belong to this farme, and that these two made one manor; and that, therefore, Smethcott was called Shotton Smethcott, for soe I finde it written".[17] He also speaks of a further tradition that, "One Bishop Rowland was sometime tenant of this farme; that hee was a Lord Marcher, and that the place of Execution was on the banke betweene Shotton and Smethcott, which I have sometimes, (though seldome) heard called the Gallow-tree banke". There is only Gough to guide one on this. By the sixteenth century there was no manorial organization here and Smethcot was quite separate from Shotton and within the chapelry. The two are not recorded together again.

The other township that lay on "the far side of the parish", within the Liberty of Shrewsbury, but served by the parish church, was Alderton. The early forms of the name are Alverton (1195) and Alverton-super-Bylemars (1280–90), suggesting to Bowcock the Anglo-Saxon personal name of Aelfhere.[18] The change to Alderton came not from the alder trees which adorn the farms today but from analogy with neighbouring Balderton. But the derivation of the name is a minor puzzle compared with the question of its origin and raison d'être as a township.

The parish boundary follows the old saltway coming from the north through Sleap and Bilmarsh and joining the Wem–Shrewsbury road just to the south of Alderton. There were only three farms within this township and the parish boundary had to be diverted from the salt-track to loop round the back of one of them, just a few yards away from Broughton farm in the parish of that name. If the parish boundaries had been drawn up with any regard to neatness, then Alderton must surely have been united with the two neighbouring and ancient settlements of Broughton and Yorton, which were much nearer to it. But Broughton did not become an independent parish until long after Alderton was founded, and by that time Alderton had become part of Myddle parish. The township is far from being unique in this; for these boundary settlements are common in ex-woodland areas.

Blakeway writes[19] that in 1195–6 Fulk fitz Warin sold Alderton to Roger de Lee, and that it was eventually granted to Wombridge Priory. At the Dissolution it was sold to Selman Wike who soon parted with it to the tenants – the two Downtons and Walter Amis, for the township already consisted of three farms. It continued to form part of the Liberty of Shrewsbury and had a joint constable with Hardwick township, which was a single farm in Hadnall's Ease more than a mile distant on the other side of Broughton and Yorton.

But although the original Alderton seems to have had no connection with the lordship of Myddle, the Downtons of Alderton Hall paid a nominal peppercorn rent for 45 acres of freehold land in Alderton to the lord of Myddle. These 45 acres formed a detached portion of the township beyond the lord's land at Bilmarsh in the far north-eastern tip of Myddle parish. The 1602 survey of Myddle lordship referred to it as "divers pastures and meadows lying in the Lordship of Myddle between Bilmarsh and Tilley park", and at that court Thomas Downton produced the original deed whereby one of the Lords Strange granted to John de la Lee, knight, lord of Alvertone, all the land tenanted by Robert Porter. As deeds were undated before the reign of Edward I (and this one bears no date), then it must date back to at least the thirteenth century, before Alderton passed from the Lees to Wombridge Priory.

Eyton believed that the whole township of Alderton was once a member of the lordship of Myddle, but that it was separated before the time of the Lords Strange. He quotes a deed to show that during the reign of Richard I, Fulk fitz Warin II sold Alderton to Reyner de Lee (now Lea Hall), and that it passed from Reyner to his lineal descendants, Thomas, Thomas, and John. For this land, the Lees paid an annual sum of one pound of pepper. He also quotes a deed of *c.* 1280–90, whereby "John de Lee, son of Thomas de Lee, gives to Stephen de Lee, his brother, certain land in Alverton super Bylemars".[20] It would seem from all this that the deeds Eyton quotes relate only to the detached portion of 45 acres, for which Thomas Downton showed the grant (or, more accurately, the confirmation) to the surveyor of 1602. These acres undoubtedly lay within the lordship of Myddle, but there is no evidence to explain the origin of the major part of the township.

A final complication about Alderton is brought to light by an undated document in the Augmentation records in the Public Record Office,[21] which reads, "The king is seized in his demesne, as of fee, of and in certain messuage[s] lands, tenements, with appurtenances, set, lying, and being in Alderton and Shifnal in the county of Salop given to and for the maintenance of one [stipendiary?] priest . . . lying within the parish church of Fesall", with a yearly value of £4 1*s.* 8*d.*, which John Downton, John Amis, and George Downton "hath entered . . . claiming the same to be their own proper inheritance". There do not seem to be any other records that shed light on this matter, and as Alderton continued to comprise just three farms held by the two Downtons and the Amis family, the dispute was probably cleared up to their satisfaction.

The remaining township that lay outside the lordship of Myddle was Balderton. Unlike Alderton and Shotton, however, it had no connection with the Liberty of Shrewsbury. 'Balder's tun' was a small Anglo-Saxon estate of about 275 acres that was unrecorded in Domesday Book. Eyton believed that two-thirds of it was probably separated from Myddle before the time of the first Lord Strange, and annexed (with Sleap Hall) to the fee of Hussey of Albright Hussey. The other third passed to the Lords Strange and was granted by them in 1175 to a William Fitz Walter of Shelvock. Four years later, this William gave his part to Haughmond Abbey, and this was confirmed by the Lords Strange. Five deeds for the period 1216–30 show how the Abbey let their lands to tenants.[22] John L'Estrange II also granted half a virgate in Webscott (1178–80) to the Abbey, with common pasture throughout the fee of Myddle for the livestock of the abbot's tenants at Balderton and Webscott. Some time later, the major part of Balderton, together with a small part of Webscott, also passed to Haughmond Abbey, which already possessed the manor of Hardwick and property in Hadnall and neighbouring Grinshill.

Haughmond Abbey was dissolved in 1541 and its property sold off during the next two years. Its lands in Balderton township were sold with Hardwick manor, for in the late sixteenth and seventeenth centuries the freeholders of Balderton paid an annual chief rent and a 'best beast' heriot to the lord of Hardwick. They also attended the Hardwick Court Baron but came under the jurisdiction of the Court Leet for the hundred of Pimhill. By the middle of the eighteenth century the tenements were engrossed into the Hall estate, which was already one of the chief seats of the parish.

Webscott and Sleap Hall were two outlying farms at opposite ends of the parish, each separated from the parent township. Both were freeholds held at small chief rents of Myddle lordship. (Only small parts of Webscott had been granted to the religious foundation, and Sleap Hall had never been alienated). It is difficult to see why either of them was joined to the township of Balderton. The 178 acres of Webscott Farm lay immediately to the south of Myddle Park and would seem to fit in perfectly with the rest of Myddle township. It was separated from Balderton by the rocky cliff of Harmer and Myddle hills and by one of the open fields of Myddle and there is no direct connecting road between the two parts of the township. The name is derived from "Wigbealdes scaga",[23] the wood of a Mercian noble – but it paid a nominal chief rent to the lord of Myddle and was not an independent estate.

Sleap Hall's attachment to the parish of Myddle is as much of a puzzle. It was separated by a brook from the township of Sleap in the parish of Loppington, to whose church it was once directly connected by the saltway. There was no such easy route to Myddle church. The saltway connected the hall to Bilmarsh and Alderton, and a cart-track also wound its way from Sleap through Brandwood, before it was obliterated in modern times by an airfield. But otherwise Sleap Hall was completely cut off beyond the woods and Myddle Pools in the north-eastern tip of the parish, "a miry place" by the brook. It was always remote from the rest of the parish, and its owners lived for most of the time in their native Cheshire. A plausible explanation is that both Sleap and Webscott were colonized from the parent village of Myddle and therefore were included within the manor, that by their common descent to the Husseys, Balderton and Sleap became united (possibly at a time when the land between them was not yet cleared), and that parts of Webscott became connected with Balderton through grants to Haughmond Abbey. The township of Balderton, in other words, was pieced together as a result of changes in ownership.

The remainder of "this side of the parish" is accounted for by the lordship of Myddle. This manor had been held by Seward before the Conquest, together with five other manors in Baschurch (later, Pimhill) hundred, but the Normans gave it to Earl Roger, who in turn granted it to Rainald the Sheriff. The Domesday entry reads: "There are 8 hides. In demesne there is 1 plough, and [there are] 8 bordars and a priest, and 2 French-born [men]. Wood[land] is there for fattening 40 swine. There is land [enough] for 20 ploughs. In the time of King Edward it was worth £6 and afterwards £4. Now 70 shillings." This brief and tantalizing glimpse is sufficient to show that the arrangements of the sixteenth and seventeenth centuries were already foreshadowed by the late eleventh century. The lord had his demesne, but it was only one-twentieth of the available land, the majority of people were tenants of the lord, with both arable land and pasturable woods to farm; and there were the two Frenchmen who were no doubt the forerunners of those freeholders who were so prominent by the time of the sixteenth century.

The Domesday manor of Myddle was acquired during the next century by the L'Estranges or Lords Strange, the Norman Lords of Knockin who gave their name to Ness Strange. They were Lords of Myddle by 1165, and nearly a hundred years later they added Ellesmere to their estates as well. One of the earliest local records is a confirmation in 1172 of a grant by the L'Estranges of the mill of Myddle to Haughmond Abbey. This mill had completely disappeared by the sixteenth century, and the lord was urged by the surveyor of 1563 to build a new windmill so that he would profit by the tolls. If the original mill was in Myddle township, it was probably a windmill, for the Pinchbrook stream looks too sluggish to power anything but the smallest undershot wheel, and the meres were stagnant pools that could not be utilized for this purpose. But there was once a water-powered mill on the site of the Marton tan-house, on the boundary stream known as the Old Mill Brook.[24] As for other manorial perquisites, at the Quo Warranto inquiry of 1292 the L'Estranges claimed infangentheof or wayf for their manors of Ness and Kinton, but not for Myddle. They only claimed free warren, and this was allowed.

Myddle was one of the many manors in the Border zone that was a Marcher lordship during the time of the Welsh wars. Like Shotton, it had its own gibbet on the hill just outside the village where both the captured enemy and those who criminally transgressed the local laws were summarily executed. The open field called Hill Field was formerly known as Gallowtree Field, and old men in Gough's day could still point out where the gallows had stood. He speaks of a tradition that all the neighbouring towns had "a piece of ground adjoining to theire houses, which was moated about with a large ditch, and fenced with a stronge ditch fence and pale, wherein they kept their cattell every night, with persons to watch them".[25] The only moated site that survives in Myddle is that which surrounds the castle, but that is hardly big enough to shelter cattle as well. This castle dates back to 1308 when one of the Lords Strange was granted a licence to crenellate his mansion in Myddle[26] – not many years after the erection of Edward I's castles in North Wales. Myddle was only a few miles from the Welsh frontier and serious measures had to be taken to defend the community. Indeed, on one occasion, in 1234, Myddle had been the scene of the signing of a two-years' truce between King Edward I and Llewelyn, Prince of Aberfraw, and Lord of Snowdon.[27]

Generation after generation of John L'Estranges continued as Lords of Myddle until the male line finally failed in the late fifteenth century and the property passed by marriage to the Stanley family, which was soon to be dignified by the title of

Earls of Derby. The Stanleys in their turn ruled these estates for just over a hundred years, until the final decade of the sixteenth century when they sold all their possessions in Shropshire to a rising star at the royal court, the Lord Keeper Egerton. He was eventually to become Lord Chancellor, and his son became the first Earl of Bridgewater. Most of these lords were non-resident; some of the early Lords Strange may have lived in Myddle for a few months at a time, but not the later ones. The comments made by the 1563 surveyor on concealed lands and arrears of rent suggest that manorial control was not always as strict as it would have been had the lord been living there. It was not until the time of the Bridgewaters that the tenants felt the effect of a demanding landlord.

In the absence of the lord, Myddle castle was the residence of the constable or castle-keeper, and also the Court House and the head farm of the demesne.[28] It served as such for 200 years or so, but when Sir Roger Kinaston was succeeded as keeper by his son, Humphrey, the castle was allowed to go to ruin. "Wild Humphrey's" riotous and dissolute life ended in his being outlawed for debt, and he was forced to abandon the castles at Knockin and Myddle to find shelter in a cave at Nesscliff. Leland found the castle "veri ruinous"[29] when he visited Myddle *c.* 1540; and today, only the red sandstone staircase stands incongruously on the hill, surrounded by the moat and the foundations of the walls. A few years after Leland's visit, a new demesne farmhouse, the Castle Farm, was built a few yards away beyond the moat. It, too, has a modern successor.

The castle and the church, together, commanded the finest site in Myddle village. The other houses straggled down the village street towards the stream, with the open fields and the woods beyond. To the west lay Myddlewood, and to the south and the east lay the demesne lands, mostly grouped together in "a pretty large parke", which was already in existence by 1333.[30] The boundaries of this park can still be clearly seen. The castle stood at its northerly edge, a lane and the Baschurch parish boundary demarcate it on the west, and the Hollins and Webscott farms adjoin it to the south. The park was once well-wooded but successive fellings had left only a coppice by the middle of the seventeenth century, and once the woods had gone, the land was largely turned over to pasture. Several other Shropshire parks were cleared of their woodland and enclosed for farming during the sixteenth and seventeenth centuries.

Despite the absence of the lord, the manor remained the essential unit of local government in Myddle throughout the sixteenth and seventeenth centuries, even though the civil parish was beginning to assume some of its responsibilities before the end. The Court Leet was functioning efficiently throughout the eighteenth century. The granting of a considerable amount of freehold land within the manor made little difference to the work of the courts, though the non-residence of the lord meant that the combined influence of the freeholders was comparatively greater, so long as they had a united viewpoint. Gough writes, "I suppose that all the lands in this Lordship did at first belong to the Lords Strange, for I have seen the antient deeds of most freeholders in this Lordship, and amongst every man's deeds the first grant was from Lord Strange . . . He gave some lands to servants, pro bono servicio, and some to chaplaines, still reserveing a certaine yearly rent and an Herriot".[31] The manorial surveys bear testimony to the accuracy of this statement.

Very little land in the township of Myddle was made free. Castle Farm and Eagle Farm, covering some 625 acres between them, both belonged to the lord and dwarfed the other farms and tenements. The Lloyds had a small freehold, and the house at the higher well was a free half-tenement that belonged to the Gittins family. But apart from the parsonage all the rest remained in the hands of the lord and was let to tenants. But further away from the village, where new land was reclaimed from the woods and marshes, it was a different story. In these new townships there was much more freehold land than there was land that was tenanted from the lord.

Newton is the most obvious example of a new colony being fostered within the manor. The lord had just one tenement of 79 acres here; the other three farms on the hill-top were all freeholds. Indeed, the original deeds of Gough's property freed him "from all reliefs, heriotts, and all manner of ayds and secular services and demands, etc."[32] His obligation was only an annual three shillings chief rent. The new township included Harmer Moss and the extensive common on Harmer Heath which between them provided cheap peat and good building stone as well as common pasture. The inhabitants of Newton also farmed the Brown Heath in Harmer at 2*s*. 8*d*. a year each, and had pasture rights in two detached portions in the woods between Houlston and Brandwood. Even after the woods had been cleared these two small areas, of 26a. 0r. 39p., and 8a. 1r. 31p. respectively, continued to belong to Newton township. Considering that there were only four original farms, no other township was so favoured in its common rights. But of all the places within the parish of Myddle this township has seen most change. The original nucleus at Newton-on-the-Hill is still approached only by a narrow lane and has preserved its seclusion, but the enclosure of Harmer Heath and its position at the Shrewsbury end of the parish has led to a lot of modern building in the southern part of the township.

Marton was another settlement that was colonized from within the parent manor. The earliest references are of 1178–1210 and of *c*. 1250 when the documents speak of la Mere. Marton is "the farm by the mere", the large glacial pool which acts as a parish boundary. Another document of *c*. 1325 refers to Bassemere, which is undoubtedly the same pool, for Bassa was the Saxon settler who founded neighbouring Baschurch.[33]

The original farm was probably on the site of Marton Hall, for this is the best site and the farm is the largest. It was probably here that John, son of William de la Mere, was living in the late twelfth century, and where his grandson and namesake later described himself rather pretentiously as "Lord of Mere". As far as the documents show, no-one else ever claimed this title. Gough, however, thought[34] that the second largest farm, Marton Farm, had once belonged to the neighbouring manor of Walford, and that it passed through marriage from the Hords of Walford and Stanwardine to the Kinastons and so to the Hanmers, who made it freehold. Similarly, he claimed that Thomas Wright had purchased the fee simple of his tenement which had also descended from the Hords. But both these farms consistently appear in the records of the lordship of Myddle; chief rents were paid and original deeds presented for inspection. It may be that these lands belonged to the Hords at one time, but they were never part of their manor of Walford.

Of all the townships within the parish of Myddle, Marton was the most compact. It was surrounded on three sides by the parishes of Baschurch and Petton and was cut off from the rest of Myddle parish by extensive, thick woods. As at Newton, the freeholders owned more land than the lord. The Atcherleys of Marton Hall were the leading family in the township from the early seventeenth century, and the Hanmers were also prominent gentry there. The Wrights, the Freemans, and the Groomes also had freehold tenements. The lord, however, extended his lands in Marton when part of Myddlewood was felled in the early sixteenth century, and again after the Enclosure Award of 1813.

The remaining unit within Myddle lordship was that of Houlston, though by the middle of the eighteenth century its farms had been engrossed and it had disappeared as a separate township. Before this had happened Gough had written: "Hulston is an hamlett in the towneship of Myddle; there is a constable, but neither pound nor Stockes, nor ever was (as I beeleive). This was one entire farme, and did beelong to the Lord Strang, and was granted to some chaplain or servant".[35] By the sixteenth century the farm was divided into four tenements, and as one was much larger than the others Gough's contemporaries thought that the original estate had been shared out between five sisters, though the proof of this is lacking. Each of the four tenements was freehold held of the manor of Myddle; two were owned by absentees, and the other two were held by the Gittins and Lloyd families of Myddle. Many of the smaller tenements within the parish were engrossed during the eighteenth and early nineteenth centuries, and because this happened at Houlston, the Tithe Award of 1838 recorded there just one farm of $148\frac{1}{2}$ acres. The original estate (if such it had been) was re-created.

By the sixteenth century the relationships of these townships to Myddle was often rather puzzling. Marton, Newton, and Houlston all seem to have been colonized from the parent village and to have remained in the lordship. Marton and Houlston were compact entities, but Newton had two detached portions that probably originated as township pastures in the woods to the north. Balderton,

Sleap Hall, and Webscott Farm were also probably colonized from Myddle, but Balderton and Sleap became alienated from the manor when they descended to the Husseys, and were joined together in one township with Webscott, which, like Balderton, was partly granted to Haughmond Abbey. Shotton and Alderton, however, lay outside the lordship in the Liberty of Shrewsbury (apart from a detached portion of Alderton which lay in Myddle lordship and which probably originated as pasture). The whole of the chapelry of Hadnall also originally lay within the Liberty of Shrewsbury, but large parts were granted to Haughmond Abbey, and after the Dissolution Hardwick township remained as an independent manor. Shotton and Alderton, therefore, do not appear to have been colonized from Myddle, and Alderton in particular is a classic example of a boundary settlement of the type that was so common in woodland areas.

4 · *The open fields*

The original farms in Myddle village were organized on an open-field basis, but by the late sixteenth century this system was defunct. In this, Myddle was typical of the rest of Shropshire, and "Gonner's conclusion that the West Midlands passed into enclosure silently and early is correct".[36] Dr Thirsk writes, "Shropshire yields good evidence of the enclosure of strips in the common fields. Agreements by deed to exchange strips and consolidate them, are plentiful in the local records of the county and were the avowed prelude to enclosure".[37] The evidence for Myddle, however, is much more piecemeal.

The 1650 demesne map marks two open fields immediately to the north of the village. There was no room for a third field; to the west lay Myddlewood, to the east was Balderton township, and south of the village street was the demesne land of Castle Farm. Faint ridge-and-furrow marks can be spotted in the demesne fields that slope down to the Pinchbrook, but these are almost certainly not associated with strips. The westerly of the two fields adjoined Myddlewood and was called Wood Field. It was separated from the other field by the Shrewsbury–Ellesmere road which was named Wood Field Lane along this stretch at the time that Gough was writing.[38] The easterly field was called Gallowtree Field in the days when Myddle was a Marcher lordship and the lord had powers of execution, but long after the gallows had ceased to be used and when they had become only a faint memory, the name was changed to Hill Field.

These two fields could only have been about a hundred acres each at the most. The lord had part of his demesne in their furlongs and strips; the 1650 map marks "a furlong in Hill Field, 16a. 1r. 22p." and "a furlong in Wood Field, 15a. 3r. 34p.", with two doles of meadow (1a. 3r. 6p. and 1a. 0r. 0p.) in the Wood Field. It also names but does not plot, "Three butts near Modlicotts oak, 0a. 3r. 32p., a furlong in Gallow Tree Field, shooting south upon Gallow tree hill, 4a. 0r. 20p.,

[and] a furlong at the east end of the field, 3a. 0r. 4p.". Altogether, the demesne covered a sizeable area of 43a. 1r. 8p. within the two open fields. The rest belonged to the original tenements of Myddle village; the 1634 rental speaks of seven farmers renting land in the Hill Furlong – one paid 4*d*., five paid 8*d*., and one paid 1*s*. 10*d*. The survey of 1640 is a little more explicit in regard to three of them; Robert More of Eagle Farm had a little meadow in the Hill Field and "certain meadowing" in the Wood Field; William Brayne held a corn meadow in the Wood Field; and John Lloyd had five measures sown in the Hill Field, 12 measures in the Wood Field, and 11 measures in the Cross Field (which was a subdivision of the Hill Field).

Long before this time the fields had ceased to be farmed upon a communal basis. The manorial records are silent about such a common organization, except for the following brief and ambiguous note made by a surveyor in 1563: "A townefeild in Middle is parcell of my lords demayne and nothinge answered for it. [According to] Richard Hodin [it] was devided amonge the tenants and every man knew his butts, and after it was so devided every housholder, cottager, and others, had pasture theare with his cattell uppon it". Whatever the system of communal farming, it appears to have been abandoned about the same time as the completion of the programme for a large-scale clearing of Myddlewood. The manorial records start just too late to confirm this, but the notes of the 1563 surveyor hint that the clearings had taken place during the lifetime of the present lord.[39] It seems likely that these new enclosures were granted to each existing farm and tenement in lieu of common grazing rights. No new smallholdings were created at this stage. So now the farmers held land in severalty as well as in the old open fields, and their new possessions meant that their strips were no longer as important. In time they became the least valuable part of the farm (judging by the rents that were paid), and as most efforts were geared towards rearing livestock these new woodland pastures, or leasows, and the common pasture rights in the remaining woods assumed a far greater importance. The open fields were no longer central to the economy.

The abandonment of the strip pattern and the creation of hedged closes came much later. Writing of the 1630s, Gough remarks: "They were walkeing along betweene two landes, or butts of corne",[40] and in the time of the Civil Wars, he mentions, "Myddle Wood Feild, which was then unincloased".[41] He goes on to speak of "a banke neare the further side of Myddle feild, where the widow Mansell has now [1701] a piece incloased". This change in the physical appearance of the fields seems to have occurred during the second part of the seventeenth century.

The secondary settlements in the parish of Myddle also had a small area of open field, though it is likely that the farmers mainly held their land in severalty right from the start. There are only a few incidental references to suggest this. By a deed of *c*. 1280–90 a messuage was granted "in the field of Alverton", and a document of 1334 speaks of "the field of Hadenhale".[42] A series of manorial paines laid in

1531 prohibited the annual enclosing of lands in the cornfield of Newton before the accustomed date, and prevented any pasturing of animals in the cornfield of Marton before the crop had been completely harvested.[43] Gough also refers to "Marton Town Meadow" and to the "town-field gate" there, and he speaks of "a butt's end of Mr Gittins land in Newton feild". But his most explicit statement is about Balderton. He writes: "Balderton feild being then open and unincloased hee [Mr Hall of Balderton Hall] sold alsoe all his feild ground to Robert Hayward, and the whoale field being now betweene three persons viz: Robert Hayward, Thomas Mather, and Richard Tyler, they agreed to exchange lands and incloase it. I was imployed by them to measure the lands and draw writeings of the exchange betweene them which I performed and the field was inclosed".[44] This must have happened sometime during the 1680s.

The original field systems within the parish of Myddle appear to be very similar to those of the Pennine foothills of, for example, south-west Yorkshire. The main settlement had its two- or three-field system, but each of the secondary hamlets had just one small arable field divided into strips, with enclosed pastures surrounding it, and the commons, woods, and wastes stretching beyond. (The manor court book of 1618 speaks of the woods as "the out groundes".) The emphasis in the outlying townships had always been on pastoral farming. (They may possibly have originated as dependent dairy-units like the 'booth', 'stall', and 'wick' settlements, and later have acquired independence.) Their open fields were never a central part of the economy as in arable areas, nor did their enclosure present the problems it did elsewhere. Most of them had gone by the beginning of the seventeenth century, and a hundred years later the enclosure of the parochial open fields was complete.

5 · *The clearing of new land*

Common rights were essential to any woodland community where the supply of farming land was limited and where the economy was geared towards the raising of livestock for the market towns. The aboriginal farms and tenements at Myddle had their arable land in the two small open fields, but were dependent upon the extensive areas of woodland and commons for grazing their animals. Domesday Book refers to pasturable woods, and Gough talks of the time when there were great benefits from having unstinted pasturage at only 4*d.* [actually 2*d.*] a swine, before the woods were felled.[45] In the manor court book for 1618 there is "A note of those swyne that were burned to have pannage and their feeding in the out groundes. The custome there beinge two pence every swyne". The list contained the names of 20 farmers who between them kept 55 swine. Four years later, a paine was laid that no-one was to gather any mast or acorns, and none was to "put to pannage any swine other than such as were by him or them there reared or bought the winter before". It had already become necessary to restrict the rights of pannage.[46]

The clearing of the woods must have gone on in fits and starts ever since the days of the original settlers. New townships started as woodland clearings and their inhabitants made piecemeal encroachments throughout medieval times. Then in the late fifteenth century Divlin Wood was felled and enclosed into tenements. The woods on Holloway Hills and at Brandwood were the next to be cleared, then two or three generations later the first attack was made on Myddlewood. All this was done in an organized manner under the supervision of the lord's representatives. It was only in the last two decades of the sixteenth century that the first wave of squatters arrived to nibble away at the fringes in a much more haphazard way. Even so, much remained in Gough's time; "For fewels, although many of the greatest woods are cut downe, yet there is sufficient left for timber and fire-boot for most tenements".[47] It was not until after the Enclosure Award of 1813 that the clearing of the woods was completed. Nowadays, only a few trees (mainly oak) are dotted about the landscape; there is nothing left that is even worthy of the name of coppice.

Holloway Hills was unusual in that no new tenement was created out of the wood that had been felled. The timber had been sold to one Medleycoate, who is recorded in the 1524 subsidy roll.[48] He cut down all the trees but one, which was left standing upon the highest point of this sandstone escarpment, between Myddle Hill and Harmer. It was known to one and all as Medleycoate's oak. The 1650 demesne map mentioned it as a landmark, but "at last some of the poore neighbours cut it downe, and converted it to fewell".[49]

Divlin Wood and Brandwood, however, were completely enclosed and divided into seven tenements. These woods had stood next to Myddlewood to the north of the Wood Field in Myddle, as far as the parish boundary with Loppington. Some of the smaller tenements in Myddle also benefited from the felling of Divlin Wood by adding a few extra acres to their lands. Divlin meant the "deep laund" or grassy place in the wood, but the name had almost fallen out of use by the time Gough was writing. The derivation of Brandwood is more difficult. It was written as Barnwood in some thirteenth-century deeds, but other early forms give it as Burntwood, and as such it was named in the 1563 survey. 'Barn', 'brand', and 'brant' are known corruptions of 'burnt', but as the wood was not finally cleared until the late fifteenth century, by which time the timber would be too valuable to remove by burning, it is likely that the name was originally applied to only a small part of the wood that was cleared in this way or which had been devastated by an accidental fire.

The Divlin–Brandwood area became something of a centre for tailor-farmers. The Hordleys of Divlin Wood were yeomen-tailors of considerable standing, and their neighbours, the Taylors, also made their living in this way, having made a tenement out of what was left of Divlin Wood when the others had completed their enclosures. A third tenement belonged to a poor weaver-labourer family, the Chidlows, but the fourth was also a sizeable affair, having been enclosed by George Watson, the bailiff of the manor. Brandwood, too, was divided into three tenements large enough to support farmer-craftsmen whose dual occupation enabled them to rank with the yeomen or the better-off husbandmen. Judging by the names of those who leased them, they, too, were all granted to existing families within the community.

A large area of the parish had now been cleared of its original woodland. There were clumps of trees still growing on the rocky ground of Harmer Heath, but the only true wood to remain was the Myddlewood that started where the gley-soils began, and which covered that part of the parish which lay between Myddle Church and Marton. Gough wrote that this was "such a stately wood, that, by report, a man might have gon along the road from Myddle almost to Marton, in a bright sun-shine day, and could not have seene the sun for the branches and leaves of trees, above three times in thatt space of ground".[50]

In the early or middle years of the sixteenth century the systematic clearing of this wood was begun. Indeed, so much was felled that the man responsible for the manorial survey in 1563 wrote in his report: "The many inclosures of Myddle wood are like to destroy the woods, but that the tenants are debarred [from] takinge any woods but underwoods". He recommended that any new leases should provide for the safeguarding of the woods. Each of the existing freeholders and tenants within the township of Myddle and Marton was given the chance of renting part of the new woodland clearings at one shilling per old customary acre per annum (i.e. 6*d*. per statutory acre)[51] in lieu of their common rights there. A considerable area of 241 acres was brought into cultivation by this organized felling of the wood.

What one suspects happened is that the lord originally allowed 30 allotments, each of 8 acres. But by the time of the 1563 survey there had been the inevitable changes of fortune in individual affairs to blur the neatness of the picture. In that year there were 28 separate units shared by 32 people in all, with the size of the allotments varying between 4 and 18 acres. One man farmed 4 acres, six had 5, one man had 6, 13 men and one pair still rented 8 acres, two had 10, one pair held 16, another pair had 17, and one man and a pair each had 18. Roger Hanmer, the leading freeholder in Marton at that time, was one of those who rented 18 acres. However, the size of the allotment did not depend upon the size of the original farm; Morgan ap Probart of Castle Farm had only five acres, and the half-tenements (such as Woulf's and Hodden's) rented eight acres, though some full-tenements had less. One can only surmise, in the absence of firm evidence, that if a tenant or freeholder did not wish, or could not afford to take all his share, then the others were given the option of renting extra land. Other families might have run into hard times since the original division and may have been forced to sell part of their lease to others. Individual fortunes were as likely to fluctuate here as they were anywhere else, and though the rent was reasonable enough the entry fine may have proved too much of an obstacle for some of the weak or unlucky ones.

The question of the entry fines to these new leasows is a puzzling one. There is no information until a survey was made in 1602 for the new lords of the manor, when it seems that an effort was being made to increase the fines. Some of the Marton freeholders resisted: Humphrey Hanmer "standeth upon the inheritance to be allowed him in respect of his common according to a composicon paying the rente"; and Edward Piers "alloweth my Lord the wood the myne the soile and craveth the pasturage and liberty to plowe accordinge to a composicon paying the rente and to bee annexed to his tenement". Humphrey Onslowe felt the same, but Mr Twyford, an absentee, was "content to referr it to his Lordship". The objectors were firmly of the opinion that their woodland clearings were in lieu of their rights of pasture; Edward Piers' comments show how they thought of the wood as having been a common. But the lord seems to have got his way in the end, and the lesser tenants of Myddlewood put up little or no resistance. A few examples from the 1602 survey will suffice. John Chaloner of Myddle paid 4*s*. 6*d*. rent and a £1 fine for his nine acres, whereas Roger Clare of Marton paid 4*s*. rent and a £4 entry fine for his, John Illedge of Brandwood was fined £2 13*s*. 4*d*. for another eight acres, while his neighbour, Richard Deakin, had to pay £7. The entry fines varied considerably, according to the value of the land.

A generation or so after this organized clearing a more piecemeal attack on the woods began. At the Court Leet of 1581[52] Ellis Hanmer was presented "for erecting of one bay of a house upon the lords waste grounde in Myddle woode". The first of a colony of squatters had arrived. They will be dealt with in more detail later; sufficient at the moment to say that a large group of immigrants of labouring rank came into the parish in two waves – in the 1580s and 1590s, and again during the Commonwealth period. Most of them erected their cottages in Myddlewood. The original clearings had been added to the existing farms and tenements, but now new small-holdings and cottages surrounded by gardens and orchards were made within the wood itself. This section of the community expanded more rapidly than any other during the late sixteenth and the seventeenth centuries, in the same way as Harmer Hill was developed in the nineteenth.

But there remained a considerable amount of common land. By the time of the Enclosure Award of 1813 there was still 132a. 1r. 27p. left of Myddlewood Common, and 236½ acres in all. There was plenty of pasture available for common grazing, and there are no records of these rights ever being stinted. A temporary crisis arose during the Civil Wars when "there was a great dearth and plague in Oswaldstree", one of Myddle's chief markets. Myddlewood Common, writes

Gough, "was cutt, and burnt, and sowed with corne. . . . The first crop was winter corne, which was a very strong crop; the next was a crop of barley, which was soe poore, that most of it was pulled up by the roote, because it was too short to bee cutt".[53] The experiment was never tried again.

This common belonged to the inhabitants of Myddle and Marton, though there were occasional attempts by people across the parish boundary in Fenemere to claim rights on it "by reason of vicinage". A letter from the Earl of Bridgewater to his agent, dated 2 March 1707, illustrates the kind of difficulty that cropped up: "You say Lord Bradford has some farmes which border upon the said common (but are not within the Lordship), but have egress and regress over the said common; by this means pretend a right of common there . . ."[54] Other commons within the lordship had the same trouble; the owners of Lea Hall and Shotton claimed vicinage rights over Harmer Heath in Newton township, the inhabitants of Balderton squabbled with Myddle township over Balderton Green, and the parishioners of Broughton staked claims to Bilmarsh Green. But disputes of this kind occurred all over the country.

Myddlewood is now completely cleared and enclosed, and many other changes have taken place since the seventeenth century. Many of the small tenements and cottages have gone – yet more victims to engrossing – and the ancient forest road that once wound its way across the common towards Oswestry was straightened out and widened by the Enclosure Commissioners, only to revert to its former character as soon as it reached Marton. But despite these changes, the area is still different from other parts of the parish.

At the Marton side of Myddlewood a small piece of common of some five or six acres was left unenclosed until 1813. This was known as Marton Moor and it was defended from enclosure by the same Marton freeholders who had stood out against entry fines for their woodland. The 1563 surveyor described it as "a common or pasture theare lyinge in a lowe ground neare adjoyning to Marton meare . . . overgrowne with bushes". As to enclosure, the surveyor struck a cautious note: in Marton, "my lord hath not passinge five tenants. If it should bee inclosed the freeholders would thinke themselves agreved for that my lord hath inclosed the most parte of Midle wood, etc." The 1602 surveyor recognized a more adamant refusal: "For this more the freeholders saye they have no more to shewe than heretofore they shewed nether will take any present course for the endinge thereof but clayme the same as their inheritance". The lord was unable to enforce his wishes until the freeholders were ready for enclosure, in 1813, when it was included as part of Myddlewood.

Another large common at Harmer Heath (85½ acres), and two smaller ones at Myddle Hill (7½ acres) and Balderton Green (11 acres) also remained until 1813. The tiny Bilmarsh Green was taken in sometime during the eighteenth century. This was another boundary settlement just to the north of Alderton. It first appears in the documents *c.* 1250–5 when John L'Estrange III gave Haughmond Abbey three acres of meadow in "Bilemersch, viz. those nearest to the acres of Thomas de Newton and of Geoffrey, in the place called Holstedemoor" [Houlston Moor?].[55] The whole of Bilmarsh Farm had once been a common, well over 100 acres in size. In addition to the farm, two squatter families – Towers the tailor, and Edward Grestocke, alias Newton, a labourer and ale-house keeper – had erected cottages and made small encroachments in Elizabethan times, but their holdings were to be swallowed up by the farm in the early years of the seventeenth century. George Watson, the Myddle bailiff, had also enclosed two marl pieces to the north, and they never formed any part of the farm. The green that remained was a constant source of trouble between Myddle and Broughton; the sort of situation that was always causing disputes in woodland areas, where boundaries were not always clearly defined. The 1563 surveyor noted that, "Bylmarsh lane [is] enclosed by certaine persons who have noe right to itt, because it is of my lords waste and within the precincts of Middle Lordship, and was never of the Sheir or Gyldalle". (By the Shire or Guildhall, he meant the adjoining Liberty of Shrewsbury.) He went on, "Thomas Rydley and [blank] Lyster have inclosed all the commons beyond Bylmarsh to which my lord's tenants were free. It is sayd the Queenes Majestie is cheife lord of the towne beyond Bylmarshe". In Gough's time, both parishes were including the green in their annual perambulations.[56]

There was a similar dispute over Balderton Green, otherwise known as Whitrishes, or Witterage Green. The Grand Jury of Myddle Court claimed that it lay within the manor, but the inhabitants of Balderton thought differently. When the dispute came to a head in 1751, William Dukes, one of the oldest men in the parish at 81 years old, was called as a witness. He said that when he went to school at old William Sturdy's house, known as the Whitrishes, by Balderton Green, the people at the Whitrishes fenced in a piece of ground at the further end of the common, but the men from Balderton Hall and the tenements there threw down the fence. He further said that neither the inhabitants of Whitrishes, Sleap Hall, Webscott Farm, nor Houlston had any right to graze sheep on Balderton Green, which belonged solely to Balderton Hall and the tenements.[57] And so the dispute dragged on.

The rocky outcrop on Myddle Hill posed no such problems, and there were only minor disputes at Harmer. The heath was poor, stony ground to the south-west of Newton township, between the Higher and Lower Ways from Shrewsbury to Myddle. It was never capable of much improvement and still remains very much as it was. But it was valuable for its "great store of free stone, very usefull for building". In Gough's time, "The inhabitants within the Mannor pay to the Lord one shilling for every hundred (that is six score) foot of stone, but Forainers paye one shilling and sixpence". Several attempts were made to find copper. In 1643, "certaine myners gott a great quantity of this stone, which was brought in carts to the warren house, and there layd up to the house wall, and proclamation made in Myddle Church, that it was treason for any one to take away without orders. Butt when the king came to Shrewsbury the myners went all for soldiers. The worke ceased, and the stones were carried to amend highwayes".[58] The Crown prerogative over copper mining was brought to an end in 1693 and a whole spate of developments then took place. In Myddle, the lord employed Derbyshire miners to sink shafts up to 60 yards deep, but the work was a failure. Finally, a deed dated 29 April 1710 allowed no less a figure than "Abraham Darby and Company of the City of Bristall" to "digg, mine, lay up, and carry away all such mines of copper ore or other mines or mineralls" on Harmer Heath and Myddle Hill.[59] But the veins were thin and the mining unprofitable.

When the Egertons purchased the manor in the late 1590s one of the first things they did was to obtain a charter for a rabbit warren on Harmer. The rights were then leased to the Twyfords (who held land in Marton) and a lodge or warren-house was built. A paine laid at the manor court in 1611 instructed that: "No man within this Lordship shall keepe any firretts or netts for the destroying of Conyes, the Warrener and his servants excepted". The warren house was let to a labourer and was regularly used as an ale-house as well. The lease of the warren quickly passed from one hand to another; to Gough's father and Thomas Jux, to Thomas Kinaston of Shotton, to Thomas Hodgkins of Webscott, and to Edward Hall of Balderton. Finally, the neighbouring landowners were so weary of the damage caused by wandering rabbits that 12 of them joined together at the end of the seventeenth century to purchase a lease in order to keep them under proper control. The lord was none too popular in this part of the parish.

So the common at Harmer was relatively unaffected by the improvements that were transforming the landscape of the rest of the parish. But the mere that lay alongside it, which gave the district its name, underwent the most radical and most successful change of all, for in the early part of the seventeenth century it was completely drained and converted to pasture. It had once held a great store of fish, especially eels, for the keeper of Myddle Castle, but after the castle had gone to ruin the fishing rights were leased to the local gentry. In 1563, Sir Andrew Corbett of Moreton Corbet and Humphrey Hanmer of Marton shared the fishing rights at £3 6*s*. 8*d*. a year, but in 1588 Mr Richard Corbett held them by himself. The 1602 survey names Robert Corbet, Esq., holding at will, "a water called the haremeare, and fishing and soyle within the bankes . . . and the cole arke and fishhouse bancke". By 1617 it was in the joint ownership of Sir Richard Corbett and Richard Kelton, gent., at the increased rent of £10, and 17 years later, when Mr Andrew Corbett had succeeded his father, the terms were the same. It was about this time that the drainage scheme was put into operation. Gough's account cannot be bettered.[60]

> Haremeare Mosse was incompassed round with the water of this Meare; howbeit, the neighbours did gett some turves upon it, which they carryed over the water in boats; butt Sir Andrew Corbett caused a large causey, or banke, to bee raised throw the water, soe that teames and carts might easily passe from Haremeare Heath to the Mosse, and the turves, (which beefore we had freely,) were sold att 8*d.* a yard, that is, 80 square yards, to cutt and lay upon, which yielded a loade for the best teame that was. Afterward, Sir Andrew Corbett and Mr. Kelton caused this Meare to bee loosed and made dry, and converted it to meadow and pasture.

The "turves" were then taken to be sold in Shrewsbury, "soe that the Turbary is much wasted and the Turfes are much dearer. Soe that a yard of peates which was formerly at 8*d.* is now sett at 2*s.*" Here are all the elements of 'improvement'. A labourer was installed in the Mear House, the boundaries were marked out with stakes, and when the mere was dry, "there were catell putt in it as a lay; and after, as it beecame dry and sound, it was divided into severall peices". Because of the peaty nature of the soil, most of it has continued to be used as pasture.

Another drainage scheme had been successfully completed several decades earlier. This had involved the glacial meres known as Myddle Pools that lay beyond the open fields where the Pinchbrook stream took its leisurely course north of the village and on towards Sleap. The meres were converted into meadows and pasture and added to existing large fields to create a new farm, called Broomhurst Farm, whose history will be examined in more detail later. (In passing, it may be noted that the adjoining fields known as the Binnings were brought into cultivation in a manner different from the rest. The 1563 surveyor mentions that these fields were given by the Lords Strange to their carriers, who operated between Myddle and Shrewsbury. Six tenants were still farming this land in 1563 without paying any rent, though their ancestors had long since ceased to carry the lord's goods to and from the market.)

Gough was unsure whether Myddle Pools were once stocked with fish, but he believed that winter fowls had gathered there. Marton Pool had the benefit of both. "It is well stored of delicate large pickerell, beesides a multytude of roach, dace, and other small fishes", wrote Gough.[61] One of the neighbouring Fenemere pools has been drained, but it is poor, peaty soil that has never been ploughed: the expected profits from converting Marton might have been too small to justify such an enterprise. The main reason why it was never drained, however, was the divided ownership. Not only did the Fenemere boundary go right through the middle of it, but the freeholders of Marton claimed half of what was left. The lord had to be content with leasing out his fishing rights to the Hanmers of Myddlewood at 10*s.* per annum. The pool still covers 45½ acres. Harmer Moss Farm enclosed 189½ acres, but it is difficult to say how much of Broomhurst Farm originally lay under water; in size it would come somewhere between the other two.

The period from the late fifteenth to the early seventeenth century witnessed the most intense reclamation of farming land from the woods and the pools. In little more than 150 years at least 1,000 new acres were brought into cultivation. The engrossing of farms and tenements during the eighteenth and early nineteenth centuries has made the first detailed account of landownership (the 1838 Tithe Award) difficult to use. But the seven new tenements within Divlin Wood and Brandwood seem to have had a combined area of just under 500 acres; the later enclosure of and encroachments upon Myddlewood, at a conservative estimate, would account for 250 new acres; and the drainage of Harmer and Myddle Pools would add another 250–300 acres. With the encroachments upon other commons such as Bilmarsh and Balderton Green, and with the felling of more timber in Myddle Park, plus all the little improvements to individual farms, the total figure would be at least 1,000 acres. If this was happening in all the woodland communities of England, or even just in a large number of them, it is easy to see why they attracted immigrants and absorbed much of the national rise in population.

CHAPTER TWO

Population and the economy

1 · *The population*

The 1524 and 1544 lay subsidies[1] are incomplete and cannot be used to give any estimated total of the population of Myddle. However, a firm base near the beginning of the period is provided by the diocesan returns of 1563.[2] At that time there were 14 households in the chapelry of Hadnall, and another 54 households in the rest of the parish. If these household figures are multiplied by five, the total population would have been about 70 for Hadnall and around 270 for the rest of the parish, giving an approximate figure of 340 for the entire parish. (It is not always possible to speak only of the part of the parish with which this history is concerned, for some figures include Hadnall.)

It is much more difficult to be precise about the number of households in later times. The 1603 diocesan returns do not survive, and neither do the protestation returns of 1641–2. Furthermore, two of the three hearth-tax returns of Charles II's reign are unsatisfactory in that they do not include the number of families who were exempt from the tax, while the useful return of 1672[3] only lists the exempted households by each hundred, and not by each parish. Some familiar Myddle names can be spotted amongst the exempt, but it is difficult to know where the parish group starts and ends in such an untidy list. The familiar names amount to only 16.5 per cent of the parish total, but as the number of exempt for the whole county averaged 23 per cent, perhaps a few more strange names, which appear neither in the parish registers nor in any other record, ought to be added. If the chapelry is excluded, Myddle had 76 taxed households, and at least another 15 that were exempt, giving a total of 91. Hadnall had 29 assessed households, and perhaps another six that were exempt if one assumes that the exempted group formed the same percentage of the total as in the rest of Myddle parish. This would give a grand total of 126 households, or a rough population figure of 630.

The hearth-tax returns can be checked against the Compton census returns of 1676,[4] which recorded 408 people in the whole parish. The census seems to have included only those who were over 16 years of age, and it has been suggested that those who were under the age of 16 accounted for roughly 40 per cent of the total population.[5] If one assumes that this was so in Myddle, and multiplies the figure accordingly, this would give a total population of about 612. This is as near to the figure from the hearth-tax returns as one could reasonably expect from such rough calculations as these.

Gough quotes a petition that was drawn up in 1693 by the inhabitants of the chapelry of Hadnall, "being thirty families".[6] This, too, was probably a round figure that does not include the poor (for 29 families were assessed in 1672). Gough claimed to have written about "all, or most part of the familyes in this side of the parish",[7] and a careful count of the number of families that he mentions as living there in 1701 comes to 85. At a minimum, therefore, there were 115 families, or a rough total population of 575, living in Myddle and Hadnall at the close of the seventeenth century. As the figures for both Myddle and the chapelry are minimal, one again comes to the conclusion that somewhere in the order of 600 people, perhaps a score or so more, were living in the parish in the late Stuart period.

A final rough check is provided by the first official census of 1801, when there were 1,141 people living in the parish. The Cambridge group has suggested[8] that the national population doubled during the eighteenth century and that a rough guide to the population of any one place in 1700 can be provided by halving the figure for 1801. This would suggest a total of about 570 in Myddle in 1700. This is very near to previous estimates, which may have been rather high in using a multiplier of five. All four indicators that have been used point to a total population of 570–630. To say that there were about 600 people living in the whole parish during the closing years of the seventeenth century, would not be far off the mark.

This means that the population of the parish rose from about 340 in 1563 to about 600 in 1700. If the chapelry of Hadnall is excluded, then the figures for the rest of the parish would show a rise from about 270 to about 450, which is an increase of around two-thirds. A preliminary look at the parish registers confirms this increase. The total number of baptism and burial entries were averaging 16 a year during the sixteenth century, rising slowly to 17.5 during the period 1600–40, then increasing sharply to 25 entries a year between 1647–60, when a large number of immigrants entered the parish, and reaching 30 a year during the last 40 years of the seventeenth century.

This population rise occurred all over Shropshire. In the diocesan census returns of 1563, there were about 800 households in the parishes and chapelries that came within the hundred of Pimhill. In the hearth-tax returns of 1672, the number of households within the same hundred totalled 1,255. The total increase in population during those 109 years was about 64 per cent, which was only slightly less than that for the parish of Myddle. A more detailed analysis of demographic trends within the parish must now be attempted, by a scrutiny of the parish registers.

The parish registers of Myddle survive in an incomplete form from the year 1541, just three years after Thomas Cromwell's order that all baptisms, burials, and marriages were to be recorded by the relevant parish authority. They have been printed by the Shropshire Parish Register Society[9] for the years 1541–1643 and 1681–1812, and the intervening years are largely covered by the bishop's transcripts now housed at the Lichfield Joint Record Office. The series is marred by a number of gaps in the recordings. Some of these are only of a few months duration, but others are more serious and last for several years. The earliest register is continuous from 1541 to 1553, but during the reign of Mary Tudor the entries cease altogether, even though the rector, John Higgins, had been regularly keeping a register ever since he had started his incumbency 18 months or so previously. He resumed his task upon the accession of Queen Elizabeth. "The Regester wantith for all the Raine of Queene Marie, beinge 5 yeares" is written on the page where the entries start again in November 1558.

There are further gaps in 1566–7, 1614–15, and 1629–31, but otherwise there are entries for nearly every month until 1638. The last illness of the rector, Ralph Kinaston, accounts for the gap between 1629 and 1631, but there are no indications as to why entries are missing for the two earlier periods. Otherwise, these early registers seem to be as complete as any others for that period. Sixteenth-century registers that survive are usually transcripts of the original entries put together in a bound volume round about the close of the century. The earliest recordings were normally made on loose sheets (which could easily be lost), so in 1597 the government ordered that all entries should be written in a special register kept for that purpose, and that transcripts of previous entries were to be made into the new volume by the minister and his churchwardens. As a further safeguard, it was also ordered that from that date transcripts of all entries were to be sent each year to the bishop of the appropriate diocese. Thus, the Myddle register for 1541 to 1599 is a series of transcripts of the original entries, with each page signed by the rector, Ralph Kinaston, and his churchwardens, Humphrey Reynolds and Richard Gough. Kinaston continued to sign each page of new entries until his death in 1629, so it is likely that he took care to see that they were accurate. His transcripts of the sixteenth-century registers are also likely to have been careful ones, but this leaves the question of how reliable were the original recordings.

Gough was of the opinion that the early registers were carefully attended to. "The Parish Register of Myddle was dilligently ordered in the times of Mr. Tho. Wilton [1568–96] and Mr. Ralph Kinaston [1596–1630] . . . In the beginning of Mr. More's time, whilest Mr. Peter Ledsham was his curate [died 1636], the Register was carefully kept; butt afterwards negligently observed, and in the War time altogether neglected".[10] Thomas More was the only absentee rector of the sixteenth and seventeenth centuries. He was ejected from both Myddle and Ellesmere during the Civil Wars, and replaced in Myddle by the puritan, Joshua Richardson. The worst gap in the registers starts during his incumbency in 1638. For the next five years there is no information about burials, but a few baptisms and marriages were entered intermittently until 1643, when the recordings cease altogether. The original register does not survive for the next generation, and there are no more entries until after Ladyday 1681. Fortunately, the gap is largely covered by the (unprinted) bishop's transcripts at Lichfield. These commence in 1647 and continue beyond 1681, but, here again, the baptismal entries between 1653 and 1659 are missing. There are also gaps in both registers and transcripts between 1686–9 (during the last illness of the rector, William Holloway) and 1704–9, but otherwise the series is complete until 1812, and beyond.

The bishop's transcripts do not survive before 1647, but where they overlap with the original register after 1681, they have been found to compare accurately, which augurs well for the reliability of those that cover the gap between 1647 and 1681. The system of registration faltered just before the outbreak of the Civil Wars, and broke down completely during it. This, of course, is a common failing. A memorandum in the registers under the year 1693 states that transcripts continued during the Civil Wars, but "Whereas in the year 1644 but one burial is entered, in the year 1645, but one christening is entered, and from the 4th. of May '86 untill Mr. Holway's burial, viz. June 25th, 1689, nothing is entered". It was the original registers, not the transcripts, that were lacking. There is nothing to suggest that the transcripts are anything but a faithful record of the original entries.

The defects in the registers obviously impair their reliability as a source of information. The gaps for the 160-year period between 1541 and 1701 amount to about 20 years for each of the three different types of entry – baptismal, burial, and marriage. This is a serious omission, amounting to one-eighth of the period. On the other hand, this is a problem common to the study of almost all parish registers, and Myddle is among the more fortunate in having registers that start as far back as 1541, while the continuous listing of occupations between 1541 and 1660 makes it a record of great value. The gaps should not lead to the rejection of the registers as worthless.

But how reliable are the entries that survive? No standard form was ever laid

1. Marton Pool. The hamlet of Marton (background) took its name from this 45½-acre pool, which in the seventeenth century was "well stored of delicate large pickerell, beesides a multytude of roach, dace, and other small fishes". The fishing rights were divided between the lord's tenant, the freeholders of Marton, and the inhabitants of Fenemere. The parish boundary passes through the middle of the pool, and this divided ownership probably explains why it was never drained.

2. Harmer Moss. View towards the Welsh hills from the southern boundary of the parish. Here a 189½-acre pool (the 'Har-mere'), used for fishing and as a turbary, was drained in the early seventeenth century and converted into pastures and meadows. To the right are the wooded slopes of Harmer Hill, in the centre background is Webscott Farm, and to the left is the Hollins.

3. The north-eastern landscape. View from Myddle Hill across the Hill Field (one of the two open fields) and the former Myddle Pools towards Houlston and Sleap. The pools were converted into meadows and pastures, which were added to existing large fields to create Broomhurst Farm. The trees in the background give some idea of the former wooded character of this area.

down until Lord Hardwicke's Marriage Act of 1753. There are, therefore, great variations in the form of the registers, not only from parish to parish, but from generation to generation within the same parish. However, the Myddle registers have only two major changes throughout the period 1541 to 1812. Up to 1660 the entries are in Latin and occupations are given; after the Restoration, the entries are in English and the occupations are omitted.

The evidence of the registers is not seriously distorted by Nonconformity, for dissenters were few in number before the nineteenth century, and, anyway, generally seem to have accepted the Anglican baptism, burial, and marriage services. What is much more difficult to determine is whether there are serious under-recordings during the periods when there are no obvious gaps in the registers. For instance, in August 1611, four lines are erased because they contain two entries that had previously been given. Was it common for entries to be inserted late? And if so, did this practice lead to some cases being forgotten altogether? There is no way of knowing, except to say that a person of a long-established Myddle family sometimes has no baptismal entry, but is later recorded as marrying or dying in the parish, or, alternatively, he is baptized, but has no burial record. This point has been argued at some length by the historical demographers. The Cambridge group has suggested[11] that the baptism registers generally under-record by some 15 per cent, and that burial totals need to be increased by about 10 per cent. J. T. Krause[12] would put these figures at a lower level, at about 10 per cent and 5 per cent, respectively. Sufficient to say at this stage that the Myddle registers certainly do not record every baptism and burial that must have taken place at the parish church.

Names that are unknown to the parish registers sometimes occur in other sources. The wills that survive at Lichfield often mention children who do not appear in the baptismal entries, or they otherwise help to unravel relationships within a family. They are also of use in naming wives, for the marriage often took place in another parish and was not recorded in Myddle. Another useful source for demographic purposes is the manorial surveys and rentals, especially such surveys as the ones of 1602 and 1638 which record copyhold leases for three lives. These lives were often those of a wife and the eldest children, and they again reveal several names that are unrecorded in the parish registers. Finally, there is the unique source of Gough's *History*. He is sometimes wrong with his genealogical details and has to be handled with great care for the sixteenth century, but time after time he explains a relationship that cannot be worked out from other sources; so much so, in fact, that one wonders how other demographers manage without a Gough. Far too many of the most obvious guesses about relationships are found to be completely wrong when checked with Gough.

The Cambridge group has maintained that the marriage registers are likely to be the most accurate of all, because of the need of a legal record of the marriage service.[13] One of the marriage partners was (and is) supposed to be resident within the parish where the ceremony took place. There were very few cases in Myddle before the Civil Wars where neither of the partners was resident in the parish, but between 1647 and 1701, 12 of the 111 marriages were between men and women, neither of whom lived in Myddle (though in every case at least one partner lived in Shropshire). Marriages between two 'outsiders' at Myddle church increased during the eighteenth century. This can only partly be explained by domestic servants returning from their place of work to marry in the church where they were baptized.[14] Even after Lord Hardwicke's Marriage Act, many names are quite strange. It seems that there were favourite churches for weddings, and that Myddle was one of them.

Baptism records are held to be the least reliable of the three. The 1538 order stated that "all christenings" were to be recorded. However, anyone could baptize a child so long as they sprinkled water and invoked the Trinity. It was the fashion in some quarters to baptize a child privately and to follow this act a few months later with public baptism. Some clergymen preferred to delay registration until the child was baptized in church, by which time he or she could be several months old. If a child died before the public baptism, he may not, therefore, be entered in the baptismal registers. However, there is no evidence that this was the practice in Myddle before the mid-eighteenth century, and then, the date of the private baptism was recorded as well as the date of the service in the church. What evidence there is suggests that parents were expected to baptize their children as soon as possible. The Salop Deanery Acta Book for 1668[15] records the presentation of Richard Clarke of Myddle at the bisop's visitation "for keeping one of his children which is at least halfe a yeare old unbaptized and the child is called by the name of Prudence". For not complying with the usual practice, Clarke was excommunicated. It is more than likely that during the sixteenth and seventeenth centuries the baptismal entries refer to children who were only a few days old, or at the most a few weeks. And during the time of the Commonwealth, in accordance with national practice, the actual births, instead of the date of baptism, were entered in the registers.[16]

Burials are usually regarded as being better-recorded than baptisms. No church service was allowed at the burial of suicides, executed criminals, excommunicates, and those who died unbaptized, but in practice most clergy recorded their burials. The Myddle registers contain references to children who died unbaptized, and during the seventeenth century, only Richard Woulf seems to have been refused burial in the churchyard. After he had killed himself by taking poison, he was interred in the traditional manner by a cross-roads, but the same night his body was removed and re-buried in his own rye-field. These burials are not recorded in the parish registers, but there is nothing else, apart from negligence, to cause under-recording.

The baptism and burial entries have been plotted in table 1.

Table 1 Baptisms and burials 1550-1700

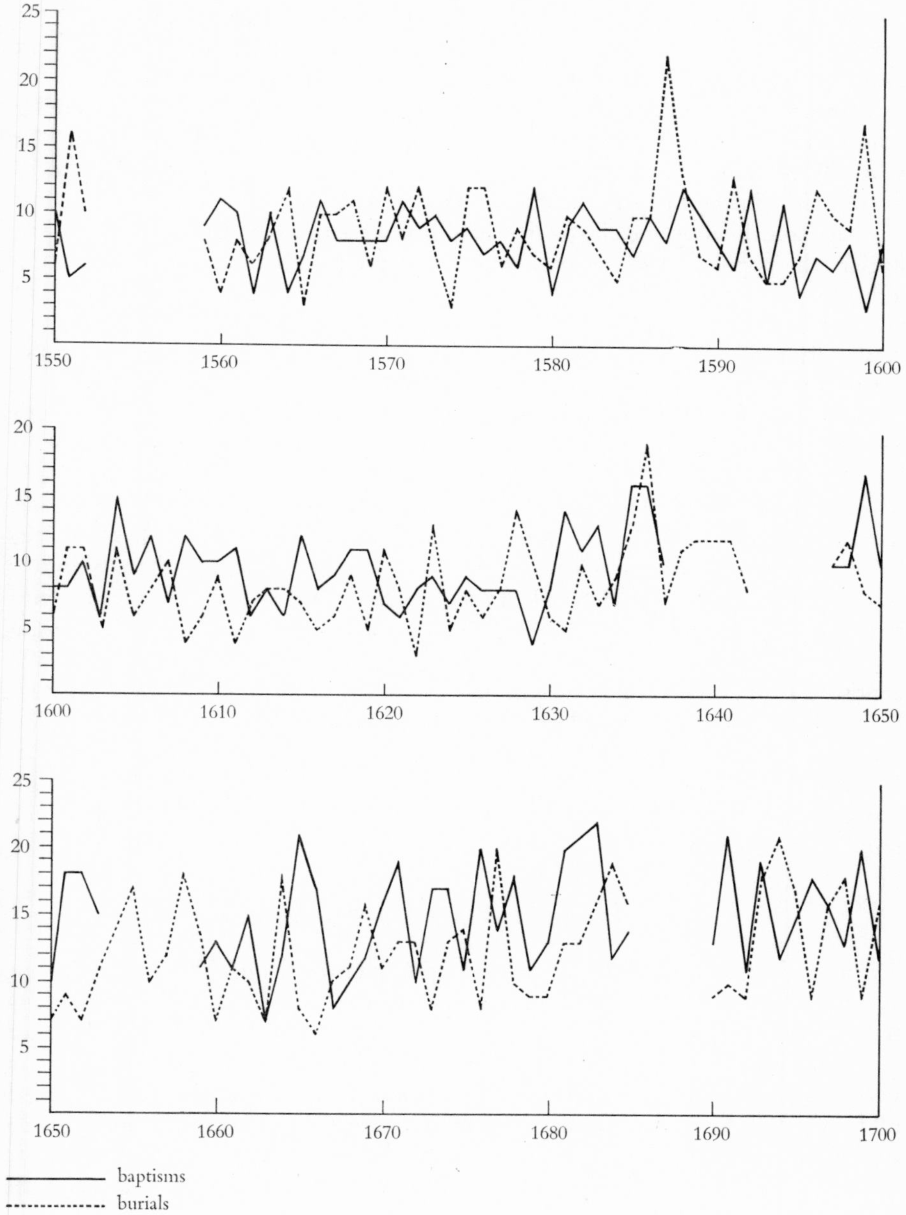

The registers reveal no significant increase in the population during the late sixteenth century. Indeed, the community was probably only just maintaining its numbers. There had possibly been some increase in the two generations before the registers begin, when many of the woods had been cleared and new lands brought into cultivation, but there were no new settlers until the 1580s and 1590s, when the first group of labourers arrived. There were 13 baptisms in 1544, and a similar number in 1549, but from that time until 1604, there were never more than 12 a year. On the other hand, burials reached peaks of 16 in 1552, 22 in 1587, and 17 in 1599, and during the period 1561–1600 there was a total of 439 burials as against 420 baptisms. Even if one allows that baptisms were more under-represented than burials, the population seems to have only just been maintaining its level, and the influx of labourers could only balance the numbers who died during the worst years of harvest failure during the 1580s and 1590s. The population rise that undoubtedly took place between 1563 and 1672 must have taken place during the seventeenth century.

The baptism rate rose slightly during the first two decades of the seventeenth century, and during the first 40 years the number of baptisms exceeded that of burials by 379 to 338. The only year with an unusually high death rate was 1636, when 19 people died. Then during the 1630s, both the baptism and burial rates started to rise as a second wave of immigrant labourers, much larger than the first, began to enter the parish. There are gaps in the registers during the Commonwealth period, just at the time when the population seems to have started rising, but when the entries recommence in 1658, it is obvious that a considerable increase had taken place. During the last 40 years of the seventeenth century there were 592 baptisms as opposed to only 462 burials. Whereas the baptism totals never rose higher than 12 in any one year between 1561 and 1600, for the corresponding period a century later it was above that figure twice as many times as it was on or below it. There were 54 households in Myddle in 1563, and about 91 in 1672, and a high proportion of these 37 new houses and cottages must have been erected about the middle of the seventeenth century.

2 · *Harvest crises and epidemics*

The annual harvest was of fundamental importance for the people of Myddle, just as it was for every other community, both urban and rural, throughout the country. The fact that Shropshire was a pastoral rather than an arable county does not lessen the importance of the harvest, for both man and beast were dependent upon good crops. A bad harvest meant that a considerable stock of cattle had to be killed off (as in 1573) for lack of fodder, and animals as well as men were more likely to succumb to disease if they were constantly under-nourished.

Professor W. G. Hoskins has shown that harvests often followed "a sequence of three or four good years in a row, or much more dramatic in their effects, three or four failures in a row".[17] A disastrous harvest would force the farmers to consume part of the seed-corn they had set aside for the following year, with the result that the next harvest would also be deficient, and so on until a prolonged spell of good weather restored the yields to their normal level. If the downward spiral was not broken by the beneficial effects of the weather, then the result was famine. This was the constant fear that explains the numerous references to the weather in seventeenth- and early-eighteenth-century diaries, and accounts for so much national legislation in the sixteenth century in particular.

It is rarely possible to tell from the registers whether a significant rise in the number of burials was due to starvation or to epidemic disease.[18] The two were often related, for under-nourishment made people less resistant to disease, and epidemics seem to have claimed most victims after the population had already been weakened in this way. Thus, there was a national famine in 1555–6 and a tremendous rise in mortality figures during the next two years as an epidemic of virulent influenza followed in the wake of near-starvation.[19] Unfortunately the Myddle registers were not kept at this time, and so there is no way of knowing whether this particular community was affected.

Parish registers rarely mention causes of death, but sometimes inferences can be made from other sources. In May 1551, nine people died in Myddle – as many as had died during the whole of the previous 14 months. The minister made no comment alongside the entries in the register, but the author of the Shrewsbury *Chronicles*[20] had this to say: "1550–1. This yeare the swetinge sycknes reignyd in England and began fyrst in thys towne of Shrowsbury, 22 March". It is very likely that the spread of this sickness caused the unusual number of deaths a few weeks later in Myddle. The sweating sickness, too, had followed three harvests that were deficient to disastrous.

The next major crisis came in 1573, though there had been several deficient harvests in between. That year, the *Chronicles* record that "mutche cattell peryshed for waunt of foode and sucker", and in the October of 1574, "The wether was gyvyn to sutche rayne . . . that many husbandmen were forsyd to keepe theire rye grownde for barleye". There was no dramatic rise in the number of burials at Myddle, but even so the total deaths for the harvest-year (i.e. August to July) in 1575 was higher than at any other time since the outbreak of sweating sickness.

There were several good harvests during the 1580s, but there was deficiency in 1585, leading to dearth in 1586. During summer and harvest time in 1585, the weather had been so bad that the farmers were unable to get in all of their corn. Much of it was flattened by the wind and rain, and even that which could be reaped and brought indoors was "scannt seasonid". February of 1586 was very frosty, so much so that it was impossible to plough the ground for rye. March was very wet, and there was a "great death of sheep all over England". In June and July, corn was very dear all over the country, especially in the western and northern parts, and a royal command had to be issued to all J.P.s to order all corn growers to stop hoarding supplies until prices were at their peak, and to bring their grain immediately to the markets to alleviate the situation. Things were beginning to look desperate at Shrewsbury, but then, towards the end of July, "the carefull zeale of master James Barker in consideration of the poore inhabytants brought from forren places one hundred strycke of Rye and selld the same in the market to the poore after the rate of 5*s*. the bushell and so brought down the price". His example was followed by the bailiffs and aldermen, and his action caused the author of the *Chronicles* to exclaim, "The Lord blesse them for theire mercyfull care and send plentie". He must have been echoed by many. During this crisis, the Myddle burial totals went up from an annual average of eight or nine to 22 during the calendar year of 1587. The harvest-year totals are high (17 and 20) for both 1586 and 1587.

For this small Shropshire community, this was the worst harvest crisis on record. However, the decade saw further hardship. The harvests between 1594 and 1597, inclusive, were disastrous on a national scale, and a serious outbreak of sheep-rot in 1594 made the situation even worse. Corn was very dear in Shrewsbury in 1595, and there was such scarcity in 1596–7 that supplies had to be imported from Danzig and Denmark, via Bristol, into Shrewsbury. The town bakers were ordered to produce special cheap bread for the poor, who "for want of the same were lycke to perrishe and were so unruly and gredie to have it so that the baylyffs 6 men and other officers had mutche a doe to serve them".

And yet again, right at the end of the century, all kinds of corn rose in price, and such was the "great want of fodder and grass" that many were "forsed to thrashe upp theire corne from stoare to feed and save their cattell for they were willinge to delyver one hallffe of their cattell to feed the oder". The *Chronicles* close in 1602 with the information that all garden seeds, such as onions, beans, and peas, had come "to no perfect perfection for lacke of warme and drie weather".

Once the *Chronicles* come to an end there is no detailed local information about the quality of the harvests, but Hoskins has shown that the same series of good and deficient crops, with occasional dearth, continued well into the eighteenth century.[21] Gaps in the Myddle registers prevent any knowledge of what happened there at the time of the next two national crises, in 1630 and 1647. There is nothing in the burial totals to suggest acute distress in the first half of the century, but the following poignant entry for 12 February 1623/4 shows that death through starvation continued to be a very real possibility: "Margaret, the wyfe of Adam Peplo, laborer [torn], his dwelling is unknowne, was found dead [torn] on the King's highe way neere Marton, and by the Judgment of men and women was starved to death". The death of an unknown wandering pauper in 1661 is the only sign in the registers of the next national famine.

A number of local people died during the disastrous harvests of 1693 and 1697. By that time the death-rate averaged 10 or 11 a year, but in the harvest-years of 1692–4 it rose to 16, 21 and 21 respectively, while between 1696 and 1699, the total burials during the harvest-years were 14, 17, 10 and 19. Throughout the sixteenth and seventeenth centuries the continual struggle to provide the bare necessities of food and drink must have been uppermost in men's minds.

Epidemic diseases were a secondary worry. An outbreak of plague in 1604 reached Myddle's chapelry of Hadnall, and William Poole, his wife, daughter, and servant, all died in the space of one month. Their names are bracketed together in the registers, with the comment in the margin: "of the plag died". But Myddle missed the other plagues that caused so much panic in Shrewsbury.[22] In 1576 the authorities became so alarmed that they ordered the destruction of all cats, and the removal of all dogs and swine. The streets were to be regularly cleaned and fires lit on alternate nights all over the town. The annual St Matthew's fair was held on common land outside the town, and the county court adjourned to the village of Meole Brace. Gough recounts what happened during a similar visitation about 1649.

> It broake out about the latter end of July, butt was concealed by the townesmen till after Lambmas faire, and on the next day after the faire they fled out of the towne in whoale shoales, soe that there was noe Markett kept there untill Candlemas following. Howbeitt, there was a small market kept on the Old Heath for things necessary for provision, and so att Monfords Bridge and in other places. There was frequent collections made in the parish churches for the relief of the poore of the town. The free-schoole was removed to the Schoole-house in Greensell; . . . The two chiefe and ablest Ministers in Shrewsbury, viz. Mr. Thomas Blake, Minister of St. Chads, and Mr. Fisher of St. Mary's removed to Myddle and dwelt both in Mr. Gittin's house att the higher well; they preached often att Myddle.[23]

Plague was not connected with harvest crises as much as were other epidemics, though Gough does refer[24] to "a great dearth and plague" in Oswestry about 1645. But though plague caused fear perhaps more than any other disease, there were other illnesses to contend with, like the sweating sickness and influenza already noted. In an age when so little was known about the causes of epidemics, many illnesses had no precise name. Thus, Andrew Bradocke "died of a sort of rambeling feavourish distemper, which raged in that country",[25] and others died of "violent fevers" or "violent distempers". Gough makes several references to such fevers, although few people seem to have died from them. When four members of the same family died inside one month in 1698 or 1699, Gough writes as if this was something quite out of the ordinary.[26] Smallpox is also mentioned as if it were commonplace, though there is little evidence that it caused many deaths in Myddle.

3 · *The economic structure*

The economy of the parish of Myddle was based upon a type of pastoral farming that produced a society with less extremes of wealth and poverty than in most contemporary arable areas. That this was so can be deduced from an analysis of the hearth-tax returns, from a study of the occupations that are listed in the parish registers, from an assessment of the total value of the personal estate that was appraised in the probate inventories, and from a few observations upon the poor-rates.

In the county of Shropshire as a whole the number of those who were too poor to pay the hearth-tax in 1672 amounted to about 23 per cent of the total number of householders. It is difficult to be precise about the number of exempt in Myddle itself, but it may have been as low as 16.5 per cent. The annual accounts of the overseers of the poor do not go back beyond the eighteenth century, but there does not seem to have been much of a pauper problem before the second wave of immigration and the subsequent population rise of the late 1630s onwards. The parish registers do not describe anyone as pauper until 1635, and Gough writes[27] that John Matthews was the only person chargeable to the parish in the 1630s, "soe that I have heard my father say that the first yeare that hee was marryed, (which was about the yeare 1633) hee payd onely four pence to the poore, and now [1701] I pay almost twenty shillings per annum". This increasing concern with the poor is also seen in the number of settlement cases with which the parish was involved during the closing years of the seventeenth century.

Nor were there as many rich people in Shropshire. The 1524 and 1544 subsidy rolls show a wide distribution of wealth, with no outstanding families in Myddle parish. And of those who paid the hearth-tax in 1672, there were 56 who paid on one hearth each, another 10 who had two each, and 10 more who had between three and seven each. No-one had anything more ostentatious, and in the whole of Pimhill hundred there were only nine households out of a total of 1,255 that had eight hearths or more. North Shropshire had fewer of the very rich and fewer of the very poor than was generally the case in the central arable areas of the country.

There were few armigerous families within the parish of Myddle at the time of the heraldic visitation of 1623.[28] William Amis of Alderton had his claims rejected, and of those who were resident within the parish, only the Gittinses of Castle Farm, the Downtons of Alderton Hall, and the Kinastons of Shotton had their pedigree allowed. The Atcherleys and the Hanmers (both of Marton) were junior branches of armigerous families whose seats were outside the parish, and other gentry families (the Corbetts, the Chambres, the Onslows, and Thorneses) held lands in Myddle but were resident elsewhere. None of the last four families ever played an important role in the life of the community, and while the others were always prominent in parochial affairs, they were never able to dominate it, either collectively or individually, in the way that a squire or lord was able to control some of the nucleated villages in the arable areas. Only the Atcherleys were able to enlarge and retain their holdings during the seventeenth century; the Kinastons left the parish, the Gittinses and the Hanmers had to part with some of their lands, and the Downtons ended in complete ruin. In a parish such as Myddle, where settlement was relatively scattered, and where there was no resident lord, there was much more independence, and a greater degree of equality than was often the case in the 'fielden' areas.

The Myddle parish registers normally included men's occupations in the entries for the period 1541 to 1660. An analysis of this information provides the best evidence for the economic structure of this woodland community that one is likely to get.

Table 2 The occupational structure, 1541–1660: an analysis of the parish registers

Period	Gentlemen		Yeomen		Husbandmen		Labourers		Craftsmen		Others		Total
	No.	%	No.	%	No.	%	No.	%	No.	%	No.	%	No.
1541–70	14	11.1	23	18.3	63	50.0	9	7.1	14	11.1	3	2.4	126
1571–1600	10	8.0	17	13.3	52	40.6	30	23.4	17	13.2	2	1.5	128
1601–30	11	7.3	43	28.3	41	27.0	33	21.7	20	13.1	4	2.6	152
1631–60	8	6.4	22	17.6	30	24.0	39	31.2	18	14.4	8	6.4	125

Notes

1 There are gaps in the registers from 1553–8, 1566–7, 1614–15, 1629–31, and 1638–47, and for baptisms between 1653 and 1659. Occupations are rarely given in the period 1631–4.

2 Each person has been counted only once for each period, but if he appears in a later period, then he has been included in that group as well.

3 If a person appears with a different occupation from the one previously given, then he has been counted for each occupation. This has rarely occurred, and does not materially affect the figures.

4 Only the males have been counted. The females appear only as 'wife', 'widow', 'spinster', or 'servant'. As the servants appear only upon marriage, or occasionally at death, the numbers do not have much meaning. There were four female servants during the first period, eleven during the second, but hardly any are recorded after 1600.

5 Everyone from the chapelry of Hadnall has been excluded. The figures relate solely to the area served by the church of Myddle.

The most significant figures are those for the labourers, and they will be commented upon in detail in chapter 5. During the mid-sixteenth century they formed only a very small group, but during the 1580s and 1590s their numbers increased considerably. A second influx during the Commonwealth period swelled their ranks until they formed almost one-third of the total population of the community. Even so, this was still considerably less than in some arable areas where over half the population were labourers during this period.[29]

This immigration of labourers obviously meant a fall in the proportion of the total numbers who were farming their own land. At the same time, there was a general improvement in economic status within this farming section of the community.

Table 3 Ranking within the farming section of the community, 1541–1660

Period	% Gentry	% Yeomen	% Husbandmen
1541–70	14.0	23.0	63.0
1571–1600	12.7	21.5	65.8
1601–30	11.6	45.2	43.2
1631–60	13.3	36.7	50.0

The term 'gentry' was used more loosely within the parish than it was by the heralds, and about one farmer in every eight was given this ranking by his neighbours. But the interesting fact that emerges from the figures is that during the early seventeenth century many farmers who had previously been described as 'husbandmen' now became known as 'yeomen'. The increasing prosperity of the average farmer is reflected in the demand for (and the ability to pay) much higher entry fines[30] for their farms and tenements during the late 1630s and the 1640s, though as several yeomen sank back to the husbandman level during the next few years, the burden may have been too much for some of them. But by the reign of Charles I there was a noticeable widening of the division between the farming class and the rising number of labourers.

The craftsmen also formed an important group throughout these 120 years, though in a woodland area such as north Shropshire one might have expected more than one in every seven or eight to be employed in this way. Their numbers include the following crafts.

Table 4 The craftsmen in the parish registers, 1541–1660

Period	Tailors	Weavers	Glovers	Carpenters	Coopers	Shoe-makers	Black-smiths	Masons
1541–70	5	3	0	1	2	1	2	0
1571–1600	8	2	0	4	1	0	1	1
1601–30	4	8	1	3	1	1	2	0
1631–60	6	6	1	1	1	1	1	1

During the sixteenth century Myddle was essentially a community of small pastoral farms and tenements, with a few large farms supporting minor gentry. As such it prospered in a mild sort of way so that by the first few decades of the seventeenth century several husbandmen were able to call themselves yeomen. An influx of labourers made the community more socially-stratified, but even so, by the time of the hearth-tax returns of 1672, Myddle and its neighbouring parishes still had few of the very rich, but also relatively few of the very poor. The probate inventories that have survived confirm the impression of a steady rise in the wealth of the farming section of the community. The median average for the total personal estate of the late-sixteenth-century inventories is about £22. During the first 40 years of the seventeenth century, this rose to around £29, and then for the last 40 years of the same century, the median average was £42. Inflation certainly accounts for a lot of this apparent rise, but even so, there was still a rise in real terms.

The farmers do not seem to have been as prosperous as the ones in Leicestershire, where the median average for personal estate rose from £14 7*s.* 11*d.* between 1500 and 1531 to £46 16*s.* 8*d.* in 1588, and to £67 2*s.* 4*d.* by 1603.[31] However, there were Shropshire men who were as wealthy as the average Leicestershire farmer, even if no-one ever approached the outstanding wealth of some individuals in the east Midlands. Two of the richest farmers in Myddle parish – Roger Maynwaring of Sleap Hall and Richard More of Castle Farm – had personal estate valued at only £20 16*s.* 4*d.* and £25 4*s.* 0*d.* respectively, in 1551 and 1553, but 20 years later, in 1572, Roger Nicholas of Balderton Hall had £119 3*s.* 0*d.*, and John Woulf, the Myddle husbandman (1574), Hugh Deakin, a Newton yeoman (1580), and George Downton of Alderton, yeoman (1587), each had between £107 and £123. The highest personal estate recorded was that of Andrew Hordley, the yeoman-tailor of Divlin Wood (1640), with £189 16*s.* 10*d.*, of which £47 5*s.* 2*d.* was in the form of debts that were owed to him. Few people had more than £100 worth of personal estate if debts are excluded. On the other hand, there appear to have been fewer of the very poor than in Leicestershire. Thomas Clare of Marton, husbandman, had only £4 13*s.* 4*d.* in personal estate in 1557, and Joan Bromley, a Myddle widow, had only £4 11*s.* 0*d.* in 1575, but after 1575 the only one with less than double figures was David ap Roberts, the Marton weaver, who died with personal estate worth £9 12*s.* 11*d.* in 1620. All the different kinds of evidence point to the fact that there were less extremes of wealth and poverty in this Shropshire woodland community than in the arable areas of the east Midlands.

The Myddle farmers and labourers worked at least in part in a money economy. This was true of all classes and was reflected in the number of bequests of money, rather than of animals or items of dress and furniture, in the wills of this period. The workings of this money economy are also seen in the portions brought by the wife upon her marriage, by the provision of credit, in the way money was readily found to pay the great increases in entry fines between 1637 and 1642, and in the examples of commutation of services and heriots to the lord for a fixed money payment. In an economy that was geared to raising livestock for the near-by markets, this is not to be wondered at.

The frequency with which debts are recorded in the probate inventories, not just in Myddle, but all over the country, suggests that it was not very difficult to obtain a loan. The provision of credit enabled people in the countryside to purchase more land, to erect new buildings, and to survive bad harvests and misfortune on their farms. Sixteen of the 53 Myddle inventories record some form of debt (either outward or inward) and one suspects that there are other inventories that ought to have recorded them. They range from a small sum of £1 3*s*. 4*d*. to bonds worth £104 10*s*. 0*d*.

Formal bonds were the most secure form of lending. They attracted the men who lived in retirement and the widows and spinsters who had money to spare, and who were able to live on the interest of their capital. When William Clayton of the Hollins, yeoman, died in 1661, his inventory simply recorded "His wearing apparell, £1," and bonds worth £104 10*s*. 0*d*. A less secure method was to lend money "without speciality". This method earned higher interest rates over a shorter period of time, but was much more risky. Richard Guest, yeoman, died in 1694 with "Good debts by specialties, £27", and "Debts in dispaire [+ 2 Books], £3". Because of the risk involved, when Thomas Atcherley of Marton lent Richard Maddox, a Myddle husbandman, the sum of £1 10*s*. 0*d*., in 1681, he insisted that the debt be recorded in the manor court.[32]

Most of the inventories simply use the general term 'debts', which could include bonds, but must also have included bills for unpaid work, and in some cases outgoing debts are known to have comprised such payments as funeral expenses, legacies, wages, rents, and heriots. They cannot be regarded as being in the same category as loans. However, there were several inventories which clearly referred to lending. In 1698 Humphrey Hanmer, gent., had "Creditts" worth £62; in 1640 Andrew Hordley, yeoman-tailor, had debts due to him worth £47 5*s*. 2*d*.; in 1587 George Downton, yeoman, was owed £37 10*s*. 8*d*.; in 1574 John Woulf, farmer, had £20 10*s*. 6*d*. due to him; in 1580 Hugh Deakyn, yeoman, was owed £18 0*s*. 4*d*.; and, in 1685 William Watson, tailor, had "1 Debt Due by Bond, £10".

The inventory of George Pickstock of Houlston, husbandman (1636), was appraised at £31 6*s*. 2*d*. The debts that he owed were then listed as follows: "Margaret Wollyston by Bond, £10, John Baylie (bond), £4, Widow Sadler (bond), £8, Tho. Hughes (bond), £12 10*s*. 0*d*., Willm. Goslinge (bond), £3, Tho. Evans (bond) £5, Michael Raphes (bond) £3, John Davies (bond), £5 13*s*. 4*d*., Tho. Groome (bond), £4, Mr Tho. Moore (bond), £5 16*s*. 8*d*.; total, £61 0*s*. 0*d*. To John Davies £2 13*s*. 4*d*., Roger Gough £2, John Baylie £2, for a Heriott £1, for Cheife rent 12*s*.; total, £8 0*s*. 4*d*. Disbursed for funerall expences 16*s*. 4*d*.".

A few of his creditors came from his own parish, but the others must have come from the wider neighbourhood.

Gough's remarks add greatly to our understanding of the credit system and the risks involved. For instance, when Thomas Hall bought Hayward's freehold tenement in Newton, he "had to borrow all the money at interest to pay for the purchase". And when the Haywards had previously bought this land from the Corbetts, a £20 debt was unpaid by them for at least 40 years.[33] There was so much buying and selling of land that borrowing facilities simply must have been readily available. Relatives frequently helped each other in these transactions, but friends and neighbours were prepared to help, provided they got an attractive rate of interest.

However, lending large sums of money could be a risky business, which occasionally brought disaster. Gough states that the fortunes of the Gittins family of Castle and Eagle farms suffered a sharp reverse in the 1630s when Richard Gittins lost a lot of money through "standing risky sureties".[34] Because of this loss the family had to relinquish the lease of Eagle farm. Then, later in the century, John Downton of Alderton Hall, who already had "great charges in the education of his children", suffered heavy financial losses through standing surety. A Chancery case, dated 14 February 1667/8, tells how he loaned £200 to his kinsman and namesake and stood security for him for a further loan of £100 from Stephen Hatchett of Lee. His losses from this were so great that he was eventually reduced to poverty, had to sell his land, and was maintained by his wife selling ale.[35] A credit system was essential to the workings of the economy, but for a few individuals the consequences could be drastic indeed.

4 · *A pastoral economy*

Shropshire was described by a member of the House of Commons in 1597 as a county consisting wholly of woodland, "bred of oxen and dairies". Throughout Elizabethan and Stuart times it was indeed, as Dr Thirsk has written, "a good example of a cattle-raising, meat-producing country".[36] But it had not always been so; before these days there had been much more of a balance between arable and pasture farming. The first settlements in Shropshire had been planted on the brown-earths, those productive, sandy soils that nourished as fine a crop as could have been found almost anywhere in the realm. And even during the years when the stress was on rearing animals, the brown-earths of Myddle continued to produce excellent crops. Gough boasted that, "The parish yields great plenty of corne, especially of the best barley, which is little inferior to the barley that is got in Wroxeter fields, which is accompted the best in Shropshire".[37] But like other woodland areas, Shropshire had to import some of her corn by the late sixteenth century, and in time of national dearth the county was amongst the first to suffer.

Such a crisis is recorded in the *Early Chronicles of Shrewsbury*, during the years 1596–7.

> This yeare there was by the baylyffs and aldermen of Shreusberie, with the commoners of the same, provision made for corne at London, the whiche cam from Danswicke, Denmarke, and those foren places to ease all England and especially London of the excessyve prices which corne bare all England over, and especially in Shreusberie, so that there was provided above 3,200 bushell at the least for Shreusberie, and cam by way by Bristowe . . .

Concentration upon beef production seems to have started during the late fifteenth and early sixteenth centuries with the clearing of immense stretches of woodland and with the draining of some of the glacial pools or meres. The woods, of course, had been used for grazing from time immemorial. Domesday Book mentions pasturable woodland, and pannage rights continued to be a great boon to the farmers until the woods were cleared. They provided beech-mast and acorns for the pigs,[38] and perhaps the hollies were used as a winter feed for sheep and cattle, as they were in other places.[39] But from Gough's comments, Myddlewood appears to have been a dense wood of little agricultural value, and while the woods of Divlin and Brandwood had grassy clearings that had been farmed from at least the thirteenth century,[40] they flourished on the same heavy gley-soils, and they, too, would have been amongst the thickest woods in north Shropshire. It seems certain that their felling was an improvement that brought an increased standard of living to all concerned. The draining of the meres led to the creation of a new farm at Harmer Moss, and a greatly extended one at Broomhurst, while all the farmers in the lordship of Myddle were allowed to rent new woodland pastures, or leasows. The common arable farming of the open fields was abandoned, and the emphasis was now on grazing, especially upon the land that had just been cleared. Like their friends and neighbours in surrounding parishes, the farmers of Myddle began to specialize in the profitable business of raising oxen, cattle, and sheep.

All this necessitated the development of the near-by market towns. Under the heading of "Natural Resources in Myddle", Gough wrote: "But the greatest convenience is the benefit of good marketts".[41] principally the one at Shrewsbury. He is worth quoting in full on this.

> There is a Markett [at Shrewsbury] on every Wednesday and Saturday for corne; and on every Saturday for cattell, besides six faires, the 1st. on Wednesday after the cloase of Easter, which is a good faire for cowes and calves, for old oxen and barren beasts; the 2nd. on Wednesday in the weeke before Whitsuntide, this is good for the same purposes; the 3rd. att Midsummer, this is good for wool, fresh oxen for the teame and barren beasts; the 4th. on Lambmas day,

> this is good for sheep, wool, and cattell; the 5th. on St. Matthew's day, Sep. 21st., a great faire for white meates and for young heifers, for then the time of laying cattell att grasse is ended and they are usually brought from the lay to this faire. The last is called St. Andrew's faire and on the day after St. Andrew's day, this is good for white meats, fatt swine, and fatt beasts.

The emphasis was plainly on rearing livestock.

Shropshire had 18 markets in the seventeenth century.[42] Wem was only a few miles from Myddle, and Gough specifically mentions Oswestry as being a convenient market for those who lived at the Marton-Myddlewood end of the parish, for they were on the market road connecting Newport and Market Drayton with Oswestry.[43] "On the 4th. of March is a good fair there for great oxen; on the 1st. of May for cowes and calves, and at St. Andrew's tide for fatt swine". The Newport butchers used to stay overnight at the Eagle and Child in Myddle, on their way back from Oswestry, and during the early seventeenth century the King's Purveyors were active in the area on the pretext of buying fat beasts for the King's household. Gough writes:

> Some of these Officers did wrong the Country very much, for the Purveyor would come to a fayre or Markett with his long Goad in his hand, and when he saw a paire of Oxen that were for his purpose, hee would lay his Goad upon them, and if they were unsold, would mark them for the King's use, unlesse the owner gave him silver persuasions to forbeare; butt if the oxen were once marked, the owner durst not sell them to any other, and the purveyor would take care not to give too much. These purveyors were likewise drovyers, who bought cattle in this country, and brought them into Kent to sell again. If the King had any of them it is likely he payd pretty well for them, but these officers being found a great nuisance both to the King and Country, were layd aside.[44]

Their activities in the area confirm what has already been said about the county's specialization in rearing beef.

An analysis of the probate inventories for the parish of Myddle amply bears out these general statements. Fifty-three inventories survive for the period 1551–1701, and 42 of these are suitable for analysis. There are 16 for the period 1551–99, another 13 for the years 1600–40, and a final 13 for the period 1664–1701. One would have liked a larger sample, but they are consistent enough to provide some useful information. They are quite definite about the concentration on meat production. In only one case – that of George Pickstock of Houlston, husbandman (1636) – is the value of the livestock less than that of the crops, and even this one may be unrealistic in that it was drawn up at the beginning of January when his stock of animals would be at its lowest, while he still had some corn left over from the previous harvest and had already sown his winter wheat. No other inventory has less than 60 per cent of the value of the farm stock devoted to animals and hay, and the majority have a much higher proportion than that.

The figures have been arrived at in the following manner. All the livestock items, including poultry and a few bees, have been listed together, with the hay that was grown for their fodder. Items listing cheese, butter, and bacon have also been added to the same amount, though in all cases it is the animals themselves that form the bulk of the total. These items have been compared with the crops and store of corn, including oats, wheat, barley, rye, peas, and blend corn. Some of these crops, of course, were principally used as fodder for the animals; the cattle would need the hay, the horses would need oats, and the peas were probably fed, at least in part, to the sheep. The *Chronicles* are eloquent on what happened when the crops failed. In 1590–1 a hard winter was followed by a drought which caused hay and fodder to be very dear and many cattle "to perrishe for waunt". A similar tale had been told several years earlier, in 1572–3: "This yeare the wynter and spring tyme was verey longe cold hard and drye so that it was verey farr in the moonthe of May before any leffe or blossom apeeryd uppon any tree, by which occasyon mutche cattell peryshed for waunte of foode and sucker". The same thing happened again in the closing years of the century: "1599–1600 . . . great want of fodder and grass . . . [farmers] forced to thrashe upp their cornne from stoare to feed and save their cattell for they were willinge to delyver one hallffe of their cattell to feed the oder". Some of the value of the corn that is listed in the inventories, therefore, could well have been added to the value of the livestock and their fodder. On the other hand, it could be argued that the draught beasts were not principally reared for their beef, and the value of the farm equipment and tools (which is usually small) has been left out of the calculations. But the general conclusions would have been much the same even if these items had been included within the total value of the crops.

The figures taken from the inventories show a remarkable consistency throughout the 150-year period. The median averages for the 16 inventories dated between 1551 and 1599 show that 87 per cent or 89 per cent of the total value of the farm stock was invested in animals and their fodder and products. The figures are roughly the same whatever the status of the person and whatever the date of the inventory. Hugh Deakin, the Newton yeoman (1580), had only 61 per cent of the value of his farm stock devoted to his animals, but nobody else had below 72 per cent. Seven people had 90 per cent or more, and five of these were amongst the first six inventories, dated between 1551 and 1563.

There was hardly any change in this respect during the seventeenth century. The median average of the 13 inventories dated between 1600 and 1640 is represented by David ap Roberts, the Marton weaver-farmer, with 87 per cent of the value of his farm stock invested in his animals. This one might expect from a weaver with only a part-time interest in farming; pastoral farming would be so much easier than ploughing and tilling the heavy clay soils of his tenement. But this concentration on pastoral farming was the norm for all classes. Humphrey Hanmer, the gentleman freeholder of Marton Farm, had 79 per cent of his farm goods invested in livestock, and the inventories of the yeomen and the husbandmen nearly all point to the same conclusion. Apart from the one exception of George Pickstock, everyone had at least two-thirds of the value of his total farm stock devoted to his animals, and most had an even higher proportion than this.

Nor is there any difference after the Restoration. The median average for the 13 inventories dated between 1664 and 1701 is 84 per cent of the value of the farm goods invested in livestock. The seven yeomen have a median average for their inventories that is exactly the same as that for the whole group, and the four husbandmen had livestock valued between 78 and 89 per cent of the total farm goods. The total range for the whole group is from 61 to 95 per cent. Throughout the whole period of 150 years the evidence of the probate inventories is quite firm. The man who represented the median average had 87 per cent of the value of his farm goods invested in livestock and their fodder and products. At no time does the median average of the various groups deviate much from this figure, and in only six of the 42 inventories was there less than 70 per cent of the farm stock invested in animals. The statistical information confirms the general impressions; the farmers of north Shropshire were principally concerned in rearing beef. On the brown-earths, however, arable farming played an important subsidiary role.

The inventories are detailed enough to allow one to tabulate the number of animals for the same three periods (see tables 5, 6 and 7 on pp. 62, 64 and 66).

The average head of cattle for the farmers of Myddle during the second half of the sixteenth century was 13.7, or 15.1 if fully-grown oxen are included. This is very close to the present national average head of 16 per farm, though of course much larger herds are now common. G. E. Fussell has suggested that the national average for the middle of the sixteenth century was only six per farm, though he warns that this is only a rough estimate as real statistics are lacking.[45] If his estimate is correct, then Myddle had more than twice the national average, and this again confirms that the area was already specializing in the rearing of beef. At Wigston Magna, in the heart of the arable Midlands, the average farm carried only about six or seven cattle in the period 1534–1602, and the farmer's livestock was worth about twice the value of his crops.[46] In the Forest of Arden, on the other hand, "seventy farmers who died between 1530 and 1569 left 989 head of cattle between them, a mean of 14.1 each".[47] The woodland areas of the west Midlands clearly practised a different type of farming from that of the typical arable villages of the country.

The truth of the Shropshire M.P.'s remarks about the breeding of oxen and the importance of dairying is borne out by the inventories. Two out of every five head of cattle were milch cows, and three out of every ten were young beasts or

Table 5 Animals in Myddle inventories, 1551–1600

Date	Name	Status	kine	heifers	calves	bulls	bullocks	beasts	oxen	horses	mares	colts	geldings	sheep	pigs	poultry	geese	bees
30 Sep. 1551	Rog. Maynwaring	gent.	4	3	–	–	–	–	4	–	1	3	1	30	–	–	–	–
6 May 1553	Richard More	gent.	13	9	5	–	–	5	6	–	1	1	–	31	★	–	–	–
6 May 1553	William Woulf	husb.	14	–	–	–	–	9	2	–	–	–	2	80	6	★	★	–
16 May 1557	Thos. Clare	husb.	3	–	1	–	–	–	–	–	1	1	–	9	1	–	–	–
16 Apr. 1563	Wm. Formston	husb.	–	–	–	–	–	7	–	–	1	–	–	–	–	–	–	–
23 Apr. 1563	Wm. Brayne	husb.	3	–	3	–	–	–	4	–	1	–	–	13	1	★	★	–
10 May 1569	John Lloyd	husb.	6	–	4	–	2	3	3	–	1	–	–	32	–	–	–	–
29 Sep. 1570	Ann Matthews	widow	–	–	1	–	2	–	–	1	–	–	–	–	1	★	–	–
17 Oct. 1572	Roger Nicholas	gent.	6	–	11	1	–	10	6	5	5	–	–	40	12	★	★	–
1 July 1573	John Woulf	husb.	20	–	10	1	–	–	4	–	2	–	–	23	13	★	★	–
18 Feb. 1575/6	John Hordley	husb.	9	–	–	–	–	–	–	–	–	–	–	–	–	★	–	★
(11 July 1579)	John Raphes	carp.	2	2	6	–	–	–	–	1	1	1	–	–	7	★	★	–
Oct. 1580	Hugh Deakin	yeo.	13	–	2	–	2	–	4	–	–	–	–	100	6	★	★	★
7 Nov. 1580	Richard Woulf	husb.	3	1	–	–	–	–	1	–	2	2	–	2	14	★	–	–
23 Oct. 1591	Richard Ash	husb.	3	2	6	–	2	–	2	–	1	2	–	–	6	–	–	–
10 Nov. 1599	Wm. Brayne	yeo.	3	–	4	–	–	3	2	–	2	–	–	–	–	–	–	–
Totals	16		102	17	53	2	8	37	38	7	19	10	3	360	67	(9)	(6)	(2)

Notes
1 There is no date on John Raphes' inventory, so the date that the will was proved is given in brackets.
2 Roger Nicholas had "ten horses and mares". These have been divided equally.
3 ★ indicates unspecified number recorded.

fully-grown oxen. Several of the calves were also being reared for the beef market. As might be expected, some of the gentry owned a considerable number of cattle. Richard More of Castle Farm (1553) had 13 kine, 9 heifers, both young and old, 6 oxen, 5 young beasts, and 5 sucking calves, in addition to his other animals; a total of 38 head of cattle on the largest farm in the parish. On the second largest farm, Roger Nicholas of Balderton Hall (1572) had 6 kine and a bull, 11 calves, 10 young beasts, and 6 oxen, that is 34 head of cattle, as well as 10 horses and mares, 40 sheep, and 12 pigs. These large herds are comparable with those of the richest farmers in the Forest of Arden.[48] But large numbers could also be raised on the smaller tenements. William Woulf (1553) had 14 kine, 9 young beasts, and 2 oxen, and 20 years later, his successor, John Woulf, kept 20 kine and a bull, 10 yearling calves, and 4 oxen, amongst his many other animals.

Oxen were used as draught beasts and sold off for meat at Shrewsbury fair when they were too old to work. Very few draught horses were kept, though it was usual to have a mare for travelling, and a few farmers reared young horses, either colts or geldings. This was only subsidiary to the rearing of cattle. Pigs were still kept in large numbers, three farmers being credited with more than a dozen, so the common pannage rights were not yet as severely restricted as they were to be. A paine laid in the Court Leet in 1622 forbade the gathering of any mast or acorns, and no-one was allowed "to put to pannage any swine other than such as were by him or them there reared or bought the wynter before".[49]

Ten of the 16 farmers kept flocks of sheep, with an average of 36 in each flock, or 22.5 if the six farmers who had none at all are included. The county of Leicestershire averaged 30 sheep per farmer as a whole in the sixteenth century, a figure that was "pulled up by the existence of a top class of big farmers who carried flocks of 200–500 sheep".[50] There was no-one of this standing in Myddle. Hugh Deakin, the Newton yeoman (1580), had a flock of 100, and William Woulf, the Myddle husbandman (1553), had 80, but there was nobody else with more than 40. Deakin also kept 21 head of cattle, 6 pigs, 21 geese, with some other poultry and a few bees, as well as a large quantity of hard corn and blend corn, with one load of peas, 12 loads of hay, and about 40 loads of dung, so he was far from being a specialist sheep-farmer. Neither was William Woulf, nor anyone else.

At first sight there seems to have been a drop in the scale of farming, and thus in the standard of living, in the first 40 years of the seventeenth century, but the sample is smaller and it includes people of a lower status than before. The ability to pay greatly increased entry fines for leases suggests that there was a steady increase in income as agricultural prices rose, and no drop in the standard of living. But the sample has a median average of only 9 head of cattle compared with 13.7 before, or 10 head if fully-grown oxen are included, compared with the previous median average of 15.1. However, there are no inventories for the largest farms during this period, and the herds of some of the tenement-farmers suggest that

Table 6 Animals in Myddle inventories, 1600–40

Date	Name	Status	kine	heifers	calves	bulls	bullocks	beasts	oxen	horses	mares	colts	geldings	sheep	pigs	poultry	geese	bees
24 Mar. 1599/1600	Ralph Lloyd	yeo.	7	1	–	–	2	11	6	1	1	–	–	87	2	★	–	–
28 Apr. 1601	Alan Chaloner	smith	3	–	–	–	–	9	–	1	–	–	–	–	–	–	–	–
10 Sep. 1604	David ap Roberts	weaver	2	1	–	–	–	–	–	–	1	–	–	12	2	–	–	–
22 Nov. 1605	Chris. Wright	yeo.	3	–	2	–	–	–	–	–	–	–	–	16	4	★	–	–
8 Jun. 1620	Robt. Amies	yeo.	3	2	–	–	2	–	–	–	1	1	–	27	–	–	–	–
4 Feb. 1625/6	Morgan Clarke	lab.	2	1	–	–	–	–	–	1	–	–	–	23	2	★	–	–
4 Sep. 1626	Anne Woulf	widow	2	–	1	–	–	4	–	–	1	–	–	–	2	★	–	–
25 Jul. 1631	Hump. Hanmer	gent.	–	–	–	–	–	5	–	–	–	–	–	11	2	★	–	–
6 Mar. 1631/2	John Clowes	husb.	9	–	4	–	–	3	4	1	–	–	–	1	–	★	–	–
2 Apr. 1634	Roger Sandford	yeo.	6	1	3	–	4	–	1	–	3	–	–	96	–	★	★	–
2 Jan. 1635/6	George Pickstock	husb.	–	1	–	–	–	–	–	–	2	3	–	–	–	–	–	–
1 Jan. 1637/8	Rich. Pickstock	husb.	2	–	–	–	–	–	–	–	–	–	–	–	–	–	–	–
16 Jul. 1640	Andrew Hordley	tailor	9	–	7	–	–	6	2	–	1	–	–	16	–	★	★	★
Totals	13		48	7	17	–	8	38	13	4	10	4	–	289	14	(7)	(2)	(1)

Note
★ indicates unspecified number recorded.

rearing was just as important as it had been before. Ralph Lloyd of Myddle, yeoman (1600), had 27 head of cattle at the time of his death, Andrew Hordley, the farmer-tailor of Divlin Wood (1640) had 24 head, and John Clowes, a Marton husbandman (1632), was rearing another 20. The emphasis on fattening rather than dairying was greater than it had been before, judging by the number of oxen and young beasts that were kept, compared with the herds of milch cows.

But the restrictions on pannage rights were beginning to affect the number of pigs that were reared. Some sixteenth-century farmers had kept more than a dozen, but now no-one had more than four, and an increasing number had none at all. If one allows for the absence of information about the big farms, then the number of horses does not seem to have changed, and the average flock of sheep was again just over 22 for the whole, or 32 for the nine men who kept them. Roger Sandford (1636) kept a flock of 96 on the same farm at Newton-on-the-Hill, where Hugh Deakin had previously kept 100, and Roger Lloyd had almost as many with 87 in Myddle. All the other flocks were as small as those belonging to most of the farmers in the sixteenth century.

Thirteen inventories are detailed enough to be analysed for the final period of 1664–1701. The average head of cattle was 13.4, with no significant change if oxen are included, for now only four were kept on all the farms put together. There were two at the Hollins in 1664, and another yoke at Newton in 1675, but no other farmer is recorded as possessing any. Nor do the numbers of horses rise to take their place as draught beasts. However, a large number of young beasts were still reared for the beef market. William Higginson of Webscott, yeoman (1664), had 13 beasts, with 15 milch cows, 3 heifers, 2 calves, and a bull; a total of 34 head of cattle. Richard Guest of Myddle, yeoman (1694), kept 7 beasts amongst his 26 head of cattle; William Turner of Alderton, yeoman (1695) had 6 beasts in his total herd of 23, and Samuel Clayton of the Hollins, also a yeoman (1664), reared 6 beasts, in addition to 14 other cattle. It is difficult to tell how many of the calves were being reared for beef and how many as milch kine, but there was a much greater production of cheese during this period, and the increased numbers of kine may be indicative of this.

Cattle remained the major source of wealth of these woodland farms throughout the Elizabethan and Stuart periods. But if the evidence of the inventories is to be believed, then there was a drastic reduction in the flocks of sheep that were kept after the Restoration. The overall average was now only 9.5 per farm, or 20.7 for those who kept them. Only Thomas Hancocks of Newton (1675) kept 50, and nobody else had more than 35. A much larger and wider sample than this would be needed to draw any reliable conclusions, and, indeed, the ten yeomen whose inventories survive from 1705 to 1732 kept upon average 24.8 sheep overall, or 41.2 for the six who kept them. Two of these men had flocks of 90 and 120, though the others had much fewer. In other words, the pattern in the early

Table 7 Animals in Myddle inventories, 1664–1701

Date	Name	Status	kine	heifers	calves	bulls	bullocks	beasts	oxen	horses	mares	colts	geldings	sheep	pigs	poultry	geese	bees
15 Jan. 1663/4	Sam. Clayton	yeo.	8	–	4	–	–	6	2	–	–	2	–	35	1	–	–	–
18 Jan. 1663/4	Wm. Higginson	yeo.	15	3	2	1	–	13	–	1	2	1	–	–	4	★	★	–
20 Aug. 1674	Step. Formston	yeo.	5	–	4	–	–	6	–	–	1	–	–	–	4	–	–	–
16 Aug. 1675	Thos. Hancocks	husb.	4	2	1	–	–	–	2	–	1	–	–	50	5	–	–	–
14 Dec. 1683	Mich. Brayne	yeo.	1	–	–	–	–	1	–	–	1	1	–	–	1	–	–	★
16 Mar. 1684/5	Francis Smith	husb.	4	–	2	–	–	4	–	–	–	3	–	–	3	–	–	–
13 May 1685	Wm. Watson	tailor	5	4	–	–	–	–	–	1	1	1	–	10	1	–	–	–
22 Apr. 1692	Francis Clarke	husb.	3	–	1	–	4	–	–	1	–	–	–	20	1	★	★	–
(5 Jun. 1694)	Dan. Tildsley	husb.	3	–	5	–	–	2	–	2	1	–	–	8	2	–	–	–
15 Jun. 1694	Rich. Guest	yeo.	13	–	5	1	–	7	–	–	2	4	–	–	4	★	–	–
16 Jan. 1694/5	Wm. Turner	yeo.	7	–	6	–	4	6	–	–	4	3	–	–	18	★	–	–
12 Aug. 1698	Bart. Mansell	yeo.	–	–	–	–	–	–	–	–	–	2	–	–	8	★	★	–
5 Jun. 1701	Wm. Bickley	yeo.	5	–	3	–	–	–	–	1	–	–	–	1	–	–	–	–
Totals	13		73	9	33	2	8	45	4	6	13	17	–	124	52	(5)	(3)	(1)

eighteenth century was the same as it had been 100–150 years earlier. It is likely that the same pattern was true of the late seventeenth century. Gough wrote in 1701, "There is good stoare of sheep in this Parish whose wool if washed white and well ordered is not much inferior to the wool of Baschurch and Nesse which bears the name of the best in this Country".[51] He does not mention the value of the mutton, nor whether sheep's milk was used, but with the woollen industry providing employment in Shropshire, it obviously paid to rear sheep.[52]

The evidence of the inventories for the whole 150-year period shows that a total of 562 head of cattle was kept by 42 farmers – an average of 13.4 head per farm. Of these, 120 were young beasts reared for the market, and 55 were fully-grown oxen. Throughout the period, the number of beasts remained at about the same level, but fewer and fewer oxen are recorded during the seventeenth century. Milch cows numbered 223 (the largest individual total), and there were 33 heifers and 103 calves. If the figures are analysed according to status, then the four gentlemen kept 22 head of cattle, the 11 yeomen kept 17.5 head, and the 16 husbandmen had an average of 11.75 head.

The same 42 men kept a total of 93 horses of all kinds, consisting of 17 draught horses, 42 mares, 31 colts, and 3 geldings. This suggests that there was some breeding of colts, but it was all on a small scale. The relatively low number of draught beasts is again indicative that arable farming was only of subsidiary importance, though presumably horses were loaned to those whose farms were too small to support one. Only half the farmers had inventories that recorded poultry, and only a quarter mentioned geese. Their values were always small, and it may be that the appraisers often forgot to mention them, or that they were regarded as belonging to the woman of the house. Only four of the sample kept any bees. Finally, pigs seem to increase in numbers again in the late seventeenth century, but the figures are inflated by the 18 pigs of William Turner of Alderton, who farmed outside Myddle lordship. They were not as numerous as they once had been, though most farmers kept one or two.[53]

The emphasis, then, was on producing beef and on dairying, but there were no large-scale graziers, and the typical farm spread out its investment to cover a number of different kinds of animal. The crops were only of secondary importance, but even so they added considerably to the wealth of the area. The turnover from sales of livestock and dairy produce would be too slow for a farmer to make a living without growing some crops and keeping a cow or two for sustenance. Early writers often commented upon the goodness of the corn that was produced. Leland found that around Shrewsbury in the 1540s there was "ground plentifull of Corne, wood and pasture", and Speed, writing in 1611, had this to say: "The soile is rich and standeth upon a red clay, abounding in Wheat and barley". Sixty years later, Richard Blome was full of praise for the county: "It is a fertile soil both for tillage and pasture, abounding in wheat and barley and is well cloathed with wood, [and] feedeth store of cattle".[54] Outsiders, from the arable zones of England, tended to emphasize those aspects of the farming system that were familiar to them, and may have over-emphasized the part played by crops in the local economy,[55] but even so their comments about abundant wheat and barley must not be underestimated, especially as Gough also claimed that Myddle barley was amongst the best. During the late eighteenth and early nineteenth centuries, when many smaller tenements were engrossed into larger farms, there was a great turnover to arable farming, so that by the time of the 1838 Tithe Award[56] there were 4,305 acres of arable in the parish of Myddle (including the chapelry of Hadnall), compared with only 2,127 acres of pasture and meadow, and a meagre 132 acres of wood. Bagshaw wrote in his *Directory* of 1851: "The whole county is in general well cultivated, yielding good crops of all kinds of grain, turnips, peas, and potatoes".[57] As in the fens of Lincolnshire during the same period, there had been a profound change from a pastoral economy to one based on arable farming.[58]

Perhaps the crops that so impressed outside visitors were grown on those farms that were on the brown-earths, and possibly they are under-represented in the inventories. In the records that do survive, the crops were of such relative unimportance that many of them were collectively labelled simply as "corn". Five sixteenth-century inventories do this, most of them dating from the early years. There are references to wheat and barley (and malt), to oats and a few peas, and to some blend corn; but rye and hardcorn seem to have been the most important crops. No Myddle inventory ever mentions beans, and there is certainly not the emphasis on peas and beans that there was in predominantly arable areas such as Leicestershire at this time.[59] Much of the barley that was grown was made into malt, and the rye and the wheat were used for making bread. The *Chronicles* continually refer to rye and wheat prices, and to crises which caused the prices to rise and the poor to go hungry. Such a dearth occurred in July 1586, and three years later another crisis was averted after a failure of the rye crop, "because the people put mutche barly with rie to macke breadd, yee and many made bredd of cleane barly and good bredd too, for barly was so fayre and so plentifull this yeare". Celia Fiennes was to remark over a hundred years later that rye-bread was commonly eaten in Shropshire.[60]

The inventories of the early seventeenth century are most uninformative about crops. The first ten merely list them as "corn", but two of the three later ones mention rye, oats, and peas, and one also speaks of barley and malt. The inventories of the second half of the century are similar in form; most mention corn, but only four refer specifically to rye, three each to barley and oats, and just one each to wheat and peas. As in the sixteenth century, the oats and peas seem to have been grown for fodder, the barley for brewing, and the rye and wheat for bread. The majority only grew sufficient for their own needs, though there were exceptions such as Roger Nicholas, the Balderton Hall gentleman (1572), with 100 thrave of hardcorn, 40 thrave of barley, 30 thrave of oats, and some peas and malt; or John Woulf, the Myddle husbandman (1574), who had 13 strike of rye, 10 strike of malt, and three strike of wheat in store, with another 15 strike of rye and wheat and 19 strike of barley, oats, and peas sown in his fields; or Hugh Deakin, the Newton yeoman (1580), who had grown 100 thrave of hardcorn, 112 thrave of "lent fillings", and one load of peas. These three men have already been singled out as having unusually large numbers of animals, which must have needed part of these crops as fodder. The emphasis in sixteenth- and seventeenth-century Shropshire was undoubtedly on pastoral farming. As far back as the enclosure enquiry of 1517 there had been a clear tendency to turn to grazing, and it was reported then that small areas of arable land, including parts of the hundred of Pimhill, had been enclosed and turned over to pasture.[61] Today, the emphasis has returned to arable farming, though herds of cattle and flocks of sheep still graze on the heavy gley soils.

The farmer's tools and equipment were rarely of great value in the inventories, and were often grouped together as 'implements of husbandry', with no details given. When they were described more fully, they tended to be just the fundamental items that were necessary on almost any farm. Thirteen men had ploughs, and 9 harrows are mentioned, together with 11 yokes, 3 collars, and 2 chains. As it is reasonable to suppose that some farmers had no plough of their own, but borrowed one when the occasion arose, 13 ploughs seems a high number, especially as 7 of them are recorded in the plural. On the other hand, the list covers a period of 150 years, and three of the 13 belonged to different generations of the Woulf family. Nine of the inventories recording ploughs (including all those mentioning more than one) are from the period 1551 to 1600. After that, three husbandmen had one each, in 1636, 1675, and 1685, but only one yeoman (in 1695) recorded any.

The tools include 8 bills, 5 sickles, 2 scythes, 3 hatchets, 1 adze, a mattock, a fork, a pitchfork, a spade, a shovel, and rake, and 2 "dyggs". As for transport, 8 carts are mentioned, together with 8 wains and 4 tumbrils. Ralph Lloyd of Myddle, yeoman (1600), and Widow Anne Woulf of Myddle (1626) each had "an ironbound wayne". This type of wain must have just been introduced about this time for the appraiser of the inventories to distinguish them in this manner. Only George Pickstock of Houlston, husbandman (1636), had his farm described in full, with 42 different items, worth in all £3 18*s*. 4*d*. Pickstock was the only man whose inventory listed more arable crops than livestock. He was quite untypical in having such a varied collection of tools and equipment, and most farmers seem to have been content with the bare necessities. Like the furniture and utensils in the house, the equipment was practical and unsophisticated.

In conclusion, some mention must be made of the increasing importance of dairying. Several inventories record butter, often in connection with bacon and sometimes beef, but these are items to be found in any farmhouse kitchen. It is the references to cheeses that are more interesting. They are recorded in 15 of the 42 inventories, though "cheese presses" are not found until 1694 and 1695. John Woulf, the Myddle husbandman (1574), is the first farmer to have an unusual amount of cheese. He had in his kitchen 60 cheeses valued at £3, with eight gallons of butter, some bacon, and some beef. No-one else had anything out of the ordinary until 1632, when John Clowes of Marton, husbandman, had £10 worth of cheese and butter at the time of his death. Then, in 1636, George Pickstock of Houlston, husbandman, had 14 cheeses and three pots of butter, and in 1664, William Higginson, the Webscott yeoman, had £10 worth of cheese to add to his considerable farming stock. Gough also mentions the theft of a hundredweight of cheese from Richard Tyler of Balderton, but it is not until the eighteenth century that there is evidence of production on a fairly large scale. James Fewtrell, the Brandwood yeoman (1709), had a special room known as the Cheese Chamber which contained about 10 cwt of cheese, worth £10. Samuel Wright, a Bilmarsh yeoman (1727), had £5 8*s*. 0*d*. worth of goods in his cheese chamber, and a further ten shillings' worth in his Cheese Press House and Garret. William Clayton of the Hollins, husbandman (1728), had six cwt of cheese worth £5 8*s*. 0*d*. in an upstairs room, and in 1731, John Davies, a Brandwood yeoman, had seven cheese vats in his kitchen, a cheese press in a special room, and 77 cheeses weighing 6½ cwt in a room over the kitchen. The few earlier references make one wonder about the extent of cheese-making during the previous two centuries. The values given to their cheeses suggest a scale of production comparable with that of their successors. Unfortunately, rooms are rarely named in the earlier inventories and there is no information as to when special cheese chambers were first used. Nor is there any information as to where the cheeses were marketed. Perhaps they were part of the extensive trade in so-called 'Cheshire' cheeses. But what the inventories do show is that the Shropshire M.P. who said in 1597 that his county was a woodland area specializing in breeding and dairying was speaking truly.

5 · Tenures and estates

Dr Eric Kerridge has recently[62] cleared up some of the confusion that has clouded the debate over land tenures – "that is the manners and conditions of service by which lands were held of their lords" – and estates, which were freeholds "with a term of not less than one life". Freehold estates could either be held in fee simple or fee tail (i.e. in the sense that one generally uses the word), or they could be copyholds for a life or lives. In the west Midlands it was common for such copyhold leases to be held for 99 years, determinable upon three lives, and this was the custom that became accepted in Myddle.

A survey of the lordship of Myddle, made on 6 August 1563, shows that 15 of the 42 peasants within the manor were freeholders (using the term in its generally accepted sense). Another nine freeholders lived within the parish, but outside the lordship, making a total of 24. A contemporary census of the diocese of Lichfield[63] numbered 54 households in Myddle parish (excluding the chapelry of Hadnall which had another 14 households), so the freeholders amounted to some 44 per cent of the whole community. In this, Myddle was typical of the woodland areas, where the practice had been to allow free men to make clearings in the woods at their own cost, and for their own benefit. It is not possible to say what proportion of the cultivated land was freehold, but it was considerably more than half that of the entire parish. The freeholders were a privileged and influential body of men.

However, they still owed allegiance to the manor. Most of their lands came within the lordship of Myddle, but the core of Balderton township belonged to the manor of Hardwick, and Shotton and Alderton lay within the bounds of the Liberty of Shrewsbury. The freeholders attended the Court Baron and the Court Leet and presented their deeds upon the occasion of a manorial survey, for they were just as keen as anyone else to get their claims down in writing. Their deeds were carefully guarded under lock and key and kept secure from one generation to the next. Thus, Robert Amis of Alderton (1620) left to his eldest son, William, "my cheaste or coffer with all my deeds and writtinge and all my lands".

The freeholders owed the lord a fixed chief rent and a heriot upon the death of the head of the family. The 1563 surveyor noted that, "The freeholders pay their harriott their best beast, some their best weapon, some pay certain somes of money more or lesse as their deeds shall lymitt, for their reiliffe some more and some lesse". According to Gough, "Heriot custome and Heriot covenant are the only two sorts of Heriots that are paid. The Heriot custome in this manor is the best weapon, and soe it is in all other Lordship's marches. Heriot covenant is such a weapon as an arrow, or a sum of money or such a beast or good, as is mentioned in the covenant. And this the Lord is obliged to take, although it happen to bee worse than the best weapon."[64] However, the best weapon could "bee but a pickavill, a trouse bill, or a clubbe staff, for these are weapons offensive and defensive, and such have been taken for heriots". He had seen only one grant from the Lords Strange where money was paid in lieu, but thought that if the freeholders read their deeds carefully, then several of them might find that they were freed from all payments by the original grant.

The chief rents were usually nominal ones, and Hayward's tenement in Balderton was quite exceptional in paying £14 per annum to the Lord of Hardwick. The highest free rent paid in Myddle lordship was £1 3*s*. 10*d*. for lands in Myddle and Houlston. Rents like the 3*s*. per annum paid by both the Goughs and the Hanmers were more typical, and a few paid even less than that. The Webscott chief rent was a pair of gilt spurs or 1*d*., the knightly Leas of Lea Hall paid 1*d*. for their small freehold in Myddle, and the Downtons of Alderton Hall also paid 1*d.*, in lieu of a peppercorn, for the 45 acres beyond Bilmarsh.

As long as they paid their chief rents and heriots and services (all of which were fixed), the freeholders could do as they pleased with their land. Several of them let a part or even the whole of it; the Maynwarings usually lived on their Cheshire estates and let Sleap Hall to tenants, and the four tenements in Houlston were rarely occupied by their owners. These matters were of no concern to the manorial surveyors or to the rent-collectors, and, therefore, were not written down in their records. The only way a freeholder could lose his land was through the rare occurrence of escheats. In a fee tail estate, if a man died without any qualified heirs to succeed him, then the estate passed back to the lord. The 1563 surveyor reported that this should have happened with Webscott Farm, but the Thornes family managed to retain it: "Note, that it is said that one Humphrey's son died without issue, and so it should be escheated. Note, one Thornes, a younger brother, did claim it, and my lord's ancestors entered, had, and enjoyed all the lands in Newton (parcel of the premises), and all those lands that lay in other places were not siezed into my lord ancestors' hands, and the same Thornes entered, and the rest which is now dispersed into many men's hands. Saving that for the long claiming of possession it is said it is a clear case in law".[65] The lord does not seem to have pressed his claims in this matter, but the 1563 survey contains the following entry for Marton: "Thomas Elkes for excheite lands late of Hugh Elks attaynted for fellony". Richard Ash and William Heire were also recorded as holding part of Elks' land on 21-year leases, which had been granted in 1554 and 1555.[66]

Nineteen of the 42 peasants recorded in the manorial survey of 1563 held their land on 21-year leases. Most of these were dated 20 September 1553, and as seven leases for lives were also made out on the same day, it seems that a general reorganization of tenures was being carried out.[67] Perhaps this was the first time that any such leases for either years or lives had been granted in Myddle. The only lease that was dated earlier than 1553 and recorded in the 1563 survey was the one granted in 1552 to Morgan ap Probart of Castle Farm, the chief demesne farm in the lordship. Leases for both years and lives were only just becoming common in Shropshire by the middle of the sixteenth century (though one can hardly discern a general pattern amongst so much variation from one manor to another). However, in the country at large, there were few traces of servile villeinage left by the end of the sixteenth century, and most peasants had some sort of security of possession in the form of leases.

An intermediate stage between customary tenure and the granting of leases for lives was the entering of lives on the court rolls of the manor. This method gave greater security than if one held land merely at the will of the lord and probably ensured the succession. However, by the middle of the sixteenth century, the J.P.s and the officials of the civil parishes were beginning to take over many of the functions of the manorial courts, which, therefore, no longer found it necessary to meet every three weeks. Infrequent meetings meant that the old system of recording lives became unsatisfactory, and so it was abandoned in favour of leases drawn up by the growing body of attorneys. And not only was this to the legal advantage of the tenant, but to the financial advantage of the landlord, for feudal services and dues were largely replaced by money payments, with entry fines and annual rents.

The subsequent manorial surveys are sometimes confusing to the modern reader because the old terminology continued to be used. To say, as the 1563 survey or the 1656 rental do, that some farms and tenements were held "at will", even though they had 99-year leases for three lives, is a contradiction in terms and merely a legal fiction. Professor R. H. Hilton has written[68] (of an earlier period) that life-tenures were widespread upon customary land without the landlord dropping the use of the term 'customary'. Technically, if the land was held at the will of the lord, the tenants could be ejected at any time; but this was certainly not true of land that was described in the surveys as being held at will, but which in fact was held by perfectly sound leases for three lives. There must have been some historical reasons why seven holdings were described in this way in the 1656 rental, but in practice their tenures were no different from the other farms and tenements that were also held for lives.

Another legal practice was to regard any leases that were for less than 100 years as chattels, and so it was normal for leases for lives to be styled as "leases for 99 years, determinable upon three lives". Thus, the inventory of the personal estate of Richard Guest, yeoman (1694), included "One chattle lease of his tenement grannted by the Right Honourable John, Earle of Bridgewater", even though this was a lease for three lives, which in fact constituted a freehold. Three other inventories include the value of the remainder of leases that had been granted for 21 years during the previous century; John Raphes of Marton (1579), for "the lease of his howse and tenement for 16 years yet to come, £8"; Richard Woulf of Myddle (1580), for "the reversion of the lease of his house beinge 11 yeares, £8"; and Alan Chaloner, the Myddle blacksmith (1601), for "all leases, £10".[69]

The 1563 rental that is appended to the survey merely refers to the recent clearings in Myddlewood as "new rents", but they, too, appear to have been held by leases, either for a term of 21 years, or for three lives. The surveyor was worried about the destruction of the woods, and recommended that, "If they take any leases, to make a provisoe for the savegard of the woods". When Ellis Hanmer made the first recorded encroachment in the remaining part of Myddlewood in 1581, Henry, the fourth Earl of Derby, gave him a 21-year lease. In the same year, Roger Pickstock and Alan Chaloner were granted similar leases for new cottages there.

Most of the families who took out 21-year leases in the last year of Edward VI's reign changed them to leases for three lives during the Elizabethan period. This then remained the normal way of holding land throughout the seventeenth century and for at least half of the eighteenth. It was the usual practice for the tenant to be able to add new lives or to change them when he wanted, upon payment of an entry fine, and by this system the peasants of Myddle were given real security of possession. Many families continued in their holdings until well into the seventeenth century, and some survived throughout it. Putting one's own life in a lease ensured security of possession for oneself, and to enter the lives of one's wife and eldest son established the succession. However, given the short expectancy of life of that time, it could be a chancy business. In Myddle, judging by the evaluation of entry fines in 1637, leases for three lives were regarded as being slightly superior to 21-year leases.[70] However, untimely deaths could terminate a lease in a much shorter period than this and could cause financial hardship if a new entry fine had to be paid for a new lease. The Claytons of the Hollins Farm suffered in this way in the late seventeenth century. And as the mortality rate was so high amongst the young, it was of no advantage to put young lives in the lease. Looked at from the point of view of averages for the whole community, this system of leases for lives might have been a satisfactory one, but for individual families it could be very risky indeed.

On the other hand, some families were the lucky ones whose leases lasted for much longer than 21 years. Samuel Formston had not renewed his lease for 50 years at the time that Gough was writing in 1701, and he would have done even better if he had not renewed it in the first place. Gough's explanation of the descent of this lease helps to explain how the system worked.

> This Samuel Formeston . . . enlarged his tenement in Brandwood by the addition of two peices of land called the High Hursts, which are the lands of the Earle of Bridgewater. These two peices were formerly in lease to my great grandfather, who gave the lease of them to his second son, my uncle John Gough, and hee took a new lease of them, and put in the lives of his son Richard, his daughter Mary, and my life, (I suppose his daughter Elizabeth was not then borne), but when my uncle John Gough had purchased his farme in Besford, hee sold this lease to Richard Nightingale of Myddle, and not long after Richard Nightingale sold this lease to Samuell Formeston, who to make all sure renewed the lease and putt in three lives of his owne nameing, viz. his owne, his wife's, and his daughter, Margaret; butt hee might have spared that money, for I and my Cozen Mary are yet liveing, and his money was laid out about fifty yeares ago; and although two of the lives of his nameing are yet liveing, yet one of them is about twenty yeares older than either of us. Beesides, this Samuel Formeston about twenty years (for a sume of money,) exchanged his owne life for his sonnes, butt his son dyed beefore him and soe that money was lost.[71]

From this it is obvious that any lives could be entered in a lease, and any such lease could be sold without the lord's permission. Nor had the lord any power to prevent sub-letting. These customs varied from manor to manor, but in Myddle a leaseholder for lives had relatively few restrictions on the use of his land, and could be regarded as possessing a freehold estate. When Henry, the fourth Earl of Derby, began to offer leases for lives in the 1570s and 1580s, the great majority of tenants who were holding by 21-year leases gladly took the opportunity to improve their tenure.

Many more such leases (i.e. mainly renewals) were granted in 1598 by Henry's younger son, William, somewhat incorrectly, before he became the sixth earl. He

> did grant leases of many farmes and tenements in the Lordship of Myddle, in his mother's life time, which perhaps his mother connived at, because he was much indebted, upon account of paying the portions of his Brother's daughters. After the death of his mother, William Earle of Darby sold the Lordship of Myddle to the Lord Keeper Egerton . . . Soon after the purchase, the Lord Keeper Egerton required all those leases, that were granted by William Earle of Darby, to bee surrendered up, beecause made by one that had noe power soe to doe . . . Many were surrendered and new ones granted on easy termes; but Sir Andrew Corbett, who had a lease of Haremeare, Arthur Chambre, who had a lease of Broomehurst Farme, Richard Wolfe, who had a lease of a small tenement in Myddle, now in possession of Mr Dale; and one Edge, who had a lease of a small tenement beyonde Marton, called Edge's tenement, these refused to surrender and were never questioned in law, but held out theire termes, tho some of them proved very long.[72]

The manorial rentals confirm Gough by containing a list of 42 "tenants who surrender their estates for lives" on 18 January 1599/1600. The survey of 1602 shows that this list covered nearly every farmer in the lordship, for by that time only Hanmer's, Chaloner's, and Pickstock's cottages were held on 21-year leases. The sixteenth century had seen considerable changes in tenure. By the end of it, nearly all the lord's farms and tenements were held by leases for three lives, and the peasants were now legally secure in what were in effect freehold estates, though with the important qualification that the lord could refuse to renew a lease at the end of the lives that were named in it. During the second half of the eighteenth century it became more profitable for estate owners to engross farms, and this they did as leases fell in.

The other big difference between these holdings and the ancient freeholds was that whereas an estate held by fee simple or by fee tail had a fixed and unchangeable system of nominal payments to the lord for rents and heriots, an estate held by leases for lives had an entry fine that was payable each time the lease came to have a new name inserted, and that fine was often arbitrable at the will of the lord.

Gough quotes a case from nearby Wem in the mid-seventeenth century. The Earl of Arundel, "like a right Nobleman, caused notice to bee given to all his coppyholders, that if they pleased they might enfranchise theire estates and could make them fee simple. Many embraced this motion and made their land free, butt some inconsiderate selfe-conceited persons refused, and conceived that a coppyhold estate was better than a freehold, but they found the contrary, to the great damage of theire familyes, and the ruine of some". The next Lord of Wem, Mr Daniel Wicherley of Clive,

> had a long and chargeable suite with his Coppyholders of Wem Lordshipp; they alleaged that theire custome for payment of fines att every decease and att surrender, was to bee one year's rent, according to the cheife rent which was paid yearely to the Lord of the Manor. But Mr. Wicherley pretended that it was arbitrary, not exceeding three years' rent, according to the improved rent on the full value; after a tedious suite, it was decreed that the fine should be arbitrary, butt should not exceed one year's rent on the improved rent . . . And the Coppyholders repented too late, that they had not made theire land free.

The copyholders of Myddle also had to meet large increases in entry fines in the middle seventeenth century, though Gough is entirely silent about this.

In the year 1600, Sir Thomas Egerton, the Lord Keeper (later to be Lord Chancellor), completed his purchases of the north Shropshire estates of the Derbys. A fresh survey of his new possessions was made two years later. This simply recounted the existing state of the various tenures and did not involve any scheme of re-leasing. The Myddle survey does not include many details of the various freeholds, but it is complete enough to list 51 different items of property. A total of 46 rents (for 41 different people) amounted to £40 3*s*. 7*d*., and 30 entry fines totalled £231 1*s*. 8*d*. The Derbys had treated their tenants most leniently, for these payments had remained low despite the unprecedented inflation of the late sixteenth and early seventeenth centuries which had raised agricultural prices by as much as 6½ times.[73] A few rents were increased during the next few years, but a whole generation passed by before the Egertons (by that time styled the Earls of Bridgewater) made a determined effort to increase the entry fines. Mr E. Hopkins has shown what happened on the Ellesmere estates, of which Myddle formed a part.[74]

The dowager countess of Bridgewater died in 1636, and all the leases which she had granted in her lifetime for 21 years "if she so long live" now fell in.[75] There were 52 such leases on the Ellesmere estates, though very few in Myddle. However, the earl was desperately short of money,[76] and so he took the opportunity to review the position on his estates, and determined to force his tenants to accept new leases on the best possible terms to himself. Those whose leases had fallen in had no option in the matter, and while the others could have carried on under their existing leases, they would still have been faced with steep increases once the lease expired. In particular, those who had only one life left on their leases were in a precarious position, and most preferred to settle at the same time as the others and to take out new leases rather than create a powerful enemy and risk a bigger increase in payments when their leases eventually expired. There does not seem to have been any objection to the principle that fines were arbitrable at the will of the lord. Thus, Alan Chaloner, the blacksmith, surrendered up a lease for three lives that had been granted by Henry, Earl of Derby, because only his own life was left on it, and Andrew Hordley "willingly surrendered" his own lease because he was in the same position. Only William Brayne "refused to fine or to pay an improved rent".[77]

At the same time, the earl insisted upon a gratuity of a few pounds to his eldest son, Viscount Brockley, and ordered his commissioners to define carefully the heriots and the services that were due. The rents were normally left at their old level, though they were substantially increased for the year 1638 in cases where the initial offers of increased fines were not acceptable and no new offer had been made. The fines by themselves were sufficient to bring in a large revenue. Mr Hopkins has calculated that the total fines for the Ellesmere estates amounted to only £660 19*s*. 11*d*. in 1602, but in 1637 they rose over 15 times to £10,398 13*s*. 4*d*. There were few large fines at the beginning of the century; throughout the Ellesmere estates the majority were well under £10, and in Myddle, only Castle and Broomhurst farms were in double figures. By 1637, however, it was common to find fines of between £50 and £100, and there were 23 farms that paid over £100.[78]

The first sign in the manorial records of the determination of the new lords to increase the profits of their estates had come in a rental of 1617, in a list of "Late Improvements in the said manor". Eleven holdings are mentioned, and the increases in rents were quite considerable. Hunt's tenement paid only 9*s*. rent in 1597, but now, 20 years later, the occupiers paid £4. In 1597, George Watson was paying £3 15*s*. 8*d*. and £2 8*s*. 4*d*. for two tenements, but his successors, Thomas Parr and Thomas Guest, paid £14 and £6, respectively. Hodden's tenement had also had its rent increased from 9*s*. 6*d*. to £2, and a few cottages had become more expensive to rent. Most of these rents were holding their new level in the 1634 rental, but there are signs that the lord had demanded a little too much in some cases. Parr's tenement was now farmed by John Lloyd for £10 instead of £14, and the rent of the warren on Harmer Hill was "afterwards abated thereof 20*s*." However, three years later, two men who were competing for a new lease of the warren both bid beyond the old higher level in their attempts to get a new lease.

When the lord set about raising the entry fines in 1637, nearly everyone who was renting land in Myddle was well able to afford substantial increases. The price inflation had favoured the farmers, and the area was at least moderately prosperous. William Brayne was alone in refusing to pay more than he had done, though the commissioners made an exception of Francis Trevor, a poor labourer, and left his cottage and garden at the same easy terms. (The following year, they even added more land to it.) A few examples will show just how great were the increases. At the Hollins Farm, according to the 1602 survey, Richard Powell had paid a £6 13*s.* 4*d.* entry fine and £1 3*s.* 4*d.* annual rent, but in 1637, William Clayton, while paying the same rent, offered to increase his entry fine to £160, with a £5 gratuity to Lord Brockley. The tenement farmers were induced to offer similar increases. Roger Hunt was recorded in 1602 as paying a fine of £1 13*s.* 4*d.*, but in 1637, William Hunt agreed to offer a £35 fine and a £3 gratuity. William Gosling raised his old fine from £1 to £35, with a £3 gratuity, and Thomas Hodden was prepared to raise his father's old fine of £4 to £50, with a £2 gratuity. The cottagers made similar offers in proportion to the size of their holdings. Thomas Hanmer's fine was raised from 10*s.* to £6 13*s.* 4*d.*, and Abraham Hanmer offered £6 in place of his previous 15*s.* In the 11 cases where entry fines can be compared between 1602 and 1637 without any ambiguity, the total increase is from £30 15*s.* 0*d.* to £515 13*s.* 4*d.* This is a 17-fold increase and it confirms the general accuracy of Hopkins' total figures. In addition, these 11 tenants offered a total of £21 to Viscount Brockley, and their rents had been slightly increased from £4 16*s.* 6*d.* to £5 10*s.* 0*d.*

Even so, the lord was still not satisfied, and six months later, early in 1638, his commissioners entered upon a new round of bargaining. Less than half of the tenants of the Ellesmere estates had made offers that satisfied the lord,[79] and a determined effort was made to secure a general increase of over 10 per cent. Some of the tenants were able to afford this, and, indeed, the 1637 report had shown that there was some competition for leases. Alice Gittins had offered a £100 entry fine for Eagle Farm in place of the £4 13*s.* 4*d.* fine of 1602, but despite a plea on her behalf by the steward, this was refused, and Robert More (who had only recently lost a long wrangle over the legal possession with the Gittins family) was admitted tenant with a superior offer of a £130 fine and a £5 gratuity. William Tyler also tried to enter a tenement that had once belonged to his brother and put in a bid against the existing tenant, Bartholomew Pierce. This bid, coupled with some questioning of the legality of his lease, frightened Pierce and induced him "upon better consideracon", to increase his initial offer of £30 to £40, with a £2 gratuity. In the fresh bargainings of 1638, William Tyler "came not to offer", and Pierce was finally accepted with a fine of £48. Richard Hughes had also expressed an interest in regaining a cottage that had once belonged to his family, but he, too, was outbid by the current occupier, Abraham Hanmer.

The commissioners seemed willing to listen to reason and to favour the tenants who were already in possession. Jane Clowes continued with her lease of a Marton tenement after having this comment written in the 1637 report, as if in her favour; "[she] sayeth that her late husband did build all the house in his life tyme and all outhouses upon the premisses [at his] own costs and charges, and did buy the tymber in Ruyton parke for the doeing thereof". On the other hand, it was the commissioners' job to get as much for their employer as possible. William Brayne refused to offer, but his widow eventually agreed to pay an increased fine; and Thomas Davis, who pleaded in 1637 that he was too poor to increase his payments, had paid off a third of his new £18 8*s*. 0*d*. fine by 1642.

The fresh round of bargainings in 1638 resulted in an increase of £700 in the total offers for the Ellesmere estates.[80] But this time there was much more reluctance amongst the tenants to agree so readily to new terms. Some, like Edward Meriden of Myddle, offered no more, and "cannot be ymproved because of his lease", while Thomas Atcherley's suggestion for a new fine was refused "for abuse which he offered". Many claimed that they could not afford any more, but they were usually persuaded to part with a little extra. Only Thomas Hodden, who had agreed to a £50 fine in 1637, and who claimed he was unable to increase his offer in 1638, did not end up paying more. (He was finally allowed to pay only £45.) Most farmers were still able to afford the fines that were finally squeezed out of them. William Clayton refused to increase his offer of £160 for the Hollins, but finally settled on £189; Robert More was induced to raise his offer of £130 for the Eagle farm to £150, and William Gosling, who had tried to stick out at £35 for his tenement, finally agreed on £100 12*s*. 6*d*., and had paid it all off by 1641. Clayton and More completed their payments the following year. In fact, the evidence that has survived suggests that most farmers continued to pay off their new debts over a short period of years, and did so without great difficulty. Even Alan Chaloner, who was described as a pauper in 1638 and who was stated to be unable to raise his offer of a £5 fine, finished paying off his agreed fine of £38 10*s*. 0*d*. by 1646. In the nine cases where the fines can be traced through the period 1637–42, the total offers amounted to £725 in 1637, to £758 in 1638, and to £1,264 in 1642. The resistance to increasing the initial offers had obviously been overcome.

Pressure had been brought to bear on those who had refused to increase their offers by insisting upon sharp increases in rents for the year 1638. Again, there seems to have been no complaint about the legality of this.[81] For instance, William Clayton, who had been paying an annual rent of £1 3*s*. 4*d*. for the Hollins, was obliged to pay £18 rent in 1638 when he refused to increase his fine. He soon agreed to a new lease with a further increase of £29 in the entry fine, and his rent reverted to the old level. The rents were always lowered to their old level when a satisfactory settlement had been made with the entry fines. The same effective method produced quick results amongst the other tenants. William Brayne had refused to make any offer at all, but when the rent was increased from 2*s*. 6*d*. to £7 his widow soon accepted new terms. William Gosling was brought round to the commissioners' way of thinking when his rent was increased from 4*s*. 6*d*. to £4, and with this method the lord soon achieved what was to him a satisfactory settlement.

Mr Hopkins has concluded[82] that the calculation of the fines depended upon individual circumstances, but that the lord considered a reasonable offer for a copyhold lease for three lives to be ten times the annual value of the property. This would obviously depend upon such things as the ages of the lives put in the leases, and whether there was any competition for the tenancy. The entry fines paid by William Clayton, John Gough, William Hunt, and Robert More were each between eight and ten times the annual value, but Thomas Hodden's was less than six times because of his inability to pay, while old William Gosling put three new lives (not including his own) in his new lease and was required to pay an entry fine 20 times the annual value of £5 that had been agreed upon by the commissioners in 1638.

As well as fixing the new fines, the commissioners carefully defined the services and heriots that were due, and the covenants that were agreed upon when a lease was taken. As these follow a common form, details will be taken from John Lloyd's lease, for 99 years determinable upon three lives, that was signed and sealed on 9 May 1640. In granting the lease (of a tenement in Myddle) the lord reserved all rights to the timber and underwood on the estate, with all the stone and coal in the ground beneath. He kept to himself the liberty to fish, fowl, hawk, hunt, and to carry away all the game; and could "come upon the land with servants, carts, horses, to cut, fell, etc., dig, and carry away the trees, mines, quarries and coals".[83] On his part, John Lloyd agreed to the following terms:

1. to keep his property in repair with the timber that was allowed him.
2. to use the compost that was made on his premises only upon the land he was renting.
3. not to plough meadows without licence, unless he was willing to pay an extra 5*s*. an acre rent.
4. to plant and maintain five oak, ash, or elm trees every year in "the fittest places".
5. to find a man with pike and corslet for the navy when the king demanded such service of the lord.
6. if he fell into 20 days' arrears of rent, or refused to pay or do service when required, or if he was wilfully wasteful of his land, or granted or exchanged his land without licence, or failed to pay the residue of the entry fine or the heriot, or refused to grind his corn at the lord's mill, then the lord was to re-enter the possession.
7. the ancient rights of "fire boote, hedge boote, plowboote and carteboote" were to apply, but they could only be used upon the premises.

A few other provisos were added to this list to make everything perfectly clear, without adding to the substance of the above terms.

Lloyd's heriot was to be his best beast or good, and this was payable upon the death of every tenant, whether he was solely or jointly in possession. For his services, he agreed to provide two fat capons in November, three days' work with a team when required, a man for the wars, and to grind at the lord's mill (if he had one) in Myddle. These residual feudal services and the heriot were commutated into a money payment. Finally, he agreed to pay £10 rent at Ladyday, and again at Michaelmas. His entry fine was fixed at £135, "£88 13*s.* 4*d.* whereof is payed: the remainder being £46 6*s.* 8*d.* to be paid 2 Feb. next". The lives on the lease were those of his wife, Jane, Thomas, the son of Richard Lloyd, and Alice, the daughter of Robert Lloyd. His own life was not entered.

Seven different pieces of property can be examined in detail for the period 1602–41, to show just how great were the increases in the entry fines (see table 8 on p. 82).

The initial offers of 1637 produced a total of fines 21 times higher than before. There was hardly any response to the lord's call for further offers the following year, but these seven men finally agreed upon a further increase of about 35 per cent. The final settlement produced a 30-fold increase on the fines that were in existence at the beginning of the century. It was a huge burden for the tenants to bear.

These new fines were paid off during the next few years, even though it was the period of the Civil Wars. But although the tenants seemed to have managed to pay up on this occasion, the new level of fines was not maintained. No other complete survey of the manor was made (or exists) after the middle of the seventeenth century, and there was certainly no more large-scale reorganization. The evidence has to be taken from the collection of leases that survive for the late seventeenth and early eighteenth centuries. Only a few of these can be compared with absolute certainty with the ones for the period 1637–41. Where they can be compared, the new leases were granted at greatly reduced entry fines, though at a figure still much higher than that of 1602. For instance, Eagle Farm was let to Thomas Moore in 1678 at the same rent of £1 2*s.* 0*d.*, but with an entry fine of £40, compared with the £150 that Robert More (no relation) had paid in 1641, and compared with the £4 13*s.* 4*d.* entry fine that had been paid in 1602. Two generations later, in 1735, Mr Lloyd took the Eagle Farm at £1 2*s.* 0*d.* rent and an entry fine of £50.

Other cases show a similar drop after the sharp increases of 1637–41. John Hughes had paid a 15*s.* fine for his Myddlewood cottage in 1602, Abraham Hanmer offered £6 for it in 1637 and 1638, and finally agreed upon £12 13*s.* 4*d.*, but when Thomas Hanmer took out a new lease for lives in 1736 he paid an entry fine of only £8. In the same way, Richard Lloyd paid a £60 6*s.* 8*d.* fine for his lease in 1641, but when it came up for renewal in 1684, only £12 was paid for a new fine. In 1718, Mr Watkins paid £75 for a fine, whereas Richard Groome had paid £320 for the same property in 1641. All the fines after the Restoration were on a much more modest level than before, both locally and nationally, culminating in a

Table 8 Entry fines, 1602–41

1602 tenant	Place	Fine	Rent	1637 tenant	Fine	Gratuity	Rent	1638 Fine	1641 Fine	Rent
		£ s. d.	£ s. d.		£	£	£ s. d.	£	£ s. d.	£ s. d.
Rich. Powell	Hollins Farm	6 13 4	1 3 4	Wm. Clayton	160	5	1 3 4	160	189 0 0	1 3 4
Rich. Gittins	Eagle Farm	4 13 4	14 0	Robt. More	130	5	1 2 0	130	150 0 0	1 2 0
Wm. Gosling	Myddle tenement	1 0 0	4 6	Wm. Gosling	35	3	4 6 11	35	100 12 6	1 2 0
John Hodden	Myddle tenement	4 0 0	7 0	Thos. Hodden	50	2	11 6 11	50	45 0 0	3 12 0
Roger Hunt	Myddle tenement	1 13 4	9 0	Wm. Hunt	35	3	9 0 11	40	58 0 0	9 0
Rich. Chaloner	Myddle smithy	1 0 0	2 0	Alan Chaloner	5	–	2 0 11	5	38 10 0	6 11
John Hughes	Myddlewood Cottages	15 0	1 0	Abr. Hanmer	6	–	1 4 11	6	12 13 4	1 10 0
Total 7		19 15 0			421			426	593 15 10	

government enquiry into the problem in 1673. The lord had been desperately short of money in the late 1630s and had tried to solve his problem by collecting as many fines together as he could. But this meant that this source of income had dried up for many years to come, and even when the leases eventually came up for renewal, the tenants simply could not afford to keep paying at such a high level. Future lords had to lower their demands, both in Shropshire and elsewhere in the country.

At one point during the reign of Charles II, the Earl of Bridgewater refused to set any more leases for lives,[84] and insisted upon 21-year leases. However, the old system soon came into use again. If the tenants could not afford a new fine, then they had to take their land at an annual rack-rent, as with William Clayton of the Hollins. But whatever the form of holding, the tenants seem to have been secure in their possession and in the right of the eldest son to succeed. The tenants were a remarkably stable body throughout the late sixteenth and the seventeenth centuries; much more so than the freeholders. (Not only was there a considerable turnover of the freehold lands, but during the later years of the seventeenth century some large tenements were split up and sold off in small pieces, thus increasing the number of freeholders in the parish.[85]) There seems to have been no case where the lord turned a man off his land or refused him the chance to renew his lease, and, on the whole, the freeholders seem to have been as tolerant with their tenants. Gough mentions two tenants who were ejected from Sleap Hall by the Maynwarings for being bad farmers and in arrears with the rent, and also writes that Vicar Gittins, "beeing informed that this Powell had some phanaticall opinions, would not admit him to bee his tenant".[86] (The same vicar allowed a future tenant to farm the tenement rent-free because he was so poor.) The terms by which the freeholders let their land were equally varied, with leases for lives, for 21 years, for 3 years, or tenure by rack-rent.

The system of holding leases for lives began to disappear in Shropshire as farms were engrossed during the second half of the eighteenth century, so that in 1807, Plymley could write, "Leases for lives, or for a single life, were more common than they are now",[87] and leases for 7, 14, or 21 years had largely taken their place. An observer in 1841 wrote, "The farmers are generally tenants at will, with six months notice on either side; but there is that good understanding between landlord and tenant that little inconvenience arises from the absence of leases".[88] Despite the struggle over entry fines, that good understanding was also evident in Myddle during the sixteenth and seventeenth centuries.

CHAPTER THREE

The farmers

1 · *The large farms*

In the absence of a resident lord the leadership of the parish during the sixteenth and seventeenth centuries passed to those gentry families that lived upon large farms of over 200 acres. These included three farms (Castle, Eagle, and Broomhurst) that were rented from the lord, another three farms (two at Marton and the other at Sleap) that were freehold lands which paid a nominal chief rent to the lord, and two other farms (Balderton Hall and Shotton) that were freeholds held outside the manor.

The late sixteenth and early seventeenth centuries saw the engrossing of some of these large farms and the emergence of two or three families that stood out distinct from the rest. The largest farm was created when the Gittins family of Eagle Farm became the occupiers, through marriage, of the near-by Castle Farm and so dominated the village of Myddle with an estate of some 650 acres. The owners of Balderton Hall also began to lease the adjoining Broomhurst Farm and other property until they had about 500 acres, and the Atcherleys of Marton engrossed neighbouring lands to create a farm of about 470 acres, plus a great deal of property outside the parish. The other three freeholders were not on the same scale. The Hanmers of Marton had about 268 acres, the Watkinses of Shotton had some 230 acres, and the Maynwarings of Sleap Hall had 200 acres to which they added the 61 acres of Sleap Gorse. However, these Maynwarings were of a different category from the Myddle gentry. They were absentee-owners, of armigerous rank in Cheshire, and for most of the time they let Sleap Hall to tenants.

The individual fortunes of these parochial leaders varied greatly from one generation to another. At the end of the seventeenth century only the Atcherleys were still flourishing on their engrossed farm. The Gittins family had lost money and was forced to give up Eagle Farm, while Broomhurst was split off from Balderton and the Hall was sold six times within a hundred years. On the other hand, the Hanmers remained stable at Marton and the Watkins family which came to Shotton in 1629 had been there for three generations by 1701.

Only the absentee Maynwarings had held their farm since the subsidy roll recorded names in 1524. The Gittinses had come from a tanning business in Shrewsbury sometime between 1524 and 1528,[1] and the Hanmers had arrived as younger sons of a prominent Welsh family a generation or so later. The Atcherleys did not come for another four or five decades. They, too, had made their money as tanners and continued to flourish in that way. The Watkinses were the last to arrive; also as a younger branch of a distinguished Shropshire family. The people who lived at Balderton Hall had varied backgrounds. Some were younger sons of gentry, or prosperous tradesmen; others had risen in the world by fortune and hard work or through a lucky marriage. Their personalities were as different as it would be possible to find; the virtuous Rector of Hodnet, the debauched son who fell from grace through heavy drinking and associating with prostitutes, the hard-headed businessman, the ambitious speculator, the hard-working farmer; all these at one time or other lived at Balderton Hall. And in the parish at large there was a similar variety of characters, with the same groups of good and bad, industrious and idle, fortunate and unfortunate, whatever the social group or class to which they belonged.

But if human nature was the same whatever the economic status of the individual, one's role and standing within the parish still depended upon the amount of property that one possessed. This was especially true on a larger scale than that of the parish, and it is these big landowners who are found as under-sheriffs of the county, constables of the hundred, and justices of the peace. These men were resident minor gentry who rarely held land outside the parish, but they had an importance far transcending that of the parish. They were a class apart. But in talking of classes it is easy to generalize, and it is only when each family is examined in detail that one appreciates the rich variety of experience that was possible within each class.

a. Castle and Eagle farms

The demesne land of the lordship of Myddle was leased out as one farm to the Constable or Keeper of the Castle, but after Humphrey Kinaston had allowed the castle to go to complete ruin, a new farm-house was built just outside the moat and given the name of Castle Farm. As Gough says,[2] it may be reasonably supposed that this happened during the lifetime of the succeeding tenant, Mr Richard More, who was farming the land round about the middle of the sixteenth century, and who died in 1553.

After More, Mr Morgan ap Probart, or Bayly Morgan as he was known through his office of manorial bailiff, became tenant, and he is the first to feature in the manorial rentals. In 1563 he held, at the will of the lord, a house and demesne land at the annual rent of 6*s*. 8*d*., wheat leasows at £1 6*s*. 8*d*., land in Brandwood at 2*s*. 8*d*., and in Myddlewood at 2*s*. 6*d*.; in other words, a considerable farm with several pastures in the woods as well as the demesne. However, his holdings did not include the park that usually formed such a prominent part of Castle Farm, for this was held at will at £2 p.a. by a Richard Hocknell, who is otherwise unknown. By 1588 Hocknell had disappeared from Myddle and the park had been absorbed into the Castle Farm. Bayly Morgan was by now dead, but his widow, Anne Morgan, was paying a substantially increased rent of £6 6*s*. 8*d*.

The Welsh name suggests that, like the Hanmers, the ap Probarts had originated from just across the border, possibly as younger sons. But they had no child of their own to carry on their name, and so they adopted a young kinswoman named Alice, and brought her up as their own. When she was of age she had a large farm as her marriage portion and she would have been considered a most desirable match. The man she chose – or who was chosen for her – was Richard Gittins IV, the heir of a family that had risen by trade and which had acquired the highly-sought status of gentry as freeholders and as tenants of the lord's second largest farm (the Eagle Farm*) in Myddle.[3] The marriage was to mark the height of the fortunes of the Gittins family.

Richard Gittins I had been a wealthy tanner in Shrewsbury.[4] (One hears of so many people making money through tanning during the sixteenth century.) He

* It acquired the name of Eagle Farm after the Gittins family had moved to Castle Farm and let the property to Thomas Jux, who put up the sign of the Eagle and Child (the coat of arms of the Lords Strange who had held the manor for so many centuries) and sold ale there.

Eagle Farm included the present Red Lion, but it is unlikely that this is the original inn. The Red Lion is a very long, two-storeyed building, with a modern imitation of a timber truss in the gable-end facing the street. It has a timber-frame in the square-panelling tradition of the west Midlands (16 × 4 panels in length, and 6 × 2 [originally 4?] in breadth), and is now infilled with bricks of a very pleasant texture. The main problem with this building is that there is no apparent opening other than the present door, which is uncharacteristically at the extreme far end at the front. The rear side cannot now be seen as the village school has been built right up to it, but the placing of the chimney at this side confirms that this is the original rear. The absence of a central door at the front, and the whole general appearance of the building, suggests that it was probably originally used as a barn rather than a farmhouse. Not many miles away at Shawbury there is a barn attached to a modern farmhouse that is remarkably similar in appearance, with the same proportions and the same style of timbering and infilling. Inside the Red Lion there is nothing to suggest that it was once an old farmhouse; the modern rooms are clearly not the original divisions. As a hypothesis, then, it may be suggested that the Red Lion was originally the barn belonging to the Eagle Farm.

Gittins

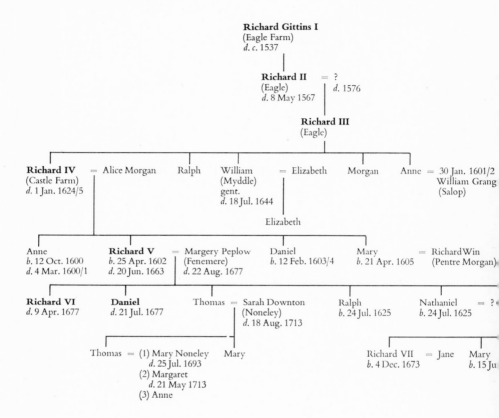

- **Richard Gittins I** (Eagle Farm) *d. c.* 1537
  - **Richard II** (Eagle) *d.* 8 May 1567 = ? *d.* 1576
    - **Richard III** (Eagle)
      - **Richard IV** (Castle Farm) *d.* 1 Jan. 1624/5 = Alice Morgan
        - Anne *b.* 12 Oct. 1600 *d.* 4 Mar. 1600/1
        - **Richard V** *b.* 25 Apr. 1602 *d.* 20 Jun. 1663 = Margery Peplow (Fenemere) *d.* 22 Aug. 1677
          - **Richard VI** *d.* 9 Apr. 1677
          - **Daniel** *d.* 21 Jul. 1677
          - Thomas = Sarah Downton (Noneley) *d.* 18 Aug. 1713
            - Thomas = (1) Mary Noneley *d.* 25 Jul. 1693 (2) Margaret *d.* 21 May 1713 (3) Anne
            - Mary
          - Ralph *b.* 24 Jul. 1625
          - Nathaniel *b.* 24 Jul. 1625 = ?
            - Richard VII *b.* 4 Dec. 1673 = Jane
            - Mary *b.* 15 Ju
        - Daniel *b.* 12 Feb. 1603/4
        - Mary *b.* 21 Apr. 1605 = Richard Win (Pentre Morgan)
      - Ralph
      - William (Myddle) gent. *d.* 18 Jul. 1644 = Elizabeth
        - Elizabeth
      - Morgan
      - Anne = 30 Jan. 1601/2 William Grang (Salop)

Note Names in bold are of those through whom the family property descended, during the period. Dates given are those of baptism (*b.*) and burial (*d.*): the symbol = indicates marriage.

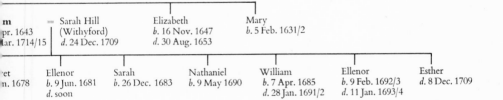

m
pr. 1643
Iar. 1714/15

= Sarah Hill
(Withyford)
d. 24 Dec. 1709

Elizabeth
b. 16 Nov. 1647
d. 30 Aug. 1653

Mary
b. 5 Feb. 1631/2

·et
n. 1678

Ellenor
b. 9 Jun. 1681
d. soon

Sarah
b. 26 Dec. 1683

Nathaniel
b. 9 May 1690

William
b. 7 Apr. 1685
d. 28 Jan. 1691/2

Ellenor
b. 9 Feb. 1692/3
d. 11 Jan. 1693/4

Esther
d. 8 Dec. 1709

		acres	roods	perches
A	The House and Homested	7	1	30
B	The Eddy Croft	8	0	39
C	The Rough Eddy Crofte	11	3	9
D	The Lower Bromy Lessow	6	2	36
E	The Way Lessow	8	1	4
F	The Moore	15	0	18
G	The Higher house ground	33	2	6
H	The Pease Lessowe	15	2	29
I	The Upper Parke	37	3	20
K	The Linch Lane	15	2	29
L	The Parke and Copse	94	0	21
M	The Hill Lessow	15	0	15
N	The Lessedge Moore	36	0	23
O	The Wheat Hill Close	12	0	0
P	A Furlong in Hill field	16	1	22
Q	A Furlong in Woodfeild	15	3	34
R	A dole of Meadow in Wood feild	1	3	6
S	ditto	1	0	0
	Land not plotted:			
	Three Butts neare Medlicotts-oake	0	3	32
	A furlong in Gallowtree Feild shooting south upon Gallowtree hill	4	0	20
	A furlong att the east end of the feild	3	0	4
		361	0	2

had bought a freehold tenement in Newton from the ancient owners, the Banasters of Hadnall, and a half tenement from them in Myddle, known as the house at the higher well. These he let to tenants. Then, he himself came to live as tenant of Eagle Farm and of eight acres of the newly-enclosed Myddlewood. This must have happened by 1528 because he was among the jurors of the manor court in that year. He was also recorded in 1537, but his widow was occupying the property in 1538. She was succeeded by her son and grandson, who were both called Richard. Richard III had been made a freeman of the Mercers' Company in 1565,[5] but he settled at Eagle Farm upon his father's death. He was also one of the five Newton farmers who rented the Brown Heath at Harmer; he renewed the lease of Eagle

Farm for three lives, and "builded the house anew and bought the Tymber at a woode sale in Myddlewood".

The two younger sons of Richard III made their living in Shrewsbury, Ralph as the High Schoolmaster, and William as a tanner. This connection with trade and the aspirations to learning remained strong with the family. There also appears to have been another son called Morgan, and a daughter named Anne who married a Shrewsbury mercer. William in fact seems to have ended his days as the gentleman tenant of Castle Farm (he died in 1644), but it was the senior branch of the family, represented in the person of Richard Gittins IV, that was generally in residence in the village. It was this "mild, peaceable, [and] charitable"[6] Richard who married Alice Morgan and inherited Castle Farm, and who later added to his freehold estate by purchasing lands in Houlston.

It is worthwhile at this point – the highest in the rise of the Gittinses – to consider just how much land they were farming in the early years of the seventeenth century. This, one cannot really do for their freeholds, but one can get a very good idea of the size of the joint Castle and Eagle farms. In 1650, no doubt as part of the programme to increase entry fines and raise the profits on the manorial estates, a survey and map was made of the demesne. This included 36 acres in the Bilmarsh–Houlston area, and 325 acres which can be clearly identified with Castle Farm in Myddle itself. The fields stretch east of the village street and south from the castle and can be readily matched with the 318½ acres of Castle Farm recorded in the Tithe Award and map of 1838, except that the huge fields of 1650 had often been cut up into smaller units by the nineteenth century. In 1650 the fields were as shown opposite (see plate 5).

Apart from the blocks of strips at the other side of the village, this was a most compact farm, suitable for a grazier, and one, moreover, that would have important rights on the near-by common pastures. Unfortunately, no inventory survives for any Gittins who lived in Myddle. The only one taken for Castle Farm is that of Richard More (1553), a previous gentleman-tenant,[7] whose speciality was rearing animals – a speciality that later tenants were likely to emulate, given good pasture ground, a demand for meat in Shrewsbury market, and a tanning business there ready to take the hides as well.

The 1650 map also enables one to pinpoint Eagle Farm as including the present Red Lion and the adjoining Alford Farm. In 1838 this farm covered just over 300 acres in the north-west of the village. Eagle Farm was always considered a sizeable one, and as no neighbouring farm had been swallowed up in the meantime, it is likely that the farm of 1838 was more or less the same compact farm it always had been. So, upon the death of his father, Richard Gittins IV had something like 625 acres upon secure lease at a low rent, with common rights of pasture and another eight acres in Myddlewood, with more freehold property in Myddle, Newton, and Houlston, rented out to sub-tenants, and a lease of part of the moss land called

Brown Heath. The extent of his financial interests in Shrewsbury is unknown, but it is hard to imagine that he did not have a finger in that pie as well. Here was obviously one of the richest men, if not the richest, in Myddle. Only the Atcherleys, tanners too, could compete.

Richard Gittins IV died in the very last days of 1624, "soe willing to forgive injuryes that he passed by many without seeming to take notice of them".[8] Unfortunately, there were men in Myddle less scrupulous than he, ready to take advantage of his mild nature. A long note by the steward of the manor tells all about the trouble he had over Eagle Farm.[9] Shortly after rebuilding this house and moving to Castle Farm he let Eagle Farm to Thomas Jux, who was descended from the Juxes of Newton and born in a cottage at the side of Houlston Lane. This Thomas, and his Welsh wife, Lowry, took the tenement at £6 a year rack-rent and kept it as an inn. But Jux, possibly overburdened with his nine children, could not make ends meet and soon ran up a debt of £28 to Gittins. Having made a bill of sale to Gittins of all his estate, Jux was given two years' grace, whereupon he "falsly sels his title to Robert Moore combininge together to defraud Gittins and puts Moore in the possession". This Robert Moore was the brother of the rector and farmer of the tithes, and was living in the Parsonage House at the time. His holy surroundings do not seem to have done much for him, for the steward goes on to say that, "Gittins heareing that Juxe was gone away by Moore's procurement, sends 2 servants no body being in the house to keepe the possession. Juxe and Moore violently brake a walle with force and drew out and hurt Gittins' servants, and forceably kept the possession untill the next session wheare they weare both Indicted and convicted by a jury and a writ of restitution was graunted in court that the possession should be redelivered to Gittins". At this point (1624) Gittins died, leaving his widow, Alice, and his son, Richard V, now 22 years old, to carry on the battle. His younger son, Daniel, had been apprenticed to a Shrewsbury draper in 1621[10] and had gone to be a merchant tailor in London, and his daughter, Mary, was soon to marry a Shropshire gentleman. Their only other child had died when she was five months old.

This fifth Richard lived to be 61 and "was of good account in his time but hee was too sociable and kinde hearted: and by strikeing hands in suretyship, hee much dampnifyed himselfe and his family. Hee did not at all derogate from the charitable, meeke and comendable moralls of his father".[11] He was soon to run into trouble in order to hang on to Eagle Farm. Moore took the case further in the courts, indeed as far as Chancery, but finally Gittins recovered possession, costs, and damages. It could not, therefore, have been this case that hit the family pockets. The steward obviously thought highly of him, asking the lord to confirm his possession, and saying that Gittins was "willing to give his lordship such fine and rent as his honnor shall thinke convenient . . . [and] hath payd all dutys to Church, king, and lord and very many lewnes [i.e. church-rates] towards the building of a

4. Aerial view of Myddle. The present Castle Farm (1) separates the church (2) from the moated site of the castle (3) and the adjacent park (4). Tyler's tenement (5) is the sole seventeenth-century farmhouse or cottage to remain standing. Top right is Wood Field (6), one of the former open fields. To the west of the church is Myddlewood (7), whose straight road and regular-shaped fields are the product of the 1813 Enclosure Award.

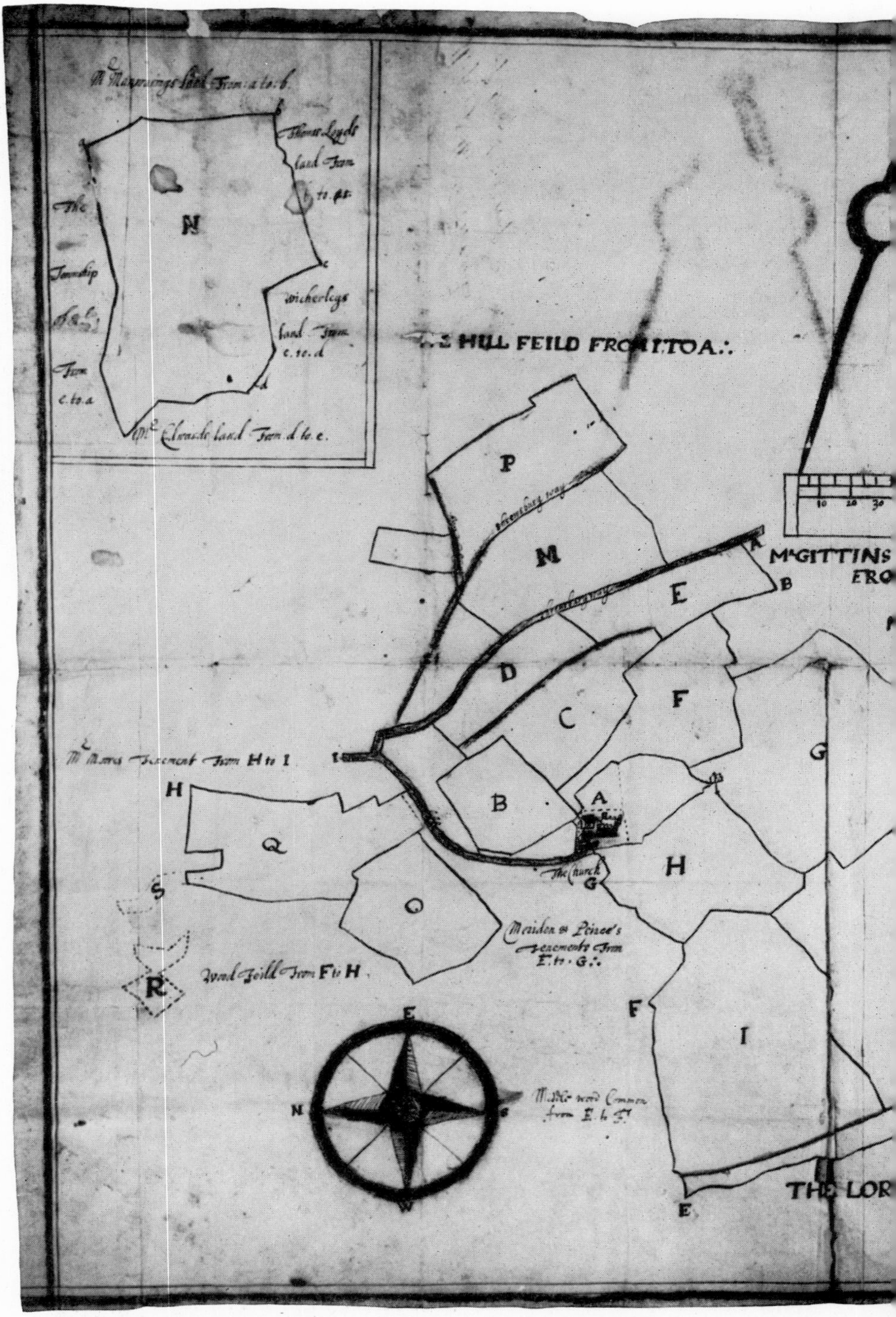

5. Demesne map, 1650. William Fowler's map of the demesne, showing the 325 acres belonging to Castle Farm, and 36 acres in the Bilmarsh–Houlston area. Many of the large fields have since been divided into smaller units. The map is an important source for identifying farms, fields, and other features. Medleycoate's oak was left standing after the wood on Holloway Hills had been felled in the early sixteenth century, but "at last some of the poore neighbours cut it downe, and converted it to fewell".

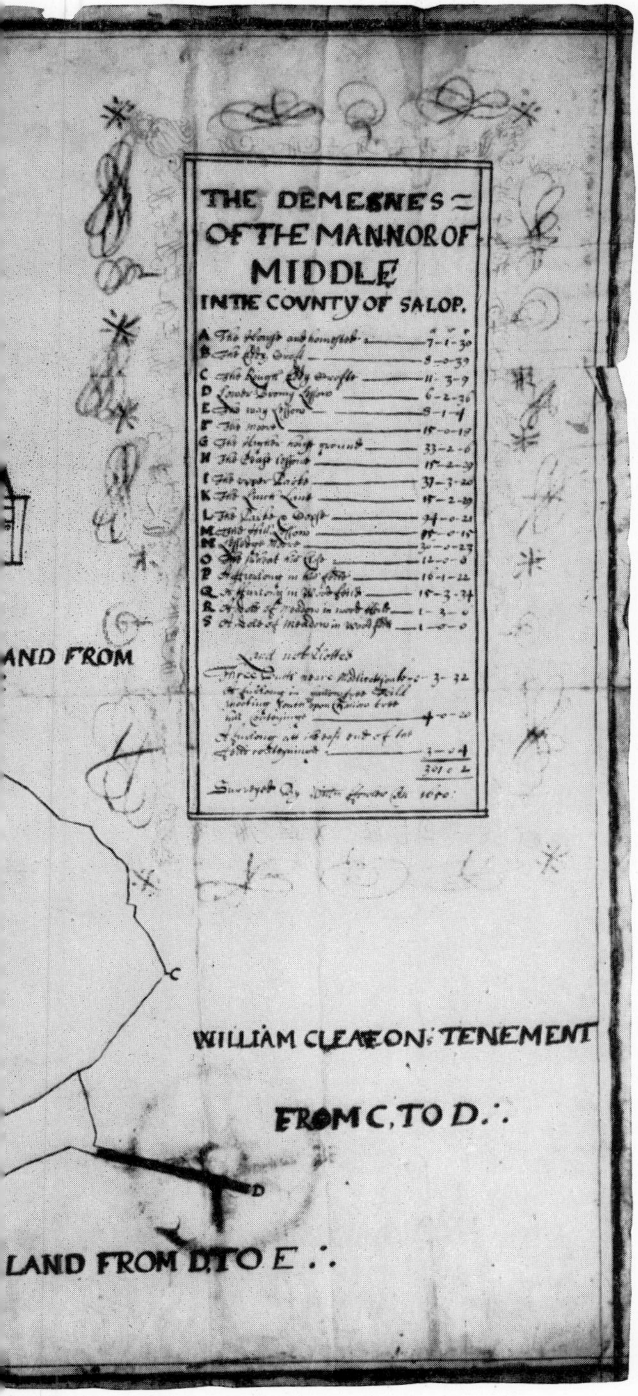

THE DEMESNES
OF THE MANNOR OF
MIDDLE
IN THE COVNTY OF SALOP.

		a. r. p.
A	The House and homestead	7-1-30
B	The litle crofte	5-0-39
C	The longe Dry crofte	11-3-9
D	Lower Dovey leasow	6-2-36
E	The way leasow	5-1-4
F	The marle	15-0-19
G	The clough way ground	33-2-6
H	The clough leasow	15-2-39
I	The vpper heath	37-3-20
K	The lower heath	15-2-39
L	The litle co Dryt	34-0-21
M	The hill leasow	11-0-15
N	The litle leasow	30-0-27
O	The litel old crofte	12-0-0
P	A meadowe in the felde	10-1-22
Q	A gardine in Wood felde	15-3-34
R	A croft of medowe in wood felde	1-2-0
S	A litle of meadow in wood felde	1-0-0

and not letten

Three litle acres middlechpahays 3-32
A litleing in parsonfree feild
making from vpon litlees tree
all contayninge 4-0-0
A gardine at litlees out of lot
litle containing 2-0-4
 ─────
 201-0-2

Surveyed By Witter afranter Jn 1650.

6. Myddle Castle. Myddle was a Marcher Lordship only a few miles from the Welsh border, so in 1308 the lord of Myddle was granted a royal licence to build a castle. Formerly the Court House, the head farm of the demesne, and the residence of the constable or castle-keeper, the building was allowed to go to ruin during the early sixteenth century. All that now remains on this moated site is the red sandstone turret staircase, looking remarkably like an eighteenth-century folly.

Steeple to Myddle Church . . . and have repayred the house and buildings at their great cost and charges".

Yet Gittins was soon to lose the Eagle Farm. There is only Gough's statement about his standing risky sureties to give any hint as to what must have happened. In 1634 widow Alice Gittins was paying her usual £6 6*s*. 8*d*. rent for Castle Farm. She also paid 14*s*. 0*d*. for Eagle Farm, with 8*s*. 0*d*. for 16 acres of woodland, 4*d*. for a house that Richard Clarke, the labourer, lived in on Harmer Hill, 3*s*. 0*d*. chief rent for the house at the higher well in Myddle, 11*s*. 6*d*. chief rent for some freehold land in Houlston, and a further 9*s*. 4*d*. rent for just over 18 acres of moorland in Houlston. By 1650 Richard Gittins V was retaining his freehold, but had relinquished all the rest except Castle Farm. Trouble seems to have been brewing in 1638, the year after the steward had spoken up for the family, for when the attempt was made to increase the entry fines, "Alice Gittins for the Egle and Child was told that her former undervaluation and offer were so much disliked that your honor purposed to take it into your lordship's hands at Our Lady day next, and she had warning to leave it at the tyme, yet I heare shee hath sowed parte of the ground with otes". Underneath was the ominous note, "Robt. More desireth to take the same at the yerely rent of £15". Moore had failed to win possession forcibly or through the courts, but now he was to enter unmolested as the Gittins family could not afford the new terms.

Moore did not survive long. After an active spell raising forces for the king in the Civil Wars, he was captured and died a prisoner, at Nantwich. He does not seem to have been liked in the parish, and his widow and children left the district for Yorkshire and sold the reversion of the lease to a John Moor (no relation) who had come to Shrewsbury and married an alderman's sister. They kept the Eagle Farm as an inn, under the new name of the Earl of Bridgewater's Arms, and, according to Gough, "the inne was in great repute in theire time".[12] Their son, Thomas, was still there at the close of the century, with a lease granted in 1678 for three lives,[13] at an annual rent of £1 2*s*. 0*d*., and an entry fine of £40.

At Castle Farm, Richard Gittins V had married Margery, the daughter of Francis Peplow, a wealthy farmer just across the parish boundary in Fenemere. She bore him six boys and two girls before his death in 1663. The eldest was Richard VI, "a good country-scoller, [who] had a strong and allmost miraculouse memory. Hee was a very religiouse person butt he was too talkative".[14] A bachelor, he died suddenly, in 1677, after a meeting of the Grand Jury for the County, and his brother, Daniel, succeeded him at Castle Farm. He too was a bachelor and he died less than four months after his brother. The property passed to the third son, Thomas, the Vicar of Loppington, but as he lived in his own parish, the youngest son, William, came to be the gentleman tenant of Castle Farm. Between the births of Thomas and William there had also been twins, but Ralph had died, and Nathaniel was provided for as Vicar of Ellesmere. Of the daughters, Elizabeth died young, and Mary "was a person of a comely countenance but somewhat crooked of Boddy. She was a modest and religiouse woman and dyed unmarryed".[15]

The son of Thomas Gittins, the vicar, was also called Thomas, and after his marriage he lived at the family freehold tenement, the house at the higher well. He does not seem to have been as placid as some of his ancestors, for the Acta books of the Bishop's Visitation Courts record a charge against him in 1699 of fighting Mr John Reynolds in Myddle churchyard.[16] His defence was "that he being run into his belly with a sword by the said John Reynolds" he thought that he had a just cause for fighting. At Castle Farm, William had taken as wife a daughter of a neighbouring farmer. He died at the age of 72 in 1715, with his wife and four of his nine children dying before him. But there were two strong branches of the Gittins family ready to continue farming the family's lands in the eighteenth century. Those wealthy Shrewsbury tanners had made a sound investment when they chose to put their money down on land in Myddle.

b. Balderton Hall and Broomhurst Farm

For many years in the sixteenth and early seventeenth centuries the owners of Balderton Hall were also the lord's tenants at the adjoining Broomhurst Farm. Before this engrossing the Hall had very little to do with the lordship of Myddle, for both it and the other small tenements of Balderton had been granted out of the manor to Haughmond Abbey during the last quarter of the twelfth century. The monks had sold their possessions sometime before the dissolution, but the new owners paid their heriots and a yearly chief rent to the Lord of the Manor of Hardwick and came under the jurisdiction not of the Lord of Myddle but of the Court Leet of the hundred of Pimhill. "Mr. Goore's Account of Balderton", which was drawn up in 1751 when the tenements were engrossed into the Hall estate, makes this explicit. "This Estate", he wrote, "ows neither suit or service to any lord but at the Court for Pimhill Hundred".[17] Balderton Hall, therefore, does not appear in the manorial records of the lordship of Myddle. However, in the late sixteenth century, its owners, the Nicholas family, are recorded paying chief rents – 4*s.* 6*d.* in 1563, then 12*s.* 0*d.* in 1588 and 1597 – for additional freehold land in Myddle and Houlston townships, and both the Nicholases and their successors, the Chambres, rented Broomhurst Farm for £3 a year.

A large part of this Broomhurst Farm had originally been a series of glacial pools, known as Myddle pools, which were connected to Harmer by the Pinchbrook stream that flows slowly through the lower end of Myddle village, then along the old boundary between the two open fields, turning north-east through the pools and the gorse, and so on out of the parish at Sleap. The survey of 1602 still referred to "all that farme called Bromehurst and Middle pooles". It was low-lying, heavy land, almost entirely used as meadow and pasture in the seventeenth century, but by 1838 the original large fields had been divided into smaller parcels, the drainage had been considerably improved, and a variety of crops were being grown alongside the permanent pastures. The older field names survive in a special survey of the farm made in 1662.[18] The names and the sizes speak for themselves.

	acres	roods	perches
1. The Broomehurst Feild	43	3	21
2. Rush Poole Meadow	26	3	4
3. The Great Poole Pasture	29	2	35
4. The Upper Little Poole Meadow	9	0	30
5. The Lower Little Poole Meadow	5	2	8
6. The Gorsty Feild	39	2	33
7. The Farthings	28	0	1
8. Taylors Feild	22	2	36
9. The first Colledge Leasow	7	0	29
10. The second Colledge Leasow	7	0	37
	200	1	34

Balderton Hall Farm was somewhat larger than this. The 1838 Tithe Award shows that there were some 275¼ acres in Balderton, and even allowing for the engrossing of the smaller tenements in 1751, it appears that about 200 acres originally belonged to the Hall. The 1563 survey also shows that Roger Nicholas held the 61 acres of Sleap Gorse from the lord, and in addition to all this there was an unspecified amount of freehold. The Nicholas family probably held something like 500 acres or more, perhaps almost 600 acres by the later years of the sixteenth century. Quite clearly, they ranked with the Gittinses as the largest landowners in the parish.

Roger Nicholas was the son of John Nicholas, who appears in the manorial rolls of 1528–38. Roger had inherited the property by 1541 and is recorded in the 1563 survey as Roger Eaton, alias Nicholas. (There are Eatons in Flintshire and Cheshire, and Eyton near by in Shropshire.) The Nicholases were not at Balderton in 1524, when Roger Maynwaring of Sleap and a Roger Gynkys and William Neuton headed the subsidy roll. Either Gynkys or Neuton was probably at Balderton, with the other at Webscott, and as there were Genckys recorded in the manorial rolls as being contemporaries of John Nicholas in 1528 and 1530, it seems likely that Nicholas had in fact succeeded Neuton some time between 1524 and 1528. The 1563 surveyor also noted that "The farthings and Taylors feild [numbers 7 and 8 in the 1662 survey, above] and 2 crofts at Middle towne and occupied by Sir Robert [. . . ?] which is a goodley livinge for any yeoman, ought to bee noe parte of that farme, but is concaeled lands from my lord and out of any rental, by that the sayd Roger [Nicholas] hath now obteined itt wherein my lord was defrauded". These fields were part of Broomhurst, and the fact that Nicholas could get away without paying rent on 50 acres, or one-quarter of this farm, is indicative of the weak manorial supervision of that time.

Roger Nicholas and his wife, Alice, had two sons and six daughters, two of whom died when they were young. One of his daughters was already married when he drew up his will in 1572. He left his other four daughters £40 apiece, with an extra £6 13*s*. 4*d*. for Ann. The rest he left to his widow and his 21-year-old son, William. The Gittins family had not yet added Castle Farm to their possessions, the Atcherleys were still at Stanwardine outside the parish, and so when Roger Nicholas died he was probably the richest man in the parish. The personal estate recorded in his inventory was valued at £119 3*s*. 0*d*., of which £79 3*s*. 4*d*. was accounted for by his farm stock. Like most farmers in Myddle, most of his capital was invested in his animals (10 horses, 6 oxen, 6 cows and a bull, 10 young beasts, 11 calves, 40 sheep, 12 swine, 10 geese, and some poultry), but he also had £10 worth of hard corn, £4 worth of barley, and some oats, peas and malt.

William Nicholas never married, and "by his greate charges in building, hee contracted much debt. Yet beeing addicted to projects, hee beecame a timber man, and purchased all the timber in Kenwick's parke, thinkeing to enrich himself by it, but it proved his ruine".[19] He was forced to sell Balderton Hall and also the lease of Broomhurst Farm to Mr Arthur Chambre of Petton. He left the district and was never heard of again, but many years later an old man in beggar's clothes was found dead by the barn and the men and women of Myddle liked to believe that it was Nicholas who had returned to die.

The full value of Gough's *History* is seen in his account of the changing ownership of Balderton Hall. After Roger Nicholas there is little that one can add to Gough's story, and without his book one would never have known that there were such a succession of owners, nor their reasons for having to leave. Gough's account can be found on pages 139–44 of his book, a synopsis of which is relevant here.

Arthur Chambre had two sons and two daughters. Judith, the youngest, probably lived at the Hall for a time, for she and her husband, Arthur Kinaston, a Shrewsbury wool merchant, baptized their daughter from Balderton in November 1604. But the property was eventually given to Arthur's youngest son, Michael, "a person of noe accompt", who was "whoally addicted to idlenesse" and debauchery. He failed to pay his father's legacies to his sisters, was sued by his brothers-in-law, and had a spell in prison. Balderton Hall had to go, though he continued to lease it for some time and he also retained the lease of Broomhurst Farm.

During the first half of the seventeenth century the Hall frequently changed hands. The next two owners, Mr John Nocke and a Mr Webbe, were wealthy Shrewsbury drapers, but each lost a great deal of money when their London connections went bankrupt. Webbe sold the estate to Mr Zankey, the Rector of Hodnet, who was "much commended for his virtue and piety", but he died soon afterwards. His widow lived many years in Balderton Hall, but one of her sons died and the other went to Ireland, so the estate was sold again, to Matthew Lath. This man had humble origins. He had been "a servant in husbandry", then he was a tenant farmer, and somehow he became wealthy enough to buy the Hall. His only child, "being a great fortune had many suitors", finally choosing Thomas Hall of Isombridge, who turned out to be a second Michael Chambre. He lived at Balderton Hall with his father-in-law, after the Restoration, "and dureing his life hee was a reasonable good husband, but after his decease hee let loose the reins to many disorderly courses, as cocking, raseing, drinking, and lewdnesse", and had a bastard child conceived and born in his own house. He finally ruined himself and was forced to sell to Robert Hayward of Balderton. He "left £400 of the price in the purchaser's hands, to the intent that the interest of it might maintaine him and his wife dureing theire lives, out of which interest shee whose portion was accompted worth £1,500 had onely £8, but shee is dead, and willingly left this troublesome world".

Robert Hayward died in 1705 and left the Hall to his nephew, another Shrewsbury draper. Meanwhile, Broomhurst Farm continued with the Chambres, though, after Michael, the family appears to have been non-resident in the parish. Broomhurst Farm and Balderton Hall were to continue under separate ownership during the eighteenth century.

c. The Atcherleys of Marton Hall

The Atcherleys were the last of the large freeholders to come into the parish of Myddle, but they were the most successful of all. By the end of the seventeenth century not only were they the dominant family at Marton, but the leading family in the entire parish. Nor did they fail after that, for they continued to prosper during the eighteenth and nineteenth centuries, as their memorials inside the parish church testify.

Like the Gittins family, they made their money out of tanning. Richard, the first of the Marton Atcherleys, was a younger brother of "the ancient and substantial family" of the Atcherleys of Stanwardine-in-the-fields, only a mile or so to the west of Marton.[20] One of this family, Sir Roger Atcherley, became Lord Mayor of London about the time the junior branch moved to Marton.[21] According to Gough, Richard Atcherley purchased lands in Marton from a David Owen and Richard Twyford, whom he supposed to have married co-heiresses, as there was only one house to these lands. Owen is never mentioned in the manorial records, and neither family is amongst those who paid the subsidies of 1524 and 1544. However, Robert Twyford was paying a chief rent of 12*d.* for his freehold in Marton in the 1563 survey, and Mr Richard Twyford was paying the same sum in 1588 and 1597, with another 4*s.* 4*d.* rent for clearings in Myddlewood. A Chancery case clears up the matter.[22] On 8 February 1612, Roger Twyford of the Inner

Atcherley

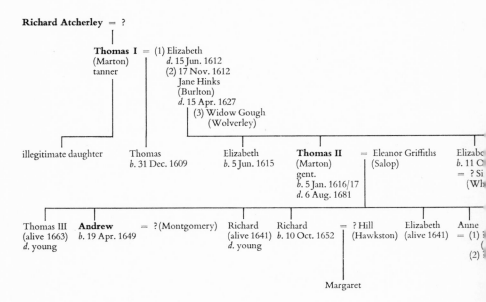

Richard Atcherley = ?

- **Thomas I** (Marton) tanner = (1) Elizabeth *d.* 15 Jun. 1612; (2) 17 Nov. 1612 Jane Hinks (Burlton) *d.* 15 Apr. 1627; (3) Widow Gough (Wolverley)
  - illegitimate daughter
  - Thomas *b.* 31 Dec. 1609
  - Elizabeth *b.* 5 Jun. 1615
  - **Thomas II** (Marton) gent. *b.* 5 Jan. 1616/17 *d.* 6 Aug. 1681 = Eleanor Griffiths (Salop)
    - Thomas III (alive 1663) *d.* young
    - **Andrew** *b.* 19 Apr. 1649 = ? (Montgomery)
    - Richard (alive 1641) *d.* young
    - Richard *b.* 10 Oct. 1652 = ? Hill (Hawkston)
      - Margaret
    - Elizabeth (alive 1641)
    - Anne = (1) ; (2)
  - Elizabe *b.* 11 C = ? Si (Wh

. 1622/3 = Roger Griffiths (Salop)

Richard = (at Wolverley)
b. 21 Aug. 1625
d. 29 Dec. 1682

ov. 1650 = (1) Nathaniel Kinaston (Montgomery)
(2) Mr Lloyd (Montgomery)

Jane
= 10 Jan. 1681/2
Mr Thomas Cole
(Salop)

Mary
= 24 Jul. 1683
Charles Chambre
(Burlton)

Sarah
d. 4 Sep. 1664

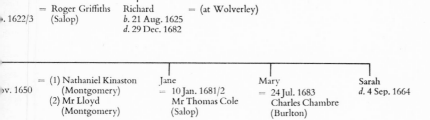

Temple, London, gent., Richard Twyford of Hawton, Shropshire, gent., and Richard Atcherley, late of Stanwardine-in-the-fields, gent. were bound unto John Windell, citizen and fishmonger of London, in the sum of £700, by which Windell bought from them a messuage or tenement in Marton occupied by William Baker and David Owen. This property changed hands several times until Richard Atcherley's son, Thomas, finally bought it in 1622, when he "doth lett and sett some parte thereof, and some parte thereof he keepeth". The Atcherleys were recorded in Marton in the survey of 1602, but it was not until 1622 that they finally bought the property that had once belonged to the Twyfords.

Thomas Atcherley I was described in the Chancery case of 1623 as a tanner. He built the picturesque house that stands right at the edge of the parish boundary, on the banks of the Old Mill Brook, and which still keeps the name of 'Tan House'. He also rented what is now Marton Hall from Lloyd Pierce, esquire, and allowed the buildings on his freehold land to decay. After the deaths of his wife, Elizabeth, and their son, Thomas, he married Jane Hinks of near-by Burlton, who bore him two sons and three daughters. He also had an illegitimate son by Edge's daughter in Marton. One of his girls died while she was still an infant, but Elizabeth grew up to marry a Whitchurch mercer, and Mary to marry a Shrewsbury alderman. Such matches are sure indications that the family was already prosperous. The younger son, Richard (1625–82) married at Wolverley and died a gentleman there. He had gone to live at Wolverley with his father who had made his third marriage to a wealthy widow there. He, too, died a gentleman.

The elder son, Thomas Atcherley II (1617–81), substantially increased the family fortunes. He purchased the freehold of the lands the family had been renting from Lloyd Pierce, and built a new house upon them. The old one was used as a malt house. Then Onslow's tenement, which lay just across the road, came on the market, and its 187½ acres[23] or so were added to Thomas's estates. By now he had something like 437 acres of freehold land in Marton as well as his tanning business. In addition, he rented some 32 acres in Myddlewood. Gough also says that he purchased the tithes of near-by Weston Lullingfields and several lands there which he proceeded to build upon, and then he purchased freehold lands and several leases in Montgomeryshire. He was also "a great dealer in timber, and bought Myddle park, and a wood in Petton, called Rowe lands". Here was an adventurous and wealthy man who was prepared to stand up to anyone. When the lord raised the entry fine to his woodland clearings in 1638, the commissioner noted, "Hee offred £20 which I refused for abuse which hee offered".[24] He was not a grasping man, but rather a man of public spirit. Gough says of him, "[He] did serve many offices with much care and faithfullnesse. Hee was three times High Constable of the Hundred of Pimhill; hee was often Churchwarden of this Parish. Hee bequeathed 24*s.* per annum to the Poore of this Parish".

He had married Eleanor, the sister of Roger Griffiths, a Shrewsbury alderman who was himself married to Mary Atcherley, Thomas's sister. They had four sons and six daughters. Sarah, and possibly Elizabeth, had died young, but Anne, Elinor, Jane, and Mary all grew up to marry gentlemen in Cheshire, Montgomeryshire, Shrewsbury, and Burlton, respectively. Thomas III was apprenticed to a Shrewsbury draper, in 1663, but he and his brother, Richard, died young. Andrew and a younger Richard grew up to maturity. This Andrew was three years the elder of the two, and upon his marriage to a rich farmer's daughter in Montgomeryshire, he was given his father's lands there. The chief farm at Marton and the lands and tithes of Weston Lullingfields were bequeathed to Richard. Thomas was much blamed in the parish for not bequeathing the chief farm to the elder son, and people wagged their heads and said that such things "doe seldom prosper". Many local Shropshire examples were quoted to show how this would bring bad luck. And for once the Jeremiahs were proved correct, for Richard died young and left a widow and a daughter. This widow married again, this time to a rich Shrewsbury grocer, and they kept the lands in Weston Lullingfields, Onslow's tenement in Marton, and the lease of another tenement, but the chief property (i.e. the Lloyd Pierce and the Twyford lands) at Marton Hall reverted to Andrew Atcherley, the elder son and only male heir. In time all the lands of his father came back to Andrew and his heirs, who continued the line into the eighteenth and nineteenth centuries.

Some of the buildings erected by the Atcherleys during the seventeenth century still survive. Their long barn at Marton was partly demolished in October 1970, and further down the lane towards Myddle, one of their tenements was considerably altered and extended during 1970–1. It originally consisted of two rooms below and two garrets above, and had the usual 'black-and-white' appearance with square-panelling and painted bricks. It is impossible to identify their seventeenth-century tenants as the Atcherleys owned more than one of these buildings.

The house which stands so attractively in its garden at the top of the bank that slopes down to the Old Mill Brook is still known as the Tan House and belonged to the owners of Marton Hall until 1954. According to Gough, Thomas Atcherley I "built a tan-house, which is now standing by the old mill brooke".[25] It must have been erected during the first three decades of the seventeenth century. The exterior walls of this building are of a high quality timber-framing on a superior-looking sandstone plinth, and, internally, the house is now of the usual three-part plan, with parlour and service ends, and a central hall with a lateral chimney-stack in the rear wall. It is the most charming house in the parish.

But the internal arrangements suggest that the present rooms are not contemporary with the shell of the building. The ceilings of the ground floor 'hall' and 'service' rooms have very thin chamfered joists (those in the 'parlour' are covered in), which in a well-timbered county like Shropshire would suggest a somewhat later date than the one that has been suggested for the shell. This is not an absolute guide, but it raises the possibility that the upper floors are a later insertion. The chimney-stack in the 'hall' is of brick construction and is unlikely to be earlier than the very late seventeenth century, if not the eighteenth. There is also a brick angle-stack in the 'parlour' which is a later insertion, as is shown by the disused peg-holes in the outer face of the rear wall. The timber-framed partition between the 'hall' and the 'parlour' is built up against this stack, and not cut away to accommodate it, as the lack of peg-holes demonstrates. All this leads to a strong presumption that the internal partitions and floors, and the chimney-stacks, were inserted in the very late seventeenth or the eighteenth century. There are no signs of any previous divisions, and one is led to wonder from the name and from Gough's account whether it was originally built as a tannery or a storage building, with perhaps some accommodation for the servants who worked there. The Atcherleys were the richest family in the parish during the seventeenth century and could well have afforded a high-class building of this kind.

d. The Hanmers of Marton

The Hanmers were the neighbours of the Atcherleys and their story is a similar one, though they never quite attained the wealth and status of the gentleman-tanners.

The original Roger Hanmer was "a younger brother of that Right Worshipful family of the Hanmers, of Hanmer in Flintshire",[26] a village that lay about 15 miles due north of Myddle. He came into the parish upon his marriage to Anne, the eldest daughter of the last of the Kinastons, ancient landowners in the parish of Myddle and a prominent name in the annals of Shropshire. A second Kinaston daughter married William Onslow of Boreatton, and they lived in the house by the beginning of the lane leading from Marton to Weston Lullingfields. This was the one already mentioned that became known as Onslow's tenement and which was bought by Thomas Atcherley. The two youngest daughters of the Kinastons sold their shares in the property to Roger Hanmer, who therefore managed to keep the major part of the old farm. This lay a bit further down the lane and is the one marked on the modern Ordnance Survey map as Marton Farm. The Hanmers must either have left or died out in the early nineteenth century, for in 1838 the farm belonged to the lord and covered 268 acres. Kinaston's original farm must, therefore, have been a large one of about 456 acres.

When the Hanmers first came to Marton they farmed much more than just their freehold land. In the manorial survey of 1563 Roger Hanmer paid a chief rent of 3*s.* for his freehold, another 9*s.* for clearings in Myddlewood, 7*s.* for two wood leasows in Brandwood, and a further £1 3*s.* 4*d.* rent for Hollins Farm. By 1588 they had relinquished the Hollins but were renting a tenement that had been escheated after Hugh Elks had murdered a servant girl. However, the Hanmers had given up all but their freehold land by 1602, and though they continued to prosper during the seventeenth century they never farmed as much land again. They were soon to be overshadowed in Marton by the newly-arrived Atcherleys.

Roger and Anne Hanmer had six sons and four daughters, most of whom seem to have died at a very early age, so that Roger may have been succeeded by his grandson, Humphrey, upon his death in 1581. The exact genealogical details of these early Hanmers are hard to come by. The parish registers contain little information,[27] but the will of Humphrey Hanmer, proved in the summer of 1631, gives his wife's name as Mary and refers to two sons, William and Thomas, a married daughter, Margery, another daughter Elizabeth, and an illegitimate daughter, Katherine. Somehow, during his lifetime the family holdings had contracted, but as he was a gentleman-freeholder of some 268 acres the family was still of considerable standing in the parish.

His son and heir, William Hanmer, married the daughter of William Baker, a Marton yeoman and head of "an ancient and flourishing family in Marton". William Hanmer described himself as a gentleman, but his marriage puts him a notch lower on the social scale than the Atcherleys. When he died in 1637 the property passed to William Hanmer II (1619–61), his eldest son. Gough was of the opinion that "His father was wanting in giveing him good learneing; but hee had good naturall parts, and for comely liniaments of body, and for a nimble strength and activity of body none in the parish exceeded him". But he died when he was only 41, leaving his Baschurch wife to live for 23 years without him. The deaths in middle age of two successive heads of the family would have made it very difficult for the Hanmers to do much more than hang on to what they had already got. The widow was living in only a one-hearth house in 1672, though by then the eldest son, Humphrey II, had inherited the farm and was paying tax on two hearths. But, though the Hanmers may not have been as prosperous as the Atcherleys, they were still confident in their description of themselves as gentlemen, and they continued to flourish in the eighteenth century.

e. Sleap Hall

Sleap Hall Farm consisted of some 200 acres, with the addition of a further 61 acres from near-by Sleap Gorse. This gorse land had been enclosed by the lords of Myddle in 1334, together with near-by Broomhurst and Gorsehurst [Gorsty?] and part of Bilmarsh. It had once been farmed by Roger Nicholas of Balderton Hall but was consistently leased to Sleap Hall from at least the early seventeenth century onwards. In practice, it had been attached to Sleap Hall many years earlier, without any rent being paid until a surveyor spotted what was going on. "There is a parcell of land in Middle Lordship called Sleaps gorse of the yerely value of £7 or £8 or better. It adioyneth neare unto the freehold of one Maynwaring there called the

Hanmer

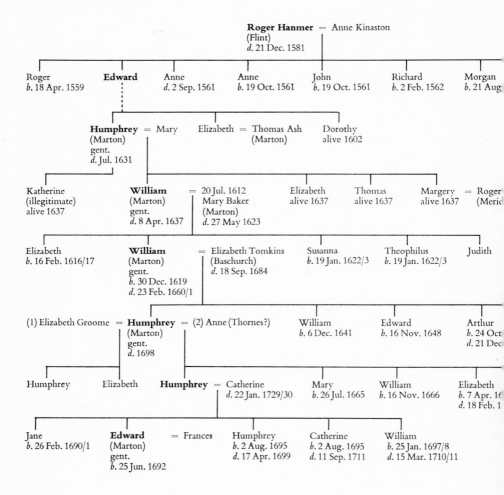

Roger Hanmer = Anne Kinaston
(Flint)
d. 21 Dec. 1581

Roger *b.* 18 Apr. 1559	**Edward**	Anne *d.* 2 Sep. 1561	Anne *b.* 19 Oct. 1561	John *b.* 19 Oct. 1561	Richard *b.* 2 Feb. 1562	Morgan *b.* 21 Aug

Humphrey = Mary Elizabeth = Thomas Ash Dorothy
(Marton) (Marton) alive 1602
gent.
d. Jul. 1631

Katherine (illegitimate) alive 1637	**William** (Marton) gent. *d.* 8 Apr. 1637	= 20 Jul. 1612 Mary Baker (Marton) *d.* 27 May 1623	Elizabeth alive 1637	Thomas alive 1637	Margery alive 1637	= Roger (Meric

Elizabeth *b.* 16 Feb. 1616/17	**William** (Marton) gent. *b.* 30 Dec. 1619 *d.* 23 Feb. 1660/1	= Elizabeth Tomkins (Baschurch) *d.* 18 Sep. 1684	Susanna *b.* 19 Jan. 1622/3	Theophilus *b.* 19 Jan. 1622/3	Judith

(1) Elizabeth Groome = **Humphrey** = (2) Anne (Thornes?) William Edward Arthur
 (Marton) *b.* 6 Dec. 1641 *b.* 16 Nov. 1648 *b.* 24 Oct
 gent. *d.* 21 Dec
 d. 1698

Humphrey	Elizabeth	**Humphrey** = Catherine *d.* 22 Jan. 1729/30	Mary *b.* 26 Jul. 1665	William *b.* 16 Nov. 1666	Elizabeth *b.* 7 Apr. 1€ *d.* 18 Feb. 1

Jane *b.* 26 Feb. 1690/1	**Edward** (Marton) gent. *b.* 25 Jun. 1692	= Frances Humphrey *b.* 2 Aug. 1695 *d.* 17 Apr. 1699	Catherine *b.* 2 Aug. 1695 *d.* 11 Sep. 1711	William *b.* 25 Jan. 1697/8 *d.* 15 Mar. 1710/11

ep. 1569 = 12 Apr. 1599 Edw. Clive, esq. (Baschurch)

Thomas
alive 1602

Margaret
b. 16 Nov. 1572

Elizabeth
b. 17 Apr. 1575
d. 18 Jun. 1575

r
lay 1653

Mary
b. 26 Apr. 1660

ar. 1672/3
Mar. 1672/3

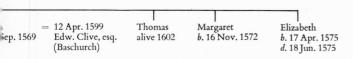

farme of Sleape but seemeth to bee noe parcell of the farme, being severed from the farme grounde by ancient and deepe dytches and mounds".[28] After a great deal of legal arguments, the Maynwarings paid rent for this as well as 2*s.* 4*d.* p.a. for their freehold.

Robert Maynwaring of Sleap apprenticed his son, John, to a Shrewsbury mercer and capper in 1512–13, and Roger Maynwaring was at Sleap when the subsidy was taken in 1524.[29] His inventory of 1551 shows that he was mainly occupied in rearing animals. He had 10 head of cattle, 30 sheep, 4 oxen, and a mare, a colt, and a gelding. He was succeeded by Mr Arthur Maynwaring, but Gough speaks of the family as being squires in Cheshire, and the farm was usually let to tenants.[30] The Groomes were yeoman-farmers here for two or three generations, followed by Rowland Plungin and his sons, Arthur and John. Arthur displeased his father by marrying a widow and so got little from him. John became the next tenant but was such a poor farmer that he fell into arrears with the rent and was evicted. He went to Balderton Hall for a time, where he spent the rest of his stock, and at the end of the seventeenth century he was living in a cottage in Myddle, maintaining himself by day labour. There is no mention of drunkenness here, nor of failure through unwise speculation, but steady decline into the labouring ranks through sheer inefficiency and lack of ability. He was followed as tenant of Sleap Hall by William Cooke, a Cheshire man, who was living "in good repute" at the turn of the century. The Maynwarings continued to live in Cheshire and had very little to do with the parish.

f. Shotton Farm

Shotton Farm formed a separate township of 230½ acres on "the far side of the parish" within the Liberty of Shrewsbury. It had no connection with Myddle lordship, but its owners and tenants worshipped in the parish church rather than in the chapel at Hadnall.

The ancient owners were the Kinastons,[31] who let it to their younger brothers until 1629 when Thomas Kinaston sold it to Mr William Watkins, the son of Mr Humphrey Watkins of Whixall. This family was to become one of the most respected in the parish, both for their abilities and for their service to the community. William Watkins was the under-sheriff of Shropshire at the time of his arrival, "but his chiefe delight was in good husbandry". One must again turn to Gough as the source of information.

> He found this farm much overgrowne with thornes, briars and rubish. He imployd many day labourers, (to whom he was a good benefactor), in cleareing and ridding his land; and having the benefitt of good marle, he much improved his land, built part of the dwelling house, and joined a brewhouse to it, which hee built of free stone. Hee built most part of the barnes, and made beast houses

> of free stone, which is a good substantial piece of building. Hee was a cheerefull, merry gentleman, and kept a plentifull table for his own family, and strangers.[32]

His wife had a similar disposition.

His three younger sons all established themselves in London, as a tradesman, a goldsmith, and "a distiller of strong waters", respectively. Two of his daughters also went to London; one to marry, and the other to be "an exchange woman". Another daughter married a Shrewsbury draper, and the fourth found a husband at Berwick, near Shrewsbury. The eldest son, Francis Watkins, followed his father's interests. "He marled several peices, and gott abundance of corne. Hee purchased lands in Tylley Parke", and certainly if he had lived he would have been "exceeding rich". His widow re-married twice; Charles Dimock of Willeton (living at Shotton in 1672), and then John Cotton, the son and heir of Richard Cotton of Haston. "Shee was much to bee comended for giving her children good education, and putt every one of them in good condition to live". The two younger sons became grocers in Shrewsbury and Bristol, the two daughters married Shropshire gentlemen, and William Watkins II inherited the farm and the family's good reputation as able farmers and kindly neighbours. Three generations had put down their roots at Shotton by the end of the seventeenth century. In time they were almost to rival the Atcherleys as the oldest family in the parish.

2 · *The small farms*

There were a few other farms within the parish of Myddle (some freehold and some held by leases for lives) that were not as large as those that belonged to these gentry, but which were still considerably larger than the tenements. Their owners were prosperous yeomen who were occasionally described as gentlemen. Indeed, the Downtons of Alderton Hall had been granted the right to display their coat of arms by the heralds in 1623.[33] Part of their lands, however, lay across the parish boundary in Broughton.

a. The Downtons of Alderton

The complicated history of Alderton township has been discussed in chapter 1. A detached portion of 45 acres of freehold land lay within the lordship of Myddle beyond Bilmarsh Farm, but the rest had been granted to Wombridge Priory and had been sold off after the Dissolution to the existing tenants, the two Downtons and the family of Amis. Gough wrote: "The family of Downtons is soe antient in this towne, that I have not heard of any that were tenants . . . before them; and such a numerouse offspring hath branched out of this family that there was three familyes of Downtons at one time in this towne", with more of them at Myddle and Webscott, "but now all these familyes are extinct, except one widow".[34]

Downton, 1

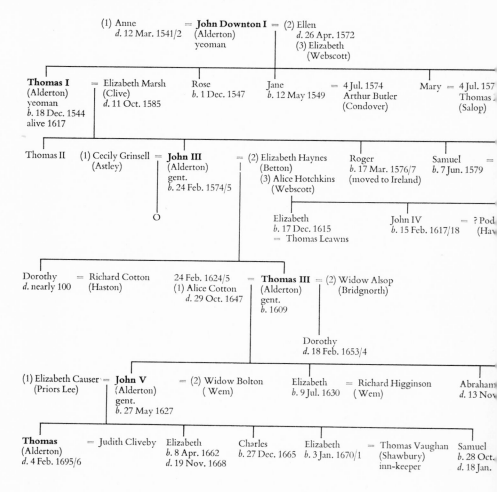

(1) Anne
d. 12 Mar. 1541/2
= **John Downton I**
(Alderton)
yeoman
= (2) Ellen
d. 26 Apr. 1572
(3) Elizabeth
(Webscott)

Thomas I
(Alderton)
yeoman
b. 18 Dec. 1544
alive 1617
= Elizabeth Marsh
(Clive)
d. 11 Oct. 1585

Rose
b. 1 Dec. 1547

Jane
b. 12 May 1549
= 4 Jul. 1574
Arthur Butler
(Condover)

Mary = 4 Jul. 157
Thomas
(Salop)

Thomas II

(1) Cecily Grinsell
(Astley)
= **John III**
(Alderton)
gent.
b. 24 Feb. 1574/5
= (2) Elizabeth Haynes
(Betton)
(3) Alice Hotchkins
(Webscott)

O

Roger
b. 17 Mar. 1576/7
(moved to Ireland)

Samuel =
b. 7 Jun. 1579

Elizabeth
b. 17 Dec. 1615
= Thomas Leawns

John IV
b. 15 Feb. 1617/18
= ? Pod
(Ha

Dorothy
d. nearly 100
= Richard Cotton
(Haston)

24 Feb. 1624/5
(1) Alice Cotton
d. 29 Oct. 1647
= **Thomas III**
(Alderton)
gent.
b. 1609
= (2) Widow Alsop
(Bridgnorth)

Dorothy
d. 18 Feb. 1653/4

(1) Elizabeth Causer
(Priors Lee)
= **John V**
(Alderton)
gent.
b. 27 May 1627
= (2) Widow Bolton
(Wem)

Elizabeth
b. 9 Jul. 1630
= Richard Higginson
(Wem)

Abraham
d. 13 No

Thomas
(Alderton)
d. 4 Feb. 1695/6
= Judith Cliveby

Elizabeth
b. 8 Apr. 1662
d. 19 Nov. 1668

Charles
b. 27 Dec. 1665

Elizabeth
b. 3 Jan. 1670/1
= Thomas Vaughan
(Shawbury)
inn-keeper

Samuel
b. 28 Oct.
d. 18 Jan.

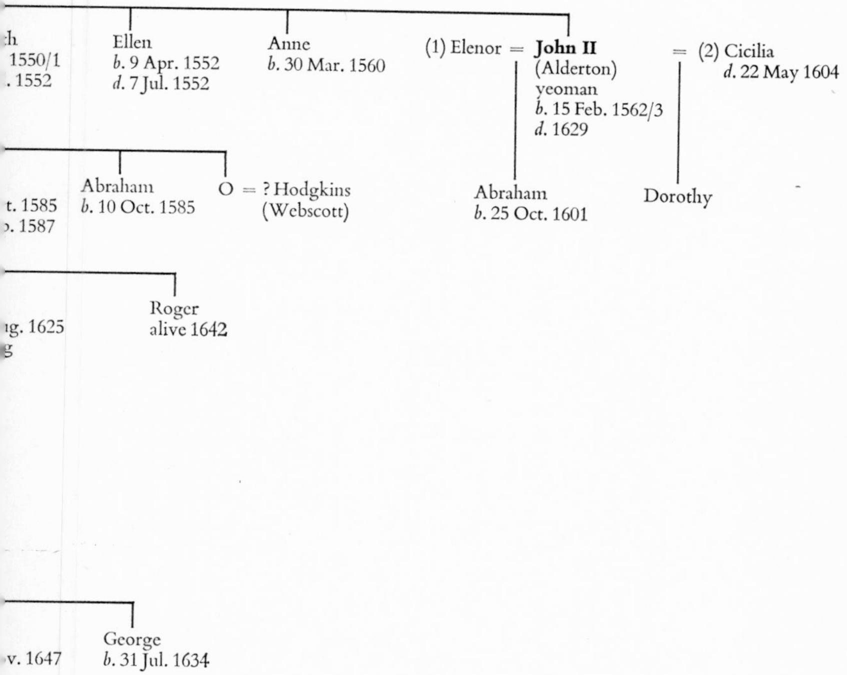
:h
1550/1
. 1552
Ellen
b. 9 Apr. 1552
d. 7 Jul. 1552
Anne
b. 30 Mar. 1560
(1) Elenor = John II
(Alderton)
yeoman
b. 15 Feb. 1562/3
d. 1629
= (2) Cicilia
d. 22 May 1604
t. 1585
›. 1587
Abraham
b. 10 Oct. 1585
O = ? Hodgkins
(Webscott)
Abraham
b. 25 Oct. 1601
Dorothy
ıg. 1625
g
Roger
alive 1642
›v. 1647
George
b. 31 Jul. 1634

The Downtons were not quite as ancient in Alderton as Gough supposed. The subsidy rolls of 1524 and 1544 mentioned only two families there – the Heylins and the Teckowes. In 1524 a Heylin lived at the chief farm and two Teckowes lived in the smaller ones. Twenty years later there were two Heylins and three Teckowes recorded. Somehow the Downtons and the Amis family had become tenants, and subsequently owners, in their place only a few years later. A Thomas Downton is recorded at Balderton in 1538 and a John Downton in Myddle in 1542. These are the earliest references to the family. By 1544 John Downton had the largest farm of 136 acres, George Downton took the smallest with 39 acres, and the remaining one of 65 acres was farmed by Walter Amis of Herefordshire, who came into the parish upon his marriage (possibly to a Teckowe).

The Amis family continued to live at Alderton throughout the late sixteenth and the seventeenth centuries. Walter purchased more lands in Loppington, and bequeathed them to his son, Thomas. He in his turn was succeeded by his son, Robert, who earned his living rearing cattle and sheep, and who passed his lands on to his son, William (1558–1654), who served as churchwarden and who was thought well of by his neighbours. The Amis family never quite reached gentry status, and William's claims were disallowed by the heralds at the visitation of 1623.[35] But they were substantial yeomen throughout this period. William's son, Robert Amis II (1608–1702), lived to be 93, and was taxed on three hearths in 1672. His son, Robert Amis III, lived at various times at Alderton, Balderton, Newton, and Broughton. One of his sons became a baker and lived well in London, another entered into service with a noble family and eventually had a farm of his own, one daughter married and went to live in Cheshire, and another brought her husband to Alderton. Two or three others died young, leaving the eldest son, William Amis II, to continue the line after his father's death in 1704.

The chief farm at Alderton consisted of 91 acres of freehold land around the Hall, another 45 acres of freehold, held at a nominal peppercorn rent from Myddle lordship, at the other side of Bilmarsh, and further land just across the parish boundary in Broughton. John Downton I,[36] yeoman, had two sons and six daughters by his second wife. His younger son, John Downton II of Alderton, yeoman (1563–1629), was renting land from the lord in 1599 and was living somewhere in Alderton, but this branch of the family came to an end upon his death in 1629. John Downton I's elder son, Thomas, was born in 1544 and was still alive in 1617. He, too, was a yeoman and was known as Bayly Downton through holding the manorial office of bailiff after Morgan ap Probart. "Hee built faire barnes and beast houses upon the farm, which are yet [1701] standing. Hee had a faire round tower of a dove house, which is now decayed". He was succeeded by his son, John III (born 1575), who became the first Downton to be described in the parish registers as 'gentleman'. He married three times, and his family seems to have prospered at Alderton. His youngest daughter, Mary, died while she was still young, but the eldest one, Dorothy, married Mr Richard Cotton of Haston and lived to be nearly 100. Elizabeth went to service with Sir Andrew Corbett and married a fellow-servant there; the youngest son, Roger, was made a freeman of the Mercers' Company of Shrewsbury in 1642;[37] and John Downton IV (born 1618), the son of the third marriage, married a Shropshire woman and bought land in near-by Noneley, but later returned to Myddle parish to live for several years at Webscott Farm. He had no surviving children at his death. The main line continued with John's half-brother, Thomas Downton III, gentleman (born 1609), who was the third of four generations to marry twice, and who, like his father, married into a family with whom he was already connected by marriage. His eldest son, John Downton V (born 1627) inherited the family freeholds.

The next generation witnessed a slump in the family's fortunes. John V married Elizabeth Causer, the only daughter of a Priors Lee joiner, who was "accompted a great fortune". Her marriage portion was given to John's mother and father, who in return gave up all their estate at Alderton. In 1672 John was living here and paying tax on four hearths. But he had "great charges in the education of his children" and heavy financial losses through paying money for sureties. He fell into debt, and though his "very discreet and provident" wife helped to maintain the family by selling ale, in the end he had to sell his land to his cousin, Mr Phillip Cotton, who let it to tenants. John's life ended miserably, for Elizabeth soon died, and he was unfortunate in his second marriage to a widow, a Wem ale-woman "with whom hee lived an unquiet life for some yeares". He finally parted from her and soon after died, much reduced in circumstances. His son, Thomas Downton IV (1641–96), a failed attorney, had so displeased his father (in the days before his bankruptcy) by marrying a woman with only £100 portion, that he had been given no land, and was forced to live on the £100 and his poor practice in Wem. However, he gradually improved his economic standing and by the end of his life he was being described as "of Alderton, yeoman". Perhaps he was the tenant at his father's old Hall. With him the main line of the Downtons came to an end.

The junior branch of the Downtons started with George Downton of Alderton, yeoman (died 1587), who was possibly the younger brother of John Downton I of Alderton Hall. George farmed 39 acres at Alderton and had the smallest of the three farms, but as his will speaks of "my landlord William Nicholas" he must have been renting land as well, most likely as sub-tenant at the adjoining Broomhurst Farm. His personal estate at his death amounted to £123 10*s*. 4*d*., a substantial sum for a yeoman of that time. He left a ewe lamb to his servant, Jane, and 5*s*. to the poor of the parish, after providing his children, Richard and Margaret, with £20 apiece, and making sure that his widow, Elizabeth, and his elder son, William, were well provided for. Two other children, John and Jane, had died many years before.

William Downton (1560–1629) was a "prudent" yeoman who rented extra land

Downton, 2

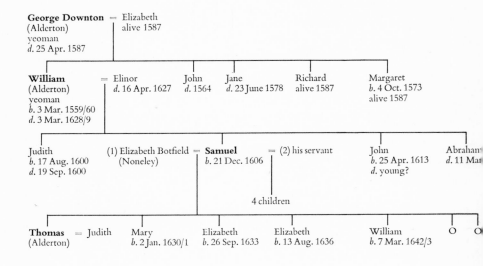

George Downton = Elizabeth
(Alderton) alive 1587
yeoman
d. 25 Apr. 1587

William = Elinor John Jane Richard Margaret
(Alderton) *d.* 16 Apr. 1627 *d.* 1564 *d.* 23 June 1578 alive 1587 *b.* 4 Oct. 1573
yeoman alive 1587
b. 3 Mar. 1559/60
d. 3 Mar. 1628/9

Judith (1) Elizabeth Botfield = **Samuel** = (2) his servant John Abraham
b. 17 Aug. 1600 (Noneley) *b.* 21 Dec. 1606 *b.* 25 Apr. 1613 *d.* 11 Mar
d. 19 Sep. 1600 *d.* young?

 4 children

Thomas = Judith Mary Elizabeth Elizabeth William O O
(Alderton) *b.* 2 Jan. 1630/1 *b.* 26 Sep. 1633 *b.* 13 Aug. 1636 *b.* 7 Mar. 1642/3

at Bilmarsh in addition to his father's land. He was succeeded by his son, Samuel, with whom the younger branch of the Downtons began its decline. Gough says he "was crooke backd, had a grim swarthy complection and long blacke haire. But hee was not so deformed in Body as debauched in behaviour . . . His prudent Father observing the idle and lewd courses of his son sought out a wife for him in time", and he married Elizabeth Botfield of Noneley, by whom he had two sons and five daughters. During her lifetime Samuel "lived in good fashion", but his wife died while the children were still young and, to the distress of his children, Samuel married his servant girl. The children all left home to go into service as soon as they could. Samuel quickly ran into debt and was forced to sell the lands he had gained by his first wife, but he could not sell his original tenement as it was bound by his first marriage settlement to his heirs. All he could do was to sell it for his life, and, hearing of this, his son, Thomas, borrowed money from his master and purchased the farm. Samuel left to sell ale in Cockshutt and for a time did well, but eventually fell into debt. He and his wife made a moonlight flit into Staffordshire, leaving their four children to be maintained by the parish. "Hee went a begging like an old decripite person and she carryed a box with pinnes . . . and laces. But after a while shee gott a new Sparke that travelled the Country and went away with him, and then this Samuel came again to Alderton to his son, Thomas, who maintained him dureing his Life".

Thomas Downton, by his parsimony and hard work, recovered much of what had been lost. He managed to pay off all the money he had borrowed and built up a good stock of cattle. But then he unexpectedly married a woman who not only brought him nothing but took away all that he had. "Her name is Judith – shee was brought up all her lifetime as servant in some alehouse or other, and shee proved such a drunken woman as hath scarce beene heard of; shee spent her husband's estate soe fast that it seemed incredible . . . Her husband paid £10 at a time for alehouse scores". Thomas died in the closing years of the seventeenth century with his possessions almost gone, for he was forced to sell his farm, to Rowland Muckleston of Oswestry. What money he had left was spent by his wife within a couple of years of his death, and in 1701 she was living poorly in a little house in Myddle. She died a widow and pauper in 1735. The decline of the Downtons was complete.

b. Bilmarsh Farm

Bilmarsh Farm had once been a common on the eastern boundary of the parish of Myddle. Freeholders at the time of the 1602 survey were able to present deeds that granted land in Bilmarsh as far back as the twelfth or thirteenth centuries, but much land remained as a common until it was finally enclosed during the sixteenth century. At the enclosure, the freeholders added extra acres to their farms and the lord created an entirely new farm for himself, which he let to tenants. The 1563 surveyor noted that "William Tentch[38] holdeth Byllmarsh and is behind for 3 years rent". He was given a new lease at £4 per annum, the same as he paid in 1588, and the same as was paid by Mr Osmary Hill in 1602. Hill extended the farm by pulling down two squatters' cottages and erecting a house in their place, in which he kept a flourishing school for the sons of gentlemen. He also purchased two other pieces of land near-by and leased a tenement in Withyford.

Sometime in the early 1650s, his son, Francis Hill, left to live at Broughton upon property he had inherited through his wife. Francis sold Bilmarsh Farm to George Reve, a Cheshire man who came into the parish as the tenant of Sleap Hall. It is difficult to say how large Bilmarsh Farm was at this time, for there had been considerable changes by the time of the 1838 Tithe Award, which provides the first definite information. But it must have covered some 100–150 acres, perhaps a little more. Reve was already tenant-farming some 260 acres at Sleap Hall, so this new lease made him a wealthy farmer, one who could rank with the largest landowners in the parish. After his death, his son, Francis, took on a new 21-year lease (as the Earl of Bridgewater would not at that time allow leases for lives). Several of Francis's sisters married "good substantial persons in this country",[39] and his son, Nathaniel, married a Shropshire woman with £100 portion. Nathaniel purchased some new land near by, at Little Bilmarsh, but when his lease on the old farm expired he refused to take a new lease unless it was on his own terms. He moved to Broughton and built a new house at Little Bilmarsh, and Thomas Hayward of neighbouring Tilley became the new tenant at Bilmarsh Farm.

What had once been stable property now changed hands as rapidly as had Balderton Hall. Upon the death of his grandfather, Hayward moved back to Tilley and sold his lease to John Waring, a Shrewsbury attorney, who may have been a relation through marriage. But Waring soon bought lands from William Crosse of Yorton and sold him the Bilmarsh lease so that he might have a place to live. This Crosse had risen from a lowly rank, but both he and his wife

> were both overmuch addicted to drunkennesse, and it is noe marvell that they consumed the marriage portion (which was considerable) in a short time, and afterwards the lands . . . hee and his wife went dayly to the ale-house, and soon after the cows went thither alsoe; and when his stocke was spent hee sold his lease to Nathaniel Reve, and removed to Shrewsbury, where he tooke a lytle house on the rack rent, and there followed the same way of drinking.

He died in a Shrewsbury alehouse.

Nathaniel Reve was the son of the Nathaniel who had refused the new lease. According to Gough, he wanted the farm for sentimental reasons. But he was handicapped by his spendthrift and crippled brother, George, and after trying to pay this brother's debts, ended up in gaol with him. He was forced to sell Little Bilmarsh and when he came out of gaol he held both Bilmarsh farms on the rack-rent. After his death, Mr Robert Finch of Cockshutt, who had loaned him £20 to buy the Bilmarsh lease, became tenant, and was there at the close of the seventeenth century.

c. The Hollins

Hollins Farm is a peculiar little adjunct to the south-west corner of Myddle parish; a rectangular limb surrounded on three sides by lands that lie in neighbouring parishes. Gough's suggestion[40] that it was a dairy house belonging to the Castle is a reasonable one, for it appears as an appendix to the Castle Farm as if pastures had been cleared of the hollies that gave it its name. It is a compact farm of 128 acres or so on the far side of the park.

There is a large turnover of names in the manorial rentals for Hollins Farm, and this does not augur well for its prosperity. The parish registers describe Thomas Kinaston, gentleman, as of the Hollins in 1541, and he may well have been there since the manorial rolls began in 1528. However, when the first manorial survey was made, in 1563, it was leased by Roger Hanmer of Marton at an annual rent of £1 3*s*. 4*d*., or 3½ nobles in the ancient reckoning. By the time of the 1588 survey it had changed hands again, for a Mr Richard Powell,[41] otherwise unknown in Myddle, was now the owner. In 1602 he was paying the same £1 3*s*. 4*d*. rent and an entry fine of £6 13*s*. 4*d*., determinable upon three lives. Roger Hanmer had changed the tenure from at will to three lives in 1568, and the terms remained the same until the new round of bargaining between 1637 and 1642. By 1634, however, the Hollins had passed to another outsider, a gentleman called John Gosse, and by 1638 it was leased by William Clayton.

The parish registers record some of the sub-tenants. As Humphrey Reynolds is referred to in 1580 and again upon his death in 1627 as being of the Hollins, it is likely that this farm was split into two, for also mentioned are John Trevor (1592), Jacob Benion (1612), and Jacob Vernon (1623). The Trevors came from Hadnall, but the other two are strange names to Myddle. Reynolds however, was here for a long time, and it was by marrying his daughter that William Clayton first became under-tenant, and then full-tenant when the lord increased the entry fines, for Gosse seems to have disappeared at just about this time. By 1641 William Clayton was paying the same annual rent of £1 3*s*. 4*d*., but the entry fine had gone up from £6 13*s*. 4*d*. to no less than £189, of which he had paid £126.

William Clayton took out a lease on the lives of three of his sons. He had eight children, but at least two, and possibly four, died while they were young. But when he, too, died in 1661, he could call himself yeoman and his small estate seemed secure. One of his sons, Richard, had caused him trouble by leaving his wife and child and going to live with another woman outside the county, and he had also been displeased when Francis, his eldest son, had married the rector's Welsh servant-girl, and he had given him little, if anything, during his life. But

Samuel had settled down to married life in Baschurch, and Isaac had had a good portion with his wife. William had £104 in bonds when he died, and after giving 40*s*. to the poor, and 5*s*. 8*d*. to the ringers, appears to have divided his property amongst his sons, so that both Isaac and Francis had half the lease each. The farm may have been originally divided into three, for Samuel died (when he was 44) at the Hollins, not much more than two years after his father, with the title of yeoman and personal estate worth £42 12*s*. 0*d*.[42]

Isaac continued to live in the old house at that standard of living which made his neighbours unsure whether to call him husbandman or yeoman. He married a Shropshire woman and had two daughters and a son, William. Meanwhile, Francis had built another small house for himself and supplemented his farm earnings by working as a tailor. He, too, had three children and the eldest was named William. In the Hearth Tax returns of 1672 Isaac had two hearths and Francis had one. Then undeserved ill luck struck them both. Gough tells the story.

> The Earle of Bridgewater's officers gave notice to the tenants that any person that had a life, or lives, in a lease, might haye them exchanged, but noe more lives putt into the lease. Upon this, Isaac Cleaton desired his Brother Francis, that hee might exchange Francis his life and putt in another, which was agreed upon; and Isaac took a new lease, and putt in his son William's life and gave securyty that Francis should hould the one halfe during his life. But it happened that Isaac dyed, and his son William proved a bad husband, and spent most of his estate and then dyed; soe that the lease was expired. The securyty given to Francis was become poore and not responsible. Francis was still living, and lost all. His son William tooke the farme on the racke rent; and dureing his father's life, which was many yeares, hee payd rent, and now, his father beeing lately dead, he holds the farme.

The manorial records help to fill in the details. The lease in which Isaac inserted his son William's name is dated 24 April 1682, and William, the son of Francis, started on a rack-rent of £20 p.a. on 10 February 1691/2. He survived, and raised a family of three daughters and two sons, who carried the Clayton name on into the eighteenth century.

d. Webscott Farm

Webscott Farm belonged in the sixteenth and seventeenth centuries to "that ancient and worthy family of the Thornses of Shelvoke",[43] who paid an annual chief rent of 1*d*. in lieu of the ancient charge of a pair of gilt spurs. The Thornses escaped having their land escheated in the middle sixteenth century, but from that time there was straightforward descent until the last of the family sold the farm to his brother-in-law, Thomas Price, near the end of the seventeenth century. The family never resided in Myddle and let their farm to tenants. It has already been suggested that the Genckys family was there in the 1520s. Originally, there were two houses on the farm: Higher Webscott on the original site, and Lower Webscott nearer Harmer. The lower house was occupied during the early seventeenth century by the Twisse family and then by Robert Orred who sold ale there until it was pulled down after the Civil Wars.

Higher Webscott was farmed by Thomas Hodgkins or Hoskins "who had a good estate in lands and houses in Ruyton". Both his son and his daughter married Downtons of Alderton. Thomas was prosperous and styled himself as gentleman, but his son and namesake fell in the way of so many others. "He was a good father and good farmer, a good Clarke, and a good companion, and that marred all. Hee spent his Estate faster than his Ancestors gott itt, and tooke noe care to leave somewhat to maintain him in his old age". He had to sell his Webscott lease and "all the household goods even to the Wainscott". He was maintained on charity by his son-in-law, but his second wife, a rich Newton widow, had "nothing to maintain herself butt what neighbours sent, [and she] dyed in a poore cottage in great poverty".

Hodgkins was succeeded at Webscott by John Downton IV and then by Richard Nightingale, who left upon his marriage. He was followed by William Higginson, yeoman, who had over £160 worth of personal estate upon his death in 1664. His son and namesake, "a painefull laboriouse man and a good husband", took a lease at an easy rack-rent for three lives and was here in 1672, but his son, John, fell into debt and had to sell the lease to a William Jenks of Stockett. At the end of the century another man, Ralph Vaughan, was tenant. The ownership of the farm had been stable, but the tenants had changed several times.

This detailed examination of the largest farms within the parish of Myddle reveals a section of the community that was far from static. Very few of the wealthiest families had been resident here for more than a century and their stories are just about as different as they can be: the man who died in a drunken stupor in a lowly Shrewsbury ale-house represents one extreme; the tanners who had risen to comparative splendour at Marton Hall and Castle Farm illustrate the other. Even if one acknowledges that some of the newcomers came from a limited group of neighbouring parishes, the mobility amongst this class was considerable.

Two families that were amongst the most stable were absentees and can therefore be excluded from the community. The Maynwarings had been at Sleap Hall as far back as 1524 and younger sons had lived there for a time, but for most of the sixteenth and throughout the seventeenth century they lived on their ancestral estates in Cheshire and let their Myddle property to tenants. The Thornses never resided at Webscott and in fact had died out altogether by the close of the seventeenth century. Only the Hanmers and the Gittinses could claim to have been resident gentry throughout Elizabethan and Stuart times. Both of them came into Myddle in the second quarter of the sixteenth century, and both expanded their estates, only to decline a little in later years. However, even after their losses, they were still acknowledged as being in the very top rank of Myddle society. The Watkins family also entered the parish upon their purchase of Shotton Hall in 1629. By the end of the century they had been there for three generations and eventually outlived both of the other two.

Both the Gittinses and the Nicholas family of Balderton Hall seemed destined to establish themselves above the other gentry families, but they were unable to retain the farms they had engrossed. The Gittinses fell back to their old level, and the Nicholases crashed into bankruptcy. Only the Atcherleys were successful in engrossing farms. Within 50 years of their arrival as younger sons of neighbouring tanners they were to be the largest landowners in the parish. By the end of the seventeenth century they may be included as a fourth family to have achieved stability here, and eventually they became the longest-established of them all.

At least some families, therefore, were both rich and stable. The Gittins family lost Eagle Farm through standing risky sureties, but were able to keep Castle Farm and their freeholds. But standing security brought about the complete downfall of the Downton family of Alderton Hall. Others, like the Claytons of the Hollins, fell upon hard times through the misfortune of two untimely deaths, and others went bankrupt through over-speculation. William Nicholas lost all at Balderton Hall, and two Shrewsbury drapers who bought the freehold of Balderton Hall in the seventeenth century both had to relinquish it when their London connections went bankrupt. All this is familiar to the person living in the twentieth century, but what is surprising is the number who literally drank themselves into debt. Thomas Hodgkins of Webscott was perhaps the worst example of all. Both he and his father could describe themselves as gentlemen, he made two good marriages, he was an able farmer and an educated and jovial man, but he ended up having to sell his furniture and depend upon charity. William Crosse of Bilmarsh drank himself into poverty and then to death, and at Balderton Hall both Michael Chambre and Thomas Hall almost ruined themselves by drinking and by their debauched behaviour. Finally, when it seemed that Thomas Downton of Alderton Hall was managing to recoup some of his father's losses he married a wife who spent all his laboriously-gathered capital at an incredible speed; "Her husband paid £10 at a time for alehouse scores".

To match the stable families were those farms with a rapid turnover of personnel. Balderton Hall was sold to one freeholder after another; the owners of Webscott had a succession of tenants to find; and the lord's steward had similar trouble with Bilmarsh. During the last quarter of the seventeenth century there were six successive tenants at Bilmarsh and five at Webscott. The chances of retaining one's possessions once the coveted rank of peasant-gentry had been reached were about 50 : 50 in Myddle during the late sixteenth and the seventeenth centuries.

CHAPTER FOUR

The tenements

1 · Distribution

The tenements were substantially smaller than the farms, but considerably larger than the cottages. Gough is careful to distinguish the three classes. Exact acreages are hard to come by as many of them had been engrossed by the time of the Tithe Award of 1838, which is the first detailed survey that is available. The lord's tenement in Newton was 79 acres at that time, and as it was surrounded by freehold lands it is likely that this was the original size. But the other tenements are unrecognizable, and only a few sizes can be worked out from the seventeenth-century manorial surveys. Bickley's tenement in Brandwood was a large one of 86 acres in 1617, and in the survey of 1602 the Watson tenement in the adjoining Divlin Wood was 88 acres. These seem to have been unusually large, and they were probably of this size because the land was amongst the poorest in the parish. Indeed, a large part of Watson's land was still described as Burlton moor.

The four tenements at Houlston could only have averaged 37 acres each, for the whole township only covered 148½ acres. In Myddle, William Gosling extended his possessions until he had a total of 58 acres, but Hodden's tenement was smaller with 44 acres, and Hunt's tenement comprised only 20 acres. Many of the poorer tenements in Myddlewood were smaller still, with several being under 10 acres. Even so, most of these lands supported husbandmen and yeomen, some of whom were also craftsmen. But younger sons and those who were dogged by ill-luck or were simply incompetent had to turn to labouring as well. For all of these tenement farmers, their common rights were of fundamental importance, for they were pastoral farmers who were dependent upon the common grazing grounds.

The village of Myddle contained two large farms (the Castle and the Eagle), while on the outskirts of the township there was the smaller farm of the Hollins. In the village there was also the parsonage and two freehold tenements (belonging to the Gittins family and the Lloyds), and six tenements and two half-tenements that were rented from the lord. This makes a total of 14 holdings, which is identical with the number recorded in the manorial rolls in 1538, but two short of the number in 1542. The lay subsidies name nine people in 1524, and 13 in 1544. By the end of the seventeenth century there were also at least six cottages in the village, but no more farms or tenements. The expansion that undoubtedly took place within the parish during the seventeenth century was mainly in the former woodland areas, and not so much within the original village. The shape of the village had already been defined by 1524.

In the hamlet of Marton during the late seventeenth century were the farm and the tenement that had been engrossed by the Atcherleys, Hanmer's Farm, a freehold tenement rented out by the Atcherleys, three other small freeholds that were owner-occupied, six tenements that were rented from the lord, and at least two cottages – a total of 15 buildings. This compares with the 11 people named in 1538, the 12 listed in 1542, and the 12 who were assessed in the lay subsidy of 1544. So, again, the population had almost reached its maximum by the reign of Henry VIII. In between Myddle and Marton, however, there were six tenements and at least eight cottages that were created during the late sixteenth and the seventeenth centuries. All these 14 properties lay in the old Myddlewood and were rented from the lord at 6*d*. an acre. They housed a group of people who were generally much poorer than the other tenement-farmers.

Near by, in Brandwood and Divlin Wood, there were six tenements of varying size, and one cottage. These woods had been felled before parts of Myddlewood were cleared and the tenements were much larger. The population pressure had not been so acute when these lands were first cultivated. A small group of tailor-farmers became established here, and some of them grew rich enough to be described as yeomen. Beyond these woods lay the township of Houlston with its four small freehold tenements, three of which were always let to tenants, and which had a considerable turnover of both owners and occupiers. Balderton also contained four small freeholds as well as its Hall until they were all engrossed into one estate in the middle of the eighteenth century. Further along the lane there were two freehold tenements and a hall in Alderton, and near by at Newton-on-the-Hill the lord held one large tenement of 79 acres, but the rest of the hamlet was farmed by three yeomen freeholders and a few cottagers.

At the most, then, there were 11 farms and 48 tenements and half-tenements within the parish, making a total of 59. Some of these, like the six small tenements in Myddlewood, were created after 1563, when the diocesan returns recorded 54 households in the parish of Myddle. But there must have been very few cottages at the time that the census was taken; the bulk of the population were farmers, and the great majority of them lived in dwellings that were smaller than the farm-houses, and which Gough distinguished as tenements. This is borne out by the analysis of occupations in the parish registers. During the seventeenth century a large number of labourers erected new cottages in the parish, but by 1701 the tenement-farmers were still the backbone of the community and (apart from one or two gentry) the longest-established families in the parish. A hundred years later, most of their lands had been engrossed and almost all of the familiar names had gone.

Comparison has already been made with the Leicestershire village of Wigston Magna, where a similar peasant body formed the real core of the community. There, the 1524 lay subsidy "brings out the character of the village as a solid community of middling-sized farmers, small yeomen and husbandmen, with no over-shadowing yeoman family at the top".[1] Only three Wigston men were taxed on lands worth over £10 per annum, nine between £5 and £9, and 30 between £2 and £4. A similar distribution of wealth is evident at Myddle. In 1524 (when there are returns for only the townships of Myddle, Balderton and Alderton), only one man was taxed on lands worth £10, one at £6 3*s*. 4*d*., four at £5, one at £3, three at £2, and seven at £1. Again, in 1544 (when returns survive for Myddle, Marton and Alderton), two Alderton men were taxed 20*d*., otherwise there was no great inequality between the six men taxed 8*d*., the one who was taxed 6*d*., and 21 others who were assessed at either 4*d*. or 2*d*. The hearth-tax returns of 1672 also reveal a community largely composed of middling farmers, with no ostentatious wealth on the one hand, and no overwhelming pauper problem on the other.

2 · *The buildings and furniture*

The few surviving buildings and the limited evidence of the probate inventories support the conclusion reached above. No medieval building remains in Myddle, but there are a few farm-houses, cottages and barns that can be dated between 1570 and 1700, the period of the national Great Rebuilding. None survives in its original form, and dating these buildings is complicated by later timber-extensions and by the amount of rebuilding in brick and stone that went on during the late eighteenth and nineteenth centuries. Nearly all the timbered houses that do survive in rural north Shropshire have been infilled with brick at some later stage, and most roofs have been re-covered with Welsh slates or with tiles, though thatch is still used at the Tan House and at the two cottages in Balderton. A modern practice is to paint the bricks white and to extend the lines of the timbers with black paint so as to give the house a more symmetrical appearance where there have been later extensions.

North Shropshire lies in an intermediate area between the Highland and Lowland zones, and so hybrid forms of building are likely to be common. At the time of the Great Rebuilding the economy was based upon pastoral farming, whereas in the second phase of rebuilding, over 200 years later, there was much more emphasis upon arable farming. However, as far as can be seen from the surviving examples, there was no great specialization of house-types, though perhaps out-houses and secondary buildings have more readily disappeared. Atcherley's long barn at Marton (which was partly demolished in October 1970), and the barn of one of the Brandwood tenements that is now known as Burlton Lane Farm, were large enough to have housed many animals as well as grain and hay, but there are no distinct pastoral farm-house-types such as the long-house of Wales or the laithe-house of the Pennines.

Some of the larger north Shropshire houses of the period of the Great Rebuilding were built of Grinshill sandstone, but the farm-houses are timber-framed in the square-panelling tradition of the west Midlands. Though there are plenty of crucks elsewhere in Shropshire, there are none in Myddle and none of the close-studding that was fashionable in the towns or in the farm-houses of eastern England. The bare timbers in one gable of the Myddlewood cottage,[2] now concealed by a lean-to constructed in the late eighteenth or early nineteenth century, suggest that the darkening of exposed timbers was a later practice. Presumably, the frames were originally filled in with wattle and daub, though this has now been replaced with brick. Neither Gough nor any other source mentions the use of brick during the seventeenth century, and so it is unlikely that this type of infilling was used in Myddle before the eighteenth century. Brick chimney stacks were possibly equally late in replacing timber ones.

The surviving tenement buildings are often difficult to analyse. Mention has already been made of the tenements leased by the Atcherleys, and there are only two other surviving examples of this type. Just down the lane from Balderton Hall is one of the freehold tenements that was engrossed into the Hall estate about the middle of the eighteenth century. It is impossible to say which of these tenements it was. The building has been considerably extended and now consists of two cottages, one of which is entered from what was possibly the original door at the front, and one from the back. The size of the original house is suggested by the presence of heavier and more robust timbers in the centre and in the part of the house furthest from the lane. The extension at the side near the lane is panelled with smaller timbers and has black lines painted over the brickwork to simulate further panelling. The roof is thatched and quite steeply pitched, but there have been so many alterations to this building that it is difficult to classify it.

A similar house stands just to the west of Myddle churchyard, by the left-hand side of the road leading to Marton. The demesne map of 1650 suggests that this was a half-tenement that belonged to the lord and which was rented out to the Tylers during the sixteenth and early seventeenth centuries, and then to the Pierce family during the rest of the century. Both of these families were farmer-tailors. Their house has been considerably altered and is now divided into two cottages. Again, the size of the original building is suggested by the larger of the timbers, and it is obvious that it has been extended both in length and in height. Only the first of the two storeys is timber-framed, though recent paintwork has been cleverly employed to suggest square-panelling all along the front. The central chimney may well be in its original position, but the upper storey, the roof, and the other chimney are all later additions. Even so, it is still basically a tenement farm-house of the late sixteenth or seventeenth century.

The documentary evidence that survives does not add a great deal to the visual record. One source that historians have found to be extremely useful in reconstructing regional building plans is the large collection of probate inventories. But in Myddle they are disappointing in this respect and give but few details about the number of rooms. The only inventory to contain any information from before the period of the Great Rebuilding is that of William Formston of Marton (1563), who seems to have had all his personal goods in "the hausse and chamber". Such a one-roomed house, chambered over, could well have been the norm for the tenement-farmers of that time, but one scrap of information is no proper guide in this matter.

The first inventory to list rooms is that of George Pickstock of Houlston, husbandman (1636), who had a simple house, with two rooms upstairs and two downstairs, and with an out-house, stable, and barn. The living room-cum-kitchen was termed the "hallhouse", as in many other parts of the country, and his downstairs bedroom was called the parlour. He had more beds in both of the chambers, which were also used for storing corn and miscellaneous items of equipment. In all this, Pickstock was probably a typical Myddle farmer and no different from peasants all over the country. Both Andrew Hordley, the yeoman-tailor of Divlin Wood (1640), and Francis Smith, a Balderton husbandman (1685), had a house and a parlour, chambered over, but in both these cases it is possible that the chamber only covered the parlour, and that the 'house' was open to the rafters in the style of earlier times.

A different terminology is used in the inventory of Richard Guest of Myddle, yeoman (1694), whose rooms were described as the house, the chamber below (which had a bed and was identical with what others termed the parlour), a milk-house (or dairy), a "room below the fire" (which also served as a bedroom), and finally, a room above the stairs (where another bed was to be found). In other words, Guest had his living room, a dairy, and two sleeping rooms downstairs, but only one room above. It is possible that other upstairs rooms had been omitted by the appraisers, but perhaps Guest had just one large room that went all the way across the house, or perhaps again there were rooms that were still open to the rafters.

Two other inventories from the earliest years of the eighteenth century give further details about rooms. William Groome of Alderton (1705) had a house and parlour, with a kitchen and a baking-house downstairs. The parlour was used as a bedroom, but the room above it seems to have been a withdrawing room, for it is styled "the house over the parlour" and it contained no bed, but just a chest, two chairs, and some cushions. Over the downstairs house and the kitchen were three "lofts" which were used as bedrooms. The difference in terminology reflects different usages. The other inventory is that of James Fewtrell of Brandwood, yeoman (1709). He had a "house place" and parlour that fulfilled the traditional functions of these rooms downstairs, and five small service rooms that acted as butteries, bake-house, work-house, and wash-house. Upstairs, there were three chambers that were used as bedrooms, and another chamber where cheese was made and stored. Judging by the value of his personal estate and the size of his farm, Fewtrell's farm-house was probably typical of the houses of the yeoman farmers at the end of the seventeenth century. But there is simply not enough information to catalogue the building revolution that occurred in Myddle, as elsewhere, during the period of the Great Rebuilding.

The probate inventories are disappointing with regard to the rooms, but they are most informative about the furniture and utensils that were kept within them. It can be seen that the rise in the standard of housing was matched by a greater accumulation of personal possessions within the home, just as it was in most other areas of the country. If the inventories of all classes for 1551–1701 are divided into three equal periods of 50 years each, then a general rise in the standard of living is quickly apparent. The *proportion* of wealth devoted to personal possessions averaged about one-quarter of the personal estate in all three periods (though there are considerable individual variations), but the *amount* of wealth invested in personal goods, and the number and variety of those goods, increased all the time. The farmers of Myddle were far wealthier in late Stuart times than their predecessors of the mid-sixteenth century.

Richard Moore, the gentleman tenant of Castle Farm, was one of the richest men in the parish at the time of his death in 1553, but his total inventory only amounted to £25 4*s*. 0*d*., and his furniture and equipment were valued at only £5 2*s*. 0*d*. Of this, £1 was accounted for by his apparel, 2*s*. by his pottery, and the rest by his "householde stuff, that is to say, bedds, and brasse, pewter, and napperyware". William Woulf, a Myddle husbandman who died in the same year, had only "housold stuffe and potts, pannes, and pewter" worth 13*s*. 4*d*., and bedding worth 10*s*., while another farmer, William Formston of Marton (1563) had simply "The goods in the hausse and chamber, that is to saye, 2 bedds and that that [sic] to they in belongethe, 2 pannes, 1 pot, 2 skellets with disshes, and other triffels in the howsse", which were assessed at £2. But only a few years later, there are definite signs of improvement. The first big inventory is that of Roger Nicholas, the gentleman-owner of Balderton Hall (1572), who had personal possessions valued at £34 3*s*. 0*d*., out of a total personal estate of £119 3*s*. 0*d*. It was his son who built the present Balderton Hall. The humbler men also prospered from that time onwards, and generally speaking, by the middle of the seventeenth century (even after one has allowed for inflation) the value of household goods was considerably higher than it had been during the first part of the reign of Queen Elizabeth. George Pickstock of Houlston (1636), for instance, was not one of the richest farmers, and never acquired the description of yeoman, but his personal goods at the time of his death were valued at £6 1*s*. 2*d*., out of a total inventory of £31–£32.

The farmers' wives did their cooking over a fire that was usually situated in the main room (and generally called 'the house'), or in the kitchen if they had one. A large iron or bronze cooking-pot or soup-pot was suspended over the fire from a hook and chain which was attached to a bar that was fastened in the chimney. Spits, or iron brooches, were supported at each side of the fire by andirons, which were large fire-dogs, with hooks to allow the spit to be adjusted to different levels. The Myddle inventories also mention bellows and tongs, and gridirons (brandards), which had long handles and could be placed over the fire to support pots and pans and kettles.

Most of the cooking utensils were made of brass; for example, Thomas Clare of Marton (1557) had "1 potte of brasse, 12*d*., [and] 2 lytell pannes of brasse, 3*s*. 4*d*." Other inventories mention dripping pans, frying pans, kettles, posnets or skellets (three-legged pans with long handles), and chafing dishes (for keeping the food warm). There are also occasional references to basins, to ewers of brass and pewter, and to "a mortar of brasse". Other utensils were of earthenware, such as the pottengers (soup bowls), while dishes, saucers, and drinking vessels were normally made of pewter, and sometimes tin. Very occasionally, the richer inhabitants had silver spoons and 'salts', and it was also common to have platters, bowls, and some dishes made of wood, which were collectively described as trynen-ware (or treenan-ware). Ann Matthews of Myddle (1570), for instance, had "17 peaces of turnd vessells", worth 4*s*. Finally, in the dairy or service-room, it was usual to find churns, cans, ladles, kimnels (tubs), and various kinds of baskets.

Some items of food were frequently recorded. Butter, cheese, and malt were both made and stored in the farm-house, salt beef, bacon, onions, and garlic hung from the ceiling, and meal and corn were stored in arks which were usually kept in a chamber. Weapons were also listed in some of the inventories: for instance, John Hordley (1577) had "a bill and 11 dusen arrowes" worth 10*d*. These weapons do not occur in the later inventories. Tables and chairs with cushions are frequently noted, but there were also several benches, stools, and forms. As in Essex, "a hard stool or bench was the poor man's seat until the early seventeenth century".[3] Storage space was provided by chests, shelves, coffers, desks, and stands, and in 1577 and 1632 dish-boards were mentioned as well as cupboards. Linen sheets were distinguished from painted cloths, as, for instance, in 1570, when widow Ann Matthews had "4 lynen clothes and 2 paynted clothes, 16*d.*", together with "8 tabell cloths and 2 napkins". Her apparel was also listed as "1 frocke, 4 petycots, a hatt, and a cape". Another widow, Joan Bromley (1576) had "2 Smockes, 2 cappes and a hatt, 2*s.* 10*d.*, 1 [?] gowne and a petycote, 4*s.* 4*d.*, 2 aprons, 2 payre of hose and a payre of shewes, 2*s.* 11*d.*, [and] 2 gownes, 20*s.*".

The beds were described in three different ways: a joined bed was one constructed by a carpenter; a standing bed was a tall bedstead with high panels at the head and foot, connected with an open-framed canopy that was covered with a cloth; and a trindle or trunkle bed was a low bed on wheels, which was used by children and servants. The mattresses and bolsters were either stuffed with feathers or flocks, and the sheets and pillow-cases ('pillowberes') were either of twill or linen. The coverings were normally described as bed-hillings. One or two rugs and carpets are mentioned, but there were no warming-pans recorded, and only one reference to close-stools (commodes) or any other method of sanitation.

The more refined articles are largely missing from the Myddle inventories. Only John Clowes (1632) and Stephen Formston (1674) had books recorded, but perhaps others were ignored; Gough mentions his books in his will, but none are mentioned in his inventory. The gap between the social standards of the bulk of the farmers and the more cultivated tastes of the time is shown by the inventory of the rector, William Holloway, who died in the autumn of 1689. His is the only inventory to list such things as a couch, a safe, a glass cage, a looking-glass, and a close-stool. For the rest of the community in the late seventeenth century the contrast with the previous century was largely a matter of quantity rather than quality. They had a few more household comforts than their ancestors, but few of the new refinements of their rector.

3 · The families

Few of the families that put down their roots in the parish of Myddle during the sixteenth and seventeenth centuries had been resident there during the previous century. The similarity with Wigston Magna is again marked. Professor W. G. Hoskins has written of the Leicestershire village, "The fifteenth century had seen an almost complete change in the village population", following the great depression after the Black Death, "but after this great re-shuffle the community settled down and stabilised itself". In 1670, about 36 of the 82 different Wigston families had been resident there for over a hundred years.[4] The tenement farmers of Myddle had tenures as secure as the freeholders and copyholders-of-inheritance of Wigston, and they, too, were remarkably stable over a long period of time.

The Goughs are a good example of one of these families. They came into the parish of Myddle in the 1530s from Tilley, where they had been copyholders of about £60 per annum.[5] Richard Gough, the first of five generations of that name, rented a tenement at Newton-on-the-Hill from the ancient owners, the Banasters, and first appears in the manorial rolls in 1538. After his death in 1575, his eldest son, Richard II, purchased this tenement, and he and his descendants appear in the manorial rentals paying a 3*s.* chief rent and 2*s.* 8*d.* for a fifth part of the Brown Heath in Harmer. The Goughs became substantial yeomen and one of the most stable and respected families in the neighbourhood. Richard Gough V, the historian, was often described as gentleman rather than yeoman, and he bought or rented adjacent pieces of property to add to his small freehold. The family was one of the oldest in the parish by the end of the seventeenth century.

According to Gough,[6] the Lloyds were possibly the most ancient family in Myddle village. They owned a freehold tenement near the north door of the church and another small freehold tenement in Houlston, which they normally let to tenants. A John Lloyd is named in the subsidy rolls of 1524 and 1544, and in the manorial rolls of 1528–42, and six generations of his direct descendants continued to live in Myddle throughout the sixteenth and seventeenth centuries. The heads of the family, and some of the younger sons, were described as farmers and eventually as yeomen, but the most junior members of all were craftsmen, such as glovers or weavers. The later generations were able to add to the modest wealth of their ancestors. When John Lloyd II died in 1568 his personal estate was valued at £20, but at the close of the century his son, Ralph, left personal goods worth over £84. During the next few years, Ralph's son, Richard, started to rent an extra 45 acres of woodland and moorland from the lord, together with another house and barn, and after the Restoration, Richard's grandson, Thomas, bought a small tenement in English Franckton and some lands in Balderton and Newton. Another Thomas lived at Myddle in 1701, while his elder brother served as rector of Petton. Between 1524 and 1701, seven generations of Lloyds had prospered in their freehold tenement and gradually added to their possessions.

The history of the Haywards is not quite so straightforward, but a branch of this family was to be found at their Balderton freehold tenement from at least 1538 until well into the eighteenth century. Thomas Hayward, yeoman (1570–1634), added to this tenement (which was held at a £14 chief rent of the manor of Hardwick, and formerly of Haughmond Abbey) by purchasing another small freehold tenement in Newton from the Corbetts of Stanwardine, in exchange for £20 and some of his Balderton lands. The Haywards never farmed this Newton tenement, but let its two cottages to labourers, weavers, and ale-sellers. Thomas's son and namesake soon resold it, only for the family to buy it back later in the century. They seem to have profited on each occasion from these speculations. They continued to live at Balderton, and Gough describes Thomas Hayward II as "a handsome, gentile man, a good country scholler and a pretty clarke. He was a person well reputed in his country and of a general acquaintance . . . He was skilled in the art of good husbandry". In addition to his Balderton and Newton possessions, he owned some land outside the parish that he had inherited from his uncle, and was able to call himself a gentleman. He married the daughter of the Shrewsbury High School master and "had a good fortune with her in money, besides houses in towne of considerable yearly value". However,

> Shee was a comely woman, but highly bredde and unfit for a country life, besides shee was shrewd with tongue, soe that they lived unquietly and uncomfortably, and their estate consumed insensibly. Hee had litle quietnesse att home which caused him to frequent publick houses merely for his naturall sustenance, and there meeting with company and beeing generally well beloved hee stayed often too long . . . This Thomas Hayward sold and consumed all his estate and was afterwards mainetained on charyty by his eldest son.[7]

But the Balderton tenement continued to be held by the Hayward family, for Thomas was able to sell it to his younger brother, Richard (1604–84), who had served as a cook at Lea Hall and then went to London to serve Bishop Juxon. During the Civil Wars he worked for William Pierpoint, a leading Parliamentarian, and upon the Restoration he returned to his old master, who was promoted to archbishop. Richard lost a lot of money through paying the debts of his younger brother, Henry, a London woodmonger, who had become bankrupt and had fled to Ireland. Richard bought the Balderton tenement and lived there for several years in retirement, "in good repute amongst his neighbours", bequeathing his property to Robert, the eldest son of his brother, Thomas, for he had no child of his own. This Robert had served an apprenticeship with a London silver refiner and followed his master's religious beliefs as a Fifth Monarchy man. His master went bankrupt and moved to Wales where he worked as a factor for Dutch merchants in the lead trade. Robert succeeded him in the post, then married a Shropshire woman and lived for a time in Shrewsbury before he inherited the tenement at Balderton. With his wife's portion he bought the Newton freehold that had once belonged to his grandfather. He, too, was childless, and so he took Robert II, the youngest son of his brother, Thomas III, a London silversmith, to be his heir, and, in 1686, set him apprentice to a white draper in Shrewsbury. The line of descent was devious, but for all their chequered history the Haywards had retained their Balderton tenement through at least six generations.

Some of the tenements held for three lives were also farmed by the families that were remarkably stable in the parish during the sixteenth and seventeenth centuries. A good example are the Braynes who lived in a house by the village street in Myddle. None of the family appears in the earliest records, but a William Brayne, husbandman, was assessed in the 1544 subsidy roll. He died in 1562, and in the survey of the following year, his widow was renting the tenement at 9*s.* per annum, with a Myddlewood leasow at 2*s.* 6*d.* p.a. She was succeeded by her son and then by her grandson, both of whom were called William. This William III had five sons and two daughters. The youngest boy, Samuel (1619–61), became the ploughboy, and then the groom, to Mr Chambre of Petton, and William IV (1612–38), the eldest surviving son, inherited the tenement at Myddle. But William died when he was only 25, leaving a poor widow (who died nine years later) and an unborn child, William V. The third son of William III was Michael Brayne (1615–83), who had been a servant to a brewer and baker in Haughmond, and who returned to Myddle upon the death of his brother, William IV. Gough regarded him as honest and peaceable, but he neglected the upbringing of his nephew, who was eventually sent away after he had been caught stealing meat (which some held he only stole through hunger). This Michael was taxed on one hearth in 1672, and though he was described as yeoman in his inventory in 1683, his personal estate was only valued at £18 7*s*. 0*d*. He had married Susan, the only child of Roger Lloyd of Myddle, who had opposed the wedding and given them nothing (though, later, he bequeathed £50 each to two of their daughters). Michael and Susan had four daughters, three of whom grew up to marry Myddle farmers, and two sons, Michael and Samuel. This Michael Brayne II (1652–95) displeased his father by marrying the bastard of a spinner called Black Nell. One of their children, Michael III (1683–1746), married in turn and carried on the family line well into the eighteenth century.

The Formstons were another long-resident family and one of the most prolific in the parish. They were tenants of the lord at Marton, where William Formston was recorded as early as 1529. By 1563 he was holding two tenements in Marton at the yearly rent of 13*s*. 4*d*., with pasture in Myddlewood rented at 5*s*. p.a. When he died in that same year he left £10 16*s*. 8*d*. worth of personal estate to his widow and their three sons, Thomas, John and Richard. This Thomas had a son and namesake who was paying an increased rent of £1 2*s*. 4*d*. and an entry fine of £6 13*s*. 4*d*. for his tenements in 1602. Thomas II had married Margery Chaloner, the daughter of the Myddle blacksmith, in 1593, and they had five sons and four daughters. Three of these children died young, but Mary married a Shropshire man, Susan married Bartholomew Pierce, a local tailor, and four boys grew up to marry and to start different branches of the family. William, Stephen and Samuel were all renting tenements from the lord in 1641, and Thomas III became a servant to Roger Kinaston of Hordley, esquire, before moving to London, where he died of the plague. His son, Thomas IV, returned to Marton for a short time, enlisted on the side of the king during the Civil Wars, and was killed in battle.

William was the eldest surviving son, and he combined working on his father's tenement at Marton with his weaving craft. He married a daughter of the junior branch of the Juxes who lived in the Houlston Lane cottage, and he and his wife settled down there for a time until he bought a tenement in Marton from Thomas Ash (who had fallen into debt), and sold the cottage to his brother-in-law,

Brayne

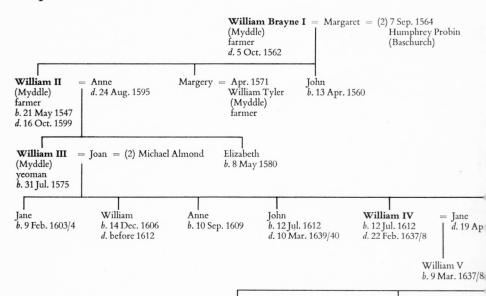

William Brayne I (Myddle) farmer *d.* 5 Oct. 1562 = Margaret = (2) 7 Sep. 1564 Humphrey Probin (Baschurch)

Children of William Brayne I and Margaret:

- **William II** (Myddle) farmer *b.* 21 May 1547 *d.* 16 Oct. 1599 = Anne *d.* 24 Aug. 1595
- Margery = Apr. 1571 William Tyler (Myddle) farmer
- John *b.* 13 Apr. 1560

Children of William II and Anne:

- **William III** (Myddle) yeoman *b.* 31 Jul. 1575 = Joan = (2) Michael Almond
- Elizabeth *b.* 8 May 1580

Children of William III and Joan:

- Jane *b.* 9 Feb. 1603/4
- William *b.* 14 Dec. 1606 *d.* before 1612
- Anne *b.* 10 Sep. 1609
- John *b.* 12 Jul. 1612 *d.* 10 Mar. 1639/40
- **William IV** *b.* 12 Jul. 1612 *d.* 22 Feb. 1637/8 = Jane *d.* 19 Ap

Child of William IV and Jane:

- William V *b.* 9 Mar. 1637/8

- Jane *b.* 30 Nov. 1642 = 24 Apr. 1668 Francis Clayton (Hollins)
- Alice *b.* 4 Aug. 1645 = 24 Ap John (Myd

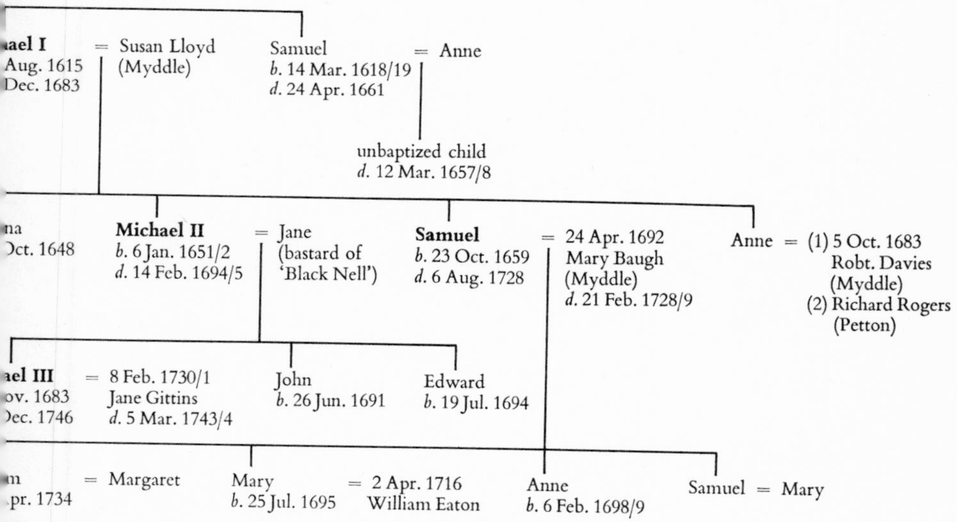
ael I
Aug. 1615
Dec. 1683
= Susan Lloyd
(Myddle)
Samuel
b. 14 Mar. 1618/19
d. 24 Apr. 1661
= Anne
unbaptized child
d. 12 Mar. 1657/8
na
Oct. 1648
Michael II
b. 6 Jan. 1651/2
d. 14 Feb. 1694/5
= Jane
(bastard of
'Black Nell')
Samuel
b. 23 Oct. 1659
d. 6 Aug. 1728
= 24 Apr. 1692
Mary Baugh
(Myddle)
d. 21 Feb. 1728/9
Anne = (1) 5 Oct. 1683
Robt. Davies
(Myddle)
(2) Richard Rogers
(Petton)
ael III
ov. 1683
Dec. 1746
= 8 Feb. 1730/1
Jane Gittins
d. 5 Mar. 1743/4
John
b. 26 Jun. 1691
Edward
b. 19 Jul. 1694
m
pr. 1734
= Margaret
Mary
b. 25 Jul. 1695
= 2 Apr. 1716
William Eaton
Anne
b. 6 Feb. 1698/9
Samuel = Mary

Formston

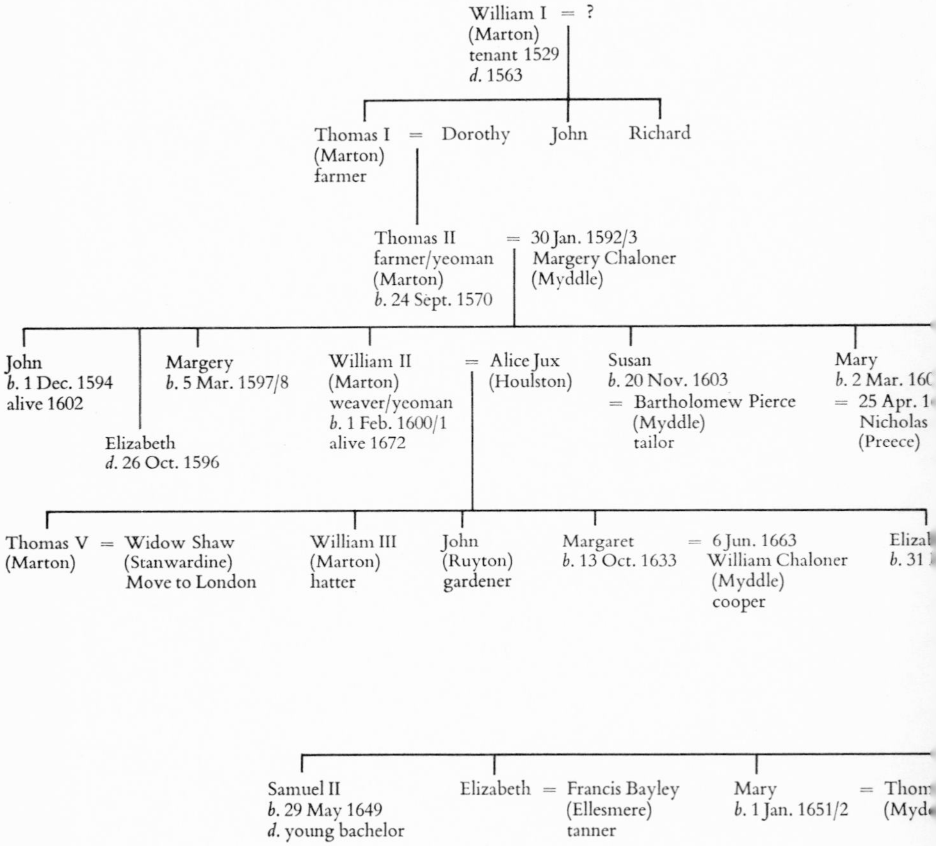
William I = ?
(Marton)
tenant 1529
d. 1563
Thomas I = Dorothy
(Marton)
farmer
John
Richard
Thomas II = 30 Jan. 1592/3
farmer/yeoman
(Marton)
b. 24 Sept. 1570
Margery Chaloner
(Myddle)
John
b. 1 Dec. 1594
alive 1602
Elizabeth
d. 26 Oct. 1596
Margery
b. 5 Mar. 1597/8
William II = Alice Jux
(Marton)
weaver/yeoman
b. 1 Feb. 1600/1
alive 1672
(Houlston)
Susan
b. 20 Nov. 1603
= Bartholomew Pierce
(Myddle)
tailor
Mary
b. 2 Mar. 16C
= 25 Apr. 1
Nicholas
(Preece)
Thomas V = Widow Shaw
(Marton)
(Stanwardine)
Move to London
William III
(Marton)
hatter
John
(Ruyton)
gardener
Margaret = 6 Jun. 1663
b. 13 Oct. 1633
William Chaloner
(Myddle)
cooper
Elizal
b. 31
Samuel II
b. 29 May 1649
d. young bachelor
Elizabeth = Francis Bayley
(Ellesmere)
tanner
Mary = Thom
b. 1 Jan. 1651/2
(Myd

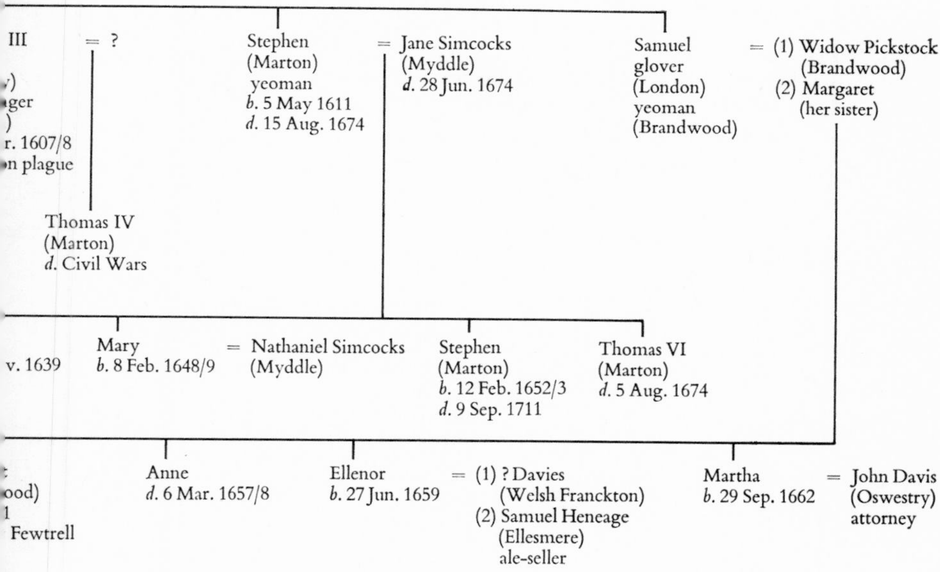
III
= ?
·)
·ger
)
r. 1607/8
·n plague
Thomas IV
(Marton)
d. Civil Wars
Stephen
(Marton)
yeoman
b. 5 May 1611
d. 15 Aug. 1674
= Jane Simcocks
(Myddle)
d. 28 Jun. 1674
Samuel
glover
(London)
yeoman
(Brandwood)
= (1) Widow Pickstock
(Brandwood)
(2) Margaret
(her sister)
v. 1639
Mary
b. 8 Feb. 1648/9
= Nathaniel Simcocks
(Myddle)
Stephen
(Marton)
b. 12 Feb. 1652/3
d. 9 Sep. 1711
Thomas VI
(Marton)
d. 5 Aug. 1674
ood)
1
Fewtrell
Anne
d. 6 Mar. 1657/8
Ellenor
b. 27 Jun. 1659
= (1) ? Davies
(Welsh Franckton)
(2) Samuel Heneage
(Ellesmere)
ale-seller
Martha
b. 29 Sep. 1662
= John Davis
(Oswestry)
attorney

Bartholomew Pierce. William Formston prospered in his new tenement and was soon able to describe himself as yeoman. But some of his children brought his name into disrepute. One of his daughters, the wife of William Chaloner, the Myddle cooper, became known as a thief and as the mother of whores. John, the youngest son, left the parish to become a gardener at Ruyton, William II became a hatter but drank himself into poverty, and the eldest son, Thomas V, married a Stanwardine widow, spent her money, and was forced to sell the tenement he had inherited from his father. After moving to Oswestry to sell ale, he fled to London to avoid his creditors, and with his departure the senior branch of the Formstons became extinct in the locality.[8]

A third son of Thomas Formston II was Stephen (1611–74), who inherited the family tenements at Marton and who was taxed upon two hearths in 1672. He left over £32 worth of personal estate and was always described as yeoman. His wife was a local girl and she bore him three sons and a daughter. John died in childhood, Thomas VI lived at Marton and was taxed on one hearth in 1672, but died about the same time as his father, Mary married into her mother's family, and Stephen II (1653–1711) fled the parish after fathering a bastard on one of his cousins. However, he must have returned later in life for he was buried in Myddle churchyard.

The youngest son of Thomas Formston II was Samuel, who was brought up as a glover. He lived with his brother, Thomas III, in London for a time, but returned upon the outbreak of plague in the 1630s. Gough describes him as "a swaggering brave young man and a crafty sutle person".[9] He married the widow of Richard Pickstock of Brandwood (the last of an ancient family there), which marriage "soe displeased the younger sister that she would not come neare them; butt the elder sister dyed not long after and left noe child beehinde her, and then Margaret the younger sister, who was soe discontented with her sister for loveing and marrying Samuel Formeston, was content to marry with him herselfe, which soon after was done". Samuel enfranchised his wife's copyhold lands in Tilley and added the High Hursts to his Brandwood tenement, so that he was soon being described as yeoman. His son and namesake, however, died before he was married, and although Samuel had six other children, all of them were girls. Five of them grew up and were married, and the tenement passed to the eldest daughter, Margaret, and her husband, James Fewtrell, a Shropshire man. At the end of the seventeenth century the Formston clan seemed to have ended through the lack of male heirs, after being so prolific in the parish for so long a time, but Stephen eventually returned and the family name was carried on until well into the nineteenth century.

Another prolific family was that of the Groomes, who for several generations had an estate in Sleap town just outside Myddle parish. It was their custom for the eldest son to inherit this estate upon marriage and for the father to 'retire' as the lessee of Sleap Hall. They continued to farm their own estate throughout the seventeenth century but lost the Sleap Hall lease after John Groome (born 1618) had farmed incompetently and had wasted most of his stock. This John's younger brother, Richard, married Margaret Clowes, the heiress of a tenement leased from the lord in Marton. They had no sons, and their five daughters all married Shropshire men from outside the parish. The youngest daughter married her cousin, Richard Groome II, the son of her uncle, John. They, too, had five daughters, and also a son to carry on the family name. A junior branch of the Groomes were weavers and labourers who rented Gittins' freehold tenement in Houlston. They, too, survived into the eighteenth century.

Finally, another long-resident family was the Tylers, who were already split into four local branches by the time of the survey of 1563. One branch lived in the chapelry of Hadnall and rose to gentry status, another prospered as freeholders in Sleap town, a third were tailor-farmers in the half-tenement just to the west of Myddle churchyard (but they died out in the seventeenth century), and a fourth held a small freehold tenement in Balderton, where they lived as yeomen well into the eighteenth century. It was this Balderton branch that became the most notorious 'Bad Family' in the parish, and more will be said about them later.

There were other tenements in the parish where the male line failed but where the property passed in unbroken descent through heiresses. For example, a tenement next to the parsonage in Myddle village remained in the hands of the Dodds and their in-laws, the Mansells, throughout the period 1524–1701. William Dodd was recorded in the 1524 subsidy roll and was at that time the constable of Myddle Castle. But the male line failed two generations later, and when his granddaughter married (in 1600) Walter Mansell of the parish of Lilleshall, the young couple inherited the tenement. Three Bartholomew Mansells in turn ensured that this family of farmers continued to lease the tenement throughout, and beyond, the seventeenth century.

The descent of a small neighbouring tenement was much more complicated. Thomas Wilton, the rector of Myddle from 1568 to 1596, built a messuage in the village and added to it a piece of Myddlewood Common that adjoined Lloyd's freehold, and for which he was paying a 6*d*. rent in 1588. After his death, a newcomer to the parish, "a covetouse, rich old fellow" called William Gosling,[10] took a new lease from the lord and steadily added to his property by renting new leasows in Myddlewood, so that by 1641 he had two cottages and 58 acres in all. His son, William, had been apprenticed to a Shrewsbury mercer in 1635, but died before his father, so William's younger daughter, Elizabeth, inherited the property. She married Peter Lloyd, a younger son of an Oswestry family, husbandman to Mr Gittins of Castle Farm, and bailiff of the lordship of Myddle. Their son died a bachelor, and so their daughter, Alice, the wife of Thomas Lovett, park-keeper at Plash, inherited the tenement. Thomas and Alice were living in Myddlewood in 1701, but their son had gone to be a soldier, and so their daughter and her husband,

Hodden

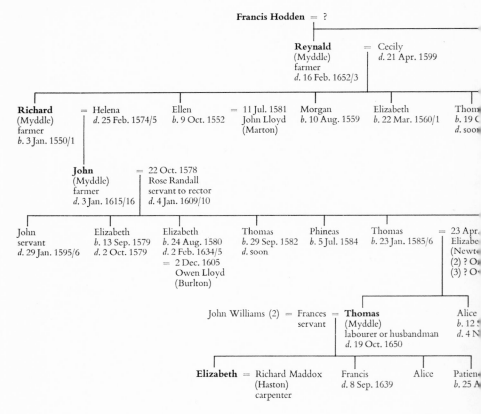

Francis Hodden = ?

Reynald (Myddle) farmer *d.* 16 Feb. 1652/3 = Cecily *d.* 21 Apr. 1599

Richard (Myddle) farmer *b.* 3 Jan. 1550/1 = Helena *d.* 25 Feb. 1574/5

Ellen *b.* 9 Oct. 1552 = 11 Jul. 1581 John Lloyd (Marton)

Morgan *b.* 10 Aug. 1559

Elizabeth *b.* 22 Mar. 1560/1

Thom *b.* 19 C *d.* soo

John (Myddle) farmer *d.* 3 Jan. 1615/16 = 22 Oct. 1578 Rose Randall servant to rector *d.* 4 Jan. 1609/10

John servant *d.* 29 Jan. 1595/6

Elizabeth *b.* 13 Sep. 1579 *d.* 2 Oct. 1579

Elizabeth *b.* 24 Aug. 1580 *d.* 2 Feb. 1634/5 = 2 Dec. 1605 Owen Lloyd (Burlton)

Thomas *b.* 29 Sep. 1582 *d.* soon

Phineas *b.* 5 Jul. 1584

Thomas *b.* 23 Jan. 1585/6 = 23 Apr. Elizabe (Newt (2) ? O (3) ? O

John Williams (2) = Frances servant = **Thomas** (Myddle) labourer or husbandman *d.* 19 Oct. 1650

Alice *b.* 12 *d.* 4 N

Elizabeth = Richard Maddox (Haston) carpenter

Francis *d.* 8 Sep. 1639

Alice

Patien *b.* 25 A

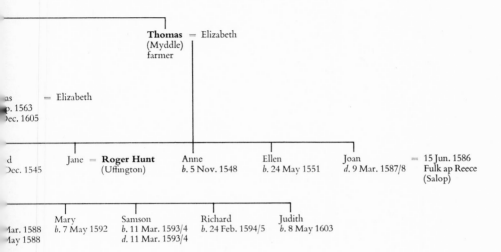

Thomas = Elizabeth
(Myddle)
farmer

as = Elizabeth
p. 1563
Dec. 1605

d
Dec. 1545

Jane = **Roger Hunt**
(Uffington)

Anne
b. 5 Nov. 1548

Ellen
b. 24 May 1551

Joan = 15 Jun. 1586
d. 9 Mar. 1587/8
Fulk ap Reece
(Salop)

Mar. 1588
May 1588

Mary
b. 7 May 1592

Samson
b. 11 Mar. 1593/4
d. 11 Mar. 1593/4

Richard
b. 24 Feb. 1594/5

Judith
b. 8 May 1603

John Huett, a Myddle blacksmith, lived in Wilton's original cottage. The property had changed hands only through the normal pattern of descent, but the absence of male heirs had brought fresh names three times during the last half-century.

Some men, like William Gosling, were able to increase the size of their holdings, but other long-established families sometimes found they had to relinquish part of their property. The Hodden family leased a tenement from the lord that was sited near the church lych gates. Richard Hodden was recorded in the manorial rolls of 1530–42, and in the subsidy roll of 1544 Francis Hodden was assessed at 8*d*., the same tax that was paid by Kinaston, Moore, Gittins, and Lloyd, the richest farmers in Myddle village. The tenement was probably divided between Francis's sons, Reynald and Thomas. Three of Thomas's children appear to have died young, another died less than two years after her marriage, and the only surviving daughter married Roger Hunt of Uffington. Late in the sixteenth century the Hunts came to live on Thomas's share of the tenement, which in 1640 was described as one wood leasow of 16 acres and a house and backside of four acres, for which the Hunts paid an entry fine of £58 and an annual rent of 9*s*. A nephew of the main line eventually inherited the property and let it to under-tenants. Meanwhile, Reynald's descendants continued to live on the 44 acres that comprised the major part of the original tenement for three more generations until the male line failed. The property passed through marriage to a Haston carpenter, and by the end of the seventeenth century it had been sold to a Shrewsbury man, who sub-let it.

Another tenement to be divided was a holding in Brandwood that the Corbetts of Stanwardine Old Hall leased from the lord and sub-let to the Bickleys. In 1617 it consisted of 86 acres and brought the lord an annual rent of 16*s*. 6*d*. The Bickleys are not recorded in the lay subsidies nor in the early manorial court rolls, but Roger Bickley, the servant of Robert Jux, was buried in 1543, and according to Gough, Thomas Bickley of Brandwood, farmer (died 1588), was his son. The manorial records confirm Gough's statement that Noneley's tenement was created out of Bickley's when Morgan Bickley (born 1578) had to part with some land to his two sisters in order to pay their legacies. The Noneleys eventually inherited one sister's part through marriage and bought the other part, but they declined to the level of labourers and poor husbandmen, and in some cases into paupers. They continued to be very poor well into the eighteenth century, but the Bickleys fared better as yeoman-tenants of what was left of the old tenement.

A final case where a tenement was divided involved property that the Wright family of farmers and labourers leased in Marton from the Corbetts, and before them from the Hords and Kinastons of Walford. They first appear in the manorial rolls of 1542, but may well have been in Marton earlier, without being recorded by the manorial stewards and rent-collectors. They continued to live on the Corbetts' land for several generations, and just after the Restoration, Thomas Wright was able to purchase the fee-simple of this tenement. But in order to pay for this, he had to sell half to Thomas Freeman, the younger son of a Wombridge family, who had married one of the Groomes of Marton. The Wrights continued in Marton until 1699, when they sold their lands to the Groomes and Freeman and left the parish their ancestors had lived in for so many generations.

A few of the most ancient families in the parish became extinct well before the end of the seventeenth century. The family of Hussey "was of great antiquity and repute in the parish" and was named in the 1524 subsidy roll for Balderton. They held a small freehold tenement there of the manor of Hardwick, and rented eight acres of pasture in Myddlewood. However, a rare case of broken marriage ended their local connection in the early seventeenth century. John Hussey had been guardian to a young woman with £100 portion, "and for covetousnesse of that money, old Hussey marryed her to his son, Richard Hussey, whilst they were under yeares of consent to marriage".[11] The marriage broke up after the girl's adultery with William Tyler, and Hussey left to serve a knight in Kent, on the recommendation of Robert Mather, who bought the Balderton tenement. Mather had come from Kent as a royal purveyor and had married into a wealthy Preston Gubbals family. His son, Thomas Mather, yeoman, was given the Balderton property and was succeeded by his son, Robert II, who died there in 1705 with personal estate worth over £72.

Not very far away at Newton-on-the-Hill, the Jux family were yeoman freeholders over five generations, but became extinct before the end of the seventeenth century. Their tenement had once belonged to the Banasters, and then to the Husseys, before being sold to outsiders. In 1550 Arthur Jux exchanged most of his lands in his native Haston for the major part of this property, and then a few years later he bought the rest of the land, and the cottage that went with it, from a Shrewsbury draper. Meanwhile, a younger branch of the family was renting a Houlston Lane cottage by 1544, but the third generation left to sell ale at the Eagle and Child, and although they had ten children the family soon died out or left the parish in search of a better life elsewhere. Four generations followed Arthur Jux at Newton. The first two did well, and the second in particular earned a good reputation as a capable churchwarden at the time of the rebuilding of the church. But the head of the third generation was "beloved of few", and his son, "by his bad courses . . . soone gott far in debt".[12] He had to sell his lands to Richard Gough, the historian, and left a poor widow and several small children upon his death. The family that had prospered at Newton for so long left the parish almost as paupers.

The Woulfs were another old family, who rented a half-tenement in Myddle village. They are first recorded in the manorial rolls of 1537, and then appear consistently as husbandmen or labourers (or in one case as a blacksmith) until the late seventeenth century. The line ended dramatically when old Richard Woulf poisoned himself rather than suffer any more abuse from his son-in-law, Richard

Clarke. Upon Woulf's death, Clarke and his wife left the parish, and a new lease was taken by the rector.

The second of three recorded suicides in Myddle ended the lease of Gossage's tenement, which lay on the opposite side of the street to the church, on the site of the present rectory. Roger Gossage was named in the subsidy roll of 1524, and was succeeded by his son and then by his grandson, a man of yeoman standing. However, the fourth generation, John Gossage, was one of the most notorious characters in the parish. He had fathered a bastard at the age of 16 and soon earned a reputation as "a drunken, debauched person". He was arrested for counterfeiting "Middle sixpences" in his back yard, but acquitted with the help of the gaoler, Edward Meriden, who bought his lease on condition that he maintained Gossage for the rest of his life. "This Edward Meriton for some while kept servants to manage this tenement; but they were such as had beene acquitted of fellony, and were continued in gaole for non-payment of fees". Meriden is recorded in the rentals as owning the lease in 1634 and 1656. Later, his son came to live here upon his marriage, and "lived very high, keeping a packe of beagles". Upon his father's death he inherited the post of Shrewsbury gaoler and sold his lease to Mr Thomas Price, who first let and then sold the lease of the tenement to Richard Eaton of Hodnett, "a drunken, debauched person", who acted for a time as manorial bailiff, and who was taxed on one hearth here in 1672. "As often as hee went to Shrewsbury, hee would bestow ale of John Gossage, whom hee called his lease, and would many times sit up drinkeing with him all night".[13] But after a drunken quarrel, Gossage swallowed arsenic and died, and Eaton's lease was terminated. He was, however, able to purchase a new lease and was succeeded by his son, who married a Brayne and had seven children to continue the family name into the eighteenth century.

Another old family which had disappeared long before the end of the seventeenth century was the Pickstocks. The senior branch rented a tenement from the lord in Brandwood and first appear in the 1563 rental, when Richard Pickstock, farmer, was paying 9*s*. rent for his tenement and a further 5*s*. for pasture in the newly-enclosed Myddlewood. Three generations succeeded Richard, and by the end of the sixteenth century they were being described as yeomen. However, Richard II died when he was only 21 and the senior branch became extinct. His uncle started a yeoman family in Haston, which survived throughout the seventeenth century, but the junior branch in Houlston did not last as long. They were labourers and poor husbandmen, originating with Richard I's younger son, but they ended in the third generation when John Pickstock "gott a wench with child and fled away".[14] His mother died a pauper in 1659 – the last of the Pickstocks in the parish of Myddle.

Two large tenements remain to be mentioned. The lord held only one tenement in the hamlet of Newton-on-the-Hill, but it was a considerable one of 79 acres. It

7. Myddle church. St Peter's church was a Saxon foundation, but nothing of the ancient fabric survives. The nave and the chancel are Victorian, but the tower was built in Grinshill stone in 1634, after the collapse of the old wooden steeple. Gough tells us that the local mason, John Dodd, "had for his wages £5 a yard for every yard from the bottom of the foundation to the toppe of the battlements".

8 and 9. Tyler's tenement. A half-tenement to the west of Myddle church held by the Tylers, then the Pierces, both farmer-tailors. The house has been considerably altered and enlarged and is now divided into cottages. The central chimney may well be in the original position, but the upper storey and the roof are later additions, with paintwork cleverly simulating timber panels.

10. The Red Lion. The Red Lion stands in Myddle village on land once belonging to Eagle Farm. Internally, there is nothing to suggest that it was once an old farm-house or inn. The absence of a central door, and the general appearance of the building, suggest that it was originally a barn built in the seventeenth century by the Gittins family or later occupants of Eagle Farm.

was leased during the sixteenth century by the Deakin family, who were recorded there in the manorial rolls of 1528. Richard, the third of the Deakins, died a yeoman in 1612, and having no children he left his property to his wife's nephew, Roger Sandford of Wellington, a wealthy man who "kept the best hospitality of any man in this Parish in his time".[15] But he, too, had no children, and his widow married Mr Hodgkins or Hoskins of Webscott Farm, who spent all her money. They were eventually forced to sell the tenement to Thomas Newans, a younger brother of the Newans of Grinshill, who "was unskilled in husbandry, though hee would talke much of it". Newans was still holding the tenement in 1656, but then went to Ireland for a time before returning to settle in Shrewsbury. He was succeeded at Newton by Francis Smith who had previously bought a small freehold tenement in Balderton, and who gave the Newton lease to his son, Daniel. This turnover in occupiers was continued in 1697 when Daniel's widow and children left upon his death and sold the lease to Richard Hatchett, the son of a wealthy Shropshire family. By that time the tenement had changed hands almost as often as some of the farms.

A tenement of 88 acres in Divlin Wood had been created relatively late during the reign of Queen Elizabeth out of the moors and commons. George Watson held this tenement in 1588, but he met with an untimely death by drowning at Harmer. The property was then split between Thomas Parr (succeeded by John Lloyd) and Thomas Guest, who was followed by his son, Richard, who worked as a badger, and then, in 1679, by Richard II (1642–94), a yeoman who left personal estate worth nearly £100. Guest's widow married Francis Watson, a Myddlewood tailor, and they were living in the tenement at the close of the seventeenth century.

4 · *Stability*

This detailed examination of the histories of each of the tenements has revealed a section of the community that was far more stable than the one immediately above it in the social scale. Whereas there were frequent changes of ownership of both the larger and smaller farms so that long-resident families stood out as being worthy of remark, with the tenements it is those that did *not* remain in the hands of the same family that are seen to be the exception. Many of the families that were there in 1701 had been there since at least 1544, if not 1524, or even earlier. It was these families that formed the core of the community, that helped to give it some sense of permanency, for as will be seen in the next chapter, the labourers and their families did not settle in the parish until comparatively late, and then they were the most mobile and unstable element of all.

This is not to imply that the husbandmen and yeomen who farmed these tenements were men of limited vision, who rarely ventured out of the parish. Several of them worked elsewhere for a time before they came into their inheritance.

Younger brothers and sisters might leave the parish altogether, or bring in outsiders upon their marriage, and the eldest son, too, often found his bride beyond the parochial boundaries, if rarely from outside his county. Individual fortunes within the family could vary as much as in any other group, and younger sons often came back into the parish to succeed to the tenement upon the premature death of the eldest.

Amongst the gentry and the substantial yeomen of the parish, fortunes were often quickly made and lost just as rapidly. There was not the scope for such extremes amongst the tenement farmers. Some, like the Lloyds or William Gosling, gradually acquired a bit more property, and others, like the Juxes or the Gossages, went to ruin, but for most of them, the material standards varied little from generation to generation. There was a general improvement in the standard of living, but this did not affect the comparative standing of these families. Most of them continued to be described as husbandmen, occasionally aspiring to the rank of yeomen, from one generation to the next. Nearly all of them had only one hearth at the time of the tax collection in 1672.

The reasons for this stability are their perseverance against decline, set against their lack of resources to expand, and the fact that their holdings were too small to attract the speculators. The tenements that were most prone to change were the freehold ones: in the sixteenth century Houlston attracted the wealthy families who were wishing to invest their money, and there were some changes in Balderton, too. However, the Goughs and Juxes of Newton, and the Haywards of Balderton, were all freeholders who were as long-resident as almost any. The lord's large tenement in Newton also changed hands frequently, but most of his tenants, especially the ones in the village of Myddle, were there for several generations, and when names did change (as, for instance, when the Mansells took over Dodd's tenement) this was often because there were no male heirs and the property had passed to a married daughter. The longevity of these families meant that they were inevitably related to each other through marriage, which strengthened the bonds between them, and increased their importance as the stable element in the community. This close-woven web of kinship will be examined in more detail in the last chapter.

CHAPTER FIVE

The craftsmen and the labourers

1 · The craftsmen

The craftsmen formed an important occupational group within the sixteenth- and seventeenth-century community of Myddle. One man in every nine was described in this way in the parish registers of the middle-sixteenth century, and one man in every seven earned his living from some craft or other a hundred years later. Perhaps one should say he earned part of his living, for these men were not divorced from the land. Most of them had at least a small-holding, while some had tenements as large as those of the husbandmen and yeomen. Nor were these craftsmen always recognizable as a separate group, for several of them were either linked by marriage to the farmers or else were younger sons who had turned to a craft for their livelihood. The families that were distinct from the rest were those who plied the same trade for generation after generation. The Chaloners were the village blacksmiths and coopers, the Raphes and Wagges were its carpenters, the Hordleys and Taylors were well-to-do yeoman-tailors, and at the other end of the scale there were poor weavers like the Parkeses of Newton and the Davieses of Myddlewood.

One would naturally expect to find a certain number of craftsmen. Blacksmiths were employed in shoeing horses and making small and varied items of iron for the farm and the home, specialist carpenters would be needed for the skilled tasks that were beyond the ordinary man, and cobblers, masons, tailors and weavers were commonly found throughout the country. So, given the fact that Myddle had so much good building stone and an abundant supply of wood, and that it was so near to the flourishing cloth market at Shrewsbury, it is perhaps surprising that it did not have many more craftsmen than it did.

For instance, in the period 1541–1660, the parish registers record only two masons. The first was John Lloyd of Myddle, who was described as pavior in 1581, and the other was Adam Dale, who worked in Myddle for a time as a mason during the Commonwealth period, sharing a cottage there with William Vaughan, a weaver. Gough also mentions the man who built the church tower in the year 1634. "The mason that built it was one John Dod, who afterwards lived at Clive. I have heard that he had for his wages £5 a yard for every yard from the bottom of the foundation to the toppe of the battlements".[1] (His mason's marks can still be clearly seen.) Gough's first item in his list of natural conveniences that the parish enjoyed was that: "There is great plenty of freestone which is very serviceable for building and soe firme that noe violence of weather will decay it; butt the longer it continues the harder it is".[2] Why, then, were there so few masons in Myddle? The stone on Harmer Hill and Myddle Hill was easy to quarry and a convenient stone to build with, but the basic building material continued to be timber. There was not enough work at any one time to employ more than a few skilled masons, and good as the local stone was, it did not compare with the famous Grinshill stone a mile or two away. Skilled masons were more likely to be found in that vicinity, at least until there was much more of a demand for building stone.

The parish registers record the names of nine carpenters, but they belonged to just two families, the Wagges and the Raphes. The coopers are the only other woodworkers to be recorded. There were no wheelwrights and no joiners, and the skills of the carpenters must have embraced all these different specializations. But even in the newly-created tenements and cottages at the edge of Myddlewood there were no recognizable groups of wood-craftsmen, though one wonders if some of the labourers were part-time woodworkers who did some carving in the evening, but who were never designated as such. The parish supported only two recognizable families of wood-craftsmen at a time.

Wagge's small tenement was enclosed out of Myddlewood by John Wagge I, sometime between 1563 and 1588. The property consisted of a cottage and eight acres of woodland, for which he paid 4*s.* 6*d.* rent. He and his wife, Alice, had ten children, five of whom died in infancy. Another girl died in her mid-30s, Rosa married Henry Taylor, a husbandman-weaver of Divlin Wood, Anne married John Raphes of Marton, the other carpenter in the parish, John Wagge II followed his father's craft at Brandwood, and the eldest son, William, inherited the family tenement and business in Myddlewood. William had three sons and at least three daughters, but only Alice seems to have survived childhood. Upon her marriage to William Parker, labourer, the family name is heard of no more.

The Raphes family were tenants of the lord in near-by Marton. They were not mentioned in the subsidy lists or the early manorial rolls, but when the manorial rentals first begin in 1563, they were paying a 6*s*. rent for their tenement in Marton. When John Raphes I died in 1578 his inventory totalled only £18 16*s*. 4*d*. (plus £8 for the remainder of his lease). His tools were valued at 10*s*., and the £2 0*s*. 8*d*. owed to him in debts presumably referred to his craft. His wife and children also earned a little money preparing material for the weaver, as the inventory mentions hemp, a wheel, and a pair of cards, but the bulk of his livelihood came from his farming activities. He owned ten head of cattle, a horse, a mare, and a colt, a sow and six pigs, seven geese, and some poultry, and he grew wheat, rye, and oats. His personal possessions were valued at only £2 16*s*. 0*d*.

Four of his seven children are not heard of again after their baptism. Katherine and Margaret both became domestic servants at Castle Farm and were married from there in 1593 and 1594. John Raphes II inherited his father's trade, married Anne Wagge in 1591, and lived on until well into his seventies. He and his wife had six sons and two daughters. The two eldest sons, John III and George, became carpenters at Marton, Michael became a tailor, Andrew became a servant to the Kinastons, and Richard, the youngest, also became a tailor and an efficient parish clerk. Richard had seven children by his first marriage, and five by his second, and it is hardly surprising to hear that he was exempted from the Hearth Tax on grounds of poverty.

John Raphes III (1592–1648) continued the main line with an only child, John IV (born 1647). This fourth John was taxed on one hearth at Marton in 1672, and was described by Gough as a peaceable man whose "phanatical opinions" kept him away from church.[3] He followed the family's craft of carpenter, married twice, and had three daughters and two sons, George and John V. Throughout the period under discussion there was at least one John Raphes at Marton who could be called upon to perform the skills of the carpenter.

Another craft family, though the line was not so long, was that of Matthews of Myddle, the village cobblers and shoemakers. An Edward Jux was a cobbler in 1553, a William Matthews in 1611, and a John Matthews in 1634 and again in 1651 (though he was described as labourer in 1649). The senior branch of the Matthews family lived at the house by the higher well and were farmers there. William Matthews was a younger brother who first appears in the manorial rentals in 1597, paying 2*s*. rent. He was paying the same sum in 1617 "for his newe howse in Midle". John Matthews was no doubt his son. "Hee was a cobbler", writes Gough, "and haveing full imployment hee followed his worke constantly and soe maintained himselfe and family".[4] His son and namesake followed him, but he had no male heirs, and at the end of the century, Thomas Highway, whose father had come into the parish upon his marriage to a Chaloner, had taken over the role of village cobbler.

Raphes

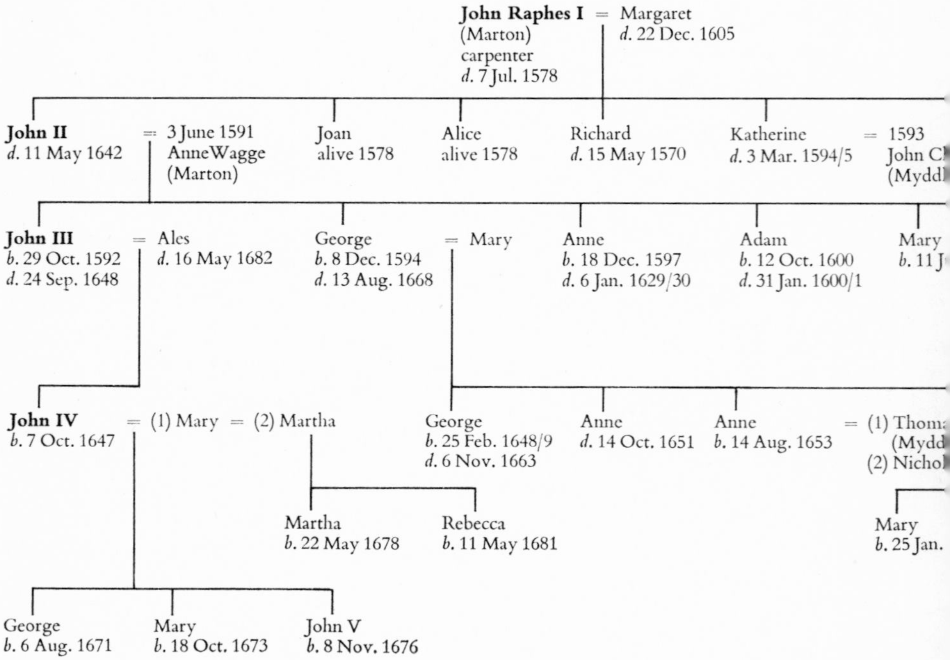
John Raphes I
(Marton)
carpenter
d. 7 Jul. 1578
=
Margaret
d. 22 Dec. 1605
John II
d. 11 May 1642
=
3 June 1591
AnneWagge
(Marton)
Joan
alive 1578
Alice
alive 1578
Richard
d. 15 May 1570
Katherine
d. 3 Mar. 1594/5
=
1593
John C
(Mydd
John III
b. 29 Oct. 1592
d. 24 Sep. 1648
=
Ales
d. 16 May 1682
George
b. 8 Dec. 1594
d. 13 Aug. 1668
=
Mary
Anne
b. 18 Dec. 1597
d. 6 Jan. 1629/30
Adam
b. 12 Oct. 1600
d. 31 Jan. 1600/1
Mary
b. 11 J
John IV
b. 7 Oct. 1647
=
(1) Mary
=
(2) Martha
George
b. 25 Feb. 1648/9
d. 6 Nov. 1663
Anne
d. 14 Oct. 1651
Anne
b. 14 Aug. 1653
=
(1) Thom
(Mydd
(2) Nichol
Martha
b. 22 May 1678
Rebecca
b. 11 May 1681
Mary
b. 25 Jan.
George
b. 6 Aug. 1671
Mary
b. 18 Oct. 1673
John V
b. 8 Nov. 1676

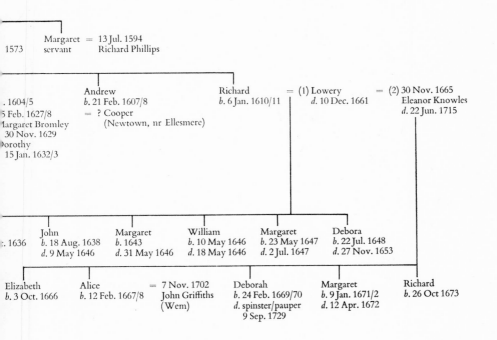

1573

Margaret = 13 Jul. 1594
servant — Richard Phillips

. 1604/5
5 Feb. 1627/8
1argaret Bromley
30 Nov. 1629
)orothy
15 Jan. 1632/3

Andrew
b. 21 Feb. 1607/8
= ? Cooper
(Newtown, nr Ellesmere)

Richard = (1) Lowery = (2) 30 Nov. 1665
b. 6 Jan. 1610/11 — *d.* 10 Dec. 1661 — Eleanor Knowles
d. 22 Jun. 1715

:. 1636

John
b. 18 Aug. 1638
d. 9 May 1646

Margaret
b. 1643
d. 31 May 1646

William
b. 10 May 1646
d. 18 May 1646

Margaret
b. 23 May 1647
d. 2 Jul. 1647

Debora
b. 22 Jul. 1648
d. 27 Nov. 1653

Elizabeth
b. 3 Oct. 1666

Alice = 7 Nov. 1702
b. 12 Feb. 1667/8 — John Griffiths
(Wem)

Deborah
b. 24 Feb. 1669/70
d. spinster/pauper
9 Sep. 1729

Margaret
b. 9 Jan. 1671/2
d. 12 Apr. 1672

Richard
b. 26 Oct 1673

The Chaloners were the village coopers and blacksmiths, and one of the most prolific families in Myddle. Their names crop up in every type of record with bewildering frequency, with five Alans, four Williams, and four Georges to confuse and frustrate the person who tries to work out the family tree. But the painstaking task is finally rewarded by a detailed picture of an 'ordinary' family of villagers – craftsmen, farmers, and labourers – over a period of 150 years. These are among the unsung countrymen who together formed the majority of England's population, and about whom we know far less than about the aristocracy and gentry.

A Roger Chaloner of Myddle, carter, married a local farmer's girl in 1569, but nothing more is heard of him. He could well have been the younger brother of Alan Chaloner, blacksmith, who founded this village dynasty. Alan married a daughter of the Tylers, the Balderton yeomen, in 1552, and erected a cottage and smithy on a waste place by the village street on the east side of Myddle church. His garden and orchard were small affairs, but he took out a 21-year lease on 3 acres of land from the newly-enclosed Myddlewood and built a barn there. So with a small farm and his blacksmith's shop, he and his wife, Elizabeth, were able to raise seven of their eight children. When he died in 1601, Alan left personal estate valued at £39 17*s.* 8*d.*, which even when one deducts the £10 for his leases and £5 for his working tools and coals, still leaves him on a more prosperous level than the labourers and many of his fellow craftsmen, and reasonably well off by the rural standards of those times. His inventory records three cows and nine beasts, a nag, corn and hay on the ground and in store, and beef and bacon, valued all together at £15 2*s.* 0*d.*; with personal possessions within the house, consisting of beds, bedding and linen, brass, pewter, and frying and dripping pans, cupboards, table, coffers, and many small items, together with his clothes, accounting for the remaining £9 15*s.* 8*d.*

In later life he had added to his two small fields, and his sons were to make considerable extensions. At the time of his death, his son, Morgan (born 1564), was no longer alive, and his only daughter, Margery, had left to marry Thomas Formston, a Marton farmer, a few weeks before her 23rd birthday. They had four sons and two daughters. Alan's widow died in the closing weeks of 1604. Alan had directed in his will that upon her death the lease of his house, and the barn in the town-end, together with the lease of a wood leasow in Marton, were to go to his youngest son, George, who had already inherited the work tools and the smithy. The eldest son, Thomas, who was almost 21 years older than George, had gone to live in Ellesmere and was given four nobles [£1 6*s.* 8*d.*] "as his childes parte". All the other children were given a shilling each, as they no doubt had been provided for earlier. The second son, John, does not appear in the baptism registers, but his marriage to Katherine Raphes, daughter of John Raphes I, the carpenter, and servant girl to Widow ap Probart of Castle Farm, is recorded in 1593. She and her newly-born son died 20 months later. John married again and he and his widow died within a few months of each other in 1627–8. This John appears in the manorial records as paying an entry fine of £1 and a yearly rent of 4*s*. 6*d*. for woodland in Myddlewood. His father was paying 7*s*. 8*d*. rent in 1588, but his widowed mother paid only 2*s*. in 1602, so John may well have inherited the land but not the smithy and the original clearings. He was described as labourer in 1595 when his father was still alive, but was entered as yeoman upon his death in 1627. As he had no children of his own, he bequeathed his property to one or more of his nephews, the sons of his brother, Richard.

The third of Alan Chaloner's sons, William, would have been unknown to us had he not been mentioned in his father's will. Three of the Chaloner boys are unrecorded in the baptism registers and Gough only knew of two of the seven, even though six of them grew to manhood. (Gough had an amazing memory but his account must be treated with caution, especially for these early generations.) The fifth son, Roger, appears to be the one who died a yeoman at Marton in 1637, but how he rose to that rank it is impossible to say. This leaves the fourth son, Richard, who is described as carter and then as cooper, and the youngest son, George, who had stayed at home to work with his father in the blacksmith's forge and who had become his own master at the age of 27. It will be convenient to deal with his side of the family first and then to come back to Richard.

George married Elinor, another of the Balderton Tylers, but died when he was only 41, leaving her to support four young children aged between two and 14. Another baby had already died. Elinor's life was marked by misfortune. A few years later she married John Gossage, one of the most disreputable members of the community, but the marriage lasted only one night. After Gossage had crowned a notorious career as a thief, drunkard, counterfeiter, and prisoner, by poisoning himself, Elinor was free to marry again; this time to Francis Davies, a Marton farmer. Her eldest son was Richard Chaloner, "an untowardly liver, very idle and extravagant, endeavouring to supply his necessytyes rather by stealeing than by his honest labour".[5] He had a bastard son, Richard, who was partly maintained by the parish and who was killed at Edgehill during the Civil Wars. Richard then came to Myddlewood, took up labouring, and married a wife who bore him two sons and three daughters. He was too poor to pay the Hearth Tax in 1663 and 1664, but was better off by 1672 when he was taxed on one hearth. He was then 71 years old, but his death is unrecorded.

George and Elinor's two daughters are not heard of again, but Alan (who was only 12 when his father died) carried on the tradition of the youngest son taking over the blacksmith's forge. He was altogether different from his brother, Richard, and took pride in his work. In 1634 he was paying an improved rent of a guinea for his forge and his new enclosure in Myddlewood, and although he was described as a pauper four years later[6] he was still able to pay an increased entry fine.

Chaloner

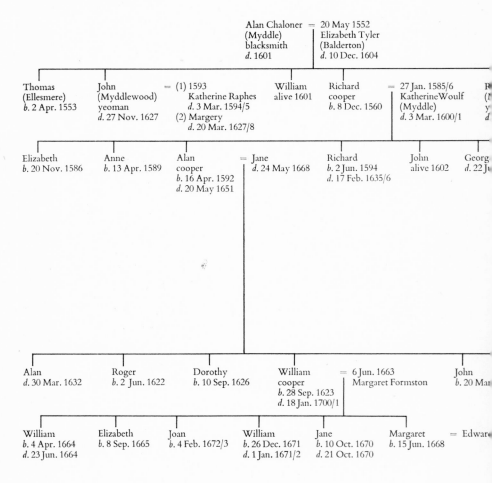

Alan Chaloner (Myddle) blacksmith *d.* 1601 = 20 May 1552 Elizabeth Tyler (Balderton) *d.* 10 Dec. 1604

- Thomas (Ellesmere) *b.* 2 Apr. 1553
- John (Myddlewood) yeoman *d.* 27 Nov. 1627 = (1) 1593 Katherine Raphes *d.* 3 Mar. 1594/5; (2) Margery *d.* 20 Mar. 1627/8
- William alive 1601
- Richard cooper *b.* 8 Dec. 1560 = 27 Jan. 1585/6 Katherine Woulf (Myddle) *d.* 3 Mar. 1600/1
  - Elizabeth *b.* 20 Nov. 1586
  - Anne *b.* 13 Apr. 1589
  - Alan cooper *b.* 16 Apr. 1592 *d.* 20 May 1651 = Jane *d.* 24 May 1668
    - Alan *d.* 30 Mar. 1632
    - Roger *b.* 2 Jun. 1622
    - Dorothy *b.* 10 Sep. 1626
    - William cooper *b.* 28 Sep. 1623 *d.* 18 Jan. 1700/1 = 6 Jun. 1663 Margaret Formston
      - William *b.* 4 Apr. 1664 *d.* 23 Jun. 1664
      - Elizabeth *b.* 8 Sep. 1665
      - Joan *b.* 4 Feb. 1672/3
      - William *b.* 26 Dec. 1671 *d.* 1 Jan. 1671/2
      - Jane *b.* 10 Oct. 1670 *d.* 21 Oct. 1670
      - Margaret *b.* 15 Jun. 1668 = Edwar
    - John *b.* 20 Mar
  - Richard *b.* 2 Jun. 1594 *d.* 17 Feb. 1635/6
  - John alive 1602
  - Georg *d.* 22 J
- R (M y *d*

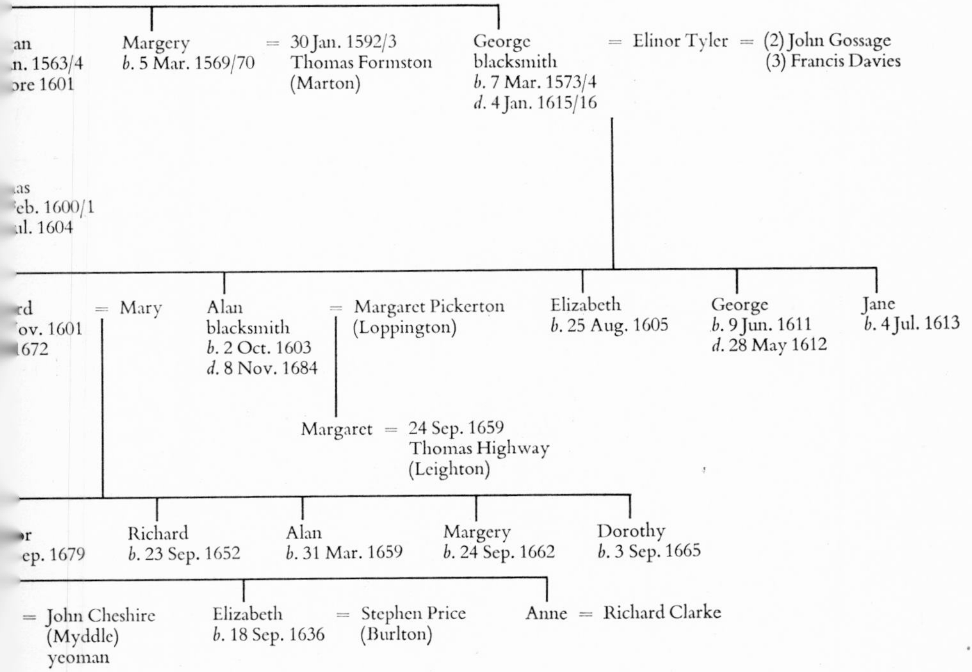
Margery
b. 5 Mar. 1569/70
= 30 Jan. 1592/3
Thomas Formston
(Marton)
George
blacksmith
b. 7 Mar. 1573/4
d. 4 Jan. 1615/16
= Elinor Tyler = (2) John Gossage
(3) Francis Davies
= Mary
Alan
blacksmith
b. 2 Oct. 1603
d. 8 Nov. 1684
= Margaret Pickerton
(Loppington)
Elizabeth
b. 25 Aug. 1605
George
b. 9 Jun. 1611
d. 28 May 1612
Jane
b. 4 Jul. 1613
Margaret = 24 Sep. 1659
Thomas Highway
(Leighton)
Richard
b. 23 Sep. 1652
Alan
b. 31 Mar. 1659
Margery
b. 24 Sep. 1662
Dorothy
b. 3 Sep. 1665
= John Cheshire
(Myddle)
yeoman
Elizabeth
b. 18 Sep. 1636
= Stephen Price
(Burlton)
Anne = Richard Clarke

His property was described in 1640 as "1 new leasowe being 4 [old] acre of woodland, 1 Barne, 1 Barne Yarde being 3 new acre of woodland, 1 Ancient cottage, 1 small [torn]". He was also presented at the manor court for "cutting, fleeinge, and burninge of the waste", and by his exertions he was safely out of poverty with one hearth in 1672. Yet he had to struggle hard for what he had, ever since his father had died. Alan lived to be 81. He was in trouble at the bishop's visitation[7] of 1665 for not attending the sacrament, but otherwise he seems to have led a life that would have been spoken of in terms of approval. He brought up a kinswoman's bastard daughter until she was able to go into service, and saw his own daughter, Margaret, married in 1659 to Thomas Highway of Leighton. The blacksmith had no son of his own, and so Highway succeeded him upon his death. Three years later, Highway, not being a blacksmith himself, was presented at the manor court for converting the smith's forge into a cottage without adding the statutory four acres of land. He seems to have had ideas about sub-letting it as a dwelling-place for some poor labourer or other, and as the Woulfs already had a new blacksmith's forge by the main road on Myddle Hill, the old smithy of the Chaloners was used no more.

The other branch of the Chaloner family began with Richard Chaloner, the cooper, of Myddlewood. Richard was born in 1560, and at the age of 25 he married Katherine, the daughter of Richard Woulf, a Myddle farmer. In 1588 he was paying only 2*s*. rent for his small piece of land, but by 1617 he had a new enclosure in Myddlewood for which he paid 39*s*. per annum, in addition to his original smallholding. Gough wrote that this new enclosure was "out of that part of Myddle Wood which lyes towards Marton, and is called the Hooke of the Wood".[8] His wife died in 1601 shortly after the birth of their seventh child. Her first had been born just over nine months after their marriage, and she had had seven children in 15 years. There is no record of what happened to the two daughters, but the youngest child, Thomas, died when he was only three, and John and George died in their youth or early manhood. Richard lived to be 41 at Myddlewood and rose from husbandman to yeoman. It might, in fact, have been he and not his father who made the new enclosure in Myddlewood. The Chaloners were renting so many new clearings in this wood that it is impossible to identify them all. However, Richard had only a daughter, Katherine, to succeed him, and as there is no record of her marriage or subsequent career, it is likely that his tenement passed to his brother, or else the option was not taken and the lease went to another family altogether.

The male line was carried on by Richard's elder brother, Alan Chaloner of Myddlewood, cooper, who was born in 1592 and died in 1651. For most of his time he lived in the woodland area and sub-let the original Chaloner cottage to Thomas Pickering, who sold ale there. Alan's wife, Jane, bore him four sons and four daughters, and survived him by 17 years. Two of the sons and one of the daughters are not heard of again after their baptisms, Alan died young, but the other four grew up and were married. Joan married John Cheshire, a Myddle yeoman, Elizabeth took Stephen Price, a Burlton blacksmith, as her husband, and they went to live in the ancient cottage that was still rented at 2*s*. per annum, while Anne married Richard Clarke, a cottager and labourer of Harmer Hill. The surviving son, William (1623–1701) did not marry until he was nearly 40, and then ended up with the unfortunate choice of Margaret Formston, and the daughters that she bore him were to break his heart. To Gough,[9] Elizabeth and Joan were "impudent whores" who had three bastards between them. One of the daughters ran away and left two of the bastards to be maintained by the parish. The other daughter was sent to Wem where she was 'last settled', presumably as a domestic servant. Two boys and another girl of William and Margaret's had died in infancy, and a third daughter, Margaret, who was different from her sisters, married Edward Baxter and lived in the old cottage at the same rent of 2*s*. a year. Before his death in 1701, William sold the lease of his tenement to his brother-in-law, Stephen Price, and so by the beginning of the eighteenth century both branches of the Chaloners had come to an end through the lack of male heirs, and it was left to cousins to come back into the parish and carry on the name.

The details of the family history of the Chaloners portray a microcosm of rural society at the farmer-craftsman-labourer level as it was in Elizabethan and Stuart England. One is struck with the way that the individual fortunes of the lowly varied as much as did those of the great. Some of the Chaloners were respected for their craft skills, others through their initiative and hard work earned the name of yeoman, but yet others through idleness or misfortune fell into poverty. There were Chaloners who lived to be 70 or 80, there were those who died in their youth or early manhood, and there were many others who never reached their first birthday. Some were fortunate in their wives; some were unusually unlucky. Some had children of whom they could be proud; some were ashamed of their offspring. Misfortune was surmounted, and misfortune became too great a burden; virtuous reputations were earned, and scandalous stories were recounted. The family was once the most prolific in the parish, but in the end the male line withered. In short, the history of the Chaloners reminds one that people living in the sixteenth and seventeenth centuries were as varied and as human as we are today.

a. The weavers and tailors

"Shrewsbury", wrote Daniel Defoe, "is indeed a beautiful, large, pleasant, populous and rich Town; full of Gentry and yet full of Trade too; for here too, is a great Manufacture, as well of Flannel, as also of white Broadcloth, which enriches all the Country round it".[10] A hundred and fifty years earlier Camden had written in much the same terms: "a fine city, well-inhabited, of good commerce, and by the industry of the citizens, their cloth manufacture, and their trade with the Welsh, very rich".[11] There is plenty of evidence that people in Myddle benefited from this trade and that some of them earned their living from it, though as a group the tailors and weavers never accounted for more than a small percentage of the community.

No Shrewsbury draper or mercer of the status of the tanners, Gittins and Atcherley, settled permanently in Myddle, but that might have happened during the middle years of the seventeenth century had not the drapers concerned, Nocke and Webbe, lost a great deal of money when their London connections went bankrupt. Balderton Hall, one of the three largest farms in the parish, had come onto the market and was bought by John Nocke, a wealthy draper in Shrewsbury, and after him by another rich draper, a Mr Webbe of Shrewsbury, but their misfortunes started soon after their purchases and so the Hall went to yet another of the seven families that were to hold it during the period 1563 to 1701. Neither Nocke nor Webbe ever lived at the Hall but were content to let it. They may never have intended to take up permanent residence there.

The Myddle gentry were sometimes connected by marriage to the Shrewsbury merchants and occasionally, like the Atcherleys, Gittinses, and Haywards, they apprenticed younger sons into the trade.[12] At a lower social level many wives and children were occupied in spinning, while most of the craftsmen combined their craft with the running of a small farm. Some of the tailors in particular were described alternatively as husbandmen or even yeomen. The trade was not by any means a mere by-employment that provided that little bit extra to keep people above the poverty line; all classes of people benefited from it.

Between 1541 and 1600 the parish registers record 13 tailors and five weavers. The first three weavers formed no permanent attachment to the parish, but the other two were the sires of families that stayed for a few generations in Myddle. William Groome of Houlston, a weaver in 1580 and still a weaver until his death in 1630, seems to have been a younger son of the yeomen at Sleap Hall. His descendants are described in the registers as labourers. The other "poor weaver" was William Parkes of Newton, held up by Gough[13] as an example of industry as none of his 11 children ever became chargeable to the parish, even though one daughter, Alice, had become crippled with rickets as a child and could not walk until she was 19. "Shee learned to knit stockens and gloves, in which imployment shee was very expert, and thereby maintained herselfe after the death of her parents". Despite the large number of children the family soon became extinct in the parish.

If one relied merely upon the evidence of the registers it would seem that only a handful of people earned their living in this way, and that the only craftsmen concerned were very poor people on much the same level as the farm labourers. But the probate inventories show that many others were involved in some way or another. Roger Nicholas, the gentleman freeholder of Balderton Hall, for instance, had three wheels, two pair of cards, two stones of wool, and forty ells of cloth recorded in his inventory in 1572. Were his female servants, one wonders, employed in carding and spinning wool during the hours when they had no domestic duties? The farmers, too, possessed wool, cards and spinning wheels. John Woulf of Myddle (1574) had a stone and a quarter of wool valued at 10*s*., and three pounds of Welsh wool valued at 5*s*.; John Raphes of Marton (1579) had hemp, a wheel, and a pair of cards; Hugh Deakin of Newton (1580) possessed four pounds of wool; Richard Woulf of Myddle (1580) owned hemp and an ell of kersey; while George Downton of Alderton (1587) had some spinning wheels, and Richard Ash of Marton (1591) owned a spinning wheel and three bags. The reference to kersey in 1580 is the only clue as to what type of cloth was being made. One would expect such a coarse material to be the standard product of the countryside, and most of the cloths made in Wales and Shropshire for the Shrewsbury staple seem to have been of this unrefined type.[14] Two other inventories mention other materials. Widow Ann Matthews (1570) had two wheels and 20 shippons of lining yarn, with which to make linings for garments; and John Hordley (1576), described as husbandman, but of a tailoring family, possessed ten ells of flax and four ells of twill, with some hemp, and three bags and a wheel.

In none of these inventories is there any mention of weavers' looms. Only the preliminary carding or heckling and the subsequent spinning were done in these homes in Myddle. The yarn would then be taken to the established weavers within the parish, or perhaps collected from these houses by the weaver or his children. There was a strict division of labour in all these processes. There was no fulling-mill at Myddle, nor has any information come to light about the task of dyeing the wool before it was finished by the Shrewsbury shearmen. The household hemp and linen goods could be completed within the parish as they did not require these processes, but everything else would have to be taken into town to be finished. The tailors probably bought their materials from the market rather than from the local craftsmen.

The tailors of Myddle were a more prosperous body than the weavers. Four of them (mainly with Welsh names) were temporary residents who are recorded only once in the registers. Three others were immigrants who settled in the parish, and the remaining six were connected with the farming families of Myddle. Some of these were younger sons who turned to the trade for employment, some eventually became farmers themselves, and others combined their craft with their farm in a most satisfactory way. The Hordleys and the Tylers are the best examples of these craftsmen-farmers.

There were Tylers who were yeomen at Balderton and others who were farmers at Myddle, as well as the tailors who rented a half-tenement in Myddle for 8*s*. a year. This was one of those ancient tenements which included land in the Hill Furlong and a part of the Binnings, and the house is still standing to the west of the churchyard. Thomas Tyler was the first of four generations of tailor-farmers;

Hordley

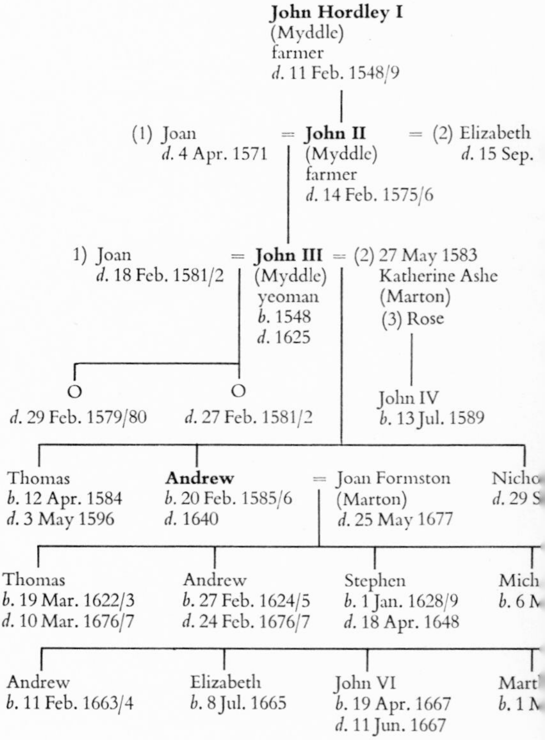
John Hordley I
(Myddle)
farmer
d. 11 Feb. 1548/9
(1) Joan
d. 4 Apr. 1571
= **John II**
(Myddle)
farmer
d. 14 Feb. 1575/6
= (2) Elizabeth
d. 15 Sep.
1) Joan
d. 18 Feb. 1581/2
= **John III**
(Myddle)
yeoman
b. 1548
d. 1625
= (2) 27 May 1583
Katherine Ashe
(Marton)
(3) Rose
O
d. 29 Feb. 1579/80
O
d. 27 Feb. 1581/2
John IV
b. 13 Jul. 1589
Thomas
b. 12 Apr. 1584
d. 3 May 1596
Andrew
b. 20 Feb. 1585/6
d. 1640
= Joan Formston
(Marton)
d. 25 May 1677
Thomas
b. 19 Mar. 1622/3
d. 10 Mar. 1676/7
Andrew
b. 27 Feb. 1624/5
d. 24 Feb. 1676/7
Stephen
b. 1 Jan. 1628/9
d. 18 Apr. 1648
Andrew
b. 11 Feb. 1663/4
Elizabeth
b. 8 Jul. 1665
John VI
b. 19 Apr. 1667
d. 11 Jun. 1667

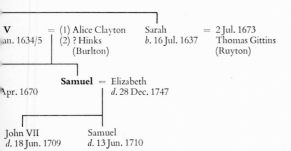

V = (1) Alice Clayton
an. 1634/5 (2) ? Hinks
(Burlton)

Sarah = 2 Jul. 1673
b. 16 Jul. 1637 Thomas Gittins
(Ruyton)

Apr. 1670

Samuel = Elizabeth
d. 28 Dec. 1747

John VII
d. 18 Jun. 1709

Samuel
d. 13 Jun. 1710

the last was William Tyler, a person "altogeather unseemely for such a calling, for hee was a bigg, tall, corpulent person, but not so bigg in body as bad in conditions". The Tylers were succeeded in their tenement by another tailor, Bartholomew Pierce.

The Hordleys were the most prosperous tailors in the parish. They rented a tenement and clearings in the old Divlin Wood by the side of the lane from Myddle to Burlton. John Hordley III (1548–1625) was the son and grandson of farmers and was himself described as yeoman upon his death, though his inventory shows that he was a craftsman as well. His son, Andrew Hordley (1585/6–1640), left personal estate worth nearly £190, which would place him well above most of the yeomen-farmers of the parish. His livestock and crops alone were valued at nearly £80, and the only items that hint at his trade are three pieces of linen cloth worth £2, wool priced at £1 13*s*. 4*d*., and debts owed to him amounting to £47 5*s*. 2*d*. Andrew's two elder sons "were rich and allways had money beefore hand".[15] They both died bachelors in their 50s, and as Stephen (also a tailor) had died at the early age of 19, and Michael had presumably died in childhood, the fifth son, John V, inherited the property and the family business.

Of the ten men who are recorded as tailors in the seventeenth century only Hugh Jones of Marton (1621) cannot be identified. All the other names have a familiar ring. Andrew Bickley of Brandwood (1571–1624) was the eldest son of a Brandwood farmer. The Brandwood–Divlin Wood area contained two or three families – the Bickleys, the Taylors, and the Hordleys – who were quite well-off as tailor-farmers. Andrew's son, William Bickley of Brandwood, was also a tailor, but William's second son was describing himself as yeoman by the end of the century. No other part of the parish had even this small concentration of craftsmen; they seem to have been scattered around indiscriminately.

Two more farmers, Thomas Mould of Myddlewood and Francis Clayton of the Hollins, appear briefly in the seventeenth-century registers as tailors. Mould's tenement was a small one of eight acres that was one of the first to be enclosed in Myddlewood. John Mould was first recorded in the manorial court rolls of 1538 and 1542, and his family continued to hold the property for several generations until the 1660s, when it passed through marriage to William Watson, another tailor, whose inventory in 1685 amounted to £42 4*s*. 4*d*., of which £10 was in a bond, and another £22 11*s*. 8*d*. was accounted for by his farm stock. But there were poorer tailors as well. Gough mentions an "idle fellow who was a taylor and went from place to place to worke in this parish, but had noe habitation".[16] There were also Michael and Richard, the two younger sons of Raphes the carpenter. This Richard was exempted from the Hearth Tax in 1664 as he "is a very poore man and hath not ground worth five shillings the yeare neither is he worth five pounds in goods".[17] The Pierce family which succeeded to Tyler's tenement also had its ups and downs; one son ended up as a soldier in Flanders and Tangiers, another fared better as the tenant of Sleap Hall, but the third worked as a labourer and lived in a cottage in Houlston Lane. He married a domestic servant, had six children, and died a pauper.

Gough briefly mentions[18] one or two tailors who lived in the parish during the closing years of the seventeenth century. Some, like Arthur Owen and Richard Rogers, never made more than a sufficient living, but those who had land and common pasture rights, like the Hordleys or Taylors, continued to live well in their woodland clearings. Abraham Taylor, who had created the family's original tenement by completing the enclosure of Divlin Wood, had been a tailor by trade as well as by name. His eldest son, Henry, had turned to weaving as well as to farming, but the other son, Richard, who had moved to Loppington, was "soe famous in that trade, that hee was of good repute in his time, and . . . had much custome, and lived in a handsome condition". Henry's son, Abraham, inherited the tenement in Divlin Wood and became a tailor too. They were never as prosperous as their neighbours, the Hordleys, but secure in their standard of living. The tailor-farmers were the wealthiest craftsmen in the parish.

Two other people appear briefly in the registers as glovers, and Gough mentions[19] a third who was living in a Myddlewood cottage in 1701. But this was only a minor occupation in the parish. As for the seventeenth-century weavers, there were 14 of them recorded between 1600 and 1660, compared with only five for the previous 60 years. Some of them were now putting down roots in the parish, such as the Parkeses of Newton, the Davieses of Marton, or the ap Robertses of Marton. David ap Roberts (1604) is the only weaver in Myddle whose inventory has survived. He had two cows, a heifer, a mare, 12 sheep, two pigs, and corn and hay, with a total value of £7 17*s*. 8*d*. The rest of his goods were valued at only £1 14*s*. 10*d*. The dual nature of the weaver-farmer's occupation is well brought out by this inventory. Looms, wool, flax, and hemp are all recorded, but the importance of the farm is shown by the much higher values of his animals and crops; and the meagre personal items that are listed show just how bare was his house and how low his standard of living.

Other poor weavers included John Dudleston, alias Hall, a weaver and "common fiddler" who lived in Castle Farm cottage, and the Davieses of Marton. Thomas Davies came from Shrewsbury in 1605 to marry Clare of Marton's only child and to live in their small tenement at the Marton end of Myddlewood. Other Davieses were recorded as weavers, and by the end of the century there were over 60 of them in the parish, working as weavers or labourers, and mostly so poor that they had to live on parish relief. Weaving remained a much poorer occupation than that of tailoring. On the other hand, a few others, like Henry Taylor and William Formston, are alternatively described as husbandmen, and John Lloyd was the younger son of an ancient and prosperous farming family in Myddle. He lived in a cottage built upon their land, and this was afterwards jointly leased by William

Bickley

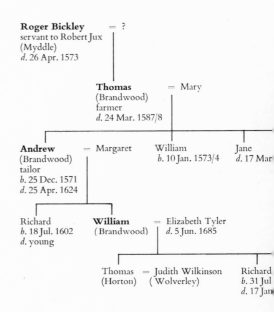

Roger Bickley = ?
servant to Robert Jux
(Myddle)
d. 26 Apr. 1573

Thomas = Mary
(Brandwood)
farmer
d. 24 Mar. 1587/8

Andrew = Margaret
(Brandwood)
tailor
b. 25 Dec. 1571
d. 25 Apr. 1624

William
b. 10 Jan. 1573/4

Jane
d. 17 Mar

Richard
b. 18 Jul. 1602
d. young

William = Elizabeth Tyler
(Brandwood)
d. 5 Jun. 1685

Thomas = Judith Wilkinson
(Horton) (Wolverley)

Richard
b. 31 Jul
d. 17 Jan

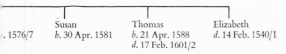

. 1576/7

Susan
b. 30 Apr. 1581

Thomas
b. 21 Apr. 1588
d. 17 Feb. 1601/2

Elizabeth
d. 14 Feb. 1540/1

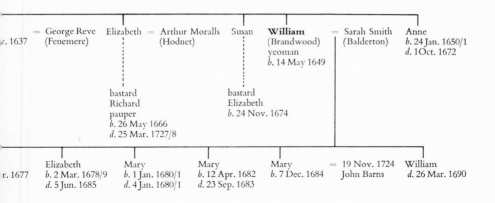

·. 1637 = George Reve (Fenemere)

Elizabeth = Arthur Moralls (Hodnet)

bastard
Richard
pauper
b. 26 May 1666
d. 25 Mar. 1727/8

Susan

bastard
Elizabeth
b. 24 Nov. 1674

William
(Brandwood)
yeoman
b. 14 May 1649
= Sarah Smith (Balderton)

Anne
b. 24 Jan. 1650/1
d. 1 Oct. 1672

r. 1677

Elizabeth
b. 2 Mar. 1678/9
d. 5 Jun. 1685

Mary
b. 1 Jan. 1680/1
d. 4 Jan. 1680/1

Mary
b. 12 Apr. 1682
d. 23 Sep. 1683

Mary
b. 7 Dec. 1684
= 19 Nov. 1724 John Barns

William
d. 26 Mar. 1690

Vaughan, a weaver, and Adam Dale, a mason. The other two men named as weavers in the registers were Alan Chaloner, the Myddlewood cooper (briefly a webster in 1633), and William Hanmer of the family of Myddlewood labourers.

The task of identifying weavers is an impossible one once the registers cease to list occupations. The names that do crop up suggest that weaving remained a poor occupation during the closing years of the seventeenth century. Gough speaks, for instance, of a poor weaver named Chidlow, who lived at Newton in a little house that had no chimney.[20] The whole drapery trade had been badly affected for a few years when Shrewsbury was a centre of military activity during the Civil Wars, but it soon recovered, so that when Robert Hayward of Balderton set his heir apprentice to a white draper, Gough could refer to it as "the wealthyest trade in Towne". But the greater part of the Myddle families that were in any way connected with the cloth trade remained involved only at the humdrum and less rewarding level of spinning and weaving.

2 · *The labourers*

The labourers form the most difficult of all the groups within the community of Myddle to identify and to comment upon in detail. They, more than any others, are recorded in only the barest details. Some probably lived in a chamber in their employer's house; others with a family of their own often lived in property that was sub-let to them. In both cases they are absent from the manorial rentals and surveys. Nor do they usually feature in the parish records (except for sparse entries in the baptism, marriage, and burial registers), for men of this class rarely became churchwardens or overseers, though they did sometimes hold the office of parish clerk. And any early records that might have shown them as recipients of charity or poor relief are lost or destroyed; only the eighteenth-century overseers' accounts and a few late-seventeenth-century apprenticeship bonds remain. They are under-represented, too, in the diocesan archives, for when they died they rarely bothered to leave a will, nor were their friends and neighbours usually called upon to draw up an inventory of their personal estate.

Fortunately, there is Gough to give family details and character sketches of some of the more unusual personalities – eccentrics like Richard Clarke, or men like Ellis Hanmer and his able family who rose out of the labouring class – but even Gough is less informative than usual when he comes to the poorer sections of the community, and most of the temporary labourers (those who did not stay in the parish for even one generation) escaped his attention altogether. On the other hand, the parish registers are unusually detailed for the sixteenth and early seventeenth centuries. From their commencement in 1541, until the Restoration of 1660, a man's occupation was normally attached to his name, and those temporary residents whom one can only suspect to be labourers in the registers of other parishes, can be definitely ascribed to this class. The occupation given in the registers provides the vital clue with which to sort out other details about the labourers from the rest of the varied information that is available.

"Shropshire", writes Dr Joan Thirsk, "was still in a semi-cleared state in the sixteenth century, affording spacious commons and waste to [the] inhabitants, and also attracting many landless migrants".[21] In a woodland area such as this, maintains Professor Alan Everitt,[22] these migrants lived in squatters' settlements in hamlets rather than in nucleated villages. This is certainly true of the parish of Myddle. There were, of course, a few cottages in the village itself, such as the tied cottage at Castle Farm, or the little apartment built on to the end of Brayne's house, but the majority lived in a colony in that part of Myddlewood which had recently been felled and cleared. The original clearings all seem to have been added to the existing farms and tenements (the 1617 rental speaks of six [old] acres of woodland "allotted to Humfry Onslowe for his land in Marton"), and there are no cottagers in the earliest rental, that of 1563. The first direct reference to a labourer coming to live in Myddlewood is in 1581 when John Ellis of Hanmer (a little village just across the border in Wales) was presented at the manorial court "for erecting of one bay of a house upon the lords waste grounde in Myddle woode".[23] Soon there were others, for the 1588 rental has a cluster of names following Ellis Hanmer as he was generally known in Myddle; John Matthews, rent 10*d*., John Hughes, 12*d*., Andrew Pickstock, 1*s*. 8*d*., and then Robert Cottrell "for a garden, 2*d*.". These are all names that at some time or other had the appendix 'labourer' in the parish registers. Later rentals speak of other families: (1602) "John Wagge,[24] all those two cottags and foure [old] acres in Middle"; (1617) "Abel Jones, for a cottage, 2*s*."; (1640) "William Parker: 1 ancient cottage with one backside containing 4 [old] acres of woodland"; and (1640) "John Gough: 1 wood leasowe containing 2 old acres or 4 new acres" in Brandwood, adjoining Myddlewood.

The reference to two old acres being the same as four new ones makes it difficult to see whether the terms of the 1589 Act, which tried to insist that new cottages should have at least four acres of land attached to them, were ever put into general effect. There do seem to have been some sporadic attempts to enforce this. In 1622, the manorial court ordered Nicholas Onslowe to eject Humphrey Clarke from the cottage he had let to him, or to provide sureties to the parish of Myddle,[25] and in 1652 Evan Jones was fined one shilling at the Quarter Sessions for erecting a cottage without the statutory four acres of land.[26] There are records of similar fines being imposed by the justices during the next century, but the only other time the manorial court seems to have attempted to enforce the statute was when Thomas Highway was fined for converting Chaloners' old smithy into a cottage in 1684.[27] There were regular fines imposed by the Court Leet for cottages on the waste, but these were merely encroachment fines – a roundabout way of getting rent. There was still plenty of land to spare, and anything that added to the manorial revenue would meet with the approval of the steward. Certainly, John Spurstowe's sixpenny rent for the Mear House (1617) suggests that he did not have much land to go with it, though Robert Cottrell probably sub-tenanted other land as well as his twopenny garden, for in later life he appears to have risen in status. But Richard Clarke's cottage on Gittins's freehold land in Newton was only built on "a butt-end".[28] Neither the lord nor the freeholders made much attempt, if any, to enforce the Act, at least, not until the middle of the seventeenth century, by which time a rising population meant that the pressure on the land was more acute and more people were having to seek parish relief.

John Spurstowe's cottage was not the only one at Harmer. Once the wooded areas were becoming filled up, the lord allowed more and more cottages to be built upon this rocky, unproductive common. In later times it provided small building plots for nineteenth-century quarrymen's cottages and for twentieth-century commuters' bungalows, but during the seventeenth century there were very few buildings here. Two others were recorded at Harmer in 1617; one belonged to Griffith ap Evan, of a line of Welsh labourers, and the other was sub-let by Richard Gittins to Richard Clarke (shortly before he moved onto Gittins's freehold land). The lord also allowed a cottage to be erected in Houlston Lane, and two more at Bilmarsh. It is difficult to give a precise number for Myddlewood, but from a careful combing of the pages of Gough there appear to have been about 14 in the year 1701.

Dr Thirsk, writing generally about woodland areas,[29] states that manorial control of the influx of landless squatters into the forests was weak, and that strong freeholders met the housing shortage by building cottages on their land to let for rent, thus often increasing the number of poor people in the parish. In Myddle the lord or his steward allowed several migrant labourers to settle upon his wastes or in his woods. It is much more difficult to pin down the number of cottages owned by the freeholders, especially as the hearth-tax returns of 1672, which might have given the precise number of households at that date, are imprecise about the number of people exempt from the tax. The freeholders paid only a nominal chief rent to the lord and there are few records (apart from Gough) of what property they let to tenants. Occasionally, the manorial rentals and surveys give a glimpse of the sub-letting of manorial lands that must have gone on. Gittins's sub-letting to Clarke has already been quoted, and the same rental of 1617 also mentions "James Wytcherley, 5 [old] acres woodland where Thomas Childlow dwelles". Gough writes[30] that Lloyd's cottage, near the Parsonage House in Myddle, was originally built for a younger brother of the Lloyds on their freehold land, but was later let to a weaver and a mason. He also remarks[31] that Davies's cottage in Marton belonged to the Atcherleys, and before them to Lloyd Pierce, esquire. There were probably several more cottages on freehold lands, for these large freeholders would need labourers to work on their estates, and it is significant that no less than 17 out of 100 or so labourers recorded in the parish registers over a period of 120 years came from the small township of Houlston which was largely freehold land owned by absentee owners. On the other hand, many of the labourers who worked on these large farms probably lived with their masters as farm-servants and not in a cottage of their own. Gough mentions pews[32] in the church reserved for the servants of large farms, and not all of these would have been female domestics. There is a lack of firm evidence here. The cottagers living on freehold land would certainly swell the ranks of those living in Myddlewood and on other manorial land, but it is doubtful whether they would exceed or even match the manorial tenants in number, and when Gough wrote about people who were labourers he largely confined his attention to the lord's tenants of the Myddlewood area, where the most conspicuous group was gathered.

The next problem concerns the standard of living of these labourers. For many of them, the wages they earned doing the many and varied tasks on the farm, from hedging and ditching, to sowing, weeding, reaping and harvesting, were supplemented by the profits of a small-holding. These consisted of just a few acres cleared from the woods, never big enough to grow corn for more than their immediate use, but sufficient to keep a few animals to care for their household wants. For these men, as for all cottagers in the woodland areas, their common rights, especially their rights of pasture, would be vital.[33] (They were not illegal squatters, but had leases for their cottages, thus acquiring common rights.) But the felling of the woods and the great influx of labourers had, of necessity, already curtailed some of these rights, especially that of pannage. The manorial courts were already imposing restrictions on this right during the reign of James I. However, there were still extensive commons upon which to pasture cattle and sheep. There were still 236½ acres of commons until the Enclosure Award of 1813, and over 132 acres of these lay close to the labouring community in Myddlewood. Only three labourers' inventories survive, but they show the importance of their livestock. This was true for the labouring classes in all regions of England and Wales.[34] Others of labouring rank had a by-employment, like weaving, to maintain them as well. Not all the craftsmen lived at this low economic level, but many of them could hardly be distinguished from the labourers except that they worked for a large part of their time at a distinctive craft.

The labourers no doubt received some of their wages in the form of provisions, but much of their weekly work was paid for in ready money. The will of Edward ap Richard, of the parish of Myddle, day labourer, proved on 11 November 1668, shows that they were used to handling money and thought naturally in those terms. Ap Richard made 18 bequests, every one in a small sum of money. No personal goods, no items of furniture, articles of dress, animals or tools, were mentioned. He starts off: "I have in the hands of William Formston of Marton" £6, of which £2 was to be set aside for his funeral expenses. He had another

£3 16*s*. 0*d*. in the hands of Stephen Formston of Marton, and further sums amounting to £4 18*s*. 4*d*. in his own possession. So he had altogether £14 14*s*. 4*d*. to share out amongst his friends, for he appears to have had no relations of his own. His friends were nearly all of the labouring class.

This total of £14 14*s*. 4*d*. is probably a fair guide to the standard of living of a seventeenth-century labourer in this area. The information is scanty and a much wider area would have to be taken to get any reliable figures, but it is probably not far off the mark to suggest that a husbandman would have personal estate worth about two-and-a-half times this amount, while the yeoman would leave something like three or four times this value. Only three labourers' inventories are available for Myddle to allow some comparison. When Morgan Clarke of Newton died in January 1626, he left personal estate worth £14 12*s*. 0*d*. Another of this clan, Francis Clarke of Newton (1692), however, was well above this figure with £23 13*s*. 8*d*., but his neighbours were unsure whether to call him labourer or husbandman. The other labourer's inventory is that of Thomas Noneley of Brandwood, who died in 1711. It reads as follows: "2 Cows £4, 1 Mare £1 10*s*. 0*d*., 1 year old Caulf 10*s*., 1 Swine 10*s*., 2 beds £1 10*s*. 0*d*., brass and pewter 8*s*., 2 iron pots 4*s*., wood vessells 3*s*., 1 box and coffer 1*s*. 6*d*., ax, hook, and shovell 2*s*., iron ware 1*s*., pair of bellows 6*d*., waring apparell 5*s*., things unseen and forgott 2*s*.; total: £9 7*s*. 0*d*." As he left all his personal estate to his wife, this is likely to be the sum total of the family's possessions, and an eloquent comment upon the poverty of some of the labouring class. His son, Thomas, was to inherit the lease after the death of his wife, and his two daughters were each given five shillings. Taking away the value of his five animals, the rest of his goods were worth only £2 17*s*. 0*d*.

Thomas Noneley's accommodation was in no way exceptional. Ellis Hanmer's original cottage of 1581 was only of one bay,[35] while another labourer, Thomas Chidlow, lived in a house at the side of Divlin Lane, which was only "a poore pitifull hutt, built up to an old oake"[36] until well into the seventeenth century. 'Soundsey' Evan Jones, a Welsh labourer, also lived for a while in a little hut in Myddlewood, but "this lytle hutt was afterwards burnt, and having a collection made in the parish and neighbourhood hee built a pretty good house".[37] Two other labouring families, the Fardos and (later) William Preece, went to the extremity of living in a cave at the Myddle end of Harmer Hill, near Lower Webscott. "This cave was formerly a hole in the rock, and was called the Goblin Hole, and afterwards was made into a habitation, and a stone chimney built up to it by one Fardo".[38] And yet this is not the whole story by any means. Labourers' houses tended to be better in the woodlands than in the 'fielden' counties,[39] and if Hanmer's cottage, which still stands so picturesquely at the side of the lane to Fenemere as it winds its way through Myddlewood, is anything to go by, then some labourers lived in well-constructed timber buildings, surrounded by an orchard and garden, and having the blessing of space. There was plenty of wood in Myddle parish with which to build such a house, and nowhere in rural Shropshire was it necessary to have those cramped, congested dwellings of the nucleated east Midlands villages. The village of Myddle itself was long and straggly, and Myddlewood, where the squatters erected their cottages, provided an attractive setting, the raw materials for building, the means of a livelihood, and room to breathe. Building and furnishing his cottage might strain a labourer's resources, especially if he had a large family to keep, but several of them were able to have a decent house. Quite probably, there was considerable differentiation within the ranks of the labourers themselves, with the Hanmers at one extreme and the Fardos at the other. Many labourers improved their lot, and they had as many ups and downs as any other section of the community.

The Hanmers' cottage is of unusual interest. Now named 'The Oaks', it can be identified with a one-bay Elizabethan labourer's cottage that was extended by the addition of another bay during the seventeenth century. According to Gough, the cottage stood "at the south side of Myddle Wood, betweene the end of the lane that goes from Myddle wood to Fennimere, and the end of the Lynch Lane".[40] With such a precise description, there can be no mistaking its identification on the 1838 Tithe Award Map and on the ground today. It is well worth describing in some detail.

It was originally rented by John Hughes, a labourer who may have been a younger son of a Haston farmer. John and his first wife, Helen, had three children born in Myddle between 1564 and 1571, but only John Hughes II (born 1571) survived infancy. By his second wife, Matilda or Maud, John I had two more children, but they, too, died young. At all the baptisms, he was described as of Myddle, labourer, but when he died in 1610 he was more precisely defined as being of Myddlewood. The cottage was not mentioned in the survey of 1563, but in 1588 John Hughes was renting a cottage at 12*d.* per annum. The rental of 1590–1 records him as paying a fourpenny rent, and another 12*d.* for land which he had ploughed up in Myddle park without the licence of the lord. The cottage stands right at the edge of the park, and it seems that the lord had allowed the original encroachment, but then charged an extra 12*d.* a year rent when Hughes broke his tenancy agreement by ploughing the land. In the survey of 1602, Hughes's property was described as a cottage or garden in Myddle, held for three lives, with an entry fine of 15*s.* The lives in the lease were those of John, Maud, and John Hughes II. This survey also had a note added to it to say that in 1641 Abraham Hanmer was holding the lease.

A rental of 1617 shows that John Hughes II was paying the same rents of 4*d.* and 12*d.* This John must have died before he was able to marry, for in 1634 Matilda (Maud) Hughes was paying the rent. She died at Myddlewood on 22 June 1635, and the cottage became vacant. Gough says[41] that Abraham Hanmer inherited the cottage by marrying Katherine Emry, but the Emrys lived across the parish boundary in Fenemere, and the Myddle parish registers for 1636 show that Abraham's wife was called Martha. But whatever the manner of inheritance, Abraham Hanmer was there in 1637, when the survey records him as holding a cottage and a garden about an acre in size at the annual rent of 16*d.* The commissioners noted that a "Richard Hughes was competitor [for a lease], who is satisfied". The Hanmers continued to hold the cottage for the rest of the seventeenth century, but by the time of the 1838 Tithe Award, Thomas Barkley (or Berkeley), the ancestor of the present owners, was the tenant.

From an examination of the existing structure[42] it would seem that the present building is twice the size of the original one. The original part nearest the lane consisted of just one ground-floor room, possibly open to the rafters. The upper floor is oddly related to the framework and may be assumed to be a later insertion, but the construction is at the moment hidden from view and one cannot be certain. The ceiling of the ground-floor room is of superior quality, with chamfered and stopped joists, and the outside walls are very strongly constructed with timbers that are ten inches wide. This original cottage was extended on the side furthest from the lane so as to form a second (smaller) ground-floor room. The present upper floor is late-nineteenth- or twentieth-century in construction, and it presumably replaced an inferior one. Whether this room was originally of one or two storeys it is not possible to say. The outer walls are of lighter construction than the other room, with the thickest timber being an eight-inch-wide stud in the gable. There can be no doubt that the present cottage was built in two parts, for the wall-plate is jointed just where the older and newer parts meet, immediately to the left of the door. However, both parts are certainly dateable between *c.* 1570 and 1700, and the whole building is basically the labourers' cottage as the Hanmers would have known it. It is far from being the hovel that labourers' cottages sometimes were, and was skilfully constructed by a craftsman. The family was safely above the poverty line with one hearth taxed in 1672, but they were always of labouring rank, even if they were amongst the most substantial of this class.

The chimney stack has been inserted into this building, for the chamfered joists of the original ground-floor room have been cut to make way for it. The stack is of stone at ground-floor level, with wooden lintels to the fireplaces, and brick above. If the cottage was already of two storeys when this took place, it is unlikely that the fire had previously been in an open hearth. Perhaps a wooden chimney on the stone base had been used, but it is impossible to say, and even so, it would still seem to have been an insertion. (The stack was inserted in such a position as to create a 'lobby entry' plan characteristic of Shropshire and Montgomeryshire.) Brick was unlikely to have been used before the end of the seventeenth century, and so both the present chimney and the brick nogging between the laths are probably dateable to the eighteenth century. The lean-to's at the back and the sides were the last parts to be added.

The number of labourers presents a problem. The general pattern for the country seems to be that in Tudor and early Stuart England the labourers formed between a quarter and a third of the entire population, with the highest proportion of labourers being found in the 'fielden' areas.[43] By the time of the Civil Wars this proportion had risen to nearly a half. The figures for Myddle do not seem to be quite as high as this, and in the early stages they were much lower. If the testimony of the baptism, burial and marriage registers is to be believed – and they are by far the most reliable guide one has – then between 1541 and 1570 only 7.1 per cent of the population were labourers. This ties in well with the evidence of the manorial rentals, for no cottagers benefited from the initial grants of land cleared from Myddlewood, and there is no definite evidence of squatter settlement there until 1581. When the labourers or cottagers appear it is in a second stage of colonization, at least a generation after the initial clearing of the woods and the draining of the meres. They appear at a time when there was a demand for labour, as farms expanded into the woods and marshes, and when a richer class of gentry had come into the parish, taking advantage of the land market and engrossing farms. This demand was met with a ready supply, for at the same time there was a national rise in the population. Increasing numbers of landless men were looking for work, and they moved into the expanding woodland regions in search of it.

By the time of the next thirty-year period (the closing decades of the sixteenth century), the proportion of labourers in the community of Myddle had risen dramatically to over a fifth and getting on for a quarter, to 23.4 per cent to be precise. The parish registers show how Ellis Hanmer was there right at the beginning of this immigration when he erected his cottage in 1581, for it was in the 1580s and the 1590s that the significant rise occurred, before it steadied down to a trickle again by the turn of the century. During the next 30 years there was some stability, or even a slight decrease, at 21.7 per cent, but then came a second wave of immigrants. A gap in the baptism registers for the early 1640s obscures the evidence, but it looks as if these new immigrants came into Myddle during the Commonwealth period until the labourers formed 31.2 per cent, or close to a third of the population. This is still somewhat lower than in other woodland areas, but it is beginning to resemble the national picture.

The labouring section could well be under-represented in the registers, as some of the temporary labourers stayed only for a very short while. Many names only appear in the registers once; often at marriage, occasionally at death, but most regularly at the baptism of a child. There must have been several others who had no cause to be recorded in the registers during their brief stay in the parish. Labourers, more than any other class, would be the most likely to be short-term residents, and the percentages that have been quoted ought to be rather higher. But even after all adjustments have been made, they still would not account for more than 40 per cent or so of the community.

Domestic servants, the female equivalent of the farm labourers, were also finding work in the parish. Several of them found a husband as well, and 14 of the first 15 servants were initially recorded in the marriage section of the registers. Morgan ap Probart and his widow Anne at Castle Farm saw seven women domestics and three male servants married from their house between 1576 and 1594. On the last occasion both were servants there. The pattern of immigration was the same as in the case of the men; there were only four domestics recorded in the first period, but 11 in the second. After 1600 they were not adequately described in the registers and no safe conclusions can be drawn.

From an analysis of the parish registers, it would seem that the population was not even maintaining itself, yet all the signs are of an expanding community competing for land. This can only point to one thing: that the population of Myddle was maintained (and possibly increased) by immigration, and that these immigrants were mostly labourers who came into the parish looking for work and who found it during periods when the native population was not able to provide it from its own numbers. The first wave came in the 1580s and 1590s, when not only was demand higher than it had been for reasons already mentioned, but when the death rate was particularly high. A harvest crisis from 1585 to 1588 had killed off nearly twice as many people as normal, and no doubt had depressed some local men into the labouring class, as well as providing opportunities for immigrants once the crisis was over. The second wave came during the Commonwealth period, after another long spell of bad harvests and higher mortality rates than usual. Following the first wave (and possibly after the second as well, though there is no evidence once the registers cease naming occupations) came a fresh period of stability, with a rising birth rate and less need for fresh immigrants to maintain the numbers. Demographic factors and the state of the economy regulated the conditions under which movement took place. But this still left plenty of scope for human initiative, good luck or bad fortune, happy accidents and personal tragedies. There were many people of all classes who came to live in Myddle during these 120 years. Some settled and prospered, some stayed but never improved their lot, while others gave up after a year or two and moved on elsewhere, never to be heard of again.

These labourers now need to be looked at in some detail so that one can find out who they were, where they came from, how long they stayed, and what happened to them and their families during their stay in Myddle. In order to make this a manageable task, these hundred or so men must be classified into various categories.

The first period (1541–70) contains only nine names, and because there are no earlier registers most of them are difficult to classify. In the first category can be placed all those who did not remain labourers all their life but who were later described as farmer or husbandman, or occasionally by a craft name. These descriptions may not always indicate changes of status but may merely be the whims of the rector or parish clerk, or the description given by a new rector or clerk. Even so, if people were uncertain whether to describe a man as husbandman or labourer, this indicates men who were better-off than the majority of labourers, and who therefore should be placed in a separate category. Only Richard Brown can be classified in this group during this early period. He was described as labourer in 1544, farmer in 1549 and 1552, but labourer again in 1565. There are no further records of the Browns; they may have moved, but the most likely explanation is that the male line died out.

The second category, and one that could well be associated with the first, is that of sons of farmers who were forced to earn their living by labouring. These were occasionally elder sons who had not yet inherited the family farm, but more often they were younger sons who only rose out of this class if death removed elder brothers and made them the heir to the family property. Several familiar names from farming stock appear only briefly as labourers, but the younger sons of some families are found in these ranks from one generation to another. Only two names appear in this first period (1541–70), but this amounts to a quarter in so small a sample. John Hughes of Myddlewood was possibly the younger son of a Haston yeoman in the chapelry of Hadnall; he is named in the registers upon his marriage to the daughter of a Newton farmer. The John Wright who baptized his daughter in 1544 was probably a younger son of the yeomen Wrights of Marton,[44] but later Wrights of Myddle appear as farmer-labourers, and so a permanent family of labouring rank could have started in this way.

A third category is those who were permanently designated as labourer. By this is meant one who remained in the parish for at least the major part of his life and who was always described as labourer. Sometimes a family remained in this class for generation after generation, but individual fortunes fluctuated as greatly then as they do today, whatever class a man might be in. There were men who successfully climbed out of this class; others were permanently in danger of poverty. John Grestocke, alias Newton, who died in 1547, appears to have been one of these, but later on Edward Grestocke, alias Newton, is listed as a farmer, and he was renting a cottage in Myddle in 1590–1. John ap Evan of Marton, who baptized his son, William, in 1560 can also be placed in this group. The connection is not certain, but there was another John ap Evan of Marton who baptized a child in 1594, and Griffith ap Evan, one of Anne ap Probart's servants, married in 1588 and stayed in the parish until his death in 1636.[45] These ap Evanses seem to belong to the same line of Welsh labourers.

A fourth and final category contains those who never rose above the rank of labourer but who appear only fleetingly in the registers. These were the mobile labourers who never put down any deep roots in the Myddle soil. Nothing is known about their fortunes in later life and very little about their previous career. Some of them died in Myddle but had not been previously recorded. There seem to be four of the 1541–70 group in this category, but the absence of previous records makes it difficult to be certain. Richard Hycockes, for instance, was described as "of Myddle" when he married a local girl in 1542, and one cannot tell whether he had spent his childhood and youth in Myddle, or whether he was a recent immigrant. He does not appear again. This sort of difficulty resolves itself in later times. Two others in this category turn up only once; Thomas Wauton of Marton upon the baptism of a child in 1570, and Humphrey Salter, the servant of Thomas Downton of Webscott, when he died in 1569. The last one, John Roberts of Marton, died in 1543. One hesitates to call him 'temporary labourer', for there was a Humphrey Roberts of Marton, farmer, with his wife and daughter in 1542, and an Alice Roberts of Marton, widow, who died in 1619. Perhaps he could be better classified as a younger son, but the proof is lacking.

So far, the system of classification has not been satisfactory, but one can speak with more confidence of the 1571–1600 group, as there are now 30 names, or nearly a quarter of those recorded in the registers. Four of these men were at one time on the husbandman level, though three of these were to end their days as labourers. A further five men appear to have been younger sons of farmers or craftsmen, while the influx of immigrants during the 1580s and 1590s led to several labourers establishing a permanent foothold in Myddle parish. Half of the 30 names between 1571 and 1600 fall within this category, and five of them had Welsh names. The Welshmen were becoming a significant element in the population, and of course there were also the prosperous Welsh Hanmers of Marton and the ap Probarts at Castle Farm who had a landed interest in the parish. Finally, there were also six temporary residents in the 1571–1600 period. Two appear in the marriage registers as the husbands of domestic servants, and both couples left the parish before any children were born. John Hodden, alias Nicholas, was the servant of William Nicholas of Balderton Hall, Thomas Gouborne came to Alderton from just outside the parish, and two others died (at Houlston and Myddlewood) in the closing years of the century.

By the early years of the seventeenth century the first great wave of immigration was over and the recorded numbers of labourers achieved some sort of stability at just over one-fifth of the population. But these figures can be deceptive; there was still mobility within the labouring class, and the actual number of temporary labourers became much higher than before.

Altogether, there are 33 names for the period 1601–30, some of whom have been mentioned before. Four men can be classified in the first category of those who rose out of the labouring class. Thomas Jux, the second son of a farmer, was a labourer upon his marriage to a Welsh girl in 1602, but by the following year he was able to describe himself as husbandman and then as innkeeper at the Eagle and

Child. The second man, William Parker of Brandwood, married Alice, the daughter of William Wagge, the carpenter. He later inherited Wagge's tenement and was able to live at a more prosperous level. Thomas Mould was the eldest son of an old farming family in Myddlewood, and once his father had died he inherited the tenement and was described as farmer himself. The other man to rise from the labouring class was Walter Mansell, who came from the parish of Lilleshall to marry Elizabeth Dodd, the heiress to a small tenement. They had eight children between 1604 and 1622, and when one of the younger ones was baptized in 1618, Mansell was described as labourer. The cost of rearing all those children must have forced him to seek additional wages on someone else's farm. But he soon recovered, and on all other occasions he was labelled husbandman.

There were also four names in the second category of younger sons of farmers, and the list of permanent labourers contains 13 names, of which Hanmer (twice), Fardo (twice), Chidlow, Clarke, and Shaw are already familiar. The other six names are new ones. Michael Crompt, alias Amon of Myddle, married a Myddle girl in April 1602, and returned to church with her to baptize their daughter 17 days later. Two other children were born, in 1604 and 1608, and though Michael is absent from later records, the burial of his widow is written into the registers for 1648. John Harries of Houlston baptized two sons and a daughter during the second decade, and two of his children married Shropshire people and continued in the parish. Another Houlston man, Thomas Mitton, baptized his child in 1624, buried her the following year, and lived on as a labourer at Houlston until 1659. Then, in 1628, a recent settler, Thomas Pickering of Myddle, married a local girl, married again after she died, and left a son, Richard, who was also to be described as labourer when he died in 1662. Myddle men were by this time becoming used to Welsh names, but in 1610 came one of the most outlandish of all – Foulk ap Preece. He came via Shrewsbury, married three times, and baptized three children at Myddle. The family settled here and in time the name softened to Preece or Price. Finally, there was John Owen of Myddle, who could perhaps come into the temporary category as he was hanged shortly before the Civil Wars. One of his sons lived on, and turns up again during the next period.

The first 30 years of the seventeenth century saw the highest number of temporary labourers. There were 12 in this group, compared with four, six, and five in the other three periods. This is at the time when the proportion of labourers in the community as a whole ceases to rise. It is true that the total number of all recorded people is a little higher during these 30 years, and that the baptisms slightly exceeded burials, but it does seem that there was less demand for extra labour than there had been, or at least that that demand had already been largely satisfied by the recent wave of immigrants. Fresh people came hopefully into the parish throughout these 30 years, but when harvests were poor and demand was slack, they were the first to go. No new clearings of the woods took place in these years, nor were the harvest fluctuations unusually severe. The community had absorbed all the labour it needed and although the farmers were prospering during these years they were unable to employ all who came in search of work. Some new names became permanent ones, but twice as many moved on in the hope of better opportunities elsewhere.

The first five temporary residents in the period 1601–30 appear only once each in the registers, and five of the others also get only a single mention. The other two were both named Griffies, but there is no evidence of any other connection. None of the 12 had an ancestor in the parish, and none seems to have perpetuated his name there. Five of them worked on freeholders' land in Houlston, with three more working at Newton, which was also mainly freehold. Only four lived in the traditional woodland area.

The final period from 1631 to 1660 is different altogether. A fresh wave of immigrants settled in the parish, and the number of temporary residents fell considerably. The situation was the same as that in the 1580s and 1590s, with the permanent labourers accounting for over half the names, with a substantial addition to their ranks from the sons of farmers. Only three men were farmer-labourers. Thomas Ash, the second son of a Marton farmer, was a labourer in 1639 but was later able to call himself husbandman. So, too, could Thomas Morris, a miller-labourer who inherited a small tenement upon his marriage. Thomas Hodden fared differently. He was the last of a long line of Myddle farmers, the only son of a husbandman. He was described as such himself in 1647, but when he died three years later he was entered in the registers as labourer. His widow was still alive in 1672 and was still able to pay the tax on her hearth, so the family had not sunk into extreme poverty.

For once there were several names (eight in all) in the second category of younger sons. Three of them came from the yeomen Trevors of Hadnall, John Matthews was a cobbler and labourer, and the younger brother of Myddle farmers, John Gough of Brandwood was the younger brother of Richard Gough IV, the Newton freeholder, John Maddox of Marton came from a farming family in Hadnall chapelry, Richard Chaloner was the cooper's son, and John Cheshire of Myddle was the son of a local yeoman.

In this period from 1631 to 1660 there are no less than 23 names within the category of permanent labourer. Three of these were Clarkes, two were Hanmers, and one was a Chidlow. There were also three Groomes whose ancestor had been a younger son, but who were now firmly within the rank of labourer. Francis Harries of Houlston, Edward Owen of Myddle, Abraham Powell of Marton, and Abel Jones of Myddlewood[46] were all sons of labourers of a previous generation. Jones is such a common Welsh name that it is impossible to say whether Richard Jones of Myddle and Evan Jones of Myddlewood were related to Abel. This Evan Jones was nicknamed 'Black Evans' to distinguish him from his namesake, nicknamed 'Soundsey Evans' [i.e. 'lucky' or 'bonny'], another Myddlewood labourer. 'Black Evans' worked as a tanner and labourer for Mr Atcherley of Marton. Gough thought him "laborious and provident",[47] and praised the tenement that he nurtured so carefully on the Marton side of Myddlewood. Another Welshman, John Griffith, may have had previous connections, but it is equally likely that he was an immigrant.

Of the new names, Roger Smith established a family in Myddle village, and Thomas Kenwicke of Myddle (whose surname suggests a Shropshire village origin for his ancestors) baptized his son and namesake in 1651, and one or the other married a Myddle woman in 1670. Gough provides a few biographical details[48] about Ralph Astley of Myddle, whose wife had previously had an illegitimate child by Sir Richard Lea, her employer at Lea Hall, who provided for the child with a lease outside Myddle parish, which the Astleys exchanged for the under-tenancy of Hunt's tenement in Myddle. The wife added to the husband's earnings by her skill at midwifery. How many other labourers' wives, one wonders, must have knitted, sewn, spun, or baked in order to keep the household going? Of the others, Stephen Davies was the son of a Shrewsbury weaver and the husband of a Marton girl; Francis Stanway of Houlston left a widow who paid tax on one hearth in 1672, and a son who was labouring towards the end of the century; Charles Reve of Myddlewood came from Fenemere, just across the parish boundary, upon his marriage to a Newton girl in 1654, and was a labourer until the day of his death in 1697; and John Williams of Myddle (one hearth in 1672) did labouring work for Mr Gittins and lived in a cottage on Myddle Hill. Gough unkindly remarked that he could speak neither good English nor good Welsh.[49]

There remains a final category of five temporary residents of labouring rank. Francis Trew of Myddlewood only appeared in the registers upon the death of his wife; John Davis, the son of Edward Davis of the parish of Kenwick, died in service at Balderton Hall; Humphrey Marter of Myddlewood baptized a son, Robert Typton baptized both a boy and a girl, and Robert Orred and his wife appeared briefly at a baptism in 1642 – he was an ale-house keeper at Lower Webscott.

What conclusions can be drawn from all this? Of the first category of people who fluctuated between the level of labourer and of farmer, seven finished up as husbandmen and five ended their days as labourers. These five could well be added to the third category of permanent labourers, and so, too, could nearly all those younger sons in the second category. Only three of the 19 definitely left the parish to seek employment elsewhere. There are a few other doubtful cases but it does seem that if younger sons were forced to earn their living by labouring, then they clung on to what was familiar to them and to the support of elder brothers in times of crisis. Most of them probably did a lot of their work on the family holding. On the other hand, there were other younger sons who were not labourers and who left the parish to take up an apprenticeship in Shrewsbury or to seek their fortune in London, or even to farm lands elsewhere. It is difficult to say whether the labourers were wise to stay in the parish; one does not know whether those who rejected the labouring life for adventure elsewhere fared any better.

The numbers in the first two categories of farmer-labourers and younger sons account for just about a third of all the recorded labourers. The rest were either immigrants or the sons and grandsons of immigrants, though by the middle of the seventeenth century several of these families had been established in the parish over a period of 60 or 70 years. On the other hand, as has been said, many temporary immigrants escaped attention in the parish registers. If one allows for these, and takes away the long-established labouring families, then one would probably still not be far out in saying that roughly two-thirds of the labouring population were immigrants.

It is an almost impossible task to try to find out where these immigrants came from. Only Gough and the marriage registers give any solid information. The easiest group to identify are the Welsh. Nine or ten different families came over the border and settled in Myddle in labourers' cottages. Some of the domestic servants who found husbands in Myddle were also Welsh girls. Some families thrived; others never left the ranks, and generation after generation served as labourers. There were also, of course, other Welshmen who came into the parish as landowners and farmers. The Hanmers of Marton and Morgan ap Probart reached the highest level, while farmers' names like Lloyd or Vaughan, and possibly Reynolds, are suggestive of Welsh origin at an earlier period. These families must have rapidly become anglicized (if they were not so before they came), even if, like the ap Probarts, they showed a preference for Welsh servants. But the labourers often remained a distinctive group, sometimes speaking English badly,[50] and possessing strange names that marked them off from the English. In time, those who stayed would become absorbed in the community, with names usually softened into their English counterparts. Gough only mentions first-generation immigrants having language difficulties, and those who grew up in Myddle probably knew Wales only as those distant hills.

Information about other groups is scanty indeed. Four labouring families came from the chapelry of Hadnall and two others came from the neighbouring parish of Baschurch. Two Welshmen came from Shrewsbury and four other families can definitely be assigned to various parts of Shropshire. This only accounts for 20 families and leaves 27 other outsiders whose origin is uncertain. A few of these have Welsh-sounding names, but they are ones that were already familiar in the border counties at that time. Even so, about a quarter of the labourers who came into Myddle during these 120 years started their journey in Wales. Further than that one cannot say, for the seventeenth century is too late a date to use surnames as proof of place of recent origin, and only a very few of these are obvious anyway.

The registers are silent about occupations during the last 40 years of the seventeenth century, but there are a few other sources that refer to at least some of the labouring class. Amongst the constable's original returns concerning the hearth tax of 1663[51] is a list of nine men and three women in the townships of Myddle, Marton, and Newton, who were discharged by certificates on the grounds of poverty. Seven names from Myddle and Newton also appear as exempt in the following year, and there are 15 recognizable names from the parish of Myddle amongst the list of exempted people in 1672. Three people appear in all three lists: Richard Raphes, Francis Davies, and Sina Davies. Richard Raphes of Myddlewood was a younger son of the carpenter, and he earned his living as a tailor and labourer, and as the parish clerk. He had married twice, and had 12 children. Francis Davies's exemption certificate of 1664 reads: he "doth not hold land worth 20*s*. per yeare to his house, neither is he worth five pounds". He was a married man, but whether his wife or any children survived him upon his death in 1674, it is not possible to say. He was one of the many Davieses who were descended from Thomas Davies of Marton, a Shrewsbury weaver who had married a Marton girl. Gough wrote: "Of these two persons, Thomas Davis and his wife, hath proceeded such a numerouse offspring in this parish, that I have heard some reckon up, takeing in wives and husbands, noe less than sixty of them, and the greater part of them have beene chargeable to the parish".[52] They earned their living as labourers or poor craftsmen. Another of this clan was Sina Davies, the widow of Thomas Davies, a poor weaver-labourer of Harmer Hill. Gough writes: "Sina Davies and her Children have for many yeares been a charge to us. Shee was a crafty, idle, dissembleing woman, and did counterfeit herselfe to bee lame, and went hopping with a staffe when men saw her, butt att other tymes could goe with it under her arme, as I myselfe have seene her, and shee had maintenance from the Parish many yeares before shee dyed".[53] Another Widow Davies was also exempt at Marton in 1663, and Thomas Davies was discharged from payment in 1672.

Of the other exempted poor, Richard Rogers of Marton (1663 and 1673) was either a tailor or a glover, for there were two people of this name living at the edge of Myddlewood. 'Soundsey' Evan Jones of Myddlewood was exempt in 1663, but after he had built a new house he was eligible for payment in 1672. And Richard Chaloner, a Myddlewood labourer, was also exempt in the early returns but paid on one hearth in 1672. There were, of course, other labourers who were always safely above the poverty line, like the Hanmers of Myddlewood, but if a labourer died before his wife, she was likely to be faced with hardship. Thus, Margery Mytton, the widow of a Houlston labourer who had died in 1659, was exempted in 1672, and so was Margaret Matthews, whose husband, John Matthews of Myddle, labourer, had died in 1666.

The 1672 list includes some labourers who had only just fallen into poverty, such as William Groome of Houlston, or Arthur Noneley of Brandwood, who had a large family of 11 children to support. Also in the list is Humphrey Beddows, a poor cobbler who had come into the parish upon his marriage to one of Sina Davies's daughters. He had fallen ill and the parish had lost their warrant of complaint against his settlement, so he could not be ejected. He never worked again, but lived the life of "an idle beggar" in his cottage on Harmer Hill. His children became a great nuisance to the overseers of the poor, for one of his daughters had an illegitimate child by a soldier, and his son, Daniel, twice ran away from the masters to whom the parish had apprenticed him, and had to be sent to the House of Correction.[54]

By the end of the century, the poor were becoming a greater problem; taxes were increasing,[55] and the resources of charities such as William Gough's were regularly used.[56] Thus, in 1682, Arthur, the son of Arthur Noneley, labourer, was apprenticed to John Ryder of Montgomeryshire, tailor, out of the funds of this charity. Richard Raphes was apprenticed to a Burlton pipemaker the following year, Francis, the son of Thomas Davies, was apprenticed to a Shrewsbury tailor in 1686, and William, the son of William Sturdy of the Whitrishes, was apprenticed to a Wem tailor in 1676. Twenty-seven such apprenticeship bonds, largely financed by the Gough charity, survive for the period 1672–1701.

By the end of the seventeenth century, the labourers were a large group within the parish of Myddle, and though no definite figures can be given, they must have formed almost half of the community. In the early and middle years of the sixteenth century they had been a very minor body, often related to the existing farming families, and thinly scattered about the parish. All that was altered after the immigration of the 1580s–90s and of the 1630s onwards. By the close of the century, the labourers were a numerous and distinctive group, and the Myddlewood area was peculiarly their own.

The detailed personal histories of three labouring families illustrate these general themes, while showing that individual fortunes could fluctuate as much as they did amongst any other section of the community. The Hanmers, the Chidlows, and the Clarkes each have very different stories.

a. The Hanmers

In 1581 Ellis Hanmer was presented at the manor court of Myddle "for erecting of one bay of a house upon the lords waste grounde in Myddle woode". He promptly paid the entry fine, and with a 21-year lease at 12*d*. per annum, he was able to set up home and start a family that was to be based in Myddlewood for about two centuries.

Hanmer is a rather late example of the derivation of a surname. To his original parishioners he was known as John Ellis, but to the men and women of Myddle he was Ellis of Hanmer, for that was the Flintshire village from whence he had come. He is described in both the parish registers and manorial records by this name. To the genealogist this is a pity, for there was another (gentry) family of Hanmers in

Myddle parish at the same time, and the names of their widows and younger children were confusingly similar to those of their less prosperous namesakes. Gough was hazy about the first two generations and puzzles one by describing the original John as a butcher.[57] The Latin used in the registers was "lanii", which suggests someone connected with the wool trade in a humble sort of way.

This John had a daughter who died in infancy, and four sons, three of whom left no record after their baptism. He was succeeded by his son and namesake, "John Ellis, alias Hanmer", who added an adjoining piece to his property and acquired a lease of the lord's fishing rights at Marton Pool. His father had been paying 3*s*. 8*d*. rent in 1588, but John's improvements meant that his annual rent was increased to 10*s*. In spite of this, at the baptism of his eldest son in 1596, and again at his own death in 1636, he was described as labourer. But he and his wife, Katherine, who was to outlive him by only 17 days, were determined that the lot of at least their eldest son, Thomas, should be a better one.

Thomas was born in 1596 and lived to be nearly 74. He was "brought up to bee a good English scholar", and after a spell as a ploughboy at Acton Hall, where he was "soe crosse among the servants that hee was turned off", he kept a petty school at Shawbury, and was employed to read the service there when the vicar was officiating at another church. He inherited his father's property in Myddlewood and was described as "clerk" in the manorial survey of 1640, when he was renting the cottage, two pieces of woodland, and the fishing rights at Marton Pool. The survey of 1637 makes it clear that the family was still living in the cottage that was erected in 1581. His son was educated at Oxford, became a Doctor of Divinity, married into a well-to-do Cheshire family, and became the minister of a church near Wrexham. This son also had a bastard son, Daniel, who was brought up by his uncle, Abraham.

John and Katherine's second son, Richard, was born in 1601. He lived for a time in Myddlewood and then at the Mear House at Harmer, and was described as labourer when his daughter was born in 1629. In 1634 he was holding a wood leasow at the improved rent of £1, but he left the county soon afterwards to find employment at Sandbach forge, where he ended his working days as overseer of the coals. The youngest son, William, died at the age of 14. The other boy was Abraham, who was born in 1604, and destined to remain a labourer all his life. He was "a litigiouse person among his neighbours, much given to law". He married the only daughter and heiress of another labourer, and went to live in the Myddlewood cottage referred to earlier. The family remained there throughout the seventeenth century and beyond. They were safely above the poverty line with one hearth taxed in 1672.

One of Abraham's sons, William, was a weaver who died in 1656 at the early age of 20. The other son, Thomas, died less than three months later, and so Abraham took his eldest brother's bastard, Daniel, and raised him up as his own.

Daniel was to marry Alice Owen of Yorton, and their eldest son, Daniel (1678–1766) carried the line on into the eighteenth century.

b. The Chidlows

Roger Chidlow of Newton appears to have been one of the immigrant labourers of the 1580s and 1590s. He first appears in a rental of 1590 when he was paying 4*d.* rent for a cottage in Newton, which he held "without licence". He was described as labourer when his wife died in 1596, but both before and after that he was called farmer or husbandman. He seems to have had three sons, James, Jacob and Thomas, but one cannot be quite sure. James Chidlow was a weaver, and Gough could remember his widow living in a little house in Newton that had no chimney. This was on Gittins's freehold land and was probably the same one that had been rented by his father. The house was later rebuilt and let to other labourers.

Jacob Chidlow was a tailor in Brandwood, but he died young, his infant son also died, and his widow soon remarried. Thomas also moved to Brandwood, where he set up home in "a poore pitifull hutt, built up to an old oake" at the side of Divlin Lane. This was later converted into a much better house, with one hearth taxed in 1672, but when the children were being born in the late 1590s and the early 1600s (and there were eight in all) they must frequently have been haunted by the spectre of poverty.

Thomas had been born in 1566 and never acquired any other label than that of labourer. The Wicherleys, and later the Lloyds, sub-let a small piece of woodland to him, and no doubt employed him on their land. The struggle to raise eight children must have been a never-ending one. Two of the younger sons and the youngest daughter probably did not survive childhood, though they may have left the parish in search of work. Roger, the eldest son, was a servant to Roger Sandford, the Newton yeoman, for many years, and died childless soon after his marriage to a woman from Acton Reynold. The second son, Thomas, found similar employment with Widow Hancox in nearby Broughton. He eventually married this widow, and after her death he worked for Captain Corbett of Shawbury Park, to whom he left all his money upon his death.

Another son, Samuel, fared well. He married an orphan girl who was working as a servant at Acton Reynold, and as they were "both provident and laborious"[58] they were able to save up a substantial sum out of their wages. When Samuel died, he left £100 to his wife, £100 to his son, and £200 to his daughter. Thrift and hard work had enabled another poor labourer's son to rise in the world. It depended very much upon individual character and temperament. His sister, Margaret, appears briefly in the registers as the mother of an illegitimate son who died only a day or two after he was born. She is not heard of again.

The two eldest sons had left home, so James, who was three or four years older than Samuel, became tenant at Brandwood after his father. He was married twice, but both his son and eldest daughter died while they were still young, and so when he died in 1676, at the age of 63, the little cottage, that had seen such a struggle to earn a living and keep children alive, passed to his other daughter and her husband, Thomas Taylor, the eldest son of their neighbour, and a tailor by trade as well as by name. He was still sub-tenanting the property at the close of the seventeenth century.

c. The Clarkes

Walter Clarke, a Shropshire day-labourer from Hadley, near Oaken Gates, came into the township of Newton round about the year 1560 in search of a job. He probably found one on the farm of Richard Gittins, freeholder and gentleman-tenant of Eagle Farm, for he and his wife, Elizabeth, set up home in a little cottage on Harmer Hill that Gittins was renting from the lord. Until the Enclosure Award of 1813, there were 85½ acres of commons on this rocky, unproductive hill, and it was to become even more of a favourite with nineteenth-century quarrymen than it was with the squatters of earlier times. Walter added a little encroachment, for which he paid an annual rent of 4*d*., and no doubt he supplemented his wages by keeping a few animals on the surrounding commons.

He married twice and had six children. At least one, and possibly three of these died in infancy, and the youngest, John, "was an innocent and went a begging in the parish".[59] The other two grew to manhood. Nothing further is heard of Thomas after the death of his unbaptized child in 1589, but there was Morgan to carry on the family line after the death of his father in 1590. Morgan was both a labourer and a weaver and was able to maintain his family just above the poverty line. He left his father's cottage and "built an house upon a butt's end of Mr. Gittins' land in Newton feild, and had onely a garden and hemp butt belonging to it". Not much; but, with his wages and his common rights, enough to enable him to marry and raise two sons and a daughter. He died intestate in 1625 or 1626, but the inventory gives an idea of his standard of living. His total personal estate was valued at £14 12*s*. 0*d*., but his farm stock and equipment accounted for £12 11*s*. 0*d*. of this. The house seems to have had only one room, or two at the most, and there was obviously little to spare for the provision of luxuries. There was nothing in the inventory to support Gough's statement that he was a weaver, but the farm stock shows a greater variety than might have been expected; there were 23 sheep, two cows and a heifer, two pigs, a horse, several hens, and some corn and hay in the field and barn. Morgan Clarke may have been renting more land than the manorial records reveal; perhaps he had taken part of Gittins's freehold, and perhaps his father had done the same before him.

His two sons, Richard and Thomas, started separate branches of the family, both of which remained in the parish. Thomas, the younger of the two, "tooke more land of Mr. Gittins, and joined it to his cottage, and made it a small tenement of about 50*s*. per annum". There was still room for advancement for a labourer by dint of hard work, but it was a slow process. Thomas was still described as labourer when he died in 1659 a few months short of his sixtieth birthday. What little property he had managed to collect was passed on to his elder son, Francis, the second of three children by his wife, Matilda, or Maud, a Welsh servant of the rector, Ralph Kinaston. The younger son, Morgan, had gone back to his mother's native land to work as a blacksmith, while Joan, the eldest child, married a man from near-by Fenemere, and settled down in a cottage in Myddlewood.

Gough says that Francis married "Elizabeth Kyffin, descended of a good, butt a decaying family in Wales", but the marriage registers call her Elizabeth Greyfeths of Newton. Perhaps he married twice, but the names sound very similar. "He had", continues Gough, "but litle portion with her butt a sad drunken woman", who on one occasion stayed all night in the ale-house. Despite this handicap, Francis seems to have consolidated the small gains of his ancestors. He paid the tax on one hearth in 1672, and although the parish registers describe him as labourer, the friends who drew up his inventory in 1692 felt that the Clarkes had finally stepped up a rung of the social ladder and now qualified for the name of husbandman. His total personal estate was valued at £23 13*s*. 8*d*., and even allowing for inflation, this was somewhat better than the £14 12*s*. 0*d*. of his grandfather in 1626. But his personal possessions were only valued at a meagre £2 6*s*. 6*d*., compared with the £21 11*s*. 2*d*. of his farm stock. The four bullocks valued at £10 seem to have made all the difference to his social status.

Like his father, Francis died just before his sixtieth birthday. One of his daughters had died in infancy, but the other two had grown up and married. In 1692 one of these married daughters was living in Welsh Hampton, but the other was only a few yards away in another cottage on Harmer Hill. The only boy in the family, Richard, entered into his father's small tenement at Newton, and in time his four children ensured that the family continued there during the eighteenth century. This younger branch never rose spectacularly, but they chose to remain in the parish, and by hard work and reasonably good health they were able to earn a moderate living.

The senior branch of the family fared somewhat differently. Morgan Clarke's elder son, Richard, married Anne Chaloner, the cooper's daughter, and built himself a house on the property she had inherited in Myddlewood. In 1640 this property was described as a cottage with a wood piece divided into three parts, while two years earlier it had been described as a messuage with 12 old acres; a large holding for a man who was still a labourer. Richard was still at Newton when his father died in 1626, and he baptized two children from there in 1621 and 1627, but as his wife's small tenement was obviously superior to the family's holding at Newton, he had moved to Myddlewood by the time his third child, Morgan, was born in 1631. His younger brother inherited the cottage at Newton.

The lord's demands for greatly increased entry fines must have caused him some hardship. Instead of buying a new lease he had to hold his land in Myddlewood at the annual rack-rent of £2 5*s*. 0*d*., but by 1651 he was ten shillings in arrears. The steward wrote, "Unless he will come to the value at racke, or fine, let it bee set away". He died three years later at the age of 61, and although his widow lived until 1672, her name does not appear in the rental of 1656. However, their great-grandson was renting the cottage in 1701, so the dispute was probably settled amicably and the property allowed to continue in the family.

Richard was still a labourer when he died. One son had died in infancy, and nothing more is heard of his daughter after her baptism, but the other son, Richard (baptized 1627), not only grew up to be one of the most unusual characters in the community of Myddle, but, thanks to Gough, to be one of the best chronicled labourers in the whole of seventeenth-century England. It is unfortunate that one does not learn from his extraordinary career much about labourers in general, for it was his more outrageous actions that commended him to Gough's attention. Only a reading of pages 106–8 in Gough's book can do him full justice.

To Gough, "Hee was naturally ingeniouse. He had a smooth way of flattering discourse, and was a perfect master in the art of dissembling". While still a youth he had carried messages for the soldiers in the Civil Wars, skilfully avoiding trouble by his talent for deceit and disguise. When the wars were over he married a woman from beyond Ellesmere, who was "very thick of hearing, butt yett she was a comely woman, and had a portion in money, which Clark quickly spent, for hee was a very drunken fellow if hee could gett money to spend. After hee had spent his wife's portion, hee came to Newton on the Hill, in a little house there under Mr. Gittin's and there hee set up a trade of making spinning wheeles. Hee was not putt apprentice to any trade, and yett he was very ingeniouse in workeing att any handycraft trade. Hee had a lytle smyth's forge, in which he made his owne tooles, and likewise knives and other small things of iron". When his second wife was carrying a dead child in her womb he made iron hooks and performed a successful operation under the midwife's direction, but he refused to repeat the operation when the same trouble arose again, and his wife died as a consequence. He married three times, had several children, and treated each wife badly. Upon his final marriage, he persuaded his father-in-law, Richard Woulf, an old widower, "to deliver all his estate to him, on condition of being maintained while he lived". But with money in his pocket, Clarke resumed his old drinking habits and so abused the old man as to make him tired of life. Woulf walked all the way to Wem, bought poison, ate it on his way home, and died in his bed. As the estate was for lives, Clarke lost all and was unable to get a new lease.

He seems to have been as opportunist in religious matters as in everything else. He and his wife, Elizabeth, had been excommunicated at the bishop's visitation in 1668 "for absenting themselves from Church", and "for keeping one of his children which is at least halfe a yeare old unbaptized". For a time he had been an Anabaptist, and then he went to near-by Stanton to join the Quakers. "Hee came home the next day a perfect Quaker in appearance, and had got their canting way of discourse as readyly as if hee had beene seven years apprentice". He was at first welcomed by the Friends, until it was found that he had borrowed several sums of money from them, and when asked for their return, he turned on these Quakers the same invective he had lately used against the ministers of the Church of England. Having been rejected by them his choice was somewhat narrowed, and so he became a Roman Catholic in name, "butt was not regarded by that party". Nor was he regarded as a true martyr when he was sentenced to be pilloried in three market towns for shouting, "I hope to see all the Protestants fry in theire owne grease beefore Michaelmas next". He received such rough treatment in the pillories of Shrewsbury and Ellesmere that he was not taken to Oswestry, for the High Sherrif "could not promise to bring him alive from amongst the inraged Welshmen".

Clarke died a few years later at Ellesmere. "His wife sold all his tooles and household goods, and went into Ireland; butt she returned very poore, and soe dyed". Their daughter and her husband, and subsequently their grandson, continued to live in the old cottage in Myddlewood. They were poorer than the other branch of the family in Newton. The recognized values of hard work and sobriety had paid off for one part of the family, but to the community of Myddle, Richard Clarke had wasted his talents and reaped a just reward for a life of selfish deceit. The incidents of his life might be recounted with vicarious pleasure, but Gough concludes in tones of disapproval.

CHAPTER SIX

The community

1 · *The mental world*

Only with Richard Gough does one have any real insight into the mind of a member of this woodland community. His conscious and unconscious beliefs and attitudes are revealed in his writings, and he can be seen to have been a very orthodox small-freeholder of the late seventeenth century. His whole outlook was shaped by his religious convictions. He was a conservative in religion and politics, upholding the Church of England and the political settlements of 1660 and 1689. His was the voice of the small-propertied classes, accepting the existing hierarchy in both church and state, proclaiming the Christian virtues and denouncing the vices, and championing the hard-working, God-fearing conformity that was preached from the pulpits.

Gough was no mere outward conformer: his whole structure of thought, his mental outlook, and his everyday actions and attitudes were dominated by his religious beliefs. People who were of excellent character, such as William Watkins of Shotton Hall, were regarded as being specially blessed by God: "It hath pleased God to give him such skill, care, and industry as his grand-father and father had". Others, like Michael Chambre of Balderton Hall, were extreme examples of the doctrine of original sin: "Soe prone is humane nature to all vice". Tragedy and misfortune were attributed to God's will without a murmur of dissent: "I intended it for my eldest son", he wrote of one tenement, "butt it pleased God that hee dyed"; and, "About the year 1649, it pleased God to visit [Shrewsbury] with the plague." Divine intervention in community matters was accepted as inevitable, for speaking of a settlement dispute, he wrote: "This was the first contest that we had and thus we lost; but thanks be to God wee never lost any afterwards". The immediacy of God in Gough's thought is apparent in his comments on the death of Richard Gittins, in Shrewsbury: "He was suddainely taken with an appoplecque fitt or some other distemp (what pleased God) which tooke not away his speach for hee cryed out suddenly (not sudden death Good Lord)".[1] Gough's character-sketches reveal a community where human nature was as rich and as varied as it is today, but the essential difference lies in the whole structure of thought, a mental environment that is foreign to most people in the twentieth century.

Divine intervention in ordinary affairs did not lead to fatalism, for it was accepted that there was a large sphere of action where men could make decisions of their own free will. This freedom was thought to be limited also by other supernatural powers, for there was a ready acceptance of superstitious beliefs. A murderer who had fled along Watling Street was arrested in Hertfordshire after his pursuers had seen "two ravens sitt upon a cocke of hay, pulling the hay with theire beaks, and making an hideouse and unusuall noyse". They found their man asleep on the hay cock and heard him confess that the ravens had followed him since the time he had committed the crime. This use of superstition to bolster traditional morality is also evident in the story of Reece Wenlock's visit to "the wise woman of Montgomery", to try to discover who had stolen his cow. "As hee went, hee putt a stone in his pockett, and tould a neighbour of his that was with him that he would know whether she were a wise woman or not, and whether she knew that hee had a stone in his pockett. And it is sayd, that when hee came to her, shee sayd, thou hast a stone in thy pockett. but itt is not soe bigge as that stone wherewith thou didst knocke out such a neighbour's harrow tines".[2] Wenlock was a notorious petty-thief, and the story is effectively told against him, supernatural powers being invoked to strengthen the traditional values of the community.[3]

In a similar way, the customary inheritance system was supported by an appeal to forces outside the control of man. Gough quotes examples to show that "such things doe seldome prosper" when primogeniture was ignored, as, for example, in the case of Thomas Atcherley. Sharp practice by James Wicherley in beating Richard Gittins to the purchase of a tenement in Houlston brought both criticism and a satisfaction that he did not prosper, for his estate "had the fate of goods not well gotten, which our English proverb sayes will not last three cropps". But Gough was somewhat unsure in this case and concluded that it was an erroneous way to judge things by the event. He was more certain in the case of Philip Huffa.[4]

Gough was alternately fascinated and doubtful when dealing with the "secretts of Philosophy". Astrology was intellectually respectable during the seventeenth century but was beginning to lose its attraction at the time that Gough was writing,[5] and this is reflected in his comments. He lists a number of important national events that had taken place on 3 September over a period of years, but then declares that "over much credit" had been given to occult philosophy. Then, when the figure 8 appeared frequently in his account of an ancestor, he paused to remark: "This may cause some that pretend to have a skill in tropomancie to say that the number 8 was criticall to him; butt the numerall letters in his name shew noe such thing". Finally, when he listed the names of all the noblemen who had died in 1701, he remarked: "Those that are curiouse in Astrologicall speculations may take notice of the seeming Prodromi of this Catastrophe Magnatum"; but he concluded: "The Prophet Jeremiah says – 'Bee not dismayed att the signes of Heaven, they are signes, butt not to bee feared'." But despite this assurance, he undoubtedly believed in a strange story concerning a farm outside the parish. He claimed that whenever the head of the household lay dying there, a pair of pigeons came to roost at the farm, and that he himself had seen them do this.[6] The appeal of the mysterious, the belief in forces outside human control, and the acceptance that there was nothing a man could do when faced by these signs, are all present in the mind of one who was amongst the best-educated and the most intelligent of the community. Amongst those of lower intelligence and little or no education, superstitious belief must have been even more readily accepted.

There is no mention of witchcraft either in Gough's account or in any other source concerning Myddle, except in the story of Reece Wenlock's journey across the border to consult the wise woman of Montgomery over his stolen cow. His long journey might suggest that there was no-one of a comparable local reputation, though Dr A. MacFarlane has shown[7] that Essex cunning-folk frequently referred their clients to outsiders who were attributed with greater powers. Certainly, there were no violent persecutions of supposed witches in Shropshire as there were in Essex, Suffolk, Lancashire, and elsewhere.

However, the ecclesiastical court records are fragmentary and the Quarter Sessions records do not survive at all for the late Elizabethan period when prosecutions were frequent in other parts of the country. The acta and comperta books for the deanery of Salop are extant for the years 1576, 1614, 1620, 1626, 1633, 1635, 1636, 1639, 1668, 1677–8, and 1679–80, and it is significant that they do not contain a single charge of witchcraft, nor is there the slightest suggestion of such associated terms as sorcery, soothsaying, cunning, or wise-woman. There are no cause papers relating to Myddle, and the only reference to witchcraft in Shropshire causes is at Wellington in 1661.[8] The only other charge that has come to notice is that recorded in the *Early Chronicles of Shrewsbury* for 1580 when "Mother Gawe" was punished in the corn market of Shrewsbury for using witchcraft in an unsuccessful attempt to cure her neighbour's sick pig.[9] The fact that this case attracted the chronicler's attention suggests that it was somewhat unusual.

This lack of evidence may simply reflect similar tolerance on the part of the authorities to that shown by the ecclesiastical courts of York.[10] However, the courts of the Salop deanery went much further than those of York and entirely excluded witch-beliefs from their attention. The silence of Gough and the chronicler confirms that there was no organized persecution, for both writers were attracted by the sensational and would surely have recorded any such trials. Gough makes no reference to any informal charges or to any village tensions that produced accusations of witchcraft. He refers to past superstitions such as a belief in fairies (which nonsense he attributes to the Catholics), but nowhere does he mention local cunning-men or soothsayers, even though he could recount tales that were well over a century old.

The tolerance shown by the authorities, therefore, may be due to the absence of any strong beliefs in witchcraft in this part of the country. If this is so, the explanation offered by Mr K. Thomas and Dr A. MacFarlane for the incidence of witchcraft persecutions elsewhere may be satisfactorily applied to explain why there was no such problem in north Shropshire. They have maintained that witch-beliefs arose out of the tensions created in local communities by the sense of guilt of those who were uncharitable towards the poor. The great majority of witchcraft accusations were directed against a pauper by someone who had previously refused to be charitable towards that person. In the Elizabethan and early Stuart period the great increase in the number of the poor brought these tensions to a head.

But in north Shropshire the poor were not so much of a problem, at least until the late seventeenth century, by which time witch-beliefs were no longer quite as tenable after the excesses of Matthew Hopkins and his fellow 'judges'. In 1633, the poor-rate in Myddle cost Gough's father only 4*d*. per annum, and the only regular pauper was blind John Matthews, who was allowed to go round the parish doing odd jobs and begging.[11] The parish registers do not describe anyone as pauper before 1635. There were many individual charitable bequests and when, in the middle of the seventeenth century, Mrs Hodgkins was reduced by her husband's excessive drinking to living in the lodge on Harmer Heath, she "had nothing to maintaine herselfe butt what neighbours sent".[12] Furthermore, (as will be seen below) it was usual for children to maintain their parents in old age and infirmity. Gough stresses the importance of charity, and the poor of the parish never became so numerous as seriously to disrupt local society.

The stability of the tenement families, all living at much the same standard of living, was the most striking feature of Tudor and Stuart Myddle. There was not that noticeable difference in the status of the *nouveau riche* and the poor as there was, for example, in Essex where there were frequent accusations of witchcraft. The immigrants were easily absorbed into local society until the second half of the seventeenth century, and when a Welsh labourer had his house destroyed by fire, the parish readily and handsomely contributed towards a new one.[13] The economic tensions that seriously divided the Essex and Suffolk villages were largely absent in north Shropshire during the time when witch-beliefs were most readily held.

Education was upheld as a great virtue, and Gough was voicing the opinion of those of his social status when he made comments like: "Shee was much to bee

11. Balderton Hall. The finest timber-framed house in the parish. Built in the medieval tradition in the 1570s or 1580s, with a central hall and off-centre entry, flanked on each side by two-storeyed cross wings. According to Gough, "William Nicholas built most part of Balderton Hall—viz. all except that crosse building, called the kitchen end". The differences in the style of the timbers confirms that one of the wings was added later. There were frequent changes of ownership after Nicholas went bankrupt.

12 and 13. The Oaks. A labourer's cottage of unusual interest. One of a number built from the 1580s onwards in Myddlewood near the parish boundary. First recorded in a rental of 1588, when it was held by John Hughes, a labourer. The timber panels reveal how the original one-bay cottage was extended on the left by the addition of an extra bay. The building is basically the labourer's cottage as the Hanmers would have known it during the seventeenth century.

14. The Tan House. In the early seventeenth century Thomas Atcherley of Marton Hall "built a tan-house, which is now standing by the old mill brooke". The internal arrangements suggest that the present rooms are not contemporary with the shell of the building. There are no signs of previous divisions, and the building seems to have been used originally for industrial purposes. (It is noteworthy that in 1637 William Wood of Wardsend, Sheffield, had "a Tan house of 3 bayes in the Tanyard" in addition to his dwelling house and outbuildings.)

comended for giveing her children good education, and putt every one of them in a good condition to live". Another widow received similar praise for making sure that her son had a good education, while, on the other hand, a father was criticized for being "wanting in giveing [his son] good learneing". There was a chance of at least a basic education for the poor as well as the rich, and some, like the Hanmers of Myddlewood, took advantage of the local petty-schools. One of these was at the Warren House at the beginning of the seventeenth century, when one Twyford "lived in good repute and taught neighbours' children to read, and his wife taught women to sew, and make needle workes". Small schools such as this were established in private houses and lasted for a few years at a time. Mr Osmary Hill of Bilmarsh "kept a very flourishing schoole att his owne house, where many gentlemen's sons of good quality were his schollers"; and a wing of Balderton Hall was used as a school for a short time towards the end of the seventeenth century. These schools did not survive the death or retirement of the master.[14]

There was no endowed school in Myddle, but there was a small school that seems to have served in a semi-official capacity. During the early years of the seventeenth century, William Hunt, the parish clerk and local tenement-farmer, was the master here. Then, Nathaniel Platt, the rector of a small benefice at Ford, supplemented his income by teaching at Myddle, and during the Civil Wars a Mr Richard Rodericke taught here and possibly served as curate as well, in the absence of the rector, Thomas More. Gough mentions that during the Commonwealth period, the old communion table was brought into the school-house for the boys to write on, and the old reading pew was brought in for the schoolmaster to sit in. Later, the parish chest was also removed from the church to the school-house. Obviously, the school was serving in some public capacity.[15]

It was at this school that Gough received his earliest education, before moving on to a small private school at Broughton, and then being educated under Robert Corbett, M.P., J.P., of Stanwardine Hall, whom he served as a clerk. Gough must have been talented to serve a man of such distinction, but this progression from village school to small private school to service in some large house may well have been normal for the sons of gentlemen and ambitious yeomen. The girls of this class also received some education, but information as to its content is entirely lacking. Possibly, quite a wide spectrum of the community received a rudimentary education, for Joshua Richardson's bequest of books to some of the poor families of the parish suggests that some humble people could read tolerably well, but, on the other hand, the numerous marks that serve as signatures in the wills, inventories, bonds, and leases of the sixteenth and seventeenth centuries show that many were unable to write their own name. Between 1660 and 1701, there are examples of 24 men and two women who could sign their names, and 10 men and five women who used a mark. The literate ones were from the gentry and the yeomen-farmers, with only Peter Lloyd from the poorer sections of the community. The illiterate ones were almost entirely from amongst the labourers and poor husbandmen, though three illiterate men, Richard Guest, Bartholomew Mansell, and John Hordley, were as prosperous as some of those who could write. Dr Margaret Spufford has shown that in seventeenth-century Cambridgeshire more people could read than write, and that some people could read but only just sign their name. The same was probably true of Myddle. Gough wrote of Thomas Highway, the parish clerk whom he considered unfit for office, "Hee can read but little . . . Hee can scarse write his owne name, or read any written hand".[16]

Gough's own training had been the usual one of grammar, Latin, the classics, law, and divinity, with some applied mathematics. This education is reflected in his writings, especially in his moral tags. He does not support his statements with biblical texts, as one might have expected, but frequently quotes old proverbs such as "Beware of him whom God hath marked", or "Hee that spilled man's blood, by man shall his blood be spilt", and "The potsherd that goes often to the well comes home broaken att last".[17] More often, he uses a classical quotation in commenting upon one of his stories. These quotations are mostly in Latin (sometimes with a translation), and his favourite authors were Ovid, Horace, Seneca, Cato, and Virgil – the pundits of ancient Rome. He also quotes Mantuan, Aristotle, Tacitus, Tiberius, and Alexander the Great, and occasionally takes his material from Chaucer, or from a moralist such as George Herbert. A few moral tags were his own. He also refers to several works that he consulted over "The Significance, Derivation, and Etymology of Severall Names of Persons and Places Mentioned in This Book", chiefly Camden, "though not a lytle out of Judge Russell's Termes of Law: Lord Cheife Justice Coke's Institutes: Judge Doddridge his Titles of Honour: Mr. Godolphin, Mr. Chamberlin and others."[18] His legal training is shown by his references to judicial precedents when pronouncing on such matters as pew disputes and manorial customs. His knowledge and his ability seem to have been put to good use by the community, for he appears as an arbitrator, a surveyor, a regular witness to deeds, wills, and such like, a counsellor over legal matters, and a man to send for when crises arose, such as when a baby was abandoned in the rector's porch. He retained his interest in his learning all his life, and in his will of 1723 he left "all my English books and of divinity" to his daughter, Joyce, and "all my Law bookes" to a young relation. How many others of his social class were as able and as knowledgeable as he was, it is impossible to say, but with a society that produced the Restoration poet, William Wycherley, it is dangerous to argue that he was altogether exceptional.

Even without such an education, the mental horizon of the men and women of Myddle was not confined to their own parish. They were conscious of the identity of their local community, but they had personal knowledge of a wider area that embraced the neighbouring parishes. They had friends and relations in several of the surrounding villages and hamlets, they had found husbands or wives there.

they were familiar with the personalities and events that provided the gossip of those places, and they were conscious of being united as a group with the same bonds and common interests.[19] This knowledge of what was happening over an area wider than that of the parish came to the assistance of Gough when he was employed in searching for the mother of a child that had been abandoned in Myddle. On the way to Shawbury,

> I happened to meet accidently with my cozen Anne Newans of Greensell [Grinshill], who upon inquiry told mee that a poore woman was delivered of a child about a fortnight agoe at a house on the side of Shawbury Heath, and when she had stayd there a weeke shee came to Greensell with her lytle child and a boy with her in side-coates, and had ribbons about the wast of his coate, and that the yong child was baptized at Greensell by Mr. Sugar then minister there, and that some servants of the towne gave the woman cloathes to wrap her child in; she stayd there a weeke and (says she) "Yesterday shee went away towards your neighbourhood".[20]

There were also the wider contacts of the market towns, especially Shrewsbury, with which everyone must have been familiar. Yet there were well-recognized differences between town and country. Thomas Hayward's wife, "beeing a towne-bred woman was unfitte for a country life; shee must be richly cloathed, fare daintily, drinke nothing butt strong waters and that not a lytle".[21] Her marriage was an unhappy one. But for all these differences there was a consciousness of Shropshire as being their 'country', for this is how they described it. They thought of themselves as being different from the Welsh (with whom they were very familiar), but Englishmen from other counties were simply described as 'foreigners'. The local units were the ones of importance in their everyday lives, and in this respect Myddle was no different from any other community in sixteenth- and seventeenth-century England.[22]

Events in north Shropshire were their immediate concern, but they were still acquainted with national events and were aware of the issues involved in the great political and religious controversies of their time. Gough's writings display a detailed knowledge of the Civil Wars, including some references to parliamentary business and to the arguments that were advanced on both sides. He was only a boy when most of the crucial events took place. Like many of his contemporaries, he thought of the reign of Queen Elizabeth as a golden age, and he firmly denounced anything that went against the religious and political settlements of his time. Oliver Cromwell and James II were anathema to him.

Gough occasionally shows a remarkably detailed awareness of some other national and foreign events. When writing about a local man who was killed in a riot on Tower Hill in 1661, Gough explains that it was started by a dispute over precedency between the ambassadors of France and Spain, and he goes on to describe the riot in great detail. On another occasion, when he was writing about the career of a man during the Protectorate, he describes the siege of Dunkirk.[23] Myddle was but a remote woodland community, but here was at least one of its members who was acquainted with national events and aware of at least some of the issues of foreign policy. Myddle was not quite as cut off from the capital as one might believe, and there was much more contact between such communities and London than used to be supposed. Mr Spufford has recently suggested that migration to London from all parts of the country was the one startling exception to the general rule of short distance migration during the seventeenth century.[24]

The evidence from Myddle bears out Dr E. A. Wrigley's thesis that many people from the provinces, at some stage or other in their life, had direct experience of living in London, though it is difficult to measure this, and not easy to see how many returned to their native parish. Dr Wrigley has argued that during the hundred years from 1650 to 1750, the surplus population of England, especially that of the Home Counties and of the Midlands, was siphoned off into the metropolis, where an immigration rate of 8,000 a year would have been needed to account for its population rise, given the fact that its death rate was so much higher than its birth rate.[25]

Gough's information is naturally largely limited to the middle and late seventeenth centuries, but even so he mentions no less than 19 families that had at least one son or daughter who went to live in London, and some of these families had several members who settled there. There were about 91 families living in Myddle at the time of the hearth-tax returns of 1672, and Gough mentions 15 of these as having at least one member who, at one time or another, had lived in London. There may have been more who had visited the place, for he often refers incidentally to the capital as if it were a commonplace that people from his parish should be there, even though the two places are some 160 miles apart. For instance, when he writes about Richard Woulf, he says, "I mett with him in London about forty yeares ago"; and on another occasion he mentions that he bought Mrs Mary Corbett's wedding ring from Richard Watkins, a London goldsmith, who was the son of William Watkins, the Shotton gentleman.[26]

Two other sons of William Watkins also settled in the capital; George as a trader, and Thomas, the youngest son, as a rich distiller. Other gentry families also established their younger sons in business there. Daniel Gittins of Castle Farm became a merchant tailor, and Humphrey Hall, the youngest of the six sons of Thomas Hall of Balderton, worked as a silversmith; "hee is a strong man, and a skillful workman, but he loves drinke too well to bee rich". (One wonders how Gough was able to give a quick character-sketch of people who lived so far away.) The Wicherleys of Houlston also sent sons to London. One was apprenticed, about the middle of the seventeenth century, into "a small trade with stuffs and serjeys" after he had fathered a bastard while still a youth, but it was not long before he sent for his girl and married her.[27] A relation of his was trained in the law at London, and yet another, William Wycherley (born at Clive but a landowner in Houlston), became a notable poet in the Restoration court.

Some farmers' boys also went to the capital in search of a fortune and a more exciting life, though this section of the community was the least likely to tear up its roots. The tenement-farmers formed the bulk of the community, but Gough refers to only six families who had members in the capital. William Preece, the son of Griffith ap Reece of Newton, was apprenticed to a London goldsmith, late in the sixteenth century. Fifty years later, Michael, the second son of Thomas Jux of Newton, yeoman, also went to serve an apprenticeship, but ended up being hanged for a crime. His nephew, Thomas Jux, was apprenticed to a London leather-seller, but he too came to an untimely end when he was killed during a riot on Tower Hill in 1661. Thomas and Samuel Formston, two of the younger sons of a Marton farmer, also went to live in the capital. Thomas was an ironmonger, but died of the plague in the 1630s, and his brother hastened away, back to his own parish.[28] One wonders whether other people lived with relations in the capital for a short while before returning to their native county.

William Lovett, the son of the Myddle bailiff, settled in London during the closing years of the seventeenth century, after serving several years as a soldier. Other boys went to be cooks. Richard Woulf served a Scottish lord in Lincoln's Inn Square and found a job there for his brother, Arthur, and Richard Hayward, a younger son of the Balderton yeoman, served Bishop Juxon before the Civil Wars and was restored to his service when he was made archbishop upon the Restoration. Richard came back to Balderton upon his retirement. His brother, Henry, was a woodmonger in London, did very well for a time, but then went bankrupt and fled to Ireland. Their niece, Elizabeth, also moved to the capital upon her second marriage, and two Haywards of the next generation served apprenticeships there to a silver wire-drawer and a silver refiner. The latter one eventually returned to Shropshire.[29]

Gough mentions two other girls who left the parish and settled in London. Henry Taylor's daughter, Mary, left Divlin Wood in the mid-seventeenth century, and Judith More of Eagle Farm removed with her husband a generation or so later.[30] Some labourers also moved on to the metropolis. There were many temporary labourers in Myddle in the late sixteenth and the seventeenth centuries, and it is impossible to say where they all came from or where they went after leaving the parish. Gough was primarily concerned with the long-established families, but he does mention three labourers who went to live in London. Richard Pickerton, whose father lived in a cottage in Myddle village in the late seventeenth century, was a hard-working man who found employment with a refiner of silver in London and did well there. After many years as a soldier and servant, Bartholomew Pierce left for London in the 1660s, rejoined the army, and was garrisoned in the Tower for some time before serving in Tangiers.[31] Finally, Mary Davis, the only child of Frank Davis of Castle Farm Cottage, married a Shropshire man in the late seventeenth century, and went with him to London, where she maintained herself very well by her own labour after his death.

Yet others fled to London to escape trouble in their own parish. Gough quotes three examples from the late seventeenth century. A second Thomas Formston left Myddle to sell ale in Oswestry, but he got so far in debt that he fled to the capital, leaving his wife behind him. About the same time, Andrew, the fifth son of Thomas Hall of Balderton, and a journeyman glover and skinner, drank himself into debt and left hurriedly for the great city. Then, Thomas Fardo of Burlton also decided to go, after fathering a bastard in Myddle parish. He became very rich in London; "it was thought that hee was worth severall thousands of pounds in houses and timber, which he had in his timber yard in Southewick. But hee broake, and was layd in prison, and died poore".[32]

Many years earlier, the rector, Thomas More, had also been forced to flee to London upon the outbreak of the Civil Wars. Earlier information is lacking. The only sixteenth-century example that Gough writes about is that of Thomas Elks of Knockin, who murdered his nephew and escaped along the road to London. He was caught in Hertfordshire, and his route had obviously been along the old Watling Street, which was a direct link between Shrewsbury and the capital. The distance might have been great, but at least there was a reasonable and direct road, judged by the standards of the sixteenth and seventeenth centuries. There was probably a regular flow of traffic along it, and Gough quotes one example of such a user; John Foden's family "came to live in Mr. Lyster's cheife farme in Broughton, where they kept a good stocke of cows and a good teame of horses with which hee carryed goods to London; they were in a very thriveing condition".[33] It was carriers such as these who escorted people to London and who delivered messages from friends and relations. Myddle was not quite as remote from the centre of national affairs as might be imagined.

The major national crisis of the period under discussion was the Civil War of the 1640s. Myddle is a good illustration of how far a rural community could be involved, actively or otherwise. And in such a time of stress, political and religious attitudes are more readily revealed.

In the summer of 1642 Charles I moved his headquarters from Nottingham to Shrewsbury, and Shropshire remained largely under Royalist control until the castle finally fell in 1645. On 2 January 1643 a form of protestation was imposed upon "many hundred inhabitants of Shrewsbury" by Sir Francis Ottley, and those who refused to sign were threatened with death.[34] The form ran:

> I, A.B., do in the presence of Almighty God protest and acknowledge without any mental reservation that I do detest and abhor the notorious rebellion which

> goes under the name of the Parliament army, and will with my whole force and means to the uttermost of my power withstand their impious rebellion against our most gracious sovereign, Lord King Charles, our Protestant religion, our laws of the land, our just privileges of Parliament, and liberty of the subject.

It was in this atmosphere that a force was raised for the king. Twenty men went from the parish of Myddle to fight on the Royalist side, and 13 of them were killed in action. Very few fought on the Parliamentary side (none was killed), and Francis Watkins of Shotton Hall was the only person of any standing in the parish to sympathize actively with the Parliamentary cause. Gough could remember as a boy seeing a great assembly on Myddle Hill that had been called to raise a force for the king.

> Sir Paul Harris sent out warrants requiring or commanding all men, both householders with theire sons, and servants, and sojourners, and others within the Hundred of Pimhill that were between the age of 16 and three score to appeare on a certaine day upon Myddle Hill. I was then a youth of about 8 or 9 years of age [1642–43], and I went to see this great show. And there I saw a multitude of men, and upon the highest banke of the hill I saw Robert More of Eagle Farm [the brother of the rector], standing with a paper in his hand, and three or four soldier's pikes, sticked upright in the ground by him; and there hee made a proclamation, that if any person would serve the King, as a soldier in the wars, hee should have 14 groats a weeke for his pay.[35]

More was soon to die in a Parliamentary gaol, and his brother was ejected from his living.

There was support for the Parliamentarians, however, in other parts of the county, and they were strong enough to establish a garrison of 200 cavalry and 400 infantry at Wem. In the spring of 1644, Prince Rupert laid siege to this garrison and on two occasions made his rendezvous on Holloway Hills. Five hundred soldiers from Warwickshire and 500 from Staffordshire were sent to relieve the garrison and the Royalists were forced to withdraw. By 27 June 1644, "the High Sheriff and gentry of Salop" were petitioning the king over the "distressed condition" of the county and the power of the rebels in it.[36] It was from the base at Wem that Shrewsbury Castle finally fell in 1645 and the skirmishing came to an end. Parliamentary control was established over the county, and one consequence for Myddle was that in the following year the absentee rector, Thomas More, was ejected from his living and the Nonconformist preacher, Joshua Richardson, was installed in his place. Of more immediate importance was the fact that a period of much inconvenience, personal tragedy, and occasional hardship had almost come to an end, though the breakdown of manorial control was to last another few years.

John, the Earl of Bridgewater, was an old man who had led a retired life upon the outbreak of the Civil Wars, but his son and namesake was an active Royalist, who was arrested in 1651.[37] After a detailed study of the Bridgewater estates in north Shropshire during the Civil Wars, Mr E. Hopkins has concluded that the wars brought four years of economic dislocation, during which time rents were uncollected, some lands were untilled, crops were damaged, and families suffered at the hands of plundering soldiers.[38] He quotes examples from a survey of 1650, when Richard Matthews of New Marton claimed to have "lost all by the wars" and could not pay the fine for a new lease; when John Tonna of Colemere "acquittances all lost by the prince's army – lost all by the warrs, not a ragg left"; and when Oliver Harrison of Kenwick Park pleaded that he was "undone by plunder and fire". These tales show the distress that could be caused to individuals, though they were not typical of north Shropshire as a whole.

The records of local administration in the 1640s cease to be as full as they had been just before the wars. After a detailed series from 1638 to 1641 there are no rentals, and very few other manorial records until 1650. There are no wills and inventories for the Civil War and Commonwealth period, though they do survive for other parts of the diocese. The parish registers also peter out during the period 1642–7, though as bishop's transcripts survive from 1647 onwards the fact that the original registers for 1647 to 1681 are missing cannot be attributed to any negligence at the time. The absence of these records suggests a breakdown in the services of the local community. Gough wrote that William Tyler refused to pay his rent to John Noneley for a tenement that he held of him, and that "Noneley knew not what to doe, it being in the heate of the warrs". Economic hardship is also suggested by the efforts made to cultivate part of Myddlewood Common towards the end of the wars, but this was a time of "great dearth and plague" in Oswestry, and harvest failure had probably resulted from natural reasons rather than from civil strife.[39] This was a time when harvests were deficient all over the country.

Gough's comments show that the suffering of some individuals was very real. Richard Wicherley of Houlston "was troubled in the time of the wars with the outrages and plunderings of soldiers on both parties (as all rich men were) and seeing his goods and horses taken away, and his money consumed in paying taxes, hee tooke an extreeme greife and dyed". Men who were neutral in their sympathies could suffer as much as the activists who found themselves on the losing side. Gough quotes another case, when Richard Hatchett of Peplow, the grandfather of a Newton man, removed from there "beefore his lease was expyred; for hee was so plagued and plundered by the soldiers in the warre time, that he was forced to remove to Shrewsbury". And Myddle suffered worst of all at the hands of one of its own sons, Nathaniel, the son of John Owen.

> The father was hang'd before the warrs, and the son deserved it in the warrs, for hee was a Cataline to his owne country. His common practice was to come

> by night with a party of horse to some neighbour's house and breake open the doores, take what they pleased, and if the man of the house was found, they carryed him to prison, from whence he could not bee released without a Ransome in money; soe that noe man here about was safe from him in his bed; and many did forsake their owne houses.[40]

Others had bedding taken for the soldiers in various garrisons, as when the Albright Hussey soldiers came to Newton, or Shrawardine Castle men came to Myddle.

This breakdown of local government may suggest one reason why the king did not find more support than he did, for in Parliament-controlled areas there was more order than this.[41] An anonymous letter, dated 1 October 1642, shows how ill-disciplined the Royalist soldiers were during the opening weeks of the wars.

> Our Country is now in a woful condition, by reason of the multitude of souldiers daily billeted upon us, both of horse and foote . . . All the Country over within 12 or 14 miles of Shrewsbury are full of Souldiers . . . we hear one outrage or other committed daily, they ride armed up and down, with swords, muskets and dragoones, to the great terror of the people, that we scarce know how in safety to go out of doors; they take men's horses, breake and pillage men's houses night and day in an unheard of maner, they pretend quarrell with the Roundheads as they call them, but for aught I see they will spare none if they may hope to have good bounty.[42]

The men who went to fight for the king were from the humblest ranks of the community. Thomas Ash of Marton had once been a yeoman-farmer, but he had fallen into debt and so he enlisted to earn a wage. But at the end of the wars "hee brought nothing home but a crazy body and many scars".[43] Thirteen others never returned; several of them were killed in minor battles in their own county, one died at Edgehill, and others were simply never heard of again and were, therefore, presumed dead. Thomas Formston was the son of a Marton farmer, Richard Chaloner was the bastard son of the Myddle cooper, Nathaniel Owen's father was John Owen who was hanged for stealing horses, Reece Vaughan was a weaver, Thomas Taylor, John Benion, and "an idle stranger" who worked at various places in the parish were tailors, John Arthurs was a servant, Thomas Hayward was the brother of an inn-keeper, and Richard and Thomas Jux were also born and bred in an inn. Finally, William Preece left his cave with his three sons to fight for his king. Two of the sons were killed, the third was hanged shortly afterwards for stealing horses, but the father survived. None of the few who fought on the Parliamentary side was killed, but John, the son of Thomas Mould of Myddlewood, was crippled with a leg wound.

All these men met their death outside the parish. "There happened noe considerable act of hostility in this parish dureing the time of the warres, save onely one small skirmage, in Myddle, part of which I saw".[44] Cornet Collins, an Irishman, often came with a party into the parish from a near-by Royalist garrison to take provisions, bedding, cattle, and anything that took his fancy. On the day before this skirmish he had been looking for bedding, and when Margaret, the wife of Alan Chaloner, the blacksmith, "had brought out and shewed him her best bedd, hee thinking it too course, cast it into the lake, before the doore, and troad it under his horse feet". The following day, Collins was again in Myddle with seven soldiers, when they were attacked by eight Parliamentarians. Collins was shot and lay dying on the very bed he had scorned, one horse was killed, and two prisoners taken. These prisoners were found to be Irish, and as a Parliamentary decree had prohibited all Irishmen from serving in the Royalist army, upon pain of death, they were summarily executed at Wem. In all, 13 Irishmen were hanged as a result of this decree, and so Prince Rupert hanged 13 Parliamentarians, taken prisoner in Shropshire, in revenge. The prince visited Myddle twice during the wars, making his rendezvous with his troops on Holloway Hills before moving on to Cockshutt.

The Civil Wars made a deep impression at the time upon the community ot Myddle. Gough writes of it as a landmark, and his numerous references show that he was fully acquainted with the issues involved and the course of national events, which are brought to life by the vividness of his boyhood memories. But the wars had little lasting effect upon the local community, and the Myddle of the Restoration period was not much different from that of the previous two generations. There was a population increase and the inevitable changes that any period of time would have brought, but during the reigns of the later Stuarts, the same families lived in the same farms, tenements, and cottages as before the wars, the land was farmed with few innovations, the church services reverted to their previous form, and the same set of officials administered the parish. Joshua Richardson lost his living by refusing to conform, but Francis Watkins took an honoured place amongst his gentry friends. No Royalists had to compound for their estates, and no Parliamentarians were penalized after the Restoration. There had been few divisions within the community during the war, and no apparent bitterness after it.

2 · *Family reconstitution*

The mental world of the people was largely conditioned by such crucial demographic factors as expectancy of life, age at marriage, and size of family. The difficult task of providing information about such matters must now be attempted.

The diocesan census returns for 1563 provide a base-figure of *c.* 340 for the total population of the parish, including the chapelry of Hadnall. Another base-figure of *c.* 600 has been estimated for the late seventeenth century, though this is not as reliable as the earlier one. These two base-figures allow some comparison to be made between the baptism, burial, and marriage rates within Myddle, and also between Myddle and other communities.

The parish registers for the period 1541–60 have too many gaps to be used satisfactorily, but the period 1561–80 seems to have been as completely recorded as one might reasonably expect. During that time there were 161 baptisms, 169 burials, and 34 marriages. Using the base-figure of *c.* 340 population, this gives a baptism-rate of 24 per 1,000, a burial-rate of 25 per 1,000, and a marriage-rate of 5 per 1,000. It is generally acknowledged that parish registers under-record both baptisms and burials, and so the figures ought to be somewhat inflated. Working on J. T. Krause's suggestion[45] that baptism figures ought to be increased by 10 per cent, and burial figures by 5 per cent, the revised birth-rate would be 28 per 1,000, and the death-rate 27 per 1,000. These are still only rough figures, for the under-representation might have been even more serious, and the base-figure of 340 may have been reached by using too high a multiplier (5) for the number of households. But even so, the figures are likely to be reliable as a rough guide, and they do show that the population was only just maintaining itself.

The Cambridge group has suggested that in rural areas the crude death-rate never fell below 15 per 1,000, and that the birth-rate was rarely below 30 per 1,000. A marriage-rate of 8 per 1,000 has been considered to be the most stable of indicators.[46] In Myddle, however, the marriage figures are the most unreliable. The 1561–80 rate of 5 per 1,000 is rather low, suggesting an *average* of five to six births per family; but a hundred years later the marriage-rate is lower still at only 3 per 1,000, and at 4 per 1,000 during the last two decades of the seventeenth century.

If the base-figure of *c.*600 is accepted for the late seventeenth century, then between 1661 and 1680 the baptism-rate was 23 per 1,000, or 26 per 1,000 if one allows the same measure of under-representation. Between 1681 and 1700 it was rather higher at 28 per 1,000, or 29 per 1,000 after adjustment. This compares with the 24 per 1,000, increased to 28 per 1,000, for 1561–80. A fairly wide margin of error must be allowed for all these figures, and, therefore, there does not seem to have been any significant change in the birth-rate between the reigns of Queen Elizabeth and the later Stuarts. During the period 1561–80, the death-rate had been 25 per 1,000, raised to 27 per 1,000. Between the years 1661 and 1680 it had dropped quite substantially to 19 or 20 per 1,000, rising again during the next 20-year period to 23 or 24 per 1,000. There does seem to have been a definite possibility that the death-rate was lower after the Restoration than it had been a hundred years earlier. The worst of the harvest crises and the most deadly of the epidemics were things of the past. But this alone cannot account for the population rise of the mid- and late seventeenth century, which was largely due to an influx of labouring families.

Some of the families of Myddle were remarkably stable over a long period of time. The tenement-farmers in particular formed the core of the community, and their property only went out of their hands upon the death of the last male heir. New owners of these tenements often turn out to have married into such a family and to have inherited the property when there was no surviving son to succeed. The contrast between such stable families and the increasing numbers of temporary migrants of labouring rank may help to explain the dichotomy between present popular belief in the permanence of village families and the findings of modern historians of large-scale mobility. Furthermore, this mobility usually took place only over a short distance, and though families may have moved out of the parish they usually remained within the neighbourhood.

An analysis of old and new names found in the baptism and burial registers between 1541 and 1701 reveals some interesting figures.

Table 9 Old and new families, 1541–1701

	Old families		New families		Old families	
Period	No.	Entries	No.	Entries	% Names	% Entries
1541–99	64	532	90	132	41.8	80.0
1600–43	61	449	83	112	42.4	80.0
1647–1701	74	909	114	212	39.4	81.1

There is remarkable consistency throughout the three periods, for the immigration of the mid-seventeenth century is balanced by the fact that some of the new immigrants of the Elizabethan period had by then settled down and become permanent residents (or 'old families') of more than one generation's standing. Only two out of every five surnames found in the registers belonged to old-established families, but if one looks at the total number of *entries* in the registers then four out of every five names are instantly recognizable as belonging to families that were often resident in the parish over five or six generations. It was they who provided the stability and continuity that one associates with a pre-industrialized community. In a real sense it was they who *were* the community.

But these stable families did have active connections with the outside world, as has been shown in the previous section. The marriage registers confirm the impression that there was regular movement between a group of parishes, and that although people were very conscious of belonging to a parochial community, they were also familiar with a wider area where they had friends and relations, and whose identity they shared. Table 10 and the map on p. 202 illustrate the marriage-pattern for those who were married in Myddle church between 1541 and 1701. It is not complete because many people from Myddle were married elsewhere, usually the men in the church of their bride. This means that there is a pronounced bias in the figures towards the group where both marriage partners were resident in the parish.

However, the geographical pattern for the origins of husbands and wives would probably not be radically altered if information were more readily available for the men.

Table 10 Origin of marriage partners, 1541–1701

	1541–99		1600–43		1647–1701	
	No.	%	No.	%	No.	%
Both partners from Myddle (inc. Hadnall)	46	41.4	22	36.1	53	47.7
Myddle woman = Shropshire man	55	49.9	36	59.0	35	31.5
Myddle woman = outsider	0	0	0	0	1	0.9
Myddle man = Shropshire woman	4	3.6	2	3.3	10	9.0
Myddle man = outsider	1	0.9	0	0	0	0
Neither in parish	5	4.5	1	1.6	12	10.8
Total	111		61		111	

In both cases where a Myddle person is recorded marrying someone from outside the county, the partner came from just across the border in Wales. Gough refers to other people whose marriages to outsiders were unrecorded in the parish registers, but in these cases nearly all the people concerned had permanently left the parish. Where neither partner was resident in Myddle, during the first hundred years all 12 people came from elsewhere in Shropshire, and during the later period, in every case, at least one of the partners was resident in the county. It can be readily seen from the table that many Myddle women found husbands not in the parish but within that wider area that embraces north Shropshire. The number of Myddle men who were married in other Shropshire churches would probably at least equal the number of men who came from neighbouring parishes to be married in Myddle. Nearly everyone found a husband or wife within a radius of ten miles of his or her dwelling, and most came from within the area centred upon the market-towns of Shrewsbury, Ellesmere, and Wem. The pattern does not change in any significant way throughout the 160-year period between 1541 and 1701.[47]

If Gough's account is used to supplement the information in the marriage registers, it can be seen that the gentry families and some of the small freeholders chose their brides and grooms from a slightly wider area than did the tenement-farmers and craftsmen. The only time that a member of the Gittins family married someone from Myddle was when Richard Gittins IV married Alice Morgan of

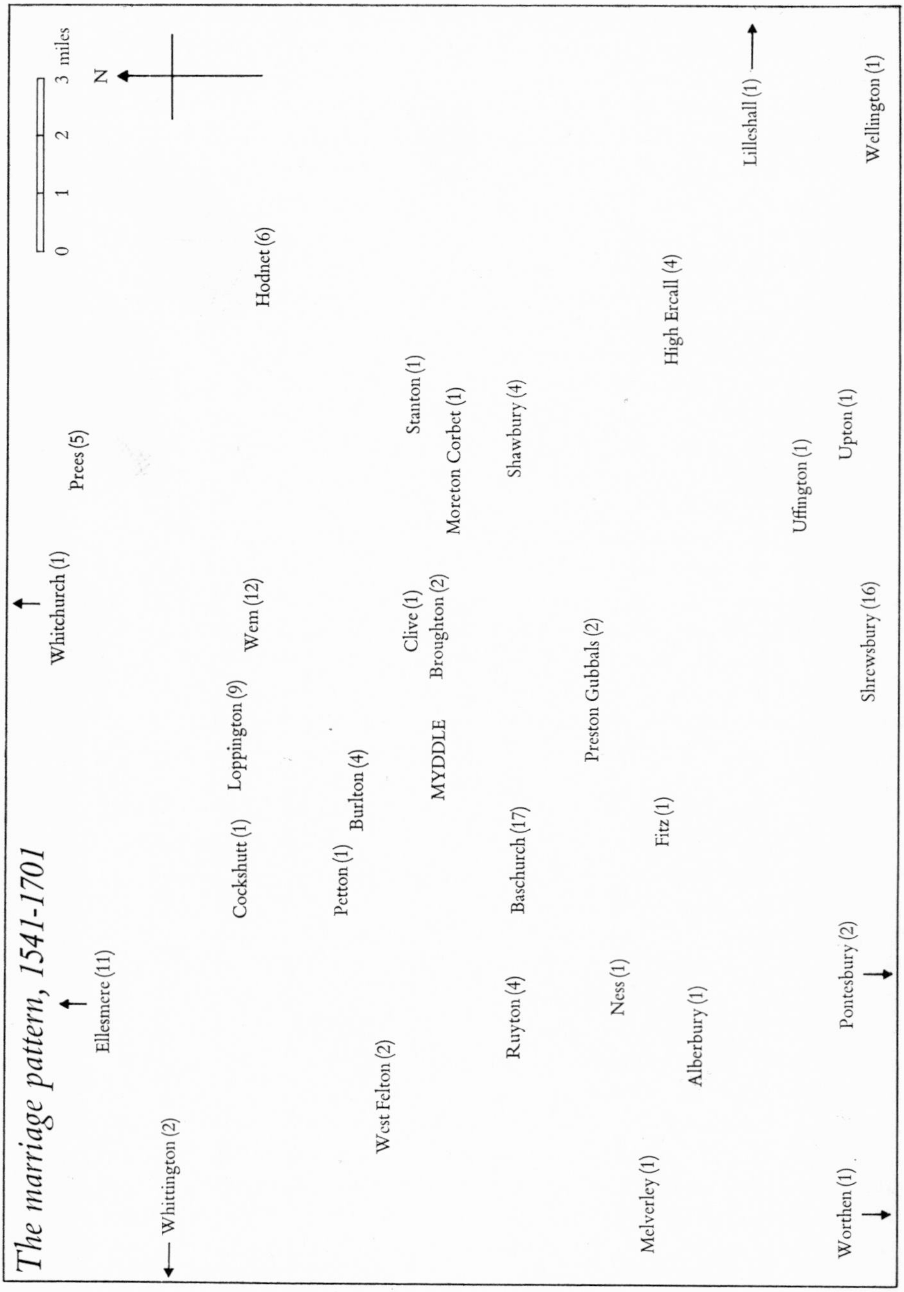

The marriage pattern, 1541-1701

Castle Farm. Otherwise, they found their partners from that wider area that included Shrewsbury, Fenemere, Pentre Morgan, Noneley, Withyford, and Ellesmere. Nor did the Atcherleys ever marry a local man or girl. On three occasions they married in Montgomeryshire (where they had close family connections), three other partners came from Shrewsbury, two from Burlton and two from Wolverley, one from Whitchurch, one from Hawkston, and one from Cheshire. Two of the Downtons married local people and two found spouses in Haston, but seven others went further afield to Shrewsbury, Clive, Condover, Hawkston, Priors Lee, Wem, and Shawbury. Their neighbours, the Amises, also married locally on two occasions, but also found brides and grooms in Shifnal, Yorton, Lilleshall, Muckleston, Lee, Cheshire, and Flintshire.

The Haywards of Balderton always chose their partners from outside the parish but within the neighbourhood, but perhaps the best illustration of all is provided by Richard Gough's own family. The Goughs were resident at Newton-on-the-Hill for several generations, but never once did they marry someone from their own parish. Their kins were widely scattered throughout north Shropshire, and brides and grooms were taken from Acton Reynold (twice), Weston Lullingfields (twice), Oswestry (twice), Ruyton, Clive, Shawbury, Little Ness, Adney, Cockshutt, Edgbolton, Peplow, Clayhowell, Measbury, Lee, and Baschurch. Richard Gough may have been very conscious of belonging to the parish of Myddle, but at the same time he had close family connections over the whole neighbourhood.

Further down the social scale, partners were chosen from a narrower geographical range. One of the Claytons found a bride in Meriden, but the other seven marriages that are recorded for this family were all with people from Myddle. The Formstons of Marton married local people on eight occasions, and also chose partners from Ellesmere (twice), Hordley, Welsh Franckton, and Oswestry. The Braynes married five local people and three others from north Shropshire; and they were typical of many others. The Chaloners, a long-resident family of blacksmiths and coopers, married 11 local men and women, another four from the neighbouring townships of Loppington and Burlton, and three more from only a few miles away.

Community ties must have been greatly strengthened by inter-marriage between the old families of the parish. The Chaloners had kinship bonds with the Tylers (twice), Formstons (twice), Woulfs, Rapheses, Pierces, Claytons, and Clarkes. The Claytons were also related through marriage to the Tylers, Juxes, Lloyds, Braynes, and Hordleys. The Formstons were married to Juxes, Pierces, Hordleys, Pickstocks, and Chaloners, and the Braynes had family ties with the Tylers, Lloyds, Claytons, Eatons, and Davieses. Marriages brought indirect connections as well: the Pierces brought the Formstons into contact with the Plungeons, and the Hordleys brought the Ashes nearer to the Formstons and Claytons. An intricate web of relationships connected all the long-established families who lived in the small farms and tenements, and personal friendships between people who were not necessarily close kins made the community even more conscious of its special identity.

Nor was there as much division between the gentry families and the rest as might be supposed from the marriage-patterns. The sharp distinctions of the nineteenth century were much more blurred in Tudor and Stuart times, when the local gentry and the tenement-farmer shared the same cultural background. The Gittins and Atcherley families married people of their own social status outside the parish, but other freeholders had kinship links with the yeomen and husbandmen, and sometimes even with the labourers. The Hanmers of Marton Farm, one of the most respected gentry families in the parish, married local people of a lower social status than themselves on at least three occasions during the first part of the seventeenth century. William Hanmer, gentleman, married Mary Baker, the daughter of a Marton yeoman, Humphrey Hanmer, gentleman, married the youngest daughter of John Groome, the Sleap Hall yeoman, and one of the Hanmer daughters married Thomas Ash, a Marton farmer.

Younger sons and daughters often had to be content with a more humble status than that of the eldest child. The Amises of Alderton could almost call themselves gentlemen, but in the 1640s two of their younger sons were cobblers. Similarly, Thomas Jux of Newton, yeoman, married Margaret Twisse of a substantial Hadnall family, early in the seventeenth century, but his sister, Alice, married a weaver. This blurring of class divisions is seen in Richard Gough's own family. His uncle, John, was "a dilligent laboriouse person, and spareing allmost to a fault", who lived in a small tenement in Brandwood as a poor husbandman and labourer. But John's brother, William "was the wealthyest man of our family", and as rich as some gentlemen.[48] Richard Gough's sister, Dorothy, also became wealthy when she married a Shropshire gentleman. Many of the younger sons of the yeomen and husbandmen earned their living as labourers, and it was quite common for a family to contain men of different occupations and social standing.

It is impossible to provide any realistic statistics about the age of marriage for Myddle men and women. Where definite information is available, the sample is far too small and the range of ages too wide to give the average any real meaning. One's impression is that most men and women in Tudor and Stuart Myddle were well into their twenties before they were married. Teenage marriages were very rare, though Gough quotes the case of a couple in his own family who were married so young "that they could not make passing thirty yeares beetweene them". They were as exceptional as another of his relations who did not marry until he was 68.[49] These impressions agree with the results of other studies, though marriage did not have to wait, as is sometimes implied, until a young man could inherit the family property from his father.[50] Newly-married couples did not normally live with their in-laws, unless an old infirm parent needed looking after, and they went to live elsewhere until the family holding was theirs. Many of them went to live out of the parish until that time, and Gough's eldest son may have been following a common practice by going to live in Shrewsbury. Gough had intended him to inherit his tenement had he not died prematurely.

Broken marriages were very rare, and though untimely death was much more common than now, some marriages lasted for quite a long time. The length of marriage can be established for 35 of the 91 households listed in the 1672 hearth-tax returns, i.e. 38½ per cent. Their average duration (both median and numerical) was 28½ years. This average might have been much lower if information was available for the other 56 households, but even so, a considerable proportion of marriages lasted long enough for both husband and wife to become grandparents, and a child had a good chance of knowing at least one grandparent on either side of the family. Sixteen couples in the 1672 profile were married for over 30 years, and of these, four were married for over 40 years. Both Michael and Susan Brayne, and Richard and Margaret Groome lived together for at least 43 years; Abraham and Martha Hanmer died within a week of each other after a marriage lasting about 49 years; and Thomas and Margaret Highway, who were married in 1659, had been married for 54 years and 2 months when Thomas died in 1714. His widow died a pauper 2½ years later. All four of these couples came from the tenement-farmer or labouring class.

Fourteen of the 69 men who are definitely known to have been husbands in 1672 were married more than once. This compares with the 21 of the 72 Clayworth (Notts.) husbands who were married at least twice.[51] Richard Rogers of Myddle-wood was married three times and outlived all his wives, and Francis Davies was living with his fourth wife at the time of his death. If a man was left a widower with young children he tended to remarry, but if his children were old enough to start work then he often remained a widower all his life. Richard Gough did not remarry although he outlived his wife by over 27 years, and Andrew Davies, who had been married for 14 years, was a widower for another 33. In the 1672 profile, William Watson, Daniel Tilsley, and Bartholomew Mansell all became widowers and remained so for over ten years, and Joan Hordley was a widow for 37 years after 18 years of marriage. She was fortunate in that her two eldest sons never married and were able to look after the family's tenement and business. Women who lost their husbands and did not remarry were in the most precarious position of all, especially if they had to rear a young family. Old age could also bring poverty, and solitary old widows were found in villages and hamlets throughout Tudor and Stuart England.

It has been estimated that roughly 70 per cent of households throughout the kingdom had children under the age of majority at any one time.[52] At least 70 of the 91 families in the 1672 list of Myddle inhabitants had children at some time or other, though the figure would have been a little lower than that at any one time.

In all the various sources there are references to at least 344 children belonging to these families, that is 4.9 per family (or 3.8 per family if one includes the households for which there is no evidence of any children). It must be stressed that these figures are minimal; there may have been other children who are not recorded. A different picture is obtained by looking at the evidence from 18 long-established families, taken for the whole period, 1524–1701. The records for these families are fuller and the average number of children per family is 5.5. These 18 families formed the core of the community; a few of them were gentry and one or two were labourers, but the majority of them were the tenement-farmers who lived and worked in the same place for generation after generation. An average of $5\frac{1}{2}$ children is probably more accurate than the lower figure taken from the full 1672 profile.

Some families were much larger than this. In the 1672 group there were ten families with just one child recorded, seven who had at least 2 children, six with 3, nine with 4, twelve with 5, nine with 6, six with 7, five with 8, one with 9, two with 10, two with 11, and another two with 12. Two of the four largest families were the result of the husband marrying twice, but the other two show what was possible if both husband and wife lived long enough for the woman to reach the end of her period of fertility. Thomas Hall of Balderton, gentleman, and his wife, Joan, had eight boys and four girls, as well as an abortive child, and at the other end of the social scale, Arthur Noneley of Brandwood, labourer, and his wife, Margaret, had seven boys and four girls. Several of the 18 long-resident families also had large families: eight of them had 7 children, ten had 8, two had 9, one had 10, and four had 11. If the available records named every child that was born, these figures might have been even higher. They confirm what has been written elsewhere about the overwhelming youthfulness of seventeenth-century society, when there were large numbers of children, but a low expectancy of life.[53] Gregory King estimated the average age in the late seventeenth century to be only $27\frac{1}{2}$ years.

The baptismal entries give some idea of how frequently children were conceived. Richard and Joan Gough had eight children born between 30 June 1663 and 10 October 1678, that is, in just over 15 years 3 months. They were baptized at intervals of $19\frac{1}{4}$ months, $36\frac{1}{2}$ months, $28\frac{1}{4}$ months, $22\frac{1}{4}$ months, 20 months, $14\frac{1}{2}$ months, and $30\frac{1}{2}$ months, which may suggest the truth of the popular idea that while a mother was suckling her child she was unlikely to conceive another. Only two of these children died in infancy or childhood.

Arthur and Margaret Noneley's children were born between 1662 and 1678, at intervals of 20 months, $17\frac{3}{4}$ months, $18\frac{1}{2}$ months, 13 months, 15 months, $24\frac{1}{4}$ months, $15\frac{3}{4}$ months, 23 months, $28\frac{1}{4}$ months, and $21\frac{3}{4}$ months. Their children were generally born at shorter intervals than were the Goughs'. John and Rose Hodden were married on 22 October 1578, had their first child $10\frac{3}{4}$ months later, and had nine more by early 1595, with another one over eight years later. One wonders whether a crude form of contraception was being practised after the birth of the tenth child, or whether Rose had abortive children who are not recorded in the registers. It is noticeable that the interval between children also increased towards the end of the reproductive life of Ralph and Rose Lloyd, who had six sons and two daughters between 1568 and 1586, born at intervals of $19\frac{1}{2}$ months, $19\frac{3}{4}$ months, $22\frac{1}{2}$ months, 26 months, $17\frac{3}{4}$ months, $34\frac{1}{4}$ months, and $49\frac{1}{4}$ months. Finally, a man who had long since ceased to father children by his first wife might start a second family when he remarried. Thus, Richard and Lowery Raphes had two sons and five daughters born between 1635 and 1648. Lowery died in 1661, and Richard married again late in 1665. He became a father again 14 months after his marriage, over 18 years after the birth of his last child, and over 31 years since he first became a father. He had five children in all by his second marriage, and his last child was born nearly 40 years after his first.

The evidence is far too slender to make any firm conclusions about whether or not brides were pregnant at the time of their wedding. One's impression is that the orthodox code of conduct was accepted and that it was rare for a woman to have conceived a child before her marriage. Nor can one give definite figures for infant mortality and the general expectancy of life. Of the 344 children born to those families who are listed in the 1672 profile, only 90 can be found in the burial registers. The amount of movement from one parish to another within the neighbourhood means that the age at death can only be established for 26.2 per cent of the profile, and that the figures are likely to be heavily biased towards those who died in infancy or early childhood before a family had moved elsewhere. Of the 59 males and 31 females in this sample, 23 died in infancy, 12 died between the ages of one and five, seven died between the ages of six and nine, nine died between the ages of ten and 19, and the remaining 31 males and eight females died after reaching maturity. In all, 28 males died before they were 20, and 31 died afterwards, whereas 23 females died in childhood or adolescence, and only eight are recorded (even under their married names) as dying in later life. Most of the girls who lived long enough to become adults must have left for some neighbouring place upon their marriage. Only 26.2 per cent can be traced from birth to death and the sample is too small to make any accurate estimate of the general expectation of life. Children frequently died in their infancy, and death could be expected at any time of life. But some lived to what would be considered an old age even today. Richard Gough was nearly 89 when he died, and there were a few others who lived into their nineties.

Those whose births are recorded but who have no entry in the Myddle burial registers account for 42 per cent of the 344 children. Of these, at least 12 of the 63 males and 17 of the 81 females grew into adults, for they can be found in the marriage registers or are known from other sources to have married. Another 13.7 per cent are only named at death, or (in the case of five men) at both marriage and death. Some of the 28 males and 19 females in this group were born outside the parish, but there are others who should have been named in the baptism registers. A further 8.1 per cent, comprising eight men and 21 women, are only mentioned at marriage, and a final 10 per cent (21 males and 13 females) do not appear in the parish registers at all, but are known only from other sources such as Gough, wills, and apprenticeship bonds. One wonders how many others are still undetected.

Fifty-eight of the 91 heads of households in the hearth-tax returns of 1672 died in Myddle, that is, 63.7 per cent. Three others died in neighbouring Broughton, and one gentleman ended his days in Oxfordshire. The other 29 (31.9 per cent) cannot be traced. Some of these almost certainly died in Myddle, but are not recorded in the burial registers. There were eight widows there in 1672, for instance, and most of them probably carried on living in their own homes until their deaths. The missing names are mostly unfamiliar ones, and one assumes that it was the poorer sections of the community who left the parish. Seven of the 15 people who were exempt from the tax cannot be traced in the burial registers. But a substantial majority of the community remained rooted in the parish, and there was certainly nothing like the rapid turnover of personnel that was characteristic of such contemporary arable villages as Clayworth (Notts.) and Cogenhoe (Northants.).

The serious under-recordings in the registers expose the limitations of family reconstitution. The parish of Myddle (and one suspects that this is true of many others) is not a satisfactory unit for attempting such work, but to analyse the whole neighbourhood of north Shropshire is a daunting task. The information one can collect about the members of a parish is far too limited to allow one to make any confident statements about matters that demand a precise answer. The technique of sampling is valuable for drawing general conclusions, in the way that one can see from the probate inventories that the farmers of Myddle followed a pastoral way of farming, but one has to be content with generalizations and the pointing out of possibilities. Sophisticated mathematical techniques do not produce convincing results if the sample is too small for obtaining precise answers to demographic queries about the exact rate of infant mortality, the normal age of marriage, and so on. This is not to dismiss family reconstitution as worthless. Far from it; other parishes may produce a more fruitful crop of statistics, and even where they do not do so, the techniques of reconstitution lead to a much greater understanding of the lives and attitudes of 'ordinary' people. But the pitfalls must be more readily pointed out, and the results treated much more cautiously than has so far been the case. In an intensive study of a community, family reconstitution is invaluable, but it must be used alongside many other techniques and seen as part of a whole. Too often, demographic analysis is made in isolation and divorced from the socio-economic history of the community that is being studied.

3 · *Kinship and neighbourliness*

Very little is known about family life and kinship during the sixteenth and seventeenth centuries. The only work to investigate the matter in depth is Dr A. Macfarlane's recent study of the diary of Ralph Josselin, a seventeenth-century Essex clergyman.[54] Diaries as detailed as this are few in number, and there is no such intimate record of the thoughts, feelings, contacts, and everyday activities of the people of Myddle. Gough was not consciously writing about such matters, and his remarks are naturally confined to his contemporaries of the late seventeenth century.

Throughout his work he is concerned with the individual families of the community. He judges them by their wealth and their social standing, by their moral virtues (or lack of them), and by the length of their residence within the parish. He frequently speaks of families being 'very ancient' in the locality, as if this was most commendable. He also approves of those who were descended from 'good' or 'substantial' families, even if sometimes they were from 'good but decaying' families. This concern with placing a man according to his birth was a common one, seen, for instance, in the case of Sir Paul Harris of Boreatton. "Hee was a person not well beloved by the antient gentry of this County, for beeing (as they termed him) but a bucke of the second head".[55]

Gough obtained much of his information from his contemporaries. (Writing about Taylor's tenement, he said, "The information that I had from Abram Taylor, the late tenant of this place is this".[56]) Even though strong bonds seem to have existed only between members of the primary family, the mental grouping of kins was a large one. Most families could go back several generations and knew of a wide range of cousins.[57] Gough could go back nearly 200 years with his own family and was fully acquainted with the personal histories of his nearest relations. He knew that his family had originated in Tilley as copyholders of about £60 p.a. and that Richard Gough I had leased his Newton tenement from the Banasters before it was made freehold by Richard II. He himself was the fifth Richard Gough of Newton. He was able to give character sketches of relations long since dead and not directly in line with him, as well as intimate sketches of the kinsmen of other families. This interest in kinship ties is a characteristic not only of Tudor and Stuart Myddle, but of many rural communities today where people are continually concerned with one another's affairs, and where conversation falls naturally into details of family history.[58] Gough was probably recounting stories that were already well known in his community.

The identification of a family with a particular farm or tenement reflected the high value that was placed upon buildings and land which had been the property of one's ancestors over several generations. "Nathaniell Reve had a desire to bee tenant of [Bilmarsh] farme, because his grandfather and father had been tenants to it before".[59] These ties were strengthened by the fact that the home was also the usual place from which one worked, the place where one spent a major part of one's life, where one was born and where one died. This was true for the substantial majority of the community of Myddle who resided on family farms. Unfortunately, there is no evidence about the ordinary working day or the rhythm of the farming year, but the comments of Gough and occasional remarks in other records illuminate the personal stories of the families of Myddle and help to focus attention upon the three crucial points of the life cycle – birth, marriage, and death.

Most women were delivered of their children by a local midwife, some of whom established a high reputation and were "of very great accompt". It was upon the advice and directions of such a midwife that Richard Clarke performed the abortion of his still-born child. The gentry families may have employed a neighbouring doctor, but there was no resident one in Myddle, and reliance was placed upon those who had successfully served one's friends and relations. Even within living memory almost all babies born in the rural Cumberland community of Gosforth "were delivered by aged women in the village who possessed no medical qualifications, but who were locally considered to be very highly skilled in midwifery". It also seems to have been the normal practice for a kinswoman to come to attend a relation during her period of labour.[60]

Childbearing was very risky. "His mother dyed in child-bedd of him", wrote Gough, and it could have been written of many others. The burial registers do not record the cause of death, but many young married women died soon after the birth of a child, or at an interval of two or three years when another child may have been due. Others were weakened or made ill by childbirth, and Gough refers to one woman who caught cold in childbearing and who was crippled for the rest of her life.[61]

Baptism followed fairly soon after birth, often within days, and certainly within weeks. The baptism of Michael Crompt's child 17 days after his marriage suggests that the service was usually held within one or two weeks of the birth. Gough queried a man's belief that he was born on St Stephen's day as this would have meant that he was over two months old before he was baptized,[62] and Richard Clarke was excommunicated for not baptizing his six-month-old daughter. At the baptism service, children were usually given names that were already popular in the family, often that of a parent or grandparent. Some families, such as the Gittinses and the Goughs, chose the same Christian name for the eldest son over several generations. It was also common for a child to be given the same name as a dead elder brother or sister, but it was not the fashion before the eighteenth century to give a child more than one Christian name. The only case to come to notice is the naming of an illegitimate child as Thomas Atcherley Edge, so that no-one could doubt who the father was.[63] This is the only time Gough refers to a baptism service actually taking place. The godfather (who named the child) was the child's grandfather.

Many of these newly-baptized infants died during their first year. Infant mortality and the more serious epidemics have already been mentioned, but there were several other illnesses to contend with, usually without the service of a doctor. Gough writes about "Dr. Eavans of Ruyton [who] was a doctor of phisicke, and in his youth was of very great accompt, and had much practice among the best men in these parts. Hee gave all his physick in powders, and made up his composition with his owne hands, not trusting to Apothecayres". But only the gentry could afford his services, and others had to rely on those (like the midwives) who had built a practical reputation for themselves. Elinor Mansell of Myddle "was very usefull and indeed famouse for her skill in surgery (which I beeleive shee learnd of her young Mistresses, the daughters of Mr. Chambre), and in that way shee did much good in the country". Mrs Julian Amies of Alderton was also "very helpfull to her neighbours in Chirurgery in which shee was very skilfull and successfull". Another surgeon had the necessary skill to fasten steel plates to the leg of George Reve, who had been crippled from birth, and with this help the leg eventually became strong enough for him to walk unaided. But there were those for whom nothing could be done. Margaret, the wife of Thomas Davies, a weaver who lived first in Newton, then in Myddlewood,

> tooke cold in childe-bearing, above twenty yeares before her death; shee was seized thereby with paine and lamenesse in her limbs, and made use of severall remedyes for cureing thereof, butt all proved ineffectual. At last, as shee was in an Apothecary's shop buying ointments and ingredients for fomentations my uncle, Mr. Richard Baddely, an able chirurgeon, saw her and asked her how shee gott her lamenesse: she sayd by takeing could in child-birth. Then says hee spare this charges and labour, for all the Doctors and Surgeons in England cannot cure it. Thou mayest live long, butt thy strength will still decay. After this shee went to lytle more charges, onely when king James II came his progresse to Shrewsbury, shee was admitted by the King's Doctors to goe to His Majesty for the Touch, which did her noe good. Shee was forced to use crootches almost 20 yeares agoe, and I thinke it is now 10 yeares since shee grew soe weake that shee was faine to bee carryed in persons' armes. About two years-and-an-halfe before her death [in 1701], shee kept her bedde continually; she was bowed soe togeather, that her knees lay closse to her brest; there was nothing but the skin and bones upon her thighs and legges. About a yeare-and-a-halfe past, her two thigh bones broake as shee lay in bedde, and one of them burst through the skin and stood out about an inch, like a dry hollow sticke, but there was noe flesh to bleed or corrupt; shee could stir noe part of her body save her head and one of her hands a lytle. When shee was dead they did not endeavour to draw her body straite, butt made a wide coffin and putt her in as shee was.[64]

Another ghastly story is also worth quoting in full for it has something to tell about the customs of the mid-seventeenth century. Richard Owen of Yorton "was seized with a violent fever" which eventually

> brought him soe weake that his speech failed and att twelve days end hee dyed, and according to the usual manner hee was laide straite upon his bedde, his eyes were closed and onely one linen sheet cast over him. Thus he continued one whoale day whilst his wife was takeing care to provide for his buriall; shee procured her sister, Jane Tyldesley of Newton, to beare her company all night for her children were yong. These two women sate by the fire all night, and about that time of night which wee account cock croweing they heard something give a great sigh. Alice Owen said it was Richard, butt Jane Tyldesley would not believe it. They tooke a candle and went into the chamber and cast the sheet from of his face and perceived noe alteration in him. Jane Tyldsley sayd it was some beast that was on the outside of the house. They tooke the candle and went round the outside of the house but found nothing. They came and sat againe by the fyre and soone after heard the same noise againe. Then they went to Richard Owen and found him all one as they left him; however they stayd by him and after some time they saw him open his mouth and give a sigh: then they warmed the bedde clothes and layd them upon him, and by that time that it was day the couler came in his face and hee opened his eyes on his owne accord, and by noone hee recovered his speech though very weakely. Hee continued weake for a long time, but at last recovered his perfect health and strength and lived after this above twenty yeares.

The practice of laying out the dead with a linen sheet must have been the usual one, for Gough goes on to quote a doctor of his youth who "was confident that many English people were buryed alive; for if they had been kept in theire warme bedds for forty-eight houres many of them would have recovered".[65]

It is likely that, as in other rural communities, kinship bonds were at their strongest at death,[66] but there is very little evidence about this or about the ceremonies associated with the burial service. Just before the Restoration, "there was three corpses buryed in Myddle churchyard att one time, by two ministers. One minister stood betweene two of the graves which were neare togeather, and read the office for both together". In the earlier years of the Commonwealth, William Tyler's daughter, the deserted wife of Richard Clayton, "was buried without any service or ceremony (according to those times). All the speech which was made att her grave was severall sad curses which her father gave against those that had brought her to her end". Gough mentions bellringers being paid immediately after the service, and the erection of "a faire Grave-stone" to a wife in the closing years of the seventeenth century. A suicide was refused burial in the churchyard and was interred, in the traditional manner, at a cross-roads, but later that night he was re-buried in his own rye-field. Suicide was very rare in seventeenth-century England, and there are only three cases in the whole of Gough's long account. John Gossage poisoned himself in a drunken stupor, Richard Woulf swallowed poison in his old age after his son-in-law had made his life a misery, and Andrew Hordley may have drowned himself upon the death of his brother.[67]

Marriages were not ordained at Myddle church during Lent, otherwise there was a fairly even distribution of weddings throughout the twelve months, with May being the most popular, and December the most unpopular. Gough complained that the "proud, foolish Girles" of his day were scorning the ancient method of calling the banns of marriage in church and were going to the expense of having a licence instead, but he makes no comments about the actual weddings, except to say of one marriage that "There was great feasting and joy att the solempnization". The better-off families provided marriage portions for their daughters, and Gough mentions sums ranging between £30 and £100. In one exceptional case, the daughter of an armigerous Shropshire family, who married the son of a wealthy Shrewsbury tanner, brought "1200 guineys, and as much silver as made her portion £1400; all payd on the wedding day". Some people married merely for the money: "shee was a harmlesse and almost helplesse woman, but hee had a great fortune with her"; and "I saw noe inducement that shee had to marry him, save his riches". But there are cases of men marrying their domestic servants (usually after the death of a first wife), and people like Thomas Downton who "unexpectedly . . . marryed a wife with nothing".[68]

Some fathers sought to guide their children when they were thinking of getting married. "His prudent Father observing the idle and lewd courses of his son [Samuel Downton] sought out a wife for him"; while Anne Baker married "more to please her father than herselfe". But her marriage failed, and so did that of Elinor Buttry, whose guardian, coveting her £100 marriage portion, married her to his son, "whilst they were under yeares of consent to marriage". Gough scathingly remarked: "Hee might . . . have taken notice of our old English proverbe, which sayes, that to marry children togeather, is the way to make whoremongers and whores; and soe it happened, for shee had noe love for her husband".[69]

But there were also cases where a son or daughter married against their parents wishes. Mary Amis married Samuel Wright "without her father's consent, which soe displeased him that hee gave his lands to Martha, the younger daughter, and married her to Edward Jenks". Michael Brayne married Susan Lloyd, "which soe displeased her father, that, allthough hee had but that onely child, yet he gave her nothing". Another member of this family of Braynes displeased his father by his marriage, and young Richard Wicherley was sent to London after fathering a bastard on one of his servant-girls, but after some time in the capital he sent for her and married her.[70]

Gough's sister also married "against consent of friends", and it was generally accepted that love should be the most important reason for marriage. The most remarkable case was that of Gough's niece who was married to a Welsh gentleman. "This couple when they were marryed were soe yong, that they could not make passing thirty yeares beetweene them, and yett neither of them were constrained by parents to marry, butt they going to schoole togeather fell in love with one another, and soe married. They live lovingly togeather, and have many children". Gough also mentions two servants who "fell in love and were married", and to his mind the ideal combination had been found by Richard Hatchett junior when he married a Shropshire woman: "Hee had a great fortune with her; butt that which is worth all, shee is a loveing wife, a discreet woman, and an excellent housewife".[71]

The ideal relationship between husband and wife was to be found in Myddle at Shotton Hall. After praising the skill and industry of William Watkins, Gough goes on to remark: "Hee is alsoe happy in a prudent, provident and discreet wife who is every way suitable for such an husband. They live very loveingly togeather, very loveing to their neighbours, and are very well beloved by theire neighbours, and they are both happy in that it hath pleased God in toaken of his love to them, and theire mutuall love one to another to blesse them with many comely and witty children". The Guests, the Ashes, and the Mansells are also commended for their happy marriages, but there were others like John Wright and his wife who "live a very unquiet and ungodly life", or Thomas Hayward's wife, who was "shrewed with tongue, soe that they lived unquietly and uncomfortably".[72]

Women had very little say in matters of public concern; they held no official positions and did not attend public meetings. Occasionally, they were called upon to witness wills or apprenticeship indentures, and the like, but only in a secondary capacity to that of their husbands. But they were normally given control over the running of the household, and were expected to provide good hospitality. When the man interfered, the housekeeping suffered. Rowland Muckleston of Alderton's first wife was "a quiett low-spirited woman, and suffered her husband to concerne himselfe with all things both within doores and without, soe that theire house-keeping was not commendable". His second wife altered all that. "Shee was a very handsome gentlewoman and of a masculine spirit, and would not suffer him to intermeddle with her concernes within doores, and shee endeavoured to keep a good house, but this caused them to keep an unquiet house, and many contests happened betweene theme which ended not without blows". Good hospitality was regarded as an essential virtue, and most men were happy to leave these matters to their wives. A few were quite dependent upon them. After Thomas Noneley's wife had died, he "went all to nought", and Thomas Downton's wife "proved a very discreet and provident woman, but theire estate being wasted, shee maintained them by selling ale".[73]

Relations between parents and their children were close and estrangements were rare. The father was not always the harsh, authoritarian figure that he is sometimes supposed to be. Richard Hayward, for example, wished to be a cook as a boy, and "his indulgent father put him to serve". Children were sometimes (though rarely) disinherited for marrying someone of whom their father disapproved, but they were usually allowed their own choice in this matter. The familial bonds were strong, and the child often repaid his parents' affection by looking after them in old age.[74]

The actions of their children sometimes caused a rift between husband and wife. Gough's brother-in-law educated his son in the best schools in the county, but became so angry at his failure and his spendthrift ways that he refused to have anything more to do with him. His wife provided their son with money and a servant and sent him to Wales, but he got no further than an ale-house just beyond Oswestry.

> It was long beefore his father would bee reconciled to him; butt att last he tooke him, putt him in a very gentile habit, gave him a good horse, and sent him to court a gentlewoman who was likely to bee a good wife for him. But this match failed: and soone after an unlucky match was made betweene him and a sister of Mr. Lloyd's, a Montgomeryshire gentleman. My brother-in-law, Glover, gave him £100 per annum att marriage, and £100 per annum att his decease; butt some yeares after, great difference happened beetweene the father and son, and alsoe betweene the son and his wife and mother in law. Butt in some kinde humour his wife's friends persuaded him to take an yearly sum to maintaine him, and to part with his wife; and the annuity being too little to supply his extravagancyes, hee lives meanely.[75]

This story has been quoted in full as this is one of the few instances where family ties are seen to be under stress, and where great efforts were made to hold the family together. It is of significance to the kinship structure and to the concept of neighbourliness that after the first rift, the young man was sent away to relations (though with money to provide for him), and that, in the last episode, his wife's friends acted to end the dispute.

It seems to have been normal for children to work on the family farm until the age of puberty, say between 13 and 15 for girls, and 15 to 17 for boys. The eldest son might remain on the farm throughout his adolescence, but unless the farm were large enough to support them younger sons were apprenticed to some neighbour or relation, or left to become servants. Girls, too, left their homes for service, though it is difficult to find any definite information about how old they were at the time. But despite these spells away from home, family links remained strong, and during their old age parents could normally expect their children to look after them. Samuel and Mary Brayne maintained his mother, "who is of great age", in his tenement in Myddle, Arthur Davies and his wife maintained her father, "who is very aged and blind, if not deaf". John and Margaret Huet looked after his father, Thomas Hall was kept by his son in part of Balderton Hall, Thomas Hayward "sold and consumed all his estate and was afterwards mainetained on charyty by his eldest son", and after Thomas Hodgkins had ruined himself by drink he went to live with his son-in-law, while his wife removed to the old Warren House, "and had nothing to maintaine herselfe butt what neighbours sent".[76] These instances show that charity was not necessarily associated with the transference of the patrimony.

Other family ties mentioned by Gough include financial help between brothers. Richard Hayward lent his brother money to set himself up in business in London, and paid his debts after he had gone bankrupt, and William Gough and his half-brother, Thomas Baker, joined their money together to pay for a lease for three lives at Sweeney. Other men secured employment for their younger brothers by their personal introductions, for if one member of a family proved to be a good servant, then it was reckoned that other members would probably work equally well. Such personal connections were of great importance in this matter.[77]

Any breaking of the kinship ties was regarded as unnatural and treated with deep suspicion.[78] When William Tyler, the most notorious character in the parish, was accused at the Assizes of sheep-stealing, his grandson, Thomas Tyler, was the chief witness, but "the Jury conceived it maliciouse, and blamed him for offering to hang his Grandfather; and soe old Tyler was acquitted". This William Tyler had used the bonds of kinship to pervert the course of justice on a previous occasion, when Richard Chaloner, his daughter's son, appeared at the Assizes for stealing a cow from one of his kinsmen. "The owner was bound to prosecute, but his uncle William Tyler tould the prosecutor that this Chaloner was his kinsman, and it would be a disgrace to him as well as to the rest of his friends to have him hanged, and that his friends would raise £5 among them to pay for the cow in case hee would forbeare the prosecution. To this the prosecutor agreed; hee received the £5. Hee preferred noe bill and Challoner was quitt by proclamation; but soone after William Tyler threatened the prosecutor that hee would ruine or hang him for takeing a bribe to save a thiefe, and by this menaceing caused the prosecutor to pay backe the £5 to Tyler".[79]

But outrageous flouting of the kinship ties sometimes caused a severing of relationships. When Michael Chambre did not pay his sister's legacies, his brothers-in-law took him to court and saw to it that he was imprisoned. There was rarely such trouble as this. The normal system of inheritance was primogeniture, with legacies for younger sons and daughters, and provision for them upon their marriage or when securing them employment. If there was no child to inherit, then a near relation was usually chosen; William Lloyd was apprenticed with his uncle in Shrewsbury, who left him his house, his shop, and his lands; and when the last of the Deakins died in 1611, he left his estate to his sister's son. Other examples could be quoted, but the most revealing comment occurs in the case of Richard Hayward, who bequeathed his tenement in Balderton to his eldest brother's son, who was well known to be an Anabaptist. He was "blamed by some gentleman of his acquaintance for soe doeing" on the grounds that his nephew was a dissenter, but "hee answeared that it was God that had given him an estate and according to the Lawes of this Land which hee beelieved were founded upon the Lawes of God, this yong man was his heire; and he did not finde by the Law that hee ought to disinherite him because hee was different from him in some opinions". The strength of his kinship ties defied any other consideration.[80]

Friends from outside the kinship group were also called upon to give advice and to help in times of difficulty. When, for instance, John Noneley was unable to get his rent from William Tyler, he "imployed freinds to compound with Tyler to be gon". Neighbours were expected to be helpful and hospitable, and these virtues were frequently extolled by Gough. Mr Kinaston, the rector, "kept good hospitality and was very charitable", but his successor, Mr More, was "blamed for his too much parsimony, or covetousenesse, and want of charity". William Watkins was a model of what a man should be, and Bartholomew Mansell "was very serviceable to his neighbours in dressing meate att feasts, and in slaughtering beeves and swine, all which he did att a very reasonable rate". Daniel Wicherley was "much commended for that hee did never contend [at law] with persons unable to deale with him, butt with great persons", but as to Richard Wicherley, "I never heard that he was commended either for his charity to the poore, his hospitality to his neighbours, nor his plentifull housekeeping for his servants".[81] Wicherley's failures demonstrate what were considered as the necessary virtues in the life of the community. A man who prospered materially was praised only if he kept good hospitality and if he was charitable to his poorer neighbours.[82] Gough mentions that John Dodd, Richard Hayward, and Thomas Lloyd each left sums, ranging between £5 and £10, to pay for bread for the poor, and it seems to have been common practice, at least in Elizabethan times, to bequeath what small sums one could afford. In 1574, John Woulf gave "to every poore body within the parishe one hoope of rye", and to each of his servants 3*s*. 4*d*. In 1587, George Downton gave to "the poore of this parish 5*s*. to be imployed as it shall seeme good to my executors", and a ewe lamb to Jane, his servant-girl. Ann Matthews's bequests in 1570 were of wider scope; she gave 1*s*. to the poor of Shrewsbury, and a further 6*s*. 8*d*. to 20 of the poorest inmates of the almshouses there, 2*s*. towards the cost of repairing Myddle church, and a hoop of rye "to every poore housholder on this side of the parishe". William Brayne (1563) also left a small sum of money towards the repair of the highways.

It became usual in England during the seventeenth century for such doles to be replaced by charitable endowments. In Myddle, the two main charities listed in Bagshaw's *Directory* of 1851[83] were the rent-charge of 24*s*. per annum left by Thomas Atcherley in 1680, and the apprenticeship-charity established by William Gough in 1669. This charity served the useful purpose of paying for poor boys in the parish to be apprenticed to some trade, and was put to regular use. Charity was one of the supreme virtues.

Gough also praises those who worked hard and skilfully, and those who were upright in their personal lives. Thomas Hayward, junior, was "a person well reputed in his country and of general acquaintance. Hee was just and faythfull in affirmeing or denying any matter in controversy, soe that lesse credit was given to some men's oathe than to his bare word". And Thomas Ash was "a proper, comely person; his father gave him good country education, which, with the benefit of a good naturall wit, a strong memory, a curteouse and mild beehaviour, a smooth and affable way of discourse, an honest and religiouse disposition, made him a compleat and hopefull young man . . . Hee was comended for avoiding that abominable sin of prophane swearing".[84]

Modern anthropologists and sociologists have stressed the role of the kinship structure in transmitting moral attitudes such as those from one generation to another. Not all children followed the way of life of their parents, but a very high proportion undoubtedly did so. Gough notes those who were the exceptions, but in his work there is the same underlying assumption that is often found in modern rural communities that kinship groups have their collective virtues and vices.[85] The careers of the offspring of William Tyler show that this influence could work against the interests of the community as well as for it, but most children were taught to accept the traditional values by the example and precepts of their parents.

4 · Power and authority

The farmhouses and cottages of the village of Myddle were overshadowed by the castle and the church in a way that symbolized the power of the lay and ecclesiastical authorities. This power was weaker than it was in many of the contemporary arable villages further east, where the squire and the parson were in everyday contact with their tenants and charges; some of the hamlets and outlying farms were contained in other manors and lay out of view more than a mile distant from the church. But this freedom from authority in the woodland communities was only relative; there was a greater sense of independence than in the 'closed' villages of the 'fielden' areas, but both lay and ecclesiastical power continued to be wielded effectively in Myddle during the sixteenth and seventeenth centuries. The manorial courts continued to function smoothly long after the decay of the castle, and the power of even an absentee-lord was seen in his successful struggle to raise entry fines in the late 1630s. The church, too, weathered the storms of the Reformation and the Civil Wars, and by the end of the seventeenth century its spiritual and moral authority within the community remained unshaken.

The church also fulfilled the role of uniting the parish into a community, a unit to which people were conscious of belonging, and which distinguished them from their neighbours in adjacent parishes. The building gave this community a united sense of continuity with the past; it had been erected by their ancestors, here they had worshipped, and here they lay buried either within or without its walls. The church also gave a sense of present unity for it served as the one meeting-place where all alike had the chance to gather together at least once a week. Smaller numbers met at the manor court, but there were no parish gilds nor any other formal body where a group was regularly assembled. When special parish-meetings were called to discuss civil business, it was within the nave of the church that people gathered. Nowhere else was the community so united, either physically or spiritually. Old and young, male and female, rich and poor, only came together as a whole for divine service on Sundays or at special church festivals.

Upon these occasions, the social gradations within the community were formalized by the strictness of the seating arrangements. There had been no pews before the Reformation, but then the gentry families led the way by installing three rows of seats. Their example was followed by the tenement-farmers, and then by the cottagers, until the church was gradually filled. Gough was very much concerned with establishing the exact ordering of the seats, and, indeed, the whole framework of his book is based upon the seating-plan. Disputes inevitably broke out as time went on, for seats were transferred not necessarily by family, but by ownership of house or cottage, and property sometimes changed hands and became divided. Furthermore, the population rise of the mid-seventeenth century put pressure on the amount of space available for new pews. These disputes could cause great bitterness of feeling; after losing a feigned action in the manor court with the Atcherleys over the right to the chief seat for Marton, the Hanmers ceased to attend Myddle church and worshipped in the neighbouring parish of Baschurch. A dispute in 1658, when William Formston wrenched off a lock on the pew door that John Downton had fitted to assert his rights (as he thought), led to a special parish meeting being called to smooth out all the problems. The meeting was attended by "a considerable part of the parish", and five orders were made, and signed by the minister, two churchwardens, and seven of the leading families. Gough's words can hardly be bettered as an unconscious revelation of the social attitudes of the time: "It was held a thing unseemly and undecent that a company of young boyes, and of persons that paid noe leawans [i.e. church-rates], should sitt (in those peiws which had been the passage) above those of the best of the parish". This concern with social status is also seen when Gough wrote in some surprise of Thomas Jux of Newton: "Hee often kept company with his betters, but shewed them noe more respecte than if they had beene his equalls or inferiors".[86]

It was also considered unseemly that Thomas Highway profited by the congestion in the church during the later years of the seventeenth century by allowing other cottagers to share his pew provided they paid him a yearly sum for this privilege.[87] This had never been done before in Myddle, and Highway (the parish clerk) was widely, but ineffectively, criticized. But even though there was no more room for any more seats, attendance at divine service was still expected. The comperta book of 1665 charged John Hoordes [Hordley?], Richard Gardner, and Alan Wright with "absenting themselves from their parish church on Sundayes and holydayes at divine service tyme", and Alan Chaloner and Robert Orred were charged with absenting themselves from the sacrament. Other cases are recorded in 1668, 1679, and 1682.[88] Provision was also made for the servants in the seating-plans, and it seems that everyone was expected to attend regularly.

The gentry would have justified the seating arrangements as being part of the natural order of things, and also by the amount of leawans, or church-rates, that they paid. These varied according to the value of one's property, and their payment was enforced by the ecclesiastical courts. In 1620, for instance, Thomas Davies appears in the comperta books for not paying his rates, and in 1668 Thomas Hall of Balderton was excommunicated for refusing to pay.[89] The property-owners or occupiers were also responsible for the maintenance and repair of the churchyard and its walls; the Brandwood tenements, for instance, had to keep in repair the six yards of walling that lay to the east end of the churchyard,[90] while the families of Hadnall chapelry had to contribute a quarter of the maintenance costs, despite having to look after their own chapel-of-ease.

Then there were also the normal payments to the rector and to the parish clerk. The rector usually received tithes in kind, and was paid 6*d.* per annum by male servants and 4*d.* by female ones. He also received the usual Easter dues and offerings and was paid by a fixed set of fees for special services. All these payments were written down with great deliberation in the church terriers. For instance, the 1699 terrier records burial fees as being 1*s.* for a churchyard burial in a coffin, or 6*d.* without a coffin, with double charges for burials inside the church. Social position as well as the ability to pay probably determined whether one was allowed burial in the nave. Thus, Roger Nicholas, the gentleman freeholder of Balderton Hall (1572), could leave his body "to be buryid in the churche of Middle at the backe of Mr. Bayley his pewe", while the wills of more humble people mention burial in the churchyard. Gough's son was buried in the chancel, and his chance remark about this suggests that some of the wealthier parishioners were being buried in the chancel, and others in the nave, by the late seventeenth century.[91]

The tithes and payments made the parish of Myddle a comfortable living. The Valor Ecclesiasticus of 1535 valued the rectory at £16 per annum, which, after deductions, left the rector a clear £12 7*s.* 2*d.* This value greatly increased as more land was brought into cultivation and more people settled in the parish. The Hadnall petitioners of 1693 claimed that their tithes were worth £50, and they amounted to only a quarter of the whole.[92] The inventory of William Holloway (1689) shows that by the late seventeenth century the rector could live in some style and that his standards of domestic comfort surpassed any in the parish.

The character and personality of the rector were obviously of prime importance in establishing the spiritual and moral tone of the community. Very little, however, is known about the rectors of Myddle other than from the pen-sketches of Gough, and the brief remarks of Foster.[93] Thomas Tonge was rector for 40 years, between 1511 and 1551, but Gough had heard of him only by name. He was succeeded by John Higgyns (1551–63), who may have been an absentee, for "Wyllyam Banester, curate" was named as the minister-in-charge at the time that the inventory of church goods was taken in 1553.[94] Then, for the next five years, Richard Foster was rector, but he too is known only by name. The first rector whom Gough could write about was Thomas Wilton, M.A., incumbent from 1568 to 1596. "He was careful to Reforme those things that through negligence were grown into disorder, and to settle things in such a way as might conduce to the future peace and benefit of the parishioners". In other words, he was a sound Anglican. The three chained books of the sixteenth century that are still kept in the church may well have been bought during his incumbency, for they are all apologies of the position adopted by the Church of England, written by Erasmus, Jewel, and Whitgift. Unfortunately, no early churchwardens' accounts survive to illuminate the progress of the Reformation, and the events were too distant for Gough to have any real knowledge of them.

Wilton was succeeded by Ralph Kinaston, M.A., rector from 1596–1629, who was descended from "the ancient and worthy family of the Kinastons of Hordley". He was born in 1560 and had graduated from St Mary Hall, Oxford, and must have served elsewhere before he came to Myddle. He had an estate in Montgomeryshire, and in addition to performing conscientiously his duties in Myddle, he was prebend of St Asaph, and a chaplain to King James I. Gough describes him as "a person of bold and undaunted spirit . . . [who] kept good hospitality and was very charitable". His gravestone is inscribed, "He had carefully and religiously performed his calling".[95]

He was followed by Thomas More, B.D. (1630–*c.* 1646), an unpopular Yorkshireman who was the first rector to be presented by the Earl of Bridgewater. He resided at Ellesmere where he had another (and better) living. He was presented at the bishop's visitation of 1633 for non-residence,[96] and it may have been from that time that he kept a curate at Myddle. His brother lived in the parsonage (and, later, at Eagle Farm) and farmed the tithes of the parish, "at a dearer value than ever they have been since sett for". More came to Myddle only once a month, riding up to the church just before the service, and leaving as soon as it had finished. He "was much comended for an excellent preacher and as much blamed for his too much parsimony, or covetousenesse, and want of charity". The chance to evict him came during the Civil Wars, for not only was he an absentee, but an ardent Royalist as well. He was forced to flee to London, and he was permanently ousted in about 1646.

The Puritan divine who replaced him was Joshua Richardson, M.A. (*c.* 1647–62), the son of Joshua Richardson of Broughton. He had graduated at Brasenose College, Oxford, and had been Vicar of Holy Cross, Shrewsbury, from 1645 to 1647. He was described in a Parliamentary Inquisition as "an able Preaching Minister",[97] and by Gough as "an able and laborious minister. His whoale employment was about the concernes of his ministry". He continued for a while after the Restoration, as the Earl of Bridgewater knew of his high reputation in the parish. He told Gough that he would willingly have conformed to the discipline and constitution of the Church of England, but he refused to subscribe to the Declaration against the Solemn League and Covenant of 1662. He was removed from his post, and after living at Broughton for a time, he removed to Alkington, near Whitchurch, where he maintained himself by teaching, until his death in 1671. He bequeathed bibles and some copies of Richard Baxter's *A Call to the Unconverted* to be given to certain poor people in the parish of Myddle. His story is typical of many other Nonconformist ministers of the time.

William Holloway, M.A. (1614–89), was the next rector. He was the son of Barnabas Holloway of Little Gaddesden, Hertfordshire, the residence of the Earl of Bridgewater. He and his brother, Thomas, graduated at Christ Church, Oxford, and both were preferred by their noble neighbour. Thomas became a vicar in Wiltshire, and William became the rector of North Cheriton in Somerset. After serving there for ten years, in 1662 he came to Myddle. To Gough, he was "short-sighted but of a discerning spirit to discover the nature and disposition of persons. He was naturally addicted to passion, which hee vented in some hasty expressions, not suffering it to gangreene into malice. Hee was easily persuaded to forgive injuries but wisely suspiciouse (for the future) of any one that had once done him a diskindnesse".[98] During his incumbency the Anglican liturgy was restored. The churchwarden's accounts for 1662 read: "Payd to John Wood, Limer, for adorning the church, £4 6*s.* 0*d.* . . . For surplice, table-cloth, carpet, silke, thred, washing, making, £4 . . . For Ale for the Joyner and Peeter Lloyde for taking up the rayles in the chancel, 1*s.*" The 1663–4 entries include: "For the Books of Homilies and Cannans, 9*s.* . . . For the new table and frame, 14*s.* . . . For the booke of Articles, 6*d.*"

The last rector of the seventeenth century was Hugh Dale, M.A. (1689–1720), the son of a Cheshire gentleman, and graduate of Brasenose College. Myddle was his first and only post, but, unfortunately, Gough makes no comment about him.

The three parish clerks whom Gough had known were from the poorer sections of the community. William Hunt was "a person very fitt for the place, as to his reading and singing with a clear and audible voice", who also kept a petty school and lived in a small tenement at the lower end of Myddle village. Richard Raphes, a poor tailor, and the son of a Marton carpenter, was also "a person in all respects well qualyfied for that office", but he was dismissed after the Restoration after remonstrating with maypole revellers, allegedly saying that it was as sinful to dance round the maypole as it was to cut off the king's head. He always denied using these words. He was replaced by Thomas Highway, "a person alltogeather unfitt for such an imployment. Hee can read but little; hee can sing but one tune of the psalmes. He can scarse write his owne name, or read any written hand". He was later given a more able assistant, and was more-or-less confined to the role of sexton by the end of the century.

Shropshire was relatively little affected by dissent during the seventeenth century. The Compton ecclesiastical census returns of 1676 number 56,923 people in the county over the age of 16, and over 98.5 per cent of these conformed to the Church of England. There were only 366 (or 0.5 per cent) Roman Catholics in the county. At Madeley, 51 of the 450 people who were counted were Catholics, and there were 30 more at Ellesmere, but nowhere else did they reach double figures. There was none in Myddle at this time, and only one or two at the most in other places. In the county as a whole in 1676 there were 644 Nonconformists, which was only about 1 per cent. Eight market towns contained 304 of them: 72 in Shrewsbury, 70 in Oswestry, 40 in Wellington, 30 each in Newport and Whitchurch, 21 each in Ludlow and St Martins, and another 20 in Ellesmere. The rest were scattered thinly over the countryside. In the parish of Myddle (including the chapelry of Hadnall) there were 398 Anglicans and 10 Nonconformists.[99] A similar picture is provided by 'John Evans' List of Dissenting Congregations', made in 1715.[100] Not until the evangelical revival of the late eighteenth century did dissent assume any real significance in Shropshire. The Old Dissent flourished in some woodland communities, but not in Myddle, nor in its neighbouring parishes.

References to dissenters are very sparse in all the records concerning the community of Myddle during the seventeenth century. After the revolutionary settlement of 1689, the house of William Cooke was twice registered at the Quarter Sessions as a place of public worship. Cooke was a Cheshire man who had just come to be tenant at Sleap Hall, and despite being a dissenter, he twice served the parish as churchwarden. There are no other indications of regular Nonconformist meeting places in the parish. The only reference in Gough to such a meeting was outside the parish in the Commonwealth era, when an Independent preacher held a four-hour prayer-meeting at the home of Mr Thomas Baker, J.P., at Sweeney. Gough had a high regard for Joshua Richardson, but was contemptuous of Catholics and of the more extreme Nonconformists. When Thomas Lovett, junior, left Myddle to enter the service of a Staffordshire Catholic, he became a convert, and in Gough's words, "leaving the relligion wherein hee was borne and baptized, hee beetooke himselfe to his beads". The Friends he dismissed as "that phanaticall, selfe-conceited sort of people called Quakers . . . [with] theire canting way of discourse", while Anabaptists and Fifth Monarchy Men were treated equally severely.[101] Gough was writing very much from the orthodox point of view, and in the absence of Nonconformist records, one simply does not know the range and depth of other opinion. But the majority of people in north Shropshire conformed to the Established Church and regularly attended its services, and both Catholicism and Dissent attracted only a handful of supporters within the parish.

Some of the surviving wills suggest a real concern with religious matters. Ann Matthews of Myddle (1570) started her will, "First I commit my soull into the handds of Allmightye god, moste certaynlye belevinge to have full reemission and forgevenes of all my sinnes, onely by the deathe and bludsheadinge of our Lorde and saivoure Jesus Christe, Item, I bequithe my body to be buryed in the churche yarde of Middle, nothinge doubtinge, but that at the laste day in the self same bodye beinge glorifyed I shall ryse agayne and see my redemer". It can be argued that this was lawyer's jargon and that other wills reveal that such phrasing was something of a standard form. Dr Margaret Spufford has recently shown[102] that sixteenth- and seventeenth-century wills in rural Cambridgeshire were drawn up by a small number of scribes. In the case of Ann Matthews, however, the handwriting and spelling give the impression that although conventional terms might be used, her will was made in genuine belief.

As far as can be seen, attendance at divine service was matched by a general acceptance of the moral teachings of the church. Myddle was far from being an idle and lawless woodland community such as Norden and other contemporary writers judged the type to be. A superficial reading of Gough might suggest great immorality, but his more scandalous passages concern only a small fraction of the community, who in no way typify the whole. The scandalous passages are the ones that catch the eye and remain in the memory, but in fact they involve only a few members of the community. In the early years of the nineteenth century, the entries in the parish registers show that about 8 per cent of the baptisms were illegitimate, and by 1861 in the Ellesmere district (which included Myddle) more than 10 per cent of births were illegitimate.[103] This is very high for a rural area of that time. However, these figures are in no way typical of the community of Myddle during the sixteenth and seventeenth centuries, for the entries in the parish registers suggest that illegitimacy was then under 1 per cent. There is a noticeable rise in the illegitimacy rates in the parish registers of the late eighteenth and early nineteenth centuries. In Tudor and Stuart Myddle the orthodox moral code was accepted by nearly everyone, regardless of class, and equally regardless of time. There were certain 'bad families' and a few notorious individuals, as in many other communities, both then and now, but the crime rate seems to have been lower, and the moral code more strictly observed, than is the case in much of the England of today.

Present understanding of the motives for crime and immorality is imperfect, so how much more difficult it is to try to understand the reasons why people turned to crime and ignored the moral standards of the age of the Tudors and Stuarts. There were the usual petty thieves, both male and female, and there were those who were compulsive stealers. Reece Wenlock of the Mear House, and his two sons, Reece and John, "never stole any considerable goods, but were night walkers, and robbed oarchyards and gardens, and stole hay out of meadows, and corne when it was cutt in the feilds, and any small things that persons by carelessnesse had left out of doors". The father was cured of stealing hedge timber when a neighbour filled a stick with gunpowder, which exploded when Wenlock stole it and put it in his oven. Another compulsive petty thief was John Aston, a Houlston labourer, who was "a sort of a silly fellow, very idle and much given to stealing of poultry and small things". He was frequently warned by his neighbours, but continued to steal and was eventually tried at Shrewsbury. He was saved by the jury valuing the poultry he had stolen at only 11*d*., "att which the judge laught heartily and said he was glad to heare that cocks and henns were soe cheap in this country". This experience made Aston more careful, "butt hee left not his old trade whoally".[104]

This type of person was regarded with amused contempt and much tolerance, but there were others who led a more organized life of crime. John Gossage of Myddle was "a drunken, debauched person", well known for his criminal activities, and eventually imprisoned for counterfeiting. But "the falsest theife that ever I heard of in this parish" was John Owen of Myddle, who slept by day and stole by night. His speciality was cattle- and horse-stealing, but he was eventually apprehended upon hiding a stolen horse in some rough ground of George Pickstock's at Houlston, a favourite reception place of his. He was tried and hanged at Shrewsbury, and "great numbers of people went to see his execution and to heare his confession, which they say was very large".[105] The only other person to be sentenced to death in the parish was Hugh Elks of Marton who had murdered a servant-girl there when she had recognized him in the act of stealing. But vicious crime such as this was most unusual.

The sexual code of the church was accepted by all sections of the community. Broken marriages and cases of adultery were rare, and the illegitimacy-rate in the sixteenth and seventeenth centuries was low. There were few cases that were brought before the ecclesiastical courts. Judith Welch was charged with fornication in the comperta books of 1682, and 17 years later, Arthur Davies and Jane Morris were called to answer a charge of "liveing together in open fornication"; a charge that was repeated on three occasions during the following year.[106] There are one or two earlier references to illegitimate children, but on the whole, the records of the ecclesiastical courts do not suggest much immorality. Nor do the parish registers name many bastards, and Gough's stories are limited to a few exceptional families.

The ones he does refer to are treated in the most scathing manner. Elizabeth, the daughter of William Tyler and the wife of William Bickley, "was accounted a lewd woman, and had severall daughters who had noe better a repute . . . Shee was more commendable for her beauty than her chastity, and was the ruin of the family". Margaret Formston, the wife of William Chaloner, the Myddle cooper, "left three daughters, two of which are as impudent whores as any in the country". And Michael Chambre of Balderton Hall "was whoally addicted to idlenesse, and therefore noe marvel that hee was lasciviouse . . . His lewd consorts were such ugly nasty bawds, that they might almost resemble uglinesse itselfe, and such as were the very scorne of the greatest and vilest debauchees of those times". It is very noticeable that when the largest landowners in the county fathered bastards they escaped the strictures of Gough.[107]

In his study of the modern Suffolk village of 'Akenfield' Ronald Blythe quotes a magistrate as saying: "In the village there was always the Bad Family. Every village had one and we knew them all. They came up [in court] over and over again, and we watched them going slowly, inevitably downhill".[108] She was sure they felt no shame. The Bad Family in the community of Myddle was sired by William Tyler of Brandwood, a person of "a meane stature, lancke haire, and a manly countenance". The Tylers were an ancient family in the parish, but only with William did they start to become notorious. He broke up a neighbour's marriage by his adultery, which ended with him fathering a bastard daughter. When this girl was grown-up, Tyler took her as his housekeeper and eventually fathered a bastard on her as well. He was also well known in the ale-houses and frequently in debt. At last, he was arrested for debt after a struggle in the churchyard one Sunday, when "the consternation and lamentation of Tyler's friends, especially the women, was such as I cannot easily demonstrate". John Gossage and some tipsy companions offered to release him, but he was safely secured. After his release, he wasted his estate on drink, but lived to an old age, passing his time by tending a little flock of sheep on the commons, and stealing those of his neighbours when the chance arose. "Hee had beene accustomed to stealeing all his lifetime, and could not forbeare in his old age". Some of Gough's stories of his trouble with his neighbours have already been recounted. The manor court books also mention a charge against him of illegally cutting down timber. He was constantly in a variety of troubles, yet he was not without his friends, as was shown at the time of his arrest.[109]

His daughter, Elizabeth, has already been mentioned. His other daughter, Anne, was abandoned by her husband, Richard Clayton. His son, Richard, was very different in character, "peaceable and well reputed among his neighbours". But Richard's son, Thomas, was of the same mould as his grandfather, and were it not for his early death in an accident at the age of 27, "hee would have beene worse than ever his Grandfather was". Two of Thomas's children are passed over without blame by Gough, but the image of the Bad Family stuck to the daughter, Sarah, who gave birth to an illegitimate child. Meanwhile, William Bickley, the grandson of William Tyler through his daughter, Elizabeth, "imitated his Grandfather's villanyes" and his three sisters "followed the mother's vices". Gough's assessment of old William Tyler was that "many had done wickedly, butt hee excelled them all".[110] There were other families, such as the Formstons of Marton, who also fulfilled the role of the Bad Family, but none was so consistently in trouble as the Tyler–Bickley clan of Brandwood.

Drink broke the Puritan ethic on many more occasions. The number of people of all classes who ruined themselves by heavy drinking is truly astonishing. In addition to the village inn, there were several ale-houses in the parish, such as at Harmer Warren House, Lower Webscott, a Bilmarsh cottage, Alderton, at the top of Myddle Hill, and again at the foot of it. There may have been more. Gough has some amazing tales to tell of the amount of drinking that went on. A drunken fight that resulted in manslaughter followed a heavy bout of drinking one afternoon in 1705. Thomas Downton's wife "went dayly to the alehouse. Her husband payd £10 att a time for alehouse scores", and eventually had to sell his lands to pay her debts. Richard Preece of Newton "proved the saddest drunkard that ever I heard of. He would never (by his good will) drinke lesse than a pint or a quart of strong ale at a draught". And David Higley of Balderton "was a good husband by fitts. What hee got with hard labor hee spent idely in the Alehouse". He was typical of many.[111]

Beer was cheap, and tea and coffee were still luxuries; it was necessary to quench the thirst produced by the consumption of salt meat and fish, and its stimulus counteracted the listlessness caused by a predominantly cereal diet. It has been estimated that during the seventeenth century one-seventh of total income was spent on drink, and that an average of between one and two pints a day was drunk by every man, woman and child in the country.[112] But it was as a social drink that it was abused. The English were notorious for consuming ale at all their business meetings, for their drunkenness at their fairs, and for their daily visits to the ale-house.

The proportion of drunkards in each class was roughly the same in Myddle, whether gentlemen, farmers, craftsmen, or labourers. Some women, too, were regular attenders at the ale-house. William Crosse of Bilmarsh and his wife "went dayly to the alehouse, and soone after the cows went thither alsoe". And Francis Clarke of Newton had a wife who was "a sad drunken woman". He went to bring her home one dark night, but she tricked him into letting her go, "ran backe to the ale-house, and boulted him out, and would not come home that night". Time and time again families were ruined by excessive drinking, or they spent the profits of their humble tenements on ale and were never able to prosper. The hours of work were long, the jobs were often tedious, and drink offered the easiest route of escape. Where else could one find such cheerful company when one's work was done? And what else could one spend one's money on? Consumer goods were few, and entertainment was not always easy to find. But the attractions of the ale-house were the ruin of some, like Thomas Hayward of Balderton, for instance. "Hee had little quietnesse att home which caused him to frequent publick houses merely for his naturall sustenance, and there meeting with company and being generally well beeloved hee stayed often too long . . . This Thomas Hayward sold and consumed all his estate and was afterwards mainetained on charyty by his eldest son".[113] In other cases, like those of Michael Chambre, Thomas Hall, John Gossage, and William Tyler, drunkenness went with immorality and sometimes crime, but there were several people who were otherwise upright and hardworking men who spent all their available money on drink, and were often ruined by it.

Pressures to conform to the values of the community came from one's kin and neighbours as well as through the parish institutions. Modern rural sociologists have shown how much other people's opinions count to a member of an interdependent community. Gossip and ridicule are often enough to deter anti-social behaviour,[114] and Gough frequently cuts a man down to size with remarks like: "This Thomas Newans was unskilled in husbandry, though hee would talke much of it". When William Preece returned from being a soldier in the Low Countries, "he told so many romanticke stories, of his strange adventures, that people gave him the name of Scoggan, by which name (at last) hee was better known than by the name of William Preece".[115] (Scoggan was the name of Edward IV's jester.) But where stricture was not enough, the Church exercised its authority through the rector and (where he had failed) in the ecclesiastical courts. The usual penalty for infringing the moral code was public penance at the time of divine service, when the guilty person stood before the congregation bare-headed, barefoot, and bare-legged, draped in a white sheet, and carrying a white wand. He had to confess his sins to the congregation, and ask them to join in his prayers for forgiveness. Failure to perform this act brought the threat of excommunication. In a society whose whole structure of thought was dominated by religion, this could be a very powerful weapon, and only those who completely rejected the authority of the Church had no fear of the ultimate threat.

The manorial courts were not concerned with spiritual and moral matters, nor did they bring pressure to bear on individuals in order to support the authority of the Church. The only cottager to be ejected for holding Nonconformist views rented his land from a freeholder (and a vicar at that). There is a letter in the manorial collection[116] that tries to discredit Alice, the wife of Griffith ap Evan, during a dispute in 1605, by calling her "a very lewde woeman, who dwelleth in a verey little tenement which is built upon the warren", but this slur does not seem to have influenced the case. The manorial courts were merely concerned with practical arrangements, albeit ones designed for the well-being of the community, in much the same way as any local authority of today. Ditches had to be scoured so that a neighbour's land would not be flooded, dogs had to be muzzled so that sheep would not be worried, and no-one was allowed to exercise his common rights in a way that would be to the disadvantage of his neighbours. With this sort of regulation, the manorial courts not only preserved the rights of the lord but administered the community fairly and efficiently. Failure to comply with the rules led not to moral pressure but to a straightforward money fine.

The farmers had their chances to take part in the local administration of both the church and the manor, and even men of lower rank occasionally filled the posts of parish clerk and manorial bailiff. The jurors on the manorial courts and the churchwardens whose names appear from time to time in the parish registers were from all sections of the farming class, including the better-off craftsmen. These official positions were coveted and gave a man some status in the community. Thus, William Parker of Myddlewood, who had inherited Wagge the carpenter's tenement through marriage, "was a person that affected to be accompted somebody in this parish, and therefore procured to bee made Bayliffe of this Manor. Hee alsoe had a great desire to bee made Churchwarden of this parish, which at last hee obtained. It was sayd that hee gave a side of bacon to Robert Moore, to the end hee would persuade his brother the Rector to choose him Churchwarden, and afterwards hee made that yeare the epoch of his computation of all accidents, and would usually say such a thing was done soe many yeares beefore or after the yeare that I was Churchwarden". The way a man fulfilled his role while in office was of greater importance to his standing than the mere attaining of the position. Peter Lloyd "was many yeares bayliffe of this manor, and discharged his place with much faythfullnesse, and was not onely just to his master, butt alsoe favorable to the tenants". Similarly, Richard Hatchett, junior, of Newton, was receiver of the rents of the lordships of Ellesmere and Myddle and was "generally well spoaken of by the tenants, for his gentle dealeing and forbearance", but Robert Wilkinson, the bailiff of Wem and Loppington, "tooke more care to gett money among the tenants than to gaine theire love or preserve his owne credit".[117]

No constable's accounts survive for Myddle and so it is impossible to say how petty justice was administered. Nor are there any records of the overseers of the highways, and the annual accounts of the overseers of the poor do not go back beyond the eighteenth century. But the great increase in population from the late 1630s onwards brought a pauper problem that had hardly existed before. The Gough family's rates rose from 4*d*. per annum in 1633 to £1 per annum in 1701, and the parish became increasingly involved in a number of settlement cases, which in the last resort were brought before the Quarter Sessions. Organizations such as this, whose power and authority covered the whole county, were served by the gentry families. Richard Gittins V, for example, "served on the Grand Jury for this County of Salop, and amongst others I [Gough] was one of his partners". The gentry, too, tried to protect the community's interests when threatened by another parish (in settlement disputes, for instance), and it was they who used their influence with the J.P.s.[118] Their personal interests were at stake, as well as those of the community at large, but they seem to have been inspired with an ideal of public service, and to have regarded it as a duty for someone in their social position.

No local community, of course, was an independent entity, and in many spheres the real decisions were made by the central government. Some laws were just a belated formalization of what was already happening in the provinces, but the local officials who administered law and order, looked after the poor, and repaired the highways, were often merely administering the consequences of national decisions. But there was still scope for initiative, and the timing and impact of, say, the Reformation, the Civil Wars, or the growing problem of the poor, varied from one locality to another. J.P.s, jurors, and parochial officials tended to act in similar ways all over the country, but local decisions were the ones that mattered to the local community.

The structure of the community of Myddle was largely informal. It is noticeable that when the rector found an abandoned child in his porch, he sent for a churchwarden to provide a nurse, but asked Atcherley and Gough, two of the leading inhabitants of the parish, who did not at that time hold formal office, to do the more serious work of finding the mother.[119] The only formal expression of the social gradations was at church, and there were no elaborate ceremonies designed to reinforce the existing structure. There were the annual perambulations of the parish (which are mentioned in the churchwardens' accounts of 1664, and in the comperta books of 1614 and 1626 when the minister was charged with non-attendance), which were still being observed at the time that Gough was writing. And there is a solitary reference in the churchwardens' accounts of 1659–60 to 8*s*. being collected as "Jole monyes at Cristide", presumably, money for Yule-tide celebrations.[120] There is no other mention of this, but it does perhaps suggest an annual ceremony involving the whole community. Gough's only reference to Christmas is that, before the Commonwealth, there was a custom "that upon Christmas day, in the afternoone after divine service, and when the minister was gone out of the churche, the clarke should sing a Christmas carroll in the churche", assisted by Richard Gittins, who was gifted with a fine bass voice, and who was one of the leading gentlemen in the parish.[121] The maypole made a reappearance after the Restoration, and there were opportunities for 'merriments' at the annual Battlefield fair, as well as the ones in Shrewsbury and the other market towns. But there were no such popular events taking place within the parish of Myddle. Formal occasions, whether serious or frivolous, were rare indeed, apart from the weekly service, but as Margaret Stacey has remarked about modern Banbury,[122] society may be informal in its structure and yet still be traditional.

The community of Myddle remained an informal and traditional society during the sixteenth and seventeenth centuries. It did not undergo radical change for another two or three generations. Then, it was destroyed by engrossing as effectively as the east Midland peasant communities were destroyed by enclosure. The small farmers were driven out, and a new society, more sharply divided between the rich and the poor, arose out of the old. Richard Gough died in 1723 on the eve of these changes, and his unique book describes a traditional way of life that was soon to be destroyed. There is still much that we do not know, and will never know, about the people of his parish. There is hardly any information, for instance, about the everyday lives of the children or about the daily routine of the adults, and we have to be satisfied with a limited understanding of the family life, the contact with friends and neighbours, and the attitudes, beliefs, and aspirations of the people of this local society. But in exploring this mental world we at last get an insight into what it must have been like to live in a rural communitv such as Myddle three or four hundred years ago.

Abbreviations

Agrarian Hist. England and Wales	*The Agrarian History of England and Wales*, ed. Joan Thirsk, vol. IV, *1500–1640* (1967)
A.H.R.	*Agricultural History Review*
B.M.	British Museum
Eyton	R. W. Eyton, *Antiquities of Shropshire*, vol. X (1860)
Gough	Richard Gough, *The Antiquityes and Memoyres of the Parish of Myddle* (1875 edn)
Lichfield J.R.O.	Lichfield Joint Record Office
P.R.O.	Public Record Office
S.A.J.	*Shropshire Archaeological Journal*
Shropshire C.R.O.	Shropshire County Record Office, Shrewsbury
V.C.H. Shropshire	*The Victoria County History of Shropshire*, vol. VIII (1968)

Notes

Introduction

1 His book was first published in an imperfect form in 1834. The complete version was published in 1875, and, again, in 1968 and 1971. The original manuscript is in Shropshire C.R.O.
2 Gough, 44.
3 *Ibid.*, 171–4.
4 W. M. Williams, *The Sociology of an English Village* (1957), 168; cf. D. Jenkins, *The Agricultural Community in South-West Wales at the Turn of the Twentieth Century* (1971), 2: "One of the distinctive features of the community was that it was 'parochial' ". See Gough, 17 and 33, for disputes about the parish boundaries.
5 Joan Thirsk, 'Seventeenth-Century Agriculture and Social Change', in Joan Thirsk (ed.), *Land, Church and People: Essays Presented to Professor H. P. R. Finberg*, *A.H.R.*, XVIII, Supplement (1970), 148–77.
6 A. H. Johnson, *The Disappearance of the Small Landowner* (1909), 78.
7 A. C. Chibnall, *Sherington, Fiefs and Fields of a Buckinghamshire Village* (1965); Margaret Spufford, *A Cambridgeshire Community, Chippenham from Settlement to Enclosure* (1965).
8 See, for instance, Joan Thirsk, *English Peasant Farming* (1957), P. A. J. Pettit, *The Royal Forests of Northamptonshire, 1558–1714* (1968), G. H. Tupling, *The Economic History of Rossendale* (1927), *Agrarian Hist. England and Wales.*
9 W. G. Hoskins, *The Midland Peasant* (1957), xvi.
10 Hoskins, *op. cit.*, 143.
11 Quoted in *Agrarian Hist. England and Wales.* See Dr Thirsk's introductory chapter on the difference between woodland and fielden communities.
12 Pettit, *op. cit.*, 145.
13 See A. M. Everitt's chapter on farm labourers in *Agrarian Hist. England and Wales.*
14 T. Rowley, *The Shropshire Landscape* (1972), 163–71.
15 *Ibid.*, 151; A. T. Gaydon (ed.), *V.C.H. Shropshire*, 185, 30, 37, 125, 253.
16 See chapter 2.
17 Rowley, *op. cit.*, 49.
18 *V.C.H. Shropshire*, 231.
19 *Ibid.*, 47, 9, 47, 95.
20 *Ibid.*, 95, 89, 47, 9, 47, 76, 121.
21 Rowley, *op. cit.*, 148.
22 *V.C.H. Shropshire*, 1, 178.

Chapter one

1 Gough, 91.
2 Shropshire C.R.O., Bridgewater Collection maps.
3 E. W. Bowcock, *Shropshire Place-Names* (1923), 160.
4 I.e., it was never part of an administrative unit where the king or some lord had hunting rights.
5 The remarks on the soils are based upon E. Compton and D. A. Osmond, *The Soils of the Wem District of Shropshire* (Soil Survey of Great Britain (Ministry of Agriculture and Fisheries), H.M.S.O., 1954).
6 *Ibid.* Gough also refers to two "Marle peices" at Bilmarsh (p. 75), and to an old marl pit at Newton (p. 10).
7 Gough, 175.
8 *Ibid.*, 12. The bishop's visitation in 1633 had noted: "The steeple [was] in decaye" (Lichfield J.R.O., B/V/I/53).
9 Gough, 45.
10 *Ibid.*, 18.
11 Lichfield J.R.O., B/V/6.
12 The foundation date is unknown, but the north and south doorways are *c.* 1190.
13 Gough, 13; P.R.O., C.2/B4/65; Lichfield J.R.O., B/V/39 (1620).
14 Lichfield J.R.O., B/V/I/48. See also B/V/I/29 (1614).
15 Bowcock, *op. cit.*, 110.
16 Eyton, 44.
17 Gough, 63.
18 Bowcock, *op. cit.*, 24–5.
19 J. B. Blakeway, *History of Shrewsbury Hundred or Liberties* (1897), 207.
20 Eyton, 79–80.
21 P.R.O., Augmentation, E.321/5/14. The spelling has been modernized.
22 Eyton, 72–6. Gough is wrong on this.
23 Bowcock, *op. cit.*, 241.
24 Gough, 10.
25 *Ibid.*, 27.
26 P.R.O., C.Ch.R.VI.94. Over 150 motte-and-bailey castles have been identified in Shropshire, but those which were not rebuilt in stone in the thirteenth and early fourteenth centuries fell into decay; T. Rowley, *The Shropshire Landscape* (1972), 82–7.
27 H. le Strange, *Le Strange Records* (1916), 101. In 1520–1 Griffith Nycknam, "a cruell and notable outlawe of Wales", was hanged, drawn, and quartered in Shrewsbury, and his head hung on the Welsh Gate (*S.A.J.*, III (1880), 253).
28 Gough, 28.
29 L. T. Smith, *The Itinerary of John Leland*, vol. V (1964), 13. See Gough, 27–8, for a description of the ruined castle.
30 Eyton, 73.
31 Gough, 23.
32 *Ibid.*, 36.
33 Bowcock, *op. cit.*, 156.

34 Gough, 45.
35 *Ibid.*, 83.
36 G. E. Fussell, 'Four Centuries of Farming Systems in Shropshire, 1500–1900', *S.A.J.*, LIV (1951–3), 1–29.
37 *Agrarian Hist. England and Wales*, 246.
38 Gough, 37.
39 Edward, Earl of Derby, was lord from 1521 to 1572. See section 5 for these clearings.
40 Gough, 92.
41 *Ibid.*, 41.
42 Eyton, 80, 58.
43 Shropshire C.R.O., Bridgewater Collection, Box 15.
44 Gough, 62.
45 *Ibid.*, 34.
46 Shropshire C.R.O., Bridgewater Collection, Box 15.
47 Gough, 175.
48 P.R.O., E.179/166/129.
49 Gough, 30.
50 *Ibid.*, 29.
51 The 1640 survey mentions that the measurements were in old customary acres which were half the size of the statutory acre. (Shropshire C.R.O., Bridgewater Collection, Box 15.)
52 Shropshire C.R.O., Bridgewater Collection, Box 345.
53 Gough, 33.
54 Shropshire C.R.O., Bridgewater Collection, Box 105.
55 Eyton, 80.
56 Gough, 33.
57 *Ibid.* Shropshire C.R.O., Bridgewater Collection, Box 105.
58 Gough, 175, 32.
59 Shropshire C.R.O., Bridgewater Collection, Box 105.
60 Gough, 30.
61 *Ibid.*, 31.

Chapter two

1 P.R.O., E.179/166/129 and E.179/166/156.
2 B.M., Harleian MS. 594, f. 160.
3 P.R.O., E.179/168/216.
4 William Salt Library, Stafford.
5 C. W. Chalklin, 'The Compton Census of 1676: The Dioceses of Canterbury and Rochester', *Kent Records*, XVII (1960), 153–74.
6 Gough, 13.
7 *Ibid.*, 44.
8 E. A. Wrigley (ed.), *Introduction to English Historical Demography* (1966), 55.
9 Shropshire Parish Register Society, *Lichfield Diocese*, vol. XIX, pt I.
10 Gough, 22.

11 Wrigley, *op. cit.*, 83.
12 J. T. Krause, 'The Changing Adequacy of English Registration, 1690–1837', in D. V. Glass and D. E. C. Eversley, *Population in History* (1965), 379–93.
13 Wrigley, *op. cit.*, 43.
14 Part of the explanation may be due to the fact that there were temporary labourers and domestic servants in Myddle (for a season) who married and were entered as living in their permanent settlements.
15 Lichfield J.R.O., B/V/I/74.
16 Gough, 22.
17 W. G. Hoskins, 'Harvest Fluctuations and English Economic History, 1620–1759', *A.H.R.* XVI, pt i (1968), 17.
18 The typical cycles are different, but not usually long enough for one to be sure.
19 Hoskins, 'Harvest Fluctuations . . .'. The following comments are based upon his articles, and upon C. J. Harrison, 'Grain Price Analysis and Harvest Qualities, 1465–1634', *A.H.R.*, XIX pt ii (1971), 135–55.
20 'The Early Chronicles of Shrewsbury', printed in *S.A.J.*, III (1880), 239–352.
21 Hoskins, 'Harvest Fluctuations . . .'.
22 J. F. D. Shrewsbury, *A History of The Bubonic Plague in the British Isles* (1970), 220.
23 Gough, 177.
24 *Ibid.*, 33.
25 *Ibid.*, 48.
26 *Ibid.*, 152.
27 *Ibid.*, 90.
28 Harleian Society, *The Visitations of Shropshire*, vols I and II (1889).
29 A. M. Everitt in *Agrarian Hist. England and Wales*, 398.
30 Even allowing for inflation – see below.
31 W. G. Hoskins, *Provincial England* (1963), 153.
32 Shropshire C.R.O., Bridgewater Collection, Box 14.
33 Gough, 79.
34 *Ibid.*, 119.
35 *Ibid.*, 139. P.R.O., C. 5/421/54.
36 *Agrarian Hist. England and Wales*, 99.
37 Gough, 175.
38 *Ibid.*
39 J. Radley, 'Holly as a Winter Feed', *A.H.R.* IX pt ii (1961), 89–92.
40 Gough, 29.
41 *Ibid.*, 175.
42 A. M. Everitt in *Agrarian Hist. England and Wales*, 470.
43 Gough, 179.
44 *Ibid.*, 74.
45 G. E. Fussell, *The English Dairy Farmer, 1500–1900* (1966), 9.
46 W. G. Hoskins, *The Midland Peasant* (1957), 159.
47 V. H. T. Skipp, 'Economic and Social Change in the Forest of Arden, 1530–1649', in Joan Thirsk (ed.), *Land, Church and People: Essays Presented to Professor H. P. R. Finberg*, *A.H.R.* XVIII, Supplement (1970), 84–111.

48 Skipp, *op. cit.*, 86.
49 Shropshire C.R.O., Bridgewater Collection, Box 15.
50 Hoskins, *The Midland Peasant*, 158.
51 Gough, 175.
52 S. Bagshaw, *History, Gazetteer, and Directory of Shropshire* (1851), 22: "The old Shropshire sheep had a black mottled face and legs, and in size were comparable with Southdowns".
53 Bagshaw, *op. cit.*, 22: "The county was formerly famous for a breed of pigs which is now almost extinct".
54 Quoted by G. E. Fussell, 'Four Centuries of Farming Systems in Shropshire, 1500–1900', *S.A.J.*, LIV (1951–3), 1–29.
55 Joan Thirsk, 'Seventeenth-Century Agriculture and Social Change', in *Land, Church and People . . .*, *op. cit.*, 148–77.
56 Lichfield J.R.O.
57 Bagshaw, *op. cit.*, 22.
58 Joan Thirsk, *English Peasant Farming* (1957); cf. J. Plymley, *General View of the Agriculture of Shropshire* (1803), 123: "The scope of Shropshire farming is perhaps less confined than that of many other counties . . . The farms, generally speaking, are arable, grazing, for hay, for the dairy, rearing, and feeding". By 1851 there had been a greater turnover to arable farming.
59 Hoskins, *Provincial England*, 149–69.
60 Quoted by Fussell, *op. cit.*
61 *Ibid.*
62 E. Kerridge, *Agrarian Problems in the Sixteenth Century and After* (1969), 33.
63 B. M. Harleian MS. 594, f. 160.
64 Gough, 34–6.
65 The spelling has been modernized.
66 Gough is wrong on the dating of this murder.
67 The date has no apparent significance in the life of the lord.
68 R. H. Hilton, *The Decline of Serfdom in Medieval England* (1969), 47.
69 Inventories should technically include chattel leases, but in practice most did not do so.
70 E. Hopkins, 'The Re-leasing of the Bridgewater Estates, 1637–42', *A.H.R.*, x (1962), 23.
71 Gough, 149.
72 *Ibid.*, 25.
73 P. Bowden in *Agrarian Hist. of England and Wales*, 594.
74 Hopkins, *op. cit.*, 14–28.
75 The legal position concerning the countess's rights is obscure.
76 Hopkins, *op. cit.*, 15. In January, 1636/7, the earl's debts amounted to £28,377.
77 *Ibid.*, 17. Only five people in the whole of the Ellesmere estates stood by their leases.
78 Hopkins, *op. cit.*, 17.
79 *Ibid.*, 19.
80 *Ibid.*
81 This was only done in Knockin and Myddle and not in the other manors that comprised the Ellesmere estates.

82 Hopkins, *op. cit.*, 22.
83 The spelling has been modernized. In 1691 William Bickley of Brandwood was accused of felling an oak tree and selling the timber in Wem; Shropshire C.R.O., Bridgewater Collection, Box 14.
84 Gough, 76.
85 *Ibid.*, 23.
86 *Ibid.*, 50, 51, 53.
87 Plymley, *op. cit.*, 135.
88 T. O. Ward, *On the Medical Topography of Shrewsbury and its Neighbourhood* (1841), 54.

Chapter three

1 Shropshire C.R.O., Bridgewater Collection, Box 14.
2 Gough, 117. The genealogies in chapters 3, 4, and 5 have been largely compiled from Gough, the parish registers, wills and inventories, manorial rentals and surveys, the lay subsidy lists and a few other documents. See Gough's index for his family accounts (though his genealogies need to be treated with caution).
3 At the 1623 visitation the Gittinses traced their family pedigree back through several generations, the first eight of whom were Welsh; *Harleian Society, The Visitations of Shropshire*, 199.
4 Gough, 118.
5 W. A. Leighton, 'The Guilds of Shrewsbury', *S.A.J.*, VIII (1885), 317, 332.
6 Gough, 119.
7 His farmstock comprised 6 oxen worth £4, 13 cattle worth £6 1*s.* 0*d.*, 9 heifers valued at £3, 5 young beasts worth £1 5*s.* 0*d.*, 5 suckling calves worth 8*s.* 4*d.*, a mare and a colt appraised at £1, 31 sheep worth £1 10*s.* 0*d.*, swine valued at 5*s.*, and £2 worth of corn.
8 Gough, 119.
9 Shropshire C.R.O., Bridgewater Collection, Box 345.
10 M. Peele, 'Shrewsbury Drapers' Apprentices', *S.A.J.*, L (1939–40), 1–29.
11 Gough, 119.
12 *Ibid.*, 68.
13 Shropshire C.R.O., Bridgewater Collection, Box 411.
14 Gough, 119.
15 *Ibid.*, 120.
16 Lichfield J.R.O., B/V/I/96.
17 Shropshire C.R.O., Bridgewater Collection, Box 105.
18 Shropshire C.R.O., Bridgewater Collection, Box 105.
19 Gough, 140.
20 *Ibid.*, 49.
21 *Harleian Society*, *op. cit.*, 7.
22 P.R.O., C2 James I, S15/20.
23 Judging by the Tithe Award of 1838.
24 Shropshire C.R.O., Bridgewater Collection, Box 345.

25 Gough, 49. The remarks on the structure are based on the comments of my colleague, Michael Laithwaite.
26 Gough, 48.
27 *Ibid.*, 53. After a pew dispute the Hanmers worshipped at Baschurch.
28 Eyton, 73; Shropshire C.R.O., Bridgewater Collection, Box 105.
29 *S.A.J.*, VIII (1885), 331. The 1537 and 1538 lists of the manor court jurors show that there was another branch of the family in Myddle village.
30 Gough, 50–1. However, in 1655 and 1656, Henry and Edward, the sons of George Maynwaring of Sleap, gent., were apprenticed to Shrewsbury drapers. They had been born in Sandbach in 1637 and 1639, respectively (*S.A.J.*, L (1939–40)).
31 Thomas Kinaston appears in the manorial rolls of 1528–41 but the parish registers record his death at the Hollins. He also held property in Houlston.
32 Gough, 64.
33 *Harleian Society*, *op. cit.*, 167.
34 Gough, 137ff.
35 *Harleian Society*, *op. cit.*
36 *Ibid.*, 167, records an earlier John, the father of this John.
37 *S.A.J.*, VIII (1885), 350.
38 *Harleian Society*, *op. cit.* His claims to gentry status were disallowed in 1585.
39 Gough, 75–8.
40 *Ibid.*, 51.
41 *Harleian Society*, *op. cit.* His claims to gentry status were disallowed in 1585, when he was resident in the Liberty of Shrewsbury.
42 Samuel Clayton was taxed on one hearth in 1662, immediately after Isaac Clayton; P.R.O., E.179/255/35.
43 Gough, 120–1.

Chapter four

1 W. G. Hoskins, *The Midland Peasant* (1957), 143.
2 Now named 'The Oaks'.
3 F. W. Steer, *Farm and Cottage Inventories of Mid-Essex, 1635 to 1749* (1950), 13.
4 Hoskins, *op. cit.*, 96.
5 See F. M. and A. V. Gough, 'The Goughs of Myddle and their Descendants', *S.A.J.*, Second Series, V (1883), 261–92, which corrects Richard Gough's account.
6 Gough, 53.
7 *Ibid.*, 124.
8 The man who had bought Ash's old tenement from Thomas Formston V was his step-son, Thomas Shaw, who had been apprenticed to William Watson, the Myddle-wood tailor. He was tenant here at the close of the seventeenth century and "lived upon it in good fashion" (Gough, 148).
9 Gough, 149.
10 *Ibid.*, 134.
11 *Ibid.*, 73.
12 *Ibid.*, 56.

13 *Ibid.*, 57–8.
14 *Ibid.*, 88.
15 *Ibid.*, 129.

Chapter five

1 Gough, 12.
2 *Ibid.*, 175.
3 *Ibid.*, 158.
4 *Ibid.*, 90.
5 *Ibid.*, 155.
6 Shropshire C.R.O., Bridgewater Collection, Box 345 (1638 survey).
7 Lichfield J.R.O., B/V/I/39.
8 Gough, 157.
9 *Ibid.*, 148.
10 D. Defoe, *A Tour through the Whole Island of Great Britain*, ed. P. Davies (1927), 474.
11 W. Camden, *Britannia* (1610), 847.
12 T. C. Mendenhall, *The Shrewsbury Drapers and the Welsh Wool Trade in the XVI and XVII Centuries* (1953), 4–5; between 1572 and 1660 40 per cent of apprentice drapers were the sons of gentry.
13 Gough, 79.
14 Mendenhall, *op. cit.*, 88.
15 Gough, 134.
16 *Ibid.*, 40.
17 P.R.O., E.179/225/24.
18 Gough, 156.
19 *Ibid.*, 33.
20 *Ibid.*, 153.
21 *Agrarian Hist. England and Wales*, 99.
22 A. M. Everitt in *Agrarian Hist. England and Wales*, 411.
23 Shropshire C.R.O., Bridgewater Collection, Box 345.
24 In later records John Wagge is described as carpenter.
25 Shropshire C.R.O., Bridgewater Collection, Box 15.
26 Shropshire C.R.O., Quarter Sessions Records.
27 Shropshire C.R.O., Bridgewater Collection, Box 14.
28 Gough, 62.
29 *Agrarian Hist. England and Wales*, 107.
30 Gough, 152.
31 *Ibid.*, 154.
32 *Ibid.*, diagram opposite p. 45.
33 A. M. Everitt in *Agrarian Hist. England and Wales.*
34 *Ibid.*, 413.
35 Shropshire C.R.O., Bridgewater Collection, Box 345.
36 Gough, 139.
37 *Ibid.*, 162.

38 *Ibid.*, 11.
39 Everitt, in *Agrarian Hist. England and Wales*, 442.
40 Gough, 160.
41 *Ibid.*, 161.
42 I am most grateful to Michael Laithwaite who surveyed the property. The comments on the structure are based on his remarks.
43 Everitt, in *Agrarian Hist. England and Wales*, 398.
44 A John Wright of Marton is named in the manorial rolls of 1542.
45 Shropshire C.R.O., Bridgewater Collection, Box 105; a letter dated 13 November 1605 mentions that Griffith ap Evan lived in "a very little Tenement which is built upon the warren".
46 In 1618 the overseers of the poor paid Abel Jones's annual rent of 12*d.* (Shropshire C.R.O., Bridgewater Collection, Box 15.)
47 Gough, 90.
48 *Ibid.*, 109.
49 *Ibid.*, 93.
50 *Ibid.*, 93, 162.
51 P.R.O., E.179/255/24. A recent article has shown the unreliability of the numbers of recorded exempt in Norfolk: J. Patten, 'The Hearth Taxes, 1662–1689', *Local Population Studies*, no. 7 (Autumn 1971), 14–27.
52 Gough, 159.
53 *Ibid.*, 169.
54 *Ibid.*, 165.
55 *Ibid.*, 90.
56 Shropshire C.R.O., 2434.
57 Gough, 160–1.
58 *Ibid.*, 160.
59 *Ibid.*, 62.

Chapter six

1 Gough, 66, 141, 56, 177, 165, 119. In August 1594, a public fast was held in Shrewsbury, when "most of the inhabitants in Salop repayrid to Sainct Maries churche there to pray and call uppon God to sennd seasonable weather to bringe in theyre corne for the comford of his people who lamenting their synns and callinge to God with sootche godly sermons" stayed in the church from 8 a.m. to 4 p.m. ('The Early Chronicles of Shrewsbury', *S.A.J.*, III (1880), 331). When "a sudden furyous fire" destroyed 162 houses in Newport in 1665, the parson wrote in the parish register, "Newport sin no more, lest a worse punishment befall thee" (E. C. Peele and R. S. Clease, *Shropshire Parish Documents*, Salop C.C., 248). The reality of the devil in people's minds is shown in another extract from the 'Chronicles', 255, when he was believed (in 1533) to have appeared in St Alkmond's church in Shrewsbury.
2 Gough, 72, 61.

3 Cf. C. M. Arensberg, *The Irish Countryman* (1937), chapter VI, 189: "The values of daily life are projected into and reinforced by the supernatural world"; see also K. Thomas, *Religion and the Decline of Magic* (1971), and J. C. Atkinson, *Forty Years in a Moorland Parish* (1891).
4 Gough, 49, 75.
5 Thomas, *op. cit.*, chapters 10 and 11.
6 Gough, 131, 104, 163–4, 47–8. The story about the pigeons is a common one.
7 A. Macfarlane, *Witchcraft in Tudor and Stuart England: A Comparative Study* (1970).
8 Lichfield J.R.O., ecclesiastical court records. The information from the cause papers was kindly supplied by Miss J. Isaac, Assistant Archivist at Lichfield.
9 'The Early Chronicles of Shrewsbury', *S.A.J.*, III (1880), 283.
10 P. Tyler, 'The Church Courts at York and Witchcraft Prosecutions, 1567–1640', *Northern History*, IV (1969), 84–110.
11 Gough, 90.
12 *Ibid.*, 121.
13 *Ibid.*, 162.
14 *Ibid.*, 65, 78, 49, 31, 75, 144.
15 *Ibid.*, 20, 162, 40, 44.
16 *Ibid.*, 40, 84, 46, 105, 19, 20; Margaret Spufford, 'The Schooling of the Peasantry in Cambridgeshire, 1575–1700', in Joan Thirsk (ed.), *Land, Church and People: Essays Presented to Professor H. P. R. Finberg, A.H.R.*, XVIII, Supplement (1970), 112–47.
17 Gough, 77, 31, 92.
18 *Ibid.*, 193.
19 Cf. D. Jenkins, *The Agricultural Community in South-West Wales at the Turn of the Twentieth Century* (1971), 7, E. W. Martin, *The Shearers and the Shorn: A Study of Life in a Devon Community* (1965), 206, and A. D. Rees, *Life in a Welsh Countryside* (2nd edn, 1951), *passim.*
20 Gough, 166.
21 *Ibid.*, 183.
22 A. M. Everitt, *Change in the Provinces: The Seventeenth Century* (1969).
23 Gough, 55, 59–60.
24 P. Spufford, 'Population Movement in Seventeenth-Century England', *Local Population Studies*, no. 4 (1970), 41–50.
25 E. A. Wrigley, 'London's Importance, 1650–1750', *Past and Present*, XXXVII (1967), 44–70.
26 Gough, 160, 64–5.
27 *Ibid.*, 119, 143–4, 84–5.
28 *Ibid.*, 11, 54, 196–8.
29 *Ibid.*, 135, 106, 122–4.
30 *Ibid.*, 151, 68.
31 *Ibid.*, 59, 60–1.
32 *Ibid.*, 148, 144, 57.
33 *Ibid.*, 162.
34 *Calendar of State Papers, Domestic Series, Charles I, (18), 1641–3*, 437.

35 Gough, 67.
36 *Calendar of State Papers, Domestic Series, Charles I, (19), 1644*, 34, 39, 111, 282–3.
37 S. Lee, *Dictionary of National Biography* (1900).
38 E. Hopkins, 'The Bridgewater Estates in North Shropshire during the Civil Wars', *S.A.J.*, LVI (1957–60), 308–13.
39 Gough, 112, 33.
40 *Ibid.*, 84, 130, 39.
41 Ex. inf. Professor A. M. Everitt.
42 Quoted by Mrs Stackhouse Acton, *The Garrisons of Shropshire during the Civil War, 1642–48* (1867), 9.
43 Gough, 147.
44 *Ibid.*, 40.
45 J. T. Krause, 'The Changing Adequacy of English Registration, 1690–1837', in D. V. Glass and D. E. C. Eversley (eds), *Population in History* (1965), 379–93.
46 E. A. Wrigley (ed.), *Introduction to English Historical Demography* (1966), 54.
47 Cf. B. A. Holderness, 'Personal Mobility in Some Rural Parishes of Yorkshire, 1777–1822', *Yorkshire Archaeological Journal*, CLXVIII (1971), 444–54.
48 Gough, 100, 103.
49 *Ibid.*, 105, 103.
50 P. Laslett, *The World We Have Lost* (1965), 90.
51 P. Laslett and J. Harrison, 'Clayworth and Cogenhoe', in H. E. Bell and R. L. Ollard (eds), *Historical Essays Presented to David Ogg* (1963).
52 Laslett, *op. cit.*, 103.
53 *Ibid.*, 104.
54 A. Macfarlane, *The Diary of Ralph Josselin: A Seventeenth-Century Essex Clergyman* (1970).
55 Gough, 67.
56 *Ibid.*, 151.
57 Cf. Jenkins, *op. cit.*, 4.
58 *Ibid.*, 159.
59 Gough, 78.
60 Gough, 109, 107, 138, 161, 133; W. M. Williams, *The Sociology of an English Village* (1957), 59.
61 Gough, 153.
62 *Ibid.*, 103.
63 *Ibid.*, 73.
64 *Ibid.*, 138, 94, 131, 73, 153.
65 *Ibid.*, 161.
66 Arensberg, *op. cit.*, 215.
67 Gough, 131, 112, 58, 107, 134. Very few seventeenth-century gravestones survive in Myddle.
68 *Ibid.*, 65, 114, 128, 148, 97.
69 *Ibid.*, 125, 97.
70 *Ibid.*, 132, 57, 84; cf. Jenkins, *op. cit.*, 129–30, Rees, *op. cit.*, 146.
71 *Ibid.*, 105, 184, 130.

72 *Ibid.*, 66, 94, 115, 147, 146, 122.
73 *Ibid.*, 128, 150, 139. In some modern rural communities it is the practice for the women to look after the poultry and pigs and to be responsible for the sale of milk and eggs; Williams, *op. cit.*, 41, Jenkins, *op. cit.*, 75. Gough refers (p. 104) to a woman hay-making in Harmer, but rarely mentions such everyday activities.
74 Gough, 123, 105.
75 *Ibid.*, 102.
76 A. Macfarlane, *The Diary of Ralph Josselin*, 92; Gough, 57, 154, 63, 143, 124, 121.
77 Gough, 123, 96.
78 Cf. Rees, *op. cit.*, 79.
79 Gough, 112, 155.
80 *Ibid.*, 141, 135, 129, 123.
81 *Ibid.*, 112, 17, 18, 94, 87, 84; cf. Arensberg, *op. cit.*, chapter II, Rees, *op. cit.*, 130.
82 Gough, 75: "Two or three of Grestock's cakes was a very acceptable present to a friend".
83 S. Bagshaw, *History, Gazetteer, and Directory of Shropshire* (1851), 248.
84 Gough, 124, 147.
85 Arensberg, *op. cit.*, 83, Jenkins, *op. cit.*, 160, Rees, *op. cit.*, 78.
86 Gough, 43, 53, 68–9, 54.
87 *Ibid.*, 115.
88 Lichfield J.R.O., B/V/I/72, 74, 81, and 87.
89 Lichfield J.R.O., B/V/I/39 and 74.
90 Myddle Parish Register extracts in *S.A.J.*, IX (1886), 236–7. The parish was presented at the bishop's visitations of 1620 and 1633 for not keeping the churchyard wall in repair; Lichfield J.R.O., B/V/I/39 and 53.
91 Gough, 105.
92 *Ibid.*, 13.
93 *Ibid.*, 15–19; J. Foster, *Alumni Oxoniensis, 1500–1714* (1968).
94 Shropshire Parish Register Society, *Lichfield Diocese*, vol. XIX, pt I, vi.
95 His son, Ralph, was made "freeman as apprentice with Mr Raphe Thurlin" of the Shrewsbury Mercers' Company in 1633 (*S.A.J.*, VIII (1885), 356).
96 Lichfield J.R.O., B/V/I/53.
97 R. A. F. Skinner, *Non-Conformity in Shropshire* (1964), 109.
98 His son, James, was apprenticed to a Shrewsbury mercer in 1675: *S.A.J.*, VIII (1885), 374.
99 William Salt Library, Stafford, Compton Census Returns.
100 Dr Williams Library, Ms. 34–4. There were Presbyterian meeting-places at Shrewsbury (440 members), Bridgnorth (120), Oswestry (120), Wem (180), Whitchurch (300), Newport (65), Wellington (42), Berrington and Leighton (74), Oldbury (400), Shifnal (36), and at Cleobury (number unrecorded); Independents at Shrewsbury (150); and Anabaptists at Shrewsbury (50) and Bridgnorth (40). Evans did not record the number of Quakers.
101 Gough, 98, 135, 107.
102 Margaret Spufford, 'The Scribes of Villagers' Wills in the Sixteenth and Seventeenth Centuries and their Influence', *Local Population Studies*, no. 7 (1971), 28–43.
103 J. M. Wilson, *Imperial Gazetteer of England and Wales* (1875), 647.

104 Gough, 61, 89.
105 *Ibid.*, 57, 91.
106 Lichfield J.R.O., B/V/I/87 and 90.
107 Gough, 113, 132, 148, 141.
108 R. Blythe, *Akenfield* (1969), 243–4.
109 Gough, 132, 112.
110 *Ibid.*, 109.
111 *Ibid.*, 32, 75, 83, 93, 108, 121, 139, 187–9, 126, 80, 122. For a comparison with nineteenth-century rural communities, see J. C. Atkinson, *Forty Years in a Moorland Parish* (1891) and A. Gatty, *A Life at One Living* (1884).
112 C. Wilson, *England's Apprenticeship, 1603–1763* (1965), 22; Thomas, *op. cit.*, 17–18.
113 Gough, 78, 124.
114 Arensberg, *op. cit.*, 107, Jenkins, *op. cit.*, 245, Rees, *op. cit.*, 148.
115 Gough, 129, 11.
116 Shropshire C.R.O., Bridgewater Collection, Box 105.
117 Gough, 156, 135, 130, 145.
118 *Ibid.*, 119, 174.
119 *Ibid.*, 166.
120 *S.A.J.*, IX (1886), 231–5; Lichfield J.R.O., B/V/I/29 and 48.
121 Gough, 20.
122 Margaret Stacey, *Tradition and Change in Modern Banbury* (1960), 182.

Bibliography

1 · *Books*

S. Acton, *The Garrisons of Shropshire during the Civil War, 1642–48* (1867).
C. M. Arensberg, *The Irish Countryman* (1937).
J. C. Atkinson, *Forty Years in a Moorland Parish* (1891).
S. Bagshaw, *History, Gazetteer and Directory of Shropshire* (1851).
J. B. Blakeway, *History of Shrewsbury Hundred or Liberties* (1897).
R. Blythe, *Akenfield* (1969).
E. W. Bowcock, *Shropshire Place-Names* (1923).
W. Camden, *Britannia* (1610).
A. C. Chibnall, *Sherington, Fiefs and Fields of a Buckinghamshire Village* (1965).
E. Compton and D. A. Osmond, *The Soils of the Wem District of Shropshire* (1954).
D. Defoe, *A Tour through the Whole Island of Great Britain*, ed. P. Davies (1927).
A. M. Everitt, *Change in the Provinces: The Seventeenth Century*, Leicester University Department of English Local History Occasional Papers, Second Series, No. 1 (1969).
R. W. Eyton, *Antiquities of Shropshire*, vol. X (1860).
J. Foster, *Alumni Oxonienses, 1500–1714* (1968).
G. E. Fussell, *The English Dairy Farmer, 1500–1900* (1966).
A. Gatty, *A Life At One Living* (1884).
A. T. Gaydon (ed.), *The Victoria County History of Shropshire*, vol. VIII (1968).
R. H. Hilton, *The Decline of Serfdom in Medieval England* (1969).
W. G. Hoskins, *The Midland Peasant* (1957).
W. G. Hoskins, *Provincial England* (1963).
D. Jenkins, *The Agricultural Community in South-West Wales at the Turn of the Twentieth Century* (1971).
A. H. Johnson, *The Disappearance of the Small Landowner* (1909).
E. Kerridge, *Agrarian Problems in the Sixteenth-Century and After* (1969).
P. Laslett, *The World We Have Lost* (1965).
S. Lee, *Dictionary of National Biography* (1900).
A. Macfarlane, *The Diary of Ralph Josselin: A Seventeenth-Century Essex Clergyman* (1970).
A. Macfarlane, *Witchcraft in Tudor and Stuart England: A Comparative Study* (1970).
E. W. Martin, *The Shearers and the Shorn: A Study of Life in a Devon Community* (1965).
T. C. Mendenhall, *The Shrewsbury Drapers and the Welsh Wool Trade in the XVI and XVII Centuries* (1953).
P. A. J. Pettit, *The Royal Forests of Northamptonshire, 1558–1714* (1968).
J. Plymley, *General View of the Agriculture of Shropshire* (1803).
A. D. Rees, *Life in a Welsh Countryside* (1951).

T. Rowley, *The Shropshire Landscape* (1972).

J. F. D. Shrewsbury, *A History of the Bubonic Plague in the British Isles* (1970).

R. A. F. Skinner, *Non-Conformity in Shropshire* (1964).

L. T. Smith (ed.), *The Itinerary of John Leland*, vol. V (1964).

Margaret Spufford, *A Cambridgeshire Community, Chippenham from Settlement to Enclosure*, Leicester University Department of English Local History Occasional Papers, First Series, No. 20 (1965).

Margaret Stacey, *Tradition and Change in Modern Banbury* (1960).

F. W. Steer, *Farm and Cottage Inventories of Mid-Essex, 1635 to 1749* (1950).

H. le Strange, *Le Strange Records* (1916).

Joan Thirsk, *English Peasant Farming* (1957).

Joan Thirsk (ed.), *The Agrarian History of England and Wales*, vol. IV, *1500–1640* (1967).

Joan Thirsk (ed.), *Land, Church and People: Essays Presented to Professor H. P. R. Finberg*, *A.H.R.*, XVIII, Supplement (1970).

K. Thomas, *Religion and the Decline of Magic* (1971).

G. H. Tupling, *The Economic History of Rossendale* (1927).

T. O. Ward, *On the Medical Topography of Shrewsbury and its Neighbourhood* (1841).

W. M. Williams, *The Sociology of an English Village* (1957).

C. Wilson, *England's Apprenticeship, 1603–1763* (1965).

J. M. Wilson, *Imperial Gazetteer of England and Wales* (1875).

E. A. Wrigley (ed.), *Introduction to English Historical Demography* (1966).

2 · *Articles*

C. W. Chalkin, 'The Compton Census of 1676: The Dioceses of Canterbury and Rochester', *Kent Records*, XVIII (1960), 153–74.

G. E. Fussell, 'Four Centuries of Farming Systems in Shropshire, 1500–1900', *S.A.J.*, LIV (1951–3), 1–29.

F. M. and A. V. Gough, 'The Goughs of Myddle and their Descendants', *S.A.J.*, V (1883), 261–92.

B. A. Holderness, 'Personal Mobility in Some Rural Parishes of Yorkshire, 1777–1822', *Yorkshire Archaeological Journal*, CLXVIII (1971), 444–54.

E. Hopkins, 'The Re-Leasing of the Bridgewater Estates, 1637–42', *A.H.R.*, X (1962), 14–28.

E. Hopkins, 'The Bridgewater Estates in North Shropshire during the Civil War', *S.A.J.*, LVI (1957–60), 308–13.

W. G. Hoskins, 'Harvest Fluctuations and English Economic History, 1480–1619', *A.H.R.*, XII, pt i (1964), 28–47, and '. . . 1620–1759', *A.H.R.*, XVI, pt i (1968), 15–31.

J. T. Krause, 'The Changing Adequacy of English Registration, 1690–1837', in D. V. Glass and D. E. C. Eversley, *Population in History* (1965).

P. Laslett and J. Harrison, 'Clayworth and Cogenhoe', in H. E. Bell and R. L. Ollard (eds), *Historical Essays Presented to David Ogg* (1963).

W. A. Leighton, 'The Guilds of Shrewsbury', *S.A.J.*, VIII (1885), 269–412.

J. Patten, 'The Hearth Taxes, 1662–1689', *Local Population Studies*, no. 7 (1971), 14–27.

M. Peele, 'Shrewsbury Drapers' Apprentices', *S.A.J.*, L (1939–40), 1–29.
J. Radley, 'Holly as a Winter Feed', *A.H.R.*, IX, pt ii (1961), 89–92.
V. H. T. Skipp, 'Economic and Social Change in the Forest of Arden, 1530–1649', in J. Thirsk (ed.), *Land, Church and People: Essays Presented to Professor H. P. R. Finberg*, *A.H.R.*, XVIII, Supplement (1970), 84–111.
Margaret Spufford, 'The Schooling of the Peasantry in Cambridgeshire, 1575–1700', in J. Thirsk (ed.), *Land, Church and People* . . ., 112–47.
Margaret Spufford, 'The Scribes of Villagers' Wills in the Sixteenth and Seventeenth Centuries and their Influence', *Local Population Studies*, no. 7 (1971), 28–43.
P. Spufford, 'Population Movement in Seventeenth-Century England', *Local Population Studies*, no. 4 (1970), 41–50.
Joan Thirsk, 'Seventeenth-Century Agriculture and Social Change', in J. Thirsk (ed.), *Land, Church and People* . . ., 148–77.
P. Tyler, 'The Church Courts at York and Witchcraft Prosecutions, 1567–1640', *Northern History*, IV (1969), 84–110.
E. A. Wrigley, 'London's Importance, 1650–1750', *Past and Present*, XXXVII (1967), 44–70.

3 · *Documentary sources*

The transcripts of Crown-copyright material in the Public Record Office and the Lichfield Joint Record Office are reproduced by permission of the Controller of H.M. Stationery Office.

1. SHROPSHIRE COUNTY RECORD OFFICE, SHREWSBURY

Bridgewater Collection, boxes 14, 15, 105, 345, 411; containing surveys, rentals, manor court books, leases, estate maps, and miscellaneous papers.
Gough's manuscript *History*.
Gough's apprenticeship charity and other bonds, S.R.O. 2434.
Enclosure Award and Maps, 1813.
Quarter Sessions records.

2. LICHFIELD JOINT RECORD OFFICE

Wills and probate inventories, Salop Deanery.
Bishop's transcripts of Myddle parish registers.
Ecclesiastical court books and visitations; B/V/I/29 to 90, B/V/6, B/V/39.
Glebe terriers, Myddle parish.
Tithe Award and Map, 1838.

3. PUBLIC RECORD OFFICE

Taxation records: E.179/166/129, E.179/166/156, E.179/168/216, E.179/255/24, E.179/255/35.
Chancery records: C.2, James I, S15/20, C.2,B4/65, C.5/421/54. C.Ch.R.VI.94.
Augmentation records: E.321/5/14.

4. BRITISH MUSEUM

1563 Diocesan census, Harleian MS. 594, f.160.

5. WILLIAM SALT LIBRARY, STAFFORD
1676 Compton ecclesiastical census, Canterbury province.

6. DR WILLIAMS LIBRARY, LONDON
MS. 34–4, John Evans' List of Dissenting Congregations, 1715.

7. LANCASHIRE RECORD OFFICE, PRESTON
Rental of Myddle Lordship, 1590–1.

8. MYDDLE PARISH CHURCH
Parish records (almost entirely after 1701).

4 · Original sources in print

Richard Gough, *The Antiquityes and Memoyres of the Parish of Myddle* (1875).
Shropshire Parish Register Society, *Lichfield Diocese*, vol. XIX, pt I (1927), containing a transcript of the Myddle parish registers.
Shropshire Archaeological Journal, IX (1886), 236–7, containing extracts from the Myddle registers.
'The Early Chronicles of Shrewsbury', in *S.A.J.*, III (1880), 239–352.
Harleian Society, *The Visitations of Shropshire*, vols I and II (1889).
Calendar of State Papers, Domestic Series, Charles I, (18) and (19).

General index

Index of names

CESTRIÆ
DENBI
FLYNT
PARS
PARS
MONTGOM.
PARS
RADNOR: PARS
OCCIDENS
INDVSTRIA NATVRAM ORNAT
Christophorus Saxton descripsit
Scala Miliariū
1 2 3 4 5 6 7 8
Remigius hogenbergius Sculpsit
Dee flu
Keriok flu
Tanot flu
Sabrina flu
Ruabon
Chirk
Llansanfride
Selattyn
OSWESTRE
Coirdigare Forest
Treuelgh Forest
Llancillyn
Llangedwen
Abertannot
Llandronio
WELSHPOOLE
Forden
MONTGOMERYE
Mydddleton hall
Llaneuan
Clune forest
The new cast
Clun cast
BISSHOPS CASTLE
Bangor
Ortonmadok
Northwood
Ellismere
Marton
New marton
Hardwick
Welsshampton
Whittenton cast
Knockin cast
Kinnerley chap
Meluerley
Abberbury
Watlesburgh cast
Causse cast
Chirbury
Lydham
Hopton cast
Bucknell
KNIGHTON